AN INTRODUCTION TO
COMPARATIVE POLITICS

AN INTRODUCTION TO COMPARATIVE POLITICS

JOHANNES LINDVALL

Department of Political Science,
University of Gothenburg

UNIVERSITY PRESS

Great Clarendon Street, Oxford, OX2 6DP,
United Kingdom

Oxford University Press is a department of the University of Oxford.
It furthers the University's objective of excellence in research, scholarship,
and education by publishing worldwide. Oxford is a registered trade mark of
Oxford University Press in the UK and in certain other countries

© Oxford University Press 2025

The moral rights of the author have been asserted

All rights reserved. No part of this publication may be reproduced, stored in a retrieval system, transmitted, used for text and data mining, or used for training artificial intelligence, in any form or by any means, without the prior permission in writing of Oxford University Press, or as expressly permitted by law, by licence or under terms agreed with the appropriate reprographics rights organization. Enquiries concerning reproduction outside the scope of the above should be sent to the Rights Department, Oxford University Press, at the address above.

You must not circulate this work in any other form
and you must impose this same condition on any acquirer

Published in the United States of America by Oxford University Press
198 Madison Avenue, New York, NY 10016, United States of America

British Library Cataloguing in Publication Data
Data available

Library of Congress Control Number: 2024951383

ISBN 978-0-19-289660-5

Printed in the UK by
Bell & Bain Ltd., Glasgow

Links to third party websites are provided by Oxford in good faith and
for information only. Oxford disclaims any responsibility for the materials
contained in any third party website referenced in this work.

The manufacturer's authorised representative in the EU for product safety is
Oxford University Press España S.A. of El Parque Empresarial San Fernando de
Henares, Avenida de Castilla, 2 – 28830 Madrid (www.oup.es/en or
product.safety@oup.com). OUP España S.A. also acts as importer into Spain
of products made by the manufacturer.

PREFACE

This book is an introduction to comparative politics, which is a field of political science that is concerned with the similarities and differences between the world's political systems. We study comparative politics to become aware of the immense variety of political life on the planet and because 'a person who knows only one country knows no countries', as the scholar of comparative politics Seymour Martin Lipset used to say.

When you've finished reading the book, you may find that you think differently about many political problems. At least that's what happened to me when I was introduced to comparative politics in the 1990s. Studying comparative politics can temper our idealism by drawing our attention to the trade-offs countries have faced as they've constructed their political institutions. But it can also guard us against cynicism, another dangerous political vice, by encouraging us to learn from others when we look for ways to reform institutions, strengthen political organizations, or improve public policies.

I've taught comparative politics for more than twenty years at three universities in Sweden and the United Kingdom. I've been responsible for introductory courses, advanced undergraduate courses, and graduate courses, and I've met many students from different walks of life who've moved on to all sorts of worthwhile pursuits after graduating. When writing this book, I've tried to follow a few simple precepts informed by my experiences as a teacher—and by my own sense of wonder as I continue to learn about the world. Get to the key concepts and problems right away. Find illustrative evidence and examples of how political systems have varied among countries and over time. Use data and case studies to try out important ideas. Keep in mind that political regimes, institutions, organizations, and policies are always changing. Figure out which questions scholars are asking right now, as they push against the boundaries of what we know.

When we study the variety of political systems around the world and throughout history, we understand our own place and time better and begin to think more clearly, responsibly, and creatively about our current problems and predicaments. That's the hope and promise of comparative politics. Let's get started.

ACKNOWLEDGEMENTS

I am grateful to Fabio Angiolillo, Andreas Bågenholm, Hanna Bäck, Michael Coppedge, Carl Dahlström, Jacob Gunderson, Elsa Hedling, Johan Hellström, Kristen Kao, Ann-Kristin Kölln, Victor Lapuente, Olof Larsson, Elena Leuschner, Staffan Lindberg, Hilma Lindskog, Ellen Lust, Jesper Strömbäck, Anders Sundell, Fredrik Söderbaum, Jan Teorell, Maya Tudor, and Felix Wiebrecht for their kind help and advice, and to Felix Bäckstedt, Linda Eitrem Holmgren, Ann-Ida Scheiber Gyllenspetz, Jasmin Rath, and Inken Schütt for excellent research assistance. I am also grateful to the team at Oxford University Press—and to the reviewers, whose thoughtful comments helped make this a much better book.

Editorial advisory panel

The author and Oxford University Press would like to thank the many members of the academic community whose generous and insightful feedback helped to shape this text, including those who wished to remain anonymous.

Many thanks to Adrian Blau (King's College London), Daniel Bochsler (Central European University), David Brockington (University of Plymouth), Anthony James Costello (Liverpool Hope University), Amina Easat-Daas (De Montfort University), Elena Gadjanova (University of Exeter), Markus Haverland (Erasmus University Rotterdam), Matthew Jones (University of Greenwich), Jeffrey Karp (Brunel University London), Giorgos Katsambekis (National Centre for Social Research, Greece (EKKE)), Hans Keman (Vrije Universiteit Amsterdam), Kevin Koehler (Leiden University), Patrick M. Kuhn (Durham University), Wang Leung Ting (University of Reading), Dr Adrian Millican (Durham University), Czeslaw Tubilewicz (University of Adelaide), Christos Vrakopoulos (University of Leeds), Günter Walzenbach (University of the West of England), and Liam Weeks (University College Cork).

Creative commons

Materials under Creative Commons licences are published in accordance with terms available at the following addresses:

CC BY 4.0 https://creativecommons.org/licenses/by/4.0/

CC BY 3.0 https://creativecommons.org/licenses/by/3.0/

CC BY 2.0 https://creativecommons.org/licenses/by/2.0/

CC BY 1.0 https://creativecommons.org/licenses/by/1.0/

CC BY-SA 4.0 https://creativecommons.org/licenses/by-sa/4.0/

CC BY-SA 3.0 https://creativecommons.org/licenses/by-sa/3.0/

CC BY-SA 2.0 https://creativecommons.org/licenses/by-sa/2.0/

CC BY-SA 1.0 https://creativecommons.org/licenses/by-sa/1.0/

Every effort has been made to trace and contact copyright holders prior to publication. If notified the publisher will undertake to rectify any errors or omissions at the earliest opportunity.

CONTENTS

A Note on the Maps		xi
List of Case Studies		xii
1	**Comparative Politics**	1
2	**Theories and Methods**	15
3	**States and Nations**	31
4	**Democracy**	50
5	**Authoritarianism**	69
6	**Federalism**	86
7	**Electoral Systems**	105
8	**Legislatures and Executives**	129
9	**Constitutions and Courts**	153
10	**Public Administration**	170
11	**Political Parties**	186
12	**Electoral Behaviour**	208
13	**Interest Groups and Protests**	225
14	**The Media**	245
15	**Public Policymaking**	262
Conclusion		281
Glossary		282
References		287
Index		298

DETAILED CONTENTS

A Note on the Maps		xi
List of Case Studies		xii
1	**Comparative Politics**	1
	1.1 Introduction	1
	1.2 Think Like a Comparativist	2
	1.3 The Basic Questions	7
	1.4 Conflicts and Institutions	9
	1.5 Getting the Most Out of This Book	11
	1.6 Conclusion	13
2	**Theories and Methods**	15
	2.1 Introduction	15
	2.2 Concepts and Theories	16
	2.3 Theories of Comparative Politics	18
	2.4 Methods	22
	2.5 Causes and Effects	27
	2.6 Conclusion	29
3	**States and Nations**	31
	3.1 Introduction	31
	3.2 The State	32
	3.3 The Growth of the State	34
	3.4 State Capacity	41
	3.5 States and Nations	46
	3.6 Conclusion	48
4	**Democracy**	50
	4.1 Introduction	50
	4.2 Rule by the People	51
	4.3 Democracy around the World	55
	4.4 Democratization	59
	4.5 Democracy's Effects	65
	4.6 Conclusion	67
5	**Authoritarianism**	69
	5.1 Introduction	69
	5.2 Varieties of Authoritarianism	70
	5.3 Hybrid Regimes	73
	5.4 How Democracies Die	77

Detailed contents   **ix**

	5.5 How Authoritarian Systems Work	81
	5.6 Conclusion	84
6	**Federalism**	86
	6.1 Introduction	86
	6.2 The Meaning of Federalism	87
	6.3 Federal and Unitary States around the World	90
	6.4 The Origins of Federalism	96
	6.5 Federalism's Effects	98
	6.6 Conclusion	102
7	**Electoral Systems**	105
	7.1 Introduction	105
	7.2 Majoritarian, Proportional, and Mixed Systems	106
	7.3 Characteristics of Electoral Systems	107
	7.4 Electoral Systems around the World	114
	7.5 Elections and Representation	120
	7.6 Conclusion	126
8	**Legislatures and Executives**	129
	8.1 Introduction	129
	8.2 Parliamentarism and Presidentialism	130
	8.3 Legislatures	136
	8.4 Executives	142
	8.5 The Relationship between the Legislature and the Executive	146
	8.6 Conclusion	150
9	**Constitutions and Courts**	153
	9.1 Introduction	153
	9.2 Constitutions	154
	9.3 High Courts	161
	9.4 Judicial Independence	163
	9.5 Judicial Review	166
	9.6 Conclusion	168
10	**Public Administration**	170
	10.1 Introduction	170
	10.2 The Need for Public Administration	171
	10.3 Public Administration around the World	174
	10.4 Corruption	179
	10.5 Delegation, Democracy, and Technocracy	183
	10.6 Conclusion	184
11	**Political Parties**	186
	11.1 Introduction	186
	11.2 What Political Parties Do	187

	11.3 How Parties Are Organized	194
	11.4 Party Families	196
	11.5 Party Systems	203
	11.6 Conclusion	206
12	**Electoral Behaviour**	208
	12.1 Introduction	208
	12.2 Studying Public Opinion	209
	12.3 Why People Vote as They Do	211
	12.4 Voter Turnout	215
	12.5 The Structure of Public Opinion	220
	12.6 Conclusion	222
13	**Interest Groups and Protests**	225
	13.1 Introduction	225
	13.2 Interest Groups and Social Movements	226
	13.3 Interest Groups around the World	230
	13.4 State–Society Relations	235
	13.5 Protests	237
	13.6 Conclusion	243
14	**The Media**	245
	14.1 Introduction	245
	14.2 The Freedom of the Press	246
	14.3 Politics and the Media	250
	14.4 Media Effects	253
	14.5 Digital and Social Media	256
	14.6 Conclusion	260
15	**Public Policymaking**	262
	15.1 Introduction	262
	15.2 Comparative Public Policy	263
	15.3 Studying Policymaking and Public Policies	267
	15.4 Getting Things Done	272
	15.5 Authoritarian Regimes and Global Challenges	275
	15.6 Conclusion	279

Conclusion	**281**
Glossary	**282**
References	**287**
Index	**298**

A NOTE ON THE MAPS

There are many maps in this book. As we examine them to learn about important differences between political systems, we need to keep in mind that there is no such thing as a neutral, objectively correct way of drawing a map of the world.

First of all, the country borders that are superimposed on the maps aren't natural, but political. We think of the world as being divided into just under 200 independent states because of historical political processes such as nation building, warfare, colonization, and decolonization. We'll discuss these processes, and how they've shaped the world, in Chapters 3 and 6.

Many country borders remain contested today. For example, there are ongoing disputes about whether Taiwan is a part of China, whether Western Sahara should be controlled by Morocco or an independent Western Saharan government, which parts of Kashmir properly belong to India, Pakistan, and China, whether there should be a Palestinian state in the West Bank and Gaza, and whether Somaliland is a part of Somalia or its own independent state. When drawing the maps in the book, I have relied on computer files maintained by the World Bank, an agency of the United Nations. I've left a few contested areas blank.

Second, whenever we draw a map, we choose how to 'project' an image of the Earth, which is a round, three-dimensional object, onto a flat, two-dimensional surface. The maps in the book use the 'Mercator' projection, which was developed by the Dutch cartographer Gerardus Mercator in the sixteenth century, and which you'll be familiar with from Google Maps and other widely used mapping services. Most other map projections make it difficult to discern the smaller countries in Europe, which would be a problem for us since we'll discuss those countries extensively. But the Mercator projection has important drawbacks. Most importantly, it makes countries close to the Earth's poles look much bigger than they are. For example, the Mercator projection makes Africa and Canada appear equally large, but Africa is actually three times larger. We'll need to keep those distortions in mind when studying the maps in this book.

Maps are indispensable tools for scholars of politics, since they allow us to display quantitative data on political systems in an accessible manner. However, they are also political constructs in themselves, subtly influencing how we see the world.

LIST OF CASE STUDIES

2.1	Two theories of how political systems work	18
2.2	Measuring corruption	26
3.1	State building in Japan	38
3.2	Gangs and the state in Mexico	44
4.1	Democratization in Benin	64
4.2	The rise and fall of democracy in Myanmar	66
5.1	One-party rule in China	71
5.2	The fate of democracy in Hungary	75
6.1	The European Union	94
6.2	War and federalism in Bosnia and Herzegovina	101
7.1	Papua New Guinea's alternative-vote system	118
7.2	New Zealand's electoral-system reform	123
8.1	When it takes a long time to form a government	147
8.2	Executive–legislative relations in Brazil	149
9.1	Constitutional reform in Zimbabwe	159
9.2	High courts and abortion	167
10.1	Officials, politicians, and Covid-19	178
10.2	Public administration in Brazil and Africa	182
11.1	BJP, the world's largest political party	190
11.2	Germany's Green Party	199
11.3	Populism then and now	201
12.1	The changing gender gap	212
12.2	High and low turnout in Norway and Algeria	217
13.1	Interest groups in Switzerland	228
13.2	Protests and constitutional reform in Chile	242
14.1	Who owns the news? Lessons from Ukraine	252
14.2	CNN or Fox News?	255
15.1	Regulating Uber in different countries	269
15.2	Reforming pensions in Europe	274

CHAPTER 1
COMPARATIVE POLITICS

CHAPTER GUIDE

1.1 Introduction
1.2 Think Like a Comparativist
1.3 The Basic Questions
1.4 Conflicts and Institutions
1.5 Getting the Most Out of This Book

1.6 Conclusion
Summary
Study Questions
Further Reading

1.1 INTRODUCTION

Every hour of every day, people live or die because of politics. Somewhere in the world, a girl is spared from a deadly communicable disease because she was vaccinated in infancy. If it weren't for her government's decision to provide vaccinations free of charge, or the public-health authorities that delivered the vaccine to her, that girl might have died. In another part of the world, a young man is killed in a civil war. If it weren't for the failure of his country's leaders to resolve political conflicts peacefully, that young man might have lived. Meanwhile, hundreds of millions of people live comfortable lives in prosperity and freedom, while countless others live desperate lives in poverty and fear. When politics doesn't make the difference between life and death, it can make the difference between a good life and a life barely worth living.

That's why comparative politics matters. It's a field of study in which we ask how different political systems have emerged, how they work, and how they shape people's lives. This is not a new endeavour. More than 2,000 years ago, the Greek philosopher Aristotle asked his students to compile information about 158 city states in the northeastern Mediterranean, generating systematic knowledge about political systems that Aristotle later put to use in his book *Politics* (*c.*350 BC). But the questions scholars of comparative politics ask have never lost their urgency, and today, in the twenty-first century, comparative politics is more relevant than ever. To understand the great political challenges of our time, we must first understand the variety of political systems in the world.

This book is meant to be read by beginners, so you don't need to know a lot about politics or social science to understand it. All you need, really, is curiosity. Intellectual curiosity is the most important quality in a student of comparative politics. It involves a willingness to learn new things, a desire to understand how the world works, and a readiness to question one's old beliefs and habitual ways of thinking. When we do comparative politics, we try to lift our eyes from our own place and time, become more aware of the world around us, and open our minds to the immense variety of political life on the planet and through history.

The goal of this chapter, and the next, is to help you orient yourself in the field of comparative politics. Section 1.2 starts with three examples of the types of research question that intrigue students and scholars of political systems. Section 1.3 describes the scholarly field of comparative politics and explains how practising it encourages us to think about the world. Section 1.4 discusses political institutions and why scholars of comparative politics are so eager to understand how institutions shape social, economic, and political conflicts. Section 1.5 gives some advice on how to make the most of this book.

1.2 THINK LIKE A COMPARATIVIST

LEARNING OUTCOMES
After reading Section 1.2, you'll be able to:
- Distinguish between different types of research question in comparative politics
- Assess different sorts of evidence about political systems.

Comparative politics is a part of political science that is concerned with similarities and differences among the world's political systems. The term 'political system' broadly refers to how political institutions are structured and how people participate in politics in a particular country. Comparative politics is a broad, diverse, and ever-changing field that encompasses a wide range of topics—from referendums to revolutions and from social classes to social media.

When comparativists study political systems, they move from a general curiosity about politics to asking specific research questions about important cross-country differences or historical trends. Formulating precise research questions is essential since studying politics systematically requires clarity about what, exactly, we want to understand. In this section, we'll explore a few facts about the world's political systems that have long interested students and scholars of comparative politics. As we examine these examples, we'll try to formulate research questions about things that intrigue us.

1.2.1 Democracy

Let's start with Figure 1.1, which distinguishes between democracies, where people can choose their political leaders in reasonably free and fair elections, and authoritarian states, where people don't have this power. For now, we'll skip over the important question of how to define and measure democracy and take the evidence in Figure 1.1 at face value (we'll come back to definitions and measures of democracy in Chapter 4). The map describes the distribution of democratic and authoritarian systems in the world, relying on a widely used indicator of democracy that was originally compiled by Boix, Miller, and Rosato (2013) and has been updated through 2020.

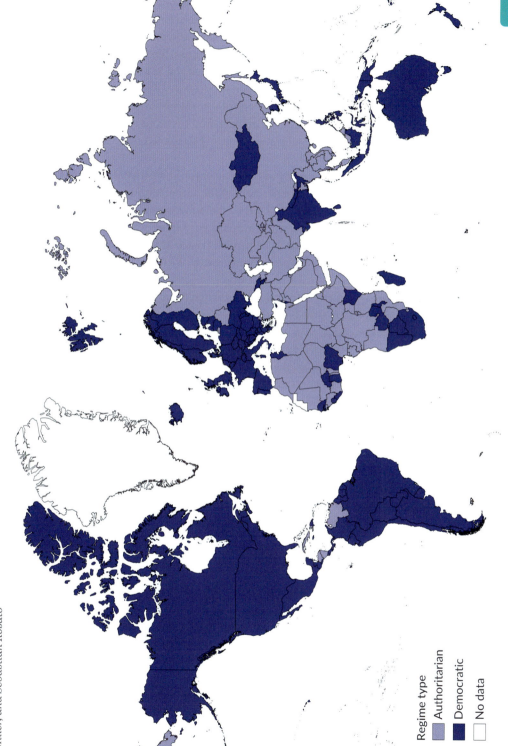

Figure 1.1 Approximately half of all countries in the world were democratic in 2020, the other half were not. *Source: Author's own work, based on data from Boix, Miller, and Rosato (2013) (updated until 2020), courtesy of 'A Complete Dataset of Political Regimes, 1800–2007' by Carles Boix, Matthew Miller, and Sebastian Rosato*

We see right away that the world's democracies are concentrated in the Americas, western and central Europe, southern Africa, Oceania, and eastern and southern Asia. India is commonly regarded as the world's largest democracy, although, as we'll see in Chapter 4, many international observers, such as the Freedom House organization and the Varieties of Democracy project, claim that India became more authoritarian in the 2010s and 2020s. India's neighbour China is not a democracy, but a closed authoritarian state.

Why are some countries democratic and others authoritarian? That's a natural question to ask after examining Figure 1.1. It's also one of the central questions of comparative politics. Let's search the map for clues. Do most democratic countries have something in common that sets them apart from authoritarian countries?

It may occur to you that many of the democratic states have high levels of **gross domestic product (GDP) per capita**, whereas many of the authoritarian states have low GDP per capita. In other words, democracies are on the whole more prosperous than authoritarian states. Because of this **correlation** (two things are correlated when they often appear together), many scholars, notably Lipset (1959), have argued that democracy ought to be seen as a byproduct of economic development and growth. We'll learn more about these relationships in Chapters 4 and 5.

But there are exceptions to the rule. For example, Saudi Arabia, an authoritarian state, has very high GDP per capita. Does the relationship between prosperity and democracy perhaps depend on the *sources* of a country's wealth? Many political scientists believe it does, holding that a dependence on natural resources is bad for democracy since governments tend to be less responsive to citizens if they don't have to tax them to fund themselves. This idea is known as 'the curse of oil' or, more generally, 'the natural-resource curse' (see, for example, Ross 2013).

After a while, your eye might be drawn to a few individual countries that differ from their neighbours in unexpected ways. Perhaps there's something that intrigues you about the north-eastern part of the map? There, wedged in between China and Russia, we find the democratic state of Mongolia. Why is it so different from its neighbours? Compared with the broad, general questions we just asked about democracy and prosperity, this question about Mongolia is narrow and specific—it's concerned with the experiences of an individual country. Scholars of comparative politics often alternate between asking broad and narrow questions about political systems, seeking to understand both general patterns and specific cases.

1.2.2 Federalism

Now let's consider another example of how different the political systems in the world are from each other. In Chapter 6, you will learn about federalism, which is a system in which political power is divided between a country's national and regional levels of government. In federal states, sub-national, regional governments have the final say on at least some important political issues. In unitary states, political power radiates outwards from the central government, and regional governments have less autonomy.

Much of the literature on federalism is concerned with federal states in North America, western Europe, South America, and Oceania, but there are federal states all over the world. Figure 1.2 presents a comparison of two of the largest states in Africa: Egypt, which is the continent's third

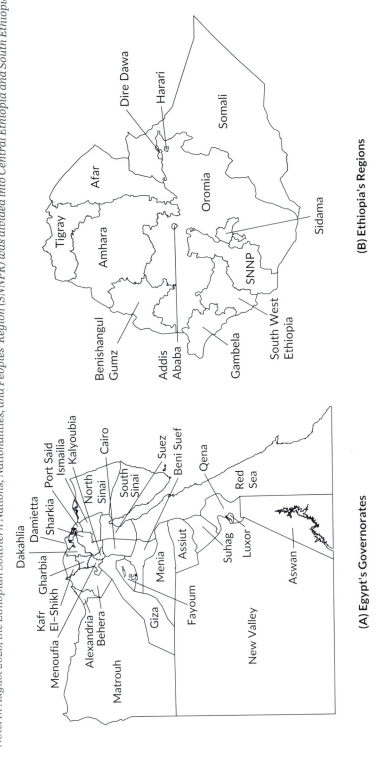

Figure 1.2 Egypt is divided into 'governorates' whereas Ethiopia, a federal state, is divided into autonomous 'regions'. *Source: Author's own work, based on data from GeoBoundaries, courtesy of William & Mary geoLab*

Note: In August 2023, the Ethiopian Southern Nations, Nationalities, and Peoples' Region (SNNPR) was divided into Central Ethiopia and South Ethiopia.

largest country by population, and Ethiopia, which is the second largest. Both countries have more than 100 million inhabitants. As Figure 1.2 shows, both Egypt and Ethiopia are subdivided into smaller geographical units, which are known as 'governorates' in Egypt and 'regions' in Ethiopia. But the roles of these smaller units are different. Egypt is a unitary state, in which regional governors are appointed by the country's president. Ethiopia, by contrast, is a federal state, where each region has its own government.

One question a student of comparative politics might ask when presented with this comparison between Egypt and Ethiopia is why one of them ended up with a federal constitution and the other didn't. That would be the same sort of question we asked about democracy and authoritarianism earlier: it's about the origins of political institutions. Another question we might ask is what *consequences* federalism has had in Ethiopia since it was introduced in the 1990s.

Ethiopia's government adopted federalism to manage conflicts between different regions and ethnic groups. Since the adoption of federalism is a common peacekeeping strategy in post-conflict societies, scholars of comparative politics are eager to learn more about the effectiveness of this remedy. Ethiopia offers a cautionary tale, since war broke out in the northern region of Tigray in 2020 between the Tigray People's Liberation Front and the central government. At least in Ethiopia, federalism doesn't appear to have solved the problem it was supposed to solve.

1.2.3 Voter turnout

The third example we'll consider in this section is the rise and fall of voter turnout among democracies. Voter turnout—or electoral participation—refers to the share of eligible voters who actually vote. Scholars of comparative politics are interested in understanding the differences in voter turnout between countries since politicians are typically more responsive to groups who participate in elections compared to those who don't. Governments in countries with high voter turnout are therefore generally more representative of the people as a whole.

But voter turnout doesn't just vary between countries; the average level of voter turnout among democracies has also changed over time. Figure 1.3 describes, for each year since 1900, the average turnout rate in the most recent **legislative election** among countries that were democratic at the time. At the beginning of the twentieth century, voter turnout in democracies averaged around 70 per cent. It increased during the inter-war period and during the first 20–30 years after the Second World War. But since the 1970s, the average turnout rate has declined from its peak of over 80 per cent and is now lower than at any other time in the past century.

Just as in the cases of democracy (Figure 1.1) and federalism (Figure 1.2), the data presented in Figure 1.3 raise intriguing research questions. Why was average turnout in democracies so low before the First World War, when many countries in the world had just become, or were becoming, democratic for the first time? Why did it increase in the inter-war period? And why has average turnout fallen in recent decades—does this trend reflect changes within democracies or new countries becoming democratic? As we'll learn in Chapter 12, scholars of comparative politics have proposed many different explanations for why turnout varies across countries and over time, and it's likely that the pattern we see in Figure 1.3 is the result of a combination of social, economic, and political factors.

Figure 1.3 Between 1900 and 2020, the average level of voter turnout among democracies first increased and then decreased. *Source: Author's own work, based on data from Coppedge et al. (2024), "V-Dem Country–Year Dataset v14" Varieties of Democracy (V-Dem) Project. https://doi.org/10.23696/mcwt-fr58*

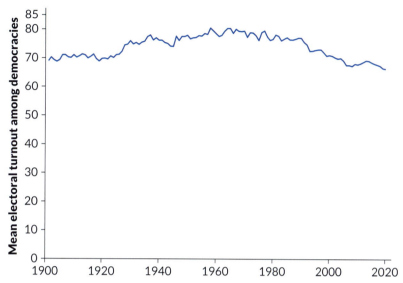

1.3 THE BASIC QUESTIONS

LEARNING OUTCOMES

After reading Section 1.3, you'll be able to:
- Describe the main fields of comparative politics
- Summarize the basic questions comparativists try to answer.

The three examples we examined in Section 1.2 were meant to give you an idea of the types of question that students and scholars of comparative politics study and are intrigued by. But the examples were also chosen to make three broad points about comparative politics as a scholarly field.

1. The examples come from different *fields* of comparative politics. The first example involved democracy and authoritarianism, which are the two main types of political **regime** among modern states. Regimes are the basic political arrangements that decide who has political power in a state. The second example involved federalism, which is a **political institution**. Institutions are rules that govern a country's political organization, and institutions such as federalism can in principle exist within both democratic and authoritarian regimes (most federations are democracies, but Ethiopia is not). The third example involved voting, which is not an institution, but a form of **behaviour**. It's something people *do*, not a rule or set of rules. Comparative politics is about regimes, institutions, and behaviour—and how they're related to each other.

2. The graphs we examined were based on different sorts of empirical *evidence*. In other words, the three examples in Section 1.2 don't just help us grasp the breadth of comparative

politics as a field of study—they also help us to distinguish between some of the methods students and scholars of comparative politics rely on. Figure 1.1 was a map that let us compare all independent states in the world in a particular year. In technical terms, we undertook a *cross-sectional* comparison of many countries. Next, we undertook a cross-sectional comparison of two particular countries—Figure 1.2 only described two states, Egypt and Ethiopia, and we didn't examine patterns in a larger dataset. Figure 1.3, finally, was a timeline that encouraged us to think about historical change, not about differences between countries. In technical terms, the comparison we undertook was *longitudinal*, not cross-sectional. We'll keep coming back to these three types of evidence throughout the book—broad comparisons, specific cases, and historical trends—and discuss their advantages and disadvantages.

3. Our discussion of democracy, federalism, and voter turnout revolved around two key *questions*. Comparative politics is a broad, diverse, and changing field of study that includes all kinds of topics, but scholars of comparative politics keep coming back to two basic questions. First, why are the political systems in the world so different from each other? Second, how do political systems shape economic, social, and political conflicts, and, ultimately, people's lives? Anyone who wishes to understand the world we live in must grapple with those questions. The first question concerns the *origins* of political institutions and systems. The second concerns the *effects* of political institutions and systems on human societies and the lives of individual people. When you've read this book, you'll have a clearer sense of how to answer both types of question.

Along the way, you will learn many things about politics and the field of comparative politics. You will become more familiar with different political systems around the world—how they've emerged, how they differ from one another, how they matter for people's lives, and what challenges they are facing today. In other words, you will be presented with a lot of *empirical evidence* about political systems: facts, figures, and stories that will help you understand politics better. You will also learn about many of the *concepts* scholars of comparative politics use to describe and analyse political systems—that is, what, precisely, they have in mind when they use terms such as 'democracy' and 'federalism'. Moreover, you will be introduced to many of the *theories* scholars use to explain how political systems work: ideas about why things happen the way they do. Finally, you will learn about the *methods* scholars of comparative politics use to describe and analyse political systems (a method, for a scholar, is a way of reaching a conclusion).

But the evidence, the concepts, the theories, and the methods aren't ends in themselves. We rely on them to answer important questions about why the world's political systems are so different and how those differences matter for political conflicts and for people's lives.

The modern field of comparative politics emerged in Europe and the Americas. It's important to acknowledge that the historical experiences of these regions—and the perspectives from which scholars have typically observed other parts of the world—have influenced the development of the concepts and theories that scholars of comparative politics rely on. Historically, comparativists have tended to take Western political institutions for granted and have often treated political institutions in other parts of the world as primitive and backward.

When writing this book, I have endeavoured to address political problems that are relevant across regions and over time and to include examples from all over the world. However, in a few important ways, the book remains quite traditional. First, although a whole chapter is devoted to authoritarian regimes and we'll keep referring to examples from these regimes throughout the book, we will pay more attention to democratic political systems. In other words, the book will focus more on the democratic half of the world than the authoritarian half. Second, much of the book is concerned with formal political institutions, and it's therefore quite 'state-centric'—it assumes that formal political institutions such as electoral rules, legislatures, governments, and courts are central to political systems. Many scholars believe that in large parts of the world, formal political institutions don't matter much in the lives of ordinary citizens since people depend more on informal institutions, kinship networks, and traditional authorities (see, for example, Lust 2022).

1.4 CONFLICTS AND INSTITUTIONS

LEARNING OUTCOMES

After reading Section 1.4, you'll be able to:
- Distinguish between different forms of social and political conflicts
- Define political institutions
- Explain how political institutions influence conflicts.

There is a deeper question we've only touched upon so far: why should we *care* about the origins and effects of political institutions and systems? There are many answers to that question (and, therefore, many good reasons to study comparative politics). In this section, we're going to concentrate on one answer, which is that we urgently need to understand how political institutions influence conflicts among different groups in society.

In all societies that have ever existed, people have had different economic interests, belonged to different ethnic groups, worshipped different gods, or spoken different languages, and therefore ended up in conflict with one another over things like land, money, status, beliefs, values, and identities. But as humans, we are also social beings who depend on each other to satisfy our basic needs. Because of this tension between competitive instincts that pull us apart and social instincts that keep us together, the basic problem in politics is how to live with conflict.

Political philosophers have grappled with the problem of conflict since long before the modern field of comparative politics emerged in the nineteenth century. It was this problem the early modern political thinker Thomas Hobbes tried to solve in his book *Leviathan*, in which he claimed that a strong state (though he didn't use the word 'state') is the only thing that can preserve humans from 'a perpetual[l] war[re] of every man against his neighbour' (Hobbes 1651, Chapter 24). The eighteenth-century philosopher Jean-Jacques Rousseau addressed the same problem in his work *The Social Contract* (1762), in which he argued that citizens must learn to look beyond their private interests to the good of the community—the *volonté générale* or 'general will'. The German philosopher Immanuel Kant (Figure 1.4) also had the same problem in mind when he observed more than 200 years ago that the basic driving force of history is the 'unsocial sociability' of humans. Though we live together in societies, Kant wrote, we are 'bound together with a mutual opposition'. In Kant's view, the only possible solution to this problem is a 'lawful . . . constitution'—that is, a set of basic rules for the political organization of society—and he argued that the problem of how to devise such a **constitution** is 'the most difficult . . . to be solved by mankind' (Kant 1784, fourth and sixth theses).

Hobbes, Rousseau, and Kant had very different ideas about how to solve the fundamental problem of how to live with conflict, but it's important to note that for all three, the solution was

Figure 1.4 According to Immanuel Kant (1724–1804), how to devise a lawful constitution is the greatest problem ever faced by mankind. *Source: Science History Images / Alamy Stock Photo*

political: it involved the organization of the state, the institutions of government, and the political practices of the community.

Those are the things modern scholars of comparative politics study, too. But our approach is different from that of political philosophers such as Hobbes, Rousseau, and Kant. We don't study states, political institutions, and political practices in the abstract. We study the similarities and differences between political systems that actually exist—or have actually existed—in order to draw lessons from those accumulated experiences.

That aim is reflected in the structure of this book. In the first few chapters, you'll learn more about the state and about political regimes such as democracy and authoritarianism, which are fundamentally different methods of dealing with conflict: in a democracy, the people vote and the majority decides; in an authoritarian state, one group of people dominates the others. In Chapters 6–10, you will learn about important political institutions such as federalism and electoral rules, which are different ways of channelling and managing conflicts within a political system (among regions in the case of federalism and among different groups of voters in the case of electoral rules). In the remaining chapters, you'll learn about things like political parties, which have emerged because of deep historical conflicts in modern societies, and political protests, which are themselves forms of political conflict.

Throughout the book, we'll keep coming back to the question of how political institutions shape social conflicts. Political institutions are often defined as 'the rules of the game in a society' (North 1990, 3), but we also use the word more broadly to refer to the organizations that embody and uphold those basic rules. Some political institutions are formal in that they're made up of well-defined rules that are laid down in a piece of legislation or a constitutional document. Others are informal, in that they're made up of conventions, traditions, and norms that aren't written down but nevertheless influence what sorts of things are seen as appropriate—or even taken for granted—in a political system.

We'll find that institutions can have at least two different types of effect. On the one hand, institutions can help societies contain, channel, and transform conflicts. In his book *Fights, Games, and Debates* (1960), the mathematician and social scientist Anatol Rapoport distinguished between three types of conflict: 'fights', 'games', and 'debates'.

- In a fight, people try to destroy each other.
- In a game, people try to defeat each other while playing by rules that are recognized and accepted by all.
- In a debate, finally, people try to change each other's minds.

We can think of political institutions as rules that transform potentially violent and dangerous 'fights' into more peaceful 'games' and 'debates'. Legislatures, which are the most important political institutions in many modern democracies (see Chapter 8), are a particularly clear example. Modern legislatures have complex rules of procedure that regulate the interactions among their members, and their other common name, 'parliaments', comes from the French word for talking, *parler*.

On the other hand, institutions can have the potentially more sinister effect of reinforcing the political, social, and economic dominance of some groups over others. This is especially clear in authoritarian regimes, in which political institutions are designed to keep one group of people in power and keep others out, but it isn't hard to find examples of institutions in democratic regimes that are set up to serve the powerful. For example, in many countries with majoritarian electoral systems, political leaders engage in a practice called 'Gerrymandering', which means redrawing the boundaries of the electoral districts to keep the ruling party in power (see Chapter 7). When we analyse the origins and effects of political institutions, we need to take into account their dual role. We wouldn't be able to live together in societies if we didn't have political institutions that regulate the conflicts among us, but those institutions often favour some groups over others.

1.5 GETTING THE MOST OUT OF THIS BOOK

LEARNING OUTCOME

After reading Section 1.5, you'll be able to:
- Make the most of the book's pedagogical features.

From Chapter 2 onwards, each chapter in this book contains a few main types of pedagogical features, which are meant to make you familiar with the modern field of comparative politics.

1.5.1 Learning from data

The map in Figure 1.1 and the graph in Figure 1.3 are based on quantitative evidence—information that can be stored numerically in a database and be analysed with the help of a computer program. Scholars of comparative politics rely more and more on quantitative evidence since it allows us to compare many countries at once, examine historical trends, and conduct systematic investigations of the origins and effects of political institutions, organizations, and events. A basic facility with quantitative evidence is fast becoming a requirement for all who study or work in politics. For better or worse, we live in a data-driven world, which is increasingly difficult to navigate for those who lack 'data literacy'—the capacity to understand and use quantitative information.

Throughout the book, you will see how comparativists use data as the basis for their conclusions about politics around the world, and how this can reveal patterns and challenge assumptions. Take note of how the studies discussed use quantitative data, and consider the approach you will take in your own research.

1.5.2 Case studies

Although comparativists rely more and more on broad comparisons among countries and data-driven analyses of long-run political trends, knowledge of individual countries, with their own particular historical experiences, social conflicts, and political traditions, remains essential for students and scholars of comparative politics. Each chapter therefore discusses many specific examples of political institutions, decisions, parties, organizations, leaders, and events. As the former Secretary-General of the United Nations, Kofi Annan, was fond of saying, in politics, 'the devil is in the details'. We'll be paying attention to details, and not just to the big picture, throughout the book.

In each chapter, there are detailed Case Studies of countries, people, or events. The Case Studies let you examine important political problems from different theoretical and empirical perspectives. Some of them put contemporary political events in historical perspective. There was a time when most textbooks in comparative politics were based on static comparisons between contemporary states. This book is based on the idea that we're better equipped to handle the challenges of today's world if we understand how political systems have changed over time and ask ourselves how they might change again in the future.

1.5.3 Research prompts

However, our main goal when we do comparative politics is to understand the contemporary world. As comparativists, we try to open our minds to the variety of political life on the planet and through history, but we do so for a specific reason: we wish to understand the political issues we're confronted with here and now. Each chapter in this book therefore includes a discussion of contemporary events, topics, and debates. In each chapter, there are also one or more Research Prompts, which ask questions that are meant to encourage you to apply the theories, concepts, and methods you're learning about in the book to important problems in today's world. The Research Prompts encourage you to go beyond the text, conducting your own research and finding new information that is relevant to the topics we discuss in the book.

1.5.4 End-of-chapter materials

At the end of each chapter, you'll find a brief Summary of the main ideas and findings as well as a few broad Study Questions, which are meant to encourage you to think about how the different themes that are covered in the chapter are related to each other. The Study Questions are similar to the Research Prompts in that they encourage you to think creatively about how to connect, apply, and develop the ideas and findings you're learning about, but they don't require you to conduct additional research. Finally, each chapter contains a short list of Further Reading for those who'd like advice on what to read next.

1.6 CONCLUSION

When you're done with this book, you'll know a great many things about the world's political systems and the changes they have experienced over the decades and centuries. One of the consequences may be that you become more aware of why politics is 'the art of the possible', as the German politician Otto von Bismarck put it a century and a half ago. Students and scholars of comparative politics typically think it's misleading to hold countries to some absolute standard. Rather than asking for perfect solutions to political problems, comparativists tend to ask practical questions. Are there countries that have improved their political systems, even if they remain far from perfect, and could other countries learn from those experiences? Studying the variety of political systems and institutions around the world gives us a sense of what's realistic and what isn't. But it can also make us aware of new ideas and opportunities.

Chapter 2 deals with the role of theories and methods in comparative politics. Chapters 3–5 deal mainly with political regimes: Chapter 3 discusses the nature of the state and the relationship between states and nations, Chapter 4 analyses the differences between democracy and authoritarianism, and Chapter 5 explains how authoritarian systems work. Chapters 6–10 deal with the most important political institutions in modern states: Chapter 6 analyses the differences between federal and unitary states, Chapter 7 deals with the rules that govern elections, Chapter 8 examines legislatures and executives, Chapter 9 studies constitutions and high courts, and Chapter 10 is concerned with public administration—the organizations that carry out government policies. Chapters 11–15, finally, are concerned with how parties, interest organizations, civil-society groups, citizens, and political leaders behave within political regimes and political institutions: Chapter 11 studies political parties, Chapter 12 deals with the political behaviour of ordinary citizens, Chapter 13 analyses the role of interest organizations and political protests, Chapter 14 studies the media, and Chapter 15 is concerned with public policymaking and the behaviour of political elites.

SUMMARY

- Comparative politics is the part of political science that investigates similarities and differences among the world's political systems.
- Students and scholars of comparative politics keep coming back to two questions: why are political systems so different, and how do political systems shape people's lives?
- Comparativists use concepts and theories to organize their thinking about politics, and research methods to analyse empirical evidence about political systems.

- In all modern societies, there are conflicts between different groups, which can be defined by class, language, religion, or ethnicity, or indeed by several of those things.
- One of the central goals of comparative politics is to understand those conflicts and to explain how they are resolved, or not resolved, in different political systems.
- Political institutions can help societies deal with conflicts between different groups by channelling and transforming those conflicts.
- But institutions are rarely neutral: they typically benefit some groups more than others and have often perpetuated oppression, injustice, and inequality.

STUDY QUESTIONS

1. Students and scholars of comparative politics are always looking for interesting similarities and differences among political systems. Consult the international section of a quality newspaper in the country you're in right now and look for an article that reports on political events in another country. Do you see an opportunity to make instructive political comparisons among countries on the basis of what you're reading?
2. The introductory sections of this chapter argued that comparativists keep coming back to two basic questions: why the world's political systems are so different from each other, and how those differences influence political conflicts and people's lives. Do you agree with this view, now that you've read a bit more about comparative politics, or are there other fundamental questions you think should be added to the list?

FURTHER READING

Aristotle, *Politics* (c.350 BC).
  A 2,300-year old analysis of the similarities and differences between political systems in the world of Classical Greece.

Carles Boix and Susan C. Stokes (eds.), *The Oxford Handbook of Comparative Politics* (2007).
  An encompassing overview of comparative politics as a scholarly field.

Daniele Caramani (ed.), *Comparative Politics* (2023), sixth edition.
  An advanced textbook with contributions from leading experts in the field.

CHAPTER 2
THEORIES AND METHODS

CHAPTER GUIDE

2.1 Introduction
2.2 Concepts and Theories
2.3 Theories of Comparative Politics
2.4 Methods
2.5 Causes and Effects

2.6 Conclusion
Summary
Study Questions
Further Reading

2.1 INTRODUCTION

Consider the knowledge of politics that a scholar of comparative politics develops. How does it differ from the knowledge journalists, pundits, and politicians have?

One tempting answer is that scholars simply know more than all those other people. Flattering though this would be, it isn't true, not really: journalists, political commentators, and politicians may not be used to thinking comparatively about the differences and similarities between political systems, as comparativists are, but they know many other useful things that scholars don't know. For example, if you want to learn about recent political events in a foreign country that interests you, you're typically better off turning to an experienced newspaper correspondent than to a university professor, since it takes a long time for information about current events to find its way into the scholarly literature.

No, what sets scholars of comparative politics apart from journalists, pundits, and politicians isn't how much they know, but how they know it. When we study comparative politics, we learn how to proceed methodically, step-by-step, as we gather information about political systems. We also learn how to give an account of our ideas, the evidence we rely on, and how we analyse that evidence. In other words, scholarly research is *systematic* and *transparent*. Scholars make it possible for others to build on what they've done, expose their ideas, evidence, and analyses to criticism, and help you decide for yourself whether you agree with the conclusions drawn.

To make their research as systematic and transparent as possible, scholars are open about the *concepts* they use, the *theories* they develop to explain why things happen, and the *methods* they rely on to draw conclusions from the empirical *evidence* they've collected. Section 2.2 explains what concepts and theories are and why they matter. Section 2.3 examines some of the main theoretical approaches in comparative politics. Section 2.4 discusses the advantages and disadvantages of different research methods and different types of evidence. Section 2.5 analyses the central methodological problem of how to study causality—the relationship between causes and effects.

2.2 CONCEPTS AND THEORIES

LEARNING OUTCOMES

After reading Section 2.2, you'll be able to:
- Define concepts
- Distinguish between different meanings of 'theory'
- Explain how scholars use theories to simplify analyses of political systems.

We're setting out to study political systems. Our first task is to explain what we mean by the words we use. We do this by defining our concepts—the ideas we use to name things and organize our thinking.

Let's take an example. In Section 1.2, we examined a map that distinguished between democracies and non-democracies. 'Democracy' is a common English word—with Greek origins—and we have a general understanding of what it means: it means the people rule. But that general idea isn't precise enough when we use the word 'democracy' in a scholarly context—for who are the people, what does it mean for them to rule, and what do they rule over? When we use a word like 'democracy' in scholarship, we must define it and say more precisely what we have in mind. If we're studying concrete examples of political systems and not just discussing democracy in the abstract, we also need to explain what we're looking for when we try to decide if countries are democratic or not. The technical term for that next step is operationalization. The scholars who came up with the data on democracy and authoritarianism that we examined in Figure 1.1 began by explaining what they meant by democracy, and then they explained how they recognized it when they saw it (see Boix, Miller, and Rosato 2013, 1525–1527, 1530–1534).

One thing to keep in mind about the concepts used in comparative politics is that many of them are best understood as ideal types: stylized, simplified models of complex phenomena. The notion of 'ideal types' was introduced by the German sociologist Max Weber more than a hundred years ago. It applies not only to comparative politics but to all the social sciences.

Ideal types aren't meant to mirror reality directly. Instead, they highlight certain essential characteristics of the objects we're studying, so we can describe and analyse them effectively. For example, as discussed in Chapter 8, scholars often categorize forms of government into parliamentary, presidential, and semi-presidential systems. These distinctions don't imply that all countries fit neatly into one of these categories (they can't), nor do they imply that all parliamentary (or presidential or semi-presidential) systems are essentially alike (they aren't). Scholars of comparative politics use these terms as analytical tools. They are helpful when students and scholars try to orient themselves amid the bewildering complexity of political institutions.

The word 'concept' derives from a Latin verb that means 'to take in'. To form a concept is to take an idea into your mind. The word we'll discuss next, 'theory', also has ancient origins. It goes back to a Greek verb that means 'to see', or 'to look at'. A theory, for a scholar of comparative politics, is a combination of ideas that help us see the world more clearly and to think systematically about how politics works. Concepts and theories are closely related, for once we have a clear sense of what we mean by a word such as 'democracy', we can begin to think of how democracy is related to other things—what causes it, for example, or what consequences it has.

That said, the word 'theory' has several different meanings in comparative politics. First, it can be used to refer to a combination of concepts that help us describe the world of politics in a systematic manner. In this sense, a theory of comparative politics is a specialized language that we use to analyse political systems and communicate ideas. Almost every section of this book is concerned with theory in this broad sense. By reading the book, you are learning a dialect of English that scholars of comparative politics use when they talk about political systems. In that dialect, common English words such as 'democracy' have more precise meanings than they do in everyday language (but, importantly, not one single meaning, since there are many different concepts of democracy). We can call this first meaning of theory 'descriptive'. Arend Lijphart's theory of consensual and majoritarian democracies, which we'll discuss in Case Study 2.1, is a theory in this sense—it lets us describe the world's democracies and compare them with each other.

Second, the word 'theory' can be used to refer to a combination of ideas that explain why things happen the way they do. We can call this second meaning of theory 'explanatory'. Let's take an example. One of the best-known ideas in comparative politics is *Duverger's Law*, named after the French political scientist Maurice Duverger. It is the claim that the electoral system influences the number of parties that can compete successfully in elections. Duverger's Law is meant to explain the empirical observation that there are typically more parties in proportional electoral systems than in majoritarian electoral systems. To do this, Duverger developed a systematic argument about how institutions, political parties, and elections work. (We'll learn more about electoral systems, political parties, party systems, and Duverger's Law in Chapters 7 and 11.) Put simply, Duverger told us a story about how parties and voters behave, which helps us make sense of why proportional electoral systems often result in more fragmented party systems than majoritarian electoral systems.

We need theories since they help us keep things simple. This might seem like a paradoxical thing to say, since many people associate the word 'theory' with something abstract and complicated, but it's true: the world of politics is so complex that we need general concepts and theories to make sense of it. We can't just learn all the details of all the political systems around the world and leave it at that. The problem isn't just that some countries are democratic and some are authoritarian or that countries have different electoral systems, forms of government, legal systems, bureaucracies, and party systems; the bigger problem is that political regimes, institutions, and party systems can be *combined* in countless different ways. If we want to understand, say, how the electoral system shapes conflicts among political parties, we need to consider not only the electoral system itself, but also the bureaucratic agencies that manage the elections, the courts that resolve disputes over electoral outcomes, how the political parties are organized, the distribution of political beliefs and attitudes in the electorate, and many other things besides. The political scientist Bo Rothstein (1996) has noted that if you start with ten different political institutions and assume that each institution can have one of two forms (think of the choice between federalism and a unitary state, for example), there are 1,024 possible combinations of the ten institutions. In other words, to understand the joint effects of ten political institutions, we don't just need to understand ten things—we need to understand more than a thousand things. (Many, many more, actually, for in the real world, political institutions can always take more than two forms.)

Figuring all this out on a case-by-case basis is too much for anyone. That's why we need theoretical ideas. We use general concepts to describe and distinguish between the different things we want to understand and describe, and we use theoretical ideas to create simple models that get at the principal mechanisms of political systems. In Case Study 2.1, you can learn about two examples of how influential scholars of comparative politics, Arend Lijphart and George Tsebelis, have tried to accomplish this goal. Lijphart and Tsebelis have very different ideas about politics, but they want to solve the same problem—how to get at the main differences among political institutions in democracies.

> **CASE STUDY 2.1**
> Two theories of how political systems work
>
> Arend Lijphart's theory of the main differences between 'consensus democracies' and 'majoritarian democracies' (2012) and George Tsebelis's theory of 'veto players' (2002) are two widely used theories of how democratic institutions work. Lijphart's and Tsebelis's approaches are different from each other—and they reach different conclusions—but they are, in a sense, trying to solve the same problem: they want to create a simplified model of the political system that can help us understand the otherwise confusing variety of political institutions in democracies.
>
> Arend Lijphart's main idea, which goes back to his comparative work on democracies in the 1980s and 1990s, is that political institutions among democracies vary in two main ways: the 'executives–parties dimension' and the 'federal–unitary dimension'. In other words, Lijphart claims that we can come up with a broad characterization of a democratic country's political system using just two concepts: the country's place on the executives–parties dimension tells us how easy it is for a single political party to control the national government, and its place on the federal–unitary dimension tells us whether the national government must engage in bargaining with other institutions and with sub-national governments to get things done. Lijphart also claims that once we've figured out where a country should be placed on the executives–parties dimension and on the federal–unitary dimension, we can make important predictions about the nature of political competition and political decision making within that country.
>
> George Tsebelis's approach to political institutions is related but different. For Tsebelis, the question we should ask ourselves if we want to understand how a political system works is how many different institutions and political parties within the system are 'veto players'—that is, how many institutions and parties need to agree before a change in public policy can be undertaken. If one party wins a majority of the seats in the legislature, that party forms a single-party majority government, and that government can't be prevented by other institutions from adopting the policies it wants (until the next election), there is only one veto player: the ruling party. By contrast, if three parties form a coalition government and the government needs to negotiate with the country's president and the upper chamber of the parliament in order to get things done, there are several veto players (five, to be exact).

2.3 THEORIES OF COMPARATIVE POLITICS

LEARNING OUTCOMES

After reading Section 2.3, you'll be able to:
- Compare different types of theory in comparative politics
- Explain which assumptions different theories make about human beings and societies.

As we discussed in Section 2.2, theories are combinations of ideas that help us to see the world more clearly and explain why things happen the way they do. Scholars of comparative politics rely on different sorts of theoretical ideas, which are based on different assumptions about the world. In this section, we'll examine some of the main types of theory that scholars of comparative politics use: rationalist, sociological, psychological, and institutionalist theories. There are other ways to categorize the main theoretical approaches in the field and there is a lot of variety *within* the main types we'll examine here, but this four-way categorization lets us distinguish between some of the main theoretical approaches in contemporary scholarship. Familiarizing yourself with these common types will make it easier for you to think through and critically evaluate the many different arguments we'll explore in the rest of the book.

We will concentrate on two basic features of different types of theory. First, like its sister disciplines economics, sociology, and psychology, political science is a social science, and one way of distinguishing between different theoretical approaches in comparative politics is to examine their assumptions about *what it means for humans to live together in societies*. Like all the other social sciences, political science is also a human science (the human sciences include the humanities—disciplines such as history, philosophy, and modern languages). Another way of distinguishing between different theoretical approaches—the one we will start with—is to ask what assumptions they make about *why humans do what they do*.

2.3.1 Rationalist theories

Rationalist theories are based on the idea that humans are forward-looking, goal-oriented, and do what they can to achieve their aims. They are called 'rationalist' since they assume that political agents do what they think will get them what they want. In the rationalist tradition, scholars typically begin by identifying the main agents in the situation they analyse—the individuals or groups of individuals whose behaviour they wish to explain—and then they make assumptions about what choices these agents are facing and what goals they have. For example, rationalist models of electoral competition are typically based on a few strong assumptions about what political parties and voters want, and on that basis, the theories explain what policies the parties adopt and how the voters choose between them.

The rationalist idea of what it means for humans to live together in societies is that human interaction is *strategic*. The goal of social-science scholarship in the rationalist tradition is to analyse what happens when rational agents need to consider what other rational agents are doing. One tool that is often used for this purpose is game theory, which is a framework that helps us explain what happens when rational agents interact with each other. George Tsebelis's theory of veto players (Case Study 2.1) is a typical example of a rationalist theory: the 'veto players' are agents who have political power, their goal is to influence public policy, and the theory helps us understand what happens when different parties and decision makers interact within a political system.

2.3.2 Sociological theories

Another tradition, which we might call the sociological tradition, makes very different assumptions about why humans do what they do and what it means for humans to live together in societies. Instead of starting from the assumption that humans are forward-looking, goal-oriented, and do what they can to reach their goals—as rationalist theories do—scholarship in the sociological tradition typically starts from the assumption that humans do what's expected of them in the culture and the institutions in which they find themselves. We each have a role to play, sociological theories say, and we play it according to the norms and expectations we perceive from others.

Sociological theories of politics don't primarily conceive of society as a place in which rational agents interact strategically with each other. Instead, they're based on the idea that humans are fundamentally shaped by their environment. What we want, what we believe, and ultimately who we are and what we do all depend on the society we're in and what we take to be normal, appropriate behaviour according to the prevailing norms in that society. There are elements of this sort of thinking in Lijphart's theory of consensus democracies and majoritarian democracies (Case Study 2.1). Lijphart argues that different kinds of institutions lead people to think of politics differently, and these differences shape political life in different countries.

2.3.3 Psychological theories

The rationalist tradition is closely related to the way economists typically think about the world, and the sociological, cultural tradition is closely related to the way sociologists typically think about things. There is a third tradition in comparative politics that has much in common with another social-science discipline, psychology, and especially with the part of psychology that is known as social psychology. Scholars of comparative politics who study politics with the help of psychological theories typically start from the assumption that what people do depends on their thoughts, feelings, beliefs, and other psychological dispositions. These drivers are the result either of biology or of the environment—or of some combination of the two—including people's upbringing and social networks.

Psychological and social-psychological approaches are particularly influential in the part of comparative politics that is known as comparative political behaviour. We'll learn more about this aspect of the subject in Chapters 12 and 13. Psychological models of political behaviour have been influential across political science ever since new survey methods that emerged in the twentieth century made it possible for scholars to study individual political behaviour among large groups of people.

2.3.4 Institutionalism

Our discussion of rationalist, cultural, and psychological approaches has shown that scholars of comparative politics often draw from other social-science disciplines when they develop theories of political systems. But they typically combine the ideas they borrow from other disciplines with arguments that are more unique to political science. Ever since the 1980s and 1990s, many scholars of comparative politics have been influenced by some form of institutionalism—the idea that political and social institutions play a central role in politics, in society, and in economic life.

Combining the idea that institutions are central to politics with the other theories we've examined in this section leads to different varieties of institutionalism (Hall and Taylor 1996). According to rationalist theories of politics, institutions are best seen as structures within which rational agents such as parties, political leaders, and interest groups interact strategically. By contrast, sociological and psychological theories see institutions as a part of the social environment that shapes social norms and influences people's goals, beliefs, expectations, and identities.

2.3.5 How to use theories

The point of distinguishing between different schools of thought within comparative politics isn't that each of us must pick a side and choose one particular way of looking at politics. As we discussed in Section 2.2, theoretical ideas are tools that we can use to tell stories about why things happen the way they do and to construct simple models of political systems. It is up to us to choose among the different tools that are available in the scholarly literature when we try to understand specific problems. Most scholars of comparative politics aren't loyal to one particular school of thought; they use different tools for different purposes, depending on the questions they try to answer. There's nothing wrong with that. Societies are complicated. Humans too are complicated, and do what they do for lots of different reasons. There are many ways to explore what it means for humans to live together in societies, and institutions can have many different effects.

To think more deeply about how different sorts of theoretical ideas can be combined, turn to Research Prompt 2.1.

>
> **RESEARCH PROMPT 2.1**
> Combining theoretical ideas
>
> On 6 January 2021, a large mob invaded the Capitol Building in Washington, DC, where the Senate and the House of Representatives were convening to certify the results of the 2020 presidential election (see Figure 2.1). The mob, which consisted of supporters of the sitting president, Donald Trump of the Republican Party, wanted to prevent Congress from formalizing the victory of the Democratic nominee, Joe Biden. When Trump ran again in 2024, one of the main messages
>
> **Figure 2.1** Supporters of Donald Trump rioting at the Capitol Building in Washington, DC, on 6 January 2021. *Source: lev radin / Shutterstock*
>
>
>
>

of the Democratic Party was that he couldn't be trusted with the presidency again because of his role in the 6 January attack on the Capitol, but it wasn't persuasive enough to dissuade voters from supporting Trump once more.

Consult the website of a reputable American newspaper or some other reliable source and analyse the information you find there on the events of 6 January 2021. Consider the actions on that day of the groups listed below:

1. The rioters
2. The Democratic Congresswomen and Congressmen
3. The Republican Congresswomen and Congressmen.

Suggest different explanations for what they did that are based on at least two of the theories of comparative politics you've read about in this section.

2.4 METHODS

LEARNING OUTCOMES

After reading Section 2.4, you'll be able to:

- Distinguish between the main types of method in comparative politics
- Weigh their advantages and disadvantages
- Describe the challenges scholars face when they gather empirical evidence about political systems.

In Section 2.2, we discussed the origins of the word 'theory' and noted that it derives from a verb that means 'to see'. The implication was that we shouldn't be intimidated by theories—they're just ways of looking at things. We shouldn't be intimidated by methods either. The word 'method' goes back to the ancient Greek words *meta*, which means 'after' or 'following', and *hodos*, which means 'way' or 'path' (Figure 2.2). In other words, having a method means something like 'following a path'—it's how we reach a conclusion. To be more specific, research methods are techniques that we use to gather and analyse empirical evidence and to draw conclusions from what we have learned about the world.

Scholars of comparative politics rely on two main types of evidence: quantitative, or 'large-N', evidence, and qualitative, or 'small-N', evidence (N is the number of **observations** that are being analysed in an empirical study). In this section, we'll outline both approaches and consider the advantages and disadvantages of each.

2.4.1 Quantitative methods: 'large-N' evidence

Many studies in comparative politics are based on quantitative, or 'large-N', evidence. This means that there are enough observations—whether they're countries, periods, regions, cities, individuals, or something else—to make it meaningful to use statistical methods. The evidence that is used

Figure 2.2 An Ancient Greek road in Ephesus, Türkiye. The word 'method' comes from the Greek for 'following' and 'path'. *Source: Aygul Sarvarova / Shutterstock*

in a study based on quantitative methods is combined into a numerical repository that is known as a dataset, which enables the researcher to examine relationships between different types of information.

To give you an idea of what a simple dataset might look like, see Table 2.1. Each row in this dataset represents a country in a particular year (e.g., Hungary in 1988, Poland in 1991). The first column lists the names of the countries, the second column shows the years, the third column contains the Boix, Miller, and Rosato (2013) democracy indicator that we illustrated in the map in Figure 1.1 in Chapter 1 (the indicator takes a value of 0 for authoritarian states and 1 for democracies), and the fourth column contains the World Bank's estimates of GDP per capita (in constant United States Dollars).

By examining the 0s and 1s in the third column, we see how Boix, Miller, and Rosato categorized the political systems of three central and eastern European countries around the fall of the Berlin Wall in 1989 and the collapse of the Soviet Union in 1991. According to their analysis, Poland adopted democracy before Hungary, with Romania following one year later. Looking at the numbers in the fourth column, we can learn more about what happened to the economies of Hungary, Poland, and Romania after their transitions to democracy. All three countries experienced economic downturns as their socialist systems began to be replaced by capitalism, with the deepest downturn in Romania, where the transition to democracy was most violent.

Technically, this is a panel dataset because it contains repeated observations of each unit (in this case, countries). In other words, there are data on Poland's, Hungary's, and Romania's democracy scores and GDP per capita for several consecutive years. There are also purely cross-sectional datasets, which contain information about several units at one point in time, and pure time-series datasets, which contain repeated observations of a single unit.

Table 2.1 Example of a dataset

Country	Year	Democracy	GDP per capita (2015 US dollars)
Hungary	1987	0	
Hungary	1988	0	
Hungary	1989	0	
Hungary	1990	1	
Hungary	1991	1	7,589
Hungary	1992	1	7,360
Poland	1987	0	
Poland	1988	0	
Poland	1989	1	
Poland	1990	1	5,111
Poland	1991	1	4,736
Poland	1992	1	4,840
Romania	1987	0	
Romania	1988	0	
Romania	1989	0	
Romania	1990	0	5,017
Romania	1991	1	4,407
Romania	1992	1	4,057

Sources: Boix, Carles, Michael Miller, and Sebastian Rosato. 'A Complete Dataset of Political Regimes, 1800–2007'. ©2013 Comparative Political Studies (democracy) and the World Bank's World Development Indicators (GDP per capita), both available via Teorell et al. (2024)

The main advantage of using large-N data and quantitative methods is that it becomes possible to combine information about many different things into a single analysis. The maps and graphs that you saw in Chapter 1 are examples of visual displays of quantitative data that make it possible to study similarities and differences between all the countries in the world. You'll find many more maps and graphs in this book. By examining similarities and differences, we can find patterns and regularities that can give us clues about how political systems work. One example is Arend Lijphart's (2012) quantitative analysis of 'patterns of democracy', which we discussed in Case Study 2.1.

2.4.2 Qualitative methods: 'small-N' evidence

The downside of using large-N evidence is that quantitative methods don't tell us much about individual observations. The main advantage of the other type of method that scholars of comparative politics rely on—small-N case studies and comparative studies—is that it *does* tell us about individual observations such as countries, periods, events, and organizations. When we use case studies and small-*N* comparative studies, we concentrate on individual cases because we want to study them in greater depth. Many influential observations in comparative politics were first made in qualitative case studies, likely because focusing our attention on nuances and details encourages us to think in new ways about how political systems work. For example, Arend Lijphart's theory of consensual and majoritarian democracies emerged from the author's early work on a single country, the Netherlands (Lijphart 1968).

When scholars of comparative politics study more than one country, period, event, or organization, they typically select their cases carefully to improve their ability to draw reliable conclusions from the comparisons they're making. One widely used method is known as the 'most similar systems design'. If we are interested in, say, the effects of the electoral system on the party system (the relationship that was studied in the middle of the twentieth century by Duverger, whose work we discussed earlier), it often makes sense to compare countries that have different electoral systems, but that are otherwise as similar as possible. That way, if their party systems are different, we can at least be reasonably confident that the difference isn't due to any of the factors that are similar across countries. Sometimes, scholars instead use the alternative 'most different systems design'. With this design, we compare countries that are alike when it comes to the variable we're interested in—such as the electoral system, to continue with our earlier example—but that are otherwise very different. If we make such a comparison and infer that the party systems in the two countries exhibit important similarities, we can at least infer that the electoral system is a more plausible explanation for those similarities than all the other factors that vary between the two contexts we're studying.

Many comparativists believe that scholarship is most likely to be successful when scholars combine quantitative and qualitative methods.

2.4.3 How comparativists collect information

Regardless of whether we use quantitative methods and gather evidence about many countries, periods, cities, or other units, or whether we engage in case studies and small-*N* comparative studies, one of the main challenges in comparative politics is to collect accurate and useful information about political systems and political behaviour. There are several problems we need to overcome to achieve this important goal.

One of the reasons this is so challenging is that it's often difficult to operationalize the concepts that scholars of comparative politics are most interested in, such as 'democracy' (see Section 2.2) or 'left', 'centre', and 'right' (see Chapter 11). Most things in politics are complex, and the empirical measure we use cannot capture all of that complexity.

Another, more practical challenge is that we often rely on information that is compiled by public organizations such as government statistics agencies. Especially in authoritarian regimes, we cannot assume that this information is reliable. The officials who compiled the information may have been under pressure from political leaders to provide information that is pleasing to the authorities and makes the country seem wealthier, happier, or more stable and peaceful than it is.

A third challenge is that it can be dangerous to conduct fieldwork and collect information about political conflicts and institutions in countries in the midst of war, or that are governed by repressive regimes (Grimm et al. 2020).

A fourth reason it's so challenging to gather accurate and useful information is that people aren't always willing to divulge the information scholars are looking for, since it might be embarrassing, compromising, or even dangerous for them to do so. An example of a field where this is a problem is in research on corruption, as we'll discuss in Case Study 2.2.

CASE STUDY 2.2
Measuring corruption

Corruption is the misuse of public office for private gain. Since corruption is illegal in most countries, it's difficult to study empirically. Most people are reluctant to volunteer information about giving or receiving bribes or engaging in other corrupt activities. To get around this problem, scholars have developed ingenious data-collection methods to learn about the prevalence of corruption in different countries.

One of the main ways to study corruption is to conduct surveys that ask individuals about their own experiences of corrupt behaviour, such as giving bribes. The challenge here is to make respondents feel that they can contribute to the survey without revealing incriminating information about themselves. Gingerich et al. (2016) review some of the methods scholars have used to get meaningful answers. Two of the most popular are the randomized-response technique and the item-count technique (also known as list experiments).

When using the randomized-response technique, the researcher tells the respondents to flip a coin secretly and to adjust their answer to a sensitive question depending on the result of the coin toss. If they get one result, say 'heads', they're asked to answer the question truthfully. If they get the other result, say 'tails', they're asked to always say 'yes' to the question, which might be 'Have you ever bribed anyone?' Since only the respondent knows what the result of the coin toss was, there is no way of determining whether a particular respondent who answered 'yes' did so because of the coin toss or because they have in fact bribed someone. But the proportion of respondents with a heads (or tails) result is likely to be similar between those who have taken bribes and those who haven't, so it remains possible to estimate the percentage of survey respondents who have given out bribes. For an example of a study that uses this technique, see Brierley (2020), who studies corrupt practices in local governments in Ghana.

When using the item-count technique, the researcher gives half of all respondents a list of non-sensitive activities and the other half a version of the list that also includes the sensitive item the researcher is interested in. Then the respondents are asked to indicate how many of the activities on the list they've engaged in. Confidentiality is again guaranteed, because in individual cases, the researcher will not know whether the total number of activities that an individual has engaged in contains the sensitive item or not. But it remains possible to estimate the proportion of all respondents who have given out bribes.

An alternative method of studying corruption is to find direct evidence of corrupt behaviour. The challenge is that finding such evidence typically requires a bit of luck. Figueroa (2021) made use of notebooks on bribes that were kept by high-level bureaucrats in Argentina and that were discovered in connection with a political scandal. With the help of these notebooks, Figueroa could describe the frequency of corruption in Argentina with great precision.

A third possible method is to calculate 'missing' public expenditure (Olken 2009, 951) by comparing officially declared expenditures with the actual amount of resources that were spent on public works. For example, Golden and Picci (2005) compare the amount of existing physical infrastructure in Italian regions with official data on the financial resources that were allocated to public investment projects, documenting that there were more missing expenditures in some regions than others.

2.5 CAUSES AND EFFECTS

LEARNING OUTCOMES

After reading Section 2.5, you'll be able to:
- Explain why correlation doesn't imply causation
- Assess the reliability of the methods scholars use to identify causal effects.

Many empirical studies in comparative politics are concerned with matters of cause and effect, or, in other words, how one thing leads to another. For example, scholars of comparative politics often ask questions about how political institutions influence important political, social, and economic outcomes. They also ask questions about where institutions come from—for example, what led some countries to adopt proportional elections when others did not. We'll come back to questions of cause and effect many times in this book.

2.5.1 Correlation and causation

Such questions are difficult to answer conclusively. As we discussed in Chapter 1, if two things seem related to each other—so if we find one, we're also likely to find the other—we say that those two things are correlated. A good example of this is the relationship between democracy and economic prosperity, which we also mentioned in Chapter 1. Most of the rich countries in the world are democratic, and most of the poor countries in the world are authoritarian. When we find that two things are correlated, it is often tempting to infer that one of them caused the other. We may want to conclude, for instance, that democracy makes countries wealthier. But that would be a hasty conclusion, which illustrates the point of the common saying that 'correlation is not causation'. Maybe prosperity comes first, with wealth making countries more democratic, and not the other way around? Or perhaps there is a third factor—such as education or culture—that explains both democracy and prosperity? Then the reason they're correlated wouldn't be that one caused the other, but that a third thing caused both.

To explore this problem in more depth, we need to state more precisely what it means for one thing to cause another. The most widely accepted definition of causality in the social sciences today is known as the **counterfactual definition of causality**. Let's say we're interested in whether an institution caused a particular outcome. According to the counterfactual theory of causality, the institution caused that outcome if the outcome would have been different in the absence of the institution—that is, if the institution had been replaced by another, or if there had been no institution at all. When we discuss causal relationships, we're always making an implicit comparison between the world as it is and the world as it might have been.

One of the implications of the counterfactual definition of causality is that we can never observe causality directly. We can only observe the world as it is, not the world as it might have been, and yet what we want to understand is the difference between those two worlds. That's the key difficulty we face when we make claims about cause-and-effect relationships.

Comparativists have long sought to overcome this problem by comparing countries with different political systems and using evidence from one country to draw conclusions about what would happen in other countries if their political systems were similar to that of the first. Let's say that we're interested in whether the electoral system influences the level of voter turnout—that is, how many of a country's eligible voters actually participate in elections (a question we'll revisit in Chapters 7 and 12). As we've already established, we can never observe the effect of the electoral system directly, since that would mean comparing an actual country, say Thailand, with an imagined version of that country in which the electoral system is different. What we can do, however, is to make an educated guess about the effects of the electoral system by undertaking other sorts of comparisons. For example, we can compare a large number countries and see if turnout is higher on average among countries with proportional elections than among countries with non-proportional electoral systems. In a study that's based on this sort of comparison, other countries are in a sense 'standing in' for the imagined case we'd ideally like to compare with the real Thailand—Thailand-with-a-different-electoral-system.

But scholars have become increasingly sceptical of this traditional approach since it's always difficult to distinguish between correlation and causation when we compare countries. There might be some deeper difference between Thailand and other countries that explains both why they have different electoral systems and why electoral behaviour varies between them. Perhaps the other countries with which we're comparing Thailand cannot 'stand in' for Thailand in the way we imagined.

2.5.2 Learning about causes and effects

Other types of method have been developed that can help us make better-educated guesses. One approach that is usually superior to static comparisons between countries is to study what happens in countries that change their institutions. If we compare the level of voter turnout before and after a change in the electoral system, we're not basing our conclusions on comparisons between different countries; we're basing them on a comparison between different periods within the same country. There is another problem, though: perhaps there were other changes that occurred at the same time as the institutional change, such as a change in leadership?

A further improvement to the method might be to compare changing trends in voter turnout across countries and see if the countries that changed their electoral systems experienced more or less voter-turnout change than countries that didn't. Let's say, for instance, that we find turnout is falling in most countries, but not in countries that adopted more proportional electoral institutions during the period we're studying. That observation might lead us to conclude that proportional elections have a positive effect on turnout. There are some problems with this approach, too—no method is perfect when it comes to studying causality—but we can at least be a little more confident than we were before.

In some cases, it's possible for political scientists to use a method that is widely used in the natural sciences to study causality: experiments. A controlled experiment is based on a comparison between two groups: the 'treatment group' and the 'control group'. The researcher subjects the treatment group to a particular change, which is not applied to the control group, in order to learn about the effects of the treatment. If the two groups were put together randomly, we can usually be quite confident that any difference between them resulted from how they were treated, and not from other factors. One way to emulate this experimental approach in comparative politics is to look for events that affected different parts of a country or different groups of people in different ways. For example, if a country changed its institutions but implemented that change at different times in different regions, it might be possible to draw conclusions about the effect of the institutional change by comparing parts of the country that were affected early with parts of the country that were affected late. In Chapter 7, we'll learn how this sort of method was used to study the relationship between electoral systems and voter turnout, and in Chapter 14, we'll learn how a similar method was used to study the effects of people's media habits on their political preferences.

But regardless of the method we use to make comparisons, we must always be cautious when we draw conclusions about causal relationships. When we speak about causal effects, we are making educated guesses, not direct observations. Being aware of this problem is an important part of a political scientist's training. Politicians, pundits, and lobbyists often make strong claims about matters of cause and effect. They want to build a case for their own favourite policies by arguing that they will have all kinds of positive consequences. Healthy scepticism is a good attitude to have when it comes to these sorts of claims.

Scepticism is also warranted when it comes to recommending institutional changes and policy changes on the basis of research within comparative politics. The difficulty of studying causality has profound implications for public policy, not least in the context of economic development (Przeworski 2004). International organizations such as the World Bank and the International Monetary Fund often recommend certain institutions and policies on the basis of causal claims. If it has been observed that rich countries tend to have certain institutions and policies in place, these organizations often suggest that other countries should adopt the same institutions and policies to promote economic growth. The fact that these recommendations are based on uncertain causal claims doesn't necessarily mean they're wrong—but it does mean we ought to be cautious.

2.6 CONCLUSION

Having read this chapter, you now know more about how scholars of comparative politics develop concepts that can be used to organize our thinking, construct theoretical arguments about politics that help us understand the workings of political systems around the world, and use quantitative evidence and case-study methods to describe and analyse political systems in different countries. You also know more about the difficulties that come with trying to answer questions about causality, or how (and whether) one thing leads to another.

Being familiar with these conceptual, theoretical, and methodological issues will provide a helpful foundation as you read the rest of this book. Starting in the next chapter—Chapter 3, which is concerned with the state—we'll place less emphasis on broad conceptual, theoretical, and methodological questions and more emphasis on the hands-on empirical and practical questions that need answering if we are to understand the political problems of today's world. But we certainly won't leave concepts, theories, and methods behind. On the contrary, we need them to answer our empirical and practical questions and to help us understand the political problems we want to analyse.

The next chapter is a case in point. To understand what the state is, we need a concept of the state. To understand what states do, we need theories of the state. To describe states, we need empirical measures of their size, scope, and capacity. And to study the origins and effects of state institutions, we need to face all the challenges that come with making arguments about causality. But now we have the tools we need for these endeavours.

SUMMARY

- If we want to study political systems in a systematic and transparent way, we need to define the concepts we use.
- We use theories of comparative politics to tell stories about how one thing leads to another and to put together simple models that help us make sense of political institutions and events in different countries.

- Some of the main theoretical approaches in comparative politics are closely related to how economists, sociologists, and psychologists think about the world; they are known as rationalist, sociological, and psychological approaches.
- Scholars of comparative politics also use institutionalist theories to develop arguments about political institutions and their effects.
- Many studies in comparative politics are based on quantitative methods that let scholars compare many countries, periods, municipalities, or other units of analysis.
- Other studies in comparative politics are based on in-depth analyses of individual countries, periods, municipalities et cetera.
- Correlation is not causation. The fact that two things usually appear together doesn't mean that one of them caused the other.
- Making educated guesses about causal relationships is a central concern for contemporary scholarship in comparative politics.

STUDY QUESTIONS

1. As we discussed in Section 2.2, the words we use to describe political systems are usually common English words that mean different things to different people and in different contexts. Compare the discussion of the word 'corruption' in a standard dictionary (such as the *Oxford English Dictionary*) with the brief discussion of how to measure corruption in Case Study 2.2. What happens when we go from the common meaning of a word like 'corruption' to the more precise meaning of that term in the empirical scholarly literature? What is gained? What is lost?

2. Take a look at the most recent issues of three leading comparative-politics journals, *Comparative Political Studies*, *Comparative Politics*, and *World Politics*. Choose one article that relies on quantitative methods (comparing many cases, perhaps using statistical techniques to analyse the data) and one article that relies on case-study methods (studying one or a few cases in greater depth). Why do you think the authors of those articles chose to use different methods? Do you agree with the choices they made?

3. Newspaper articles and columns often make causal claims about how to explain political events. See if you can find some examples of that in today's newspaper in the place where you live. Did the journalists and columnists pay attention to the fact that correlation doesn't necessarily imply causation (Section 2.5)? Can you think of a convincing way to empirically test the causal claims in the articles and columns you read?

FURTHER READING

Janet M. Box-Steffensmeier, Henry E. Brady, and David Collier (eds.), *The Oxford Handbook of Political Methodology* (2008).
Offers a broad overview of research methods in political science.

Arend Lijphart, *Patterns of Democracy* (2012).
Develops an influential theory of the differences between consensual and majoritarian democracies.

George Tsebelis, *Veto Players* (2002).
Develops a theory of which parties and institutions can prevent political change and how they use that power.

CHAPTER 3

STATES AND NATIONS

CHAPTER GUIDE

3.1 Introduction
3.2 The State
3.3 The Growth of the State
3.4 State Capacity
3.5 States and Nations

3.6 Conclusion
Summary
Study Questions
Further Reading

3.1 INTRODUCTION

Think back to the country where you grew up. Perhaps you live there still. Were there civil servants and public officials who carried out the government's policies? Were there courts that upheld the laws and settled legal disputes? Could people rely on the national, regional, and local government to provide public services such as schooling, sanitation, and policing? If the answers to those questions are all 'yes', you probably grew up in a country with a reasonably effective and capable state. For those of us with this background, it can be hard to imagine what it's like to live in a country without an effective state. It's easy to take the state for granted.

But it's a mistake to do so, and perhaps that's something you already know from personal experience. Perhaps where you grew up, civil servants and public officials couldn't, or wouldn't, carry out the government's policies, the courts didn't uphold the laws, and citizens didn't trust the government to provide essential public services. If that's your own experience of the state, you know an effective, well-functioning state doesn't exist naturally in the world; it's built, often over long periods of time.

In this chapter, you'll learn what states are, which services modern states typically provide for their citizens, and what makes strong states different from weak states. Scholars of comparative politics often use the term 'state capacity' to describe the ability of public officials to carry out government policies and provide public services, and we'll examine how state capacity has varied among countries and over time. We'll also discuss the relationship between the idea of the state and the idea of the nation. In many countries, these two ideas have been combined into the idea of a 'nation state'. That's a fairly recent idea, and one we'll want to examine carefully.

Why do we need to learn about all these things? There are two main reasons. First, the organization and capacity of the state influence people's lives directly since countries with effective states typically have higher economic growth, are more peaceful, and provide better services for their citizens. Second, the organization and capacity of the state indirectly influence all the *other* things we're studying in this book. Political leaders, parties, and interest groups fight for influence within the state since they want to use its resources and power for their own ends and purposes. We'll therefore understand modern politics better if we begin by studying the principal object of political conflicts in today's world: the modern state.

3.2 THE STATE

LEARNING OUTCOMES

After reading Section 3.2, you'll be able to:

- Define the state
- Explain the differences between states and other social organizations
- Describe the historical origins of states.

When we think of politics, we usually think of things like how a country's government is organized, how its political leaders are chosen, and what policies those leaders adopt. These are all very important topics, and we'll learn about each of them in this book. But first, let's take a step back and ask ourselves a few deeper questions. Why are there even countries in the first place? What is it that their leaders govern? And why do the policies governments adopt matter to ordinary people?

All of those questions lead us to the importance of the modern state. We tend to think of politics at the level of countries since the world is divided into just under 200 independent, territorially bounded states that are recognized as such by other states (the United Nations, which is an organization of the world's states, has 193 members). Each country has a government that controls its state apparatus, which is the combination of legal and administrative organizations that make up the state. And public policies matter to ordinary people because they're enforced and carried out by state institutions such as courts of law and government agencies. In other words, we think of modern states as organizations that control a particular territory, have governments that control their public authorities, and collect taxes from and deliver services to their citizens.

As we'll learn in later chapters, states can be structured very differently. For example, some states are federal, which means that political power is divided between the central government and regional governments (which, confusingly, are themselves often known as 'states', as in the United States of America), whereas other states are unitary, which means that power isn't divided in this way. Institutions such as governments, judiciaries, and bureaucracies can also be organized very differently. For now, however, we're discussing the general idea of the state as a composite organization that controls a particular territory, upholds laws, and carries out public policies. This idea can meaningfully be applied to political arrangements all over the world.

But it remains quite difficult to say what things states have in common that set them apart from all other social institutions and organizations. One of the reasons for this difficulty is that the nature of what we now call the state has changed greatly over the centuries. If we define the state broadly as an enduring administrative organization that is separate from individual rulers, there have been states on the planet for approximately 5,000 years, ever since complex political institutions were created for the regulation of water usage from great rivers such as the Euphrates and the Tigris in present-day Iraq, the Nile in present-day Egypt, and the Indus in present-day Pakistan. Archaeologists, historians, and social scientists don't agree on all the details of the origins of political organizations, but it remains standard to refer to the Sumerian society along the Euphrates and Tigris rivers and the Egyptian society along the Nile around 3000 BC as the world's first states (see, for example, Finer 1997, Volume I).

Five thousand years may seem like a long time, but it's only a small fraction of human history, for humans have been around for hundreds of thousands of years—as a species, we became separated from our closest relatives, the chimpanzees, approximately 6 million years ago, and it's been more than 200,000 years since anatomically modern humans, *Homo sapiens*, first appeared. It can plausibly be said that the state, with its enormous capacity for both good and evil, is the most important social institution in human history, but it's humbling to realize that there are living trees in the arid mountains of California that were already alive when the oldest states, now long gone, emerged in Africa and Asia.

When we study *modern* politics, as opposed to historical political systems, it typically makes sense to ask for something more than the presence of an enduring administrative organization when we define the state, and if we add more elements to the definition, the history of the state becomes much shorter than 5,000 years. For example, the idea that a state must be *territorial*—that each state needs to have well-defined geographical boundaries and be independent from other states—goes back a few hundred years at most.

The best-known definition of the modern state in the social sciences was proposed by the German sociologist Max Weber approximately a hundred years ago. In a speech to a group of students in Munich in early 1919, Weber argued that the defining characteristic of the modern state is that it's the only 'human community that (successfully) claims the monopoly of the legitimate use of physical force within a given territory'. Weber didn't mean to say that this is the *only* thing states do; he meant to say that their monopoly on the use of physical force is what distinguishes states from other human organizations. The important idea that all states claim a 'monopoly on violence' goes back to Weber's definition, which continues to be widely used in the social sciences to this day. It has several important implications. For example, it implies that the state's most significant challengers are organizations that claim *they* have a right to use violence to enforce their own rules. Large criminal gangs such as the Sicilian Mafia are one example. Organized groups that claim authority over parts of a state's territory are another. We'll come back to the problem of such challengers in Case Study 3.2.

Weber's definition of the state has an interesting backstory. In 1918, the year before Weber gave his speech in Munich, the German government was negotiating a peace agreement with the new communist government that had risen to power in Russia during its 1917 revolution. The Russian delegation was led by the communist leader Leon Trotsky (Figure 3.1). At one point during the negotiations, one of the German generals accused the new Russian regime of being based on violence. Trotsky replied that *every* state is based on violence. Max Weber was not a communist—he helped form one of the liberal parties in the Weimar Republic, the German political system after the First World War—but he told the Munich students that he agreed with Trotsky's view of the state (an English translation of his speech is included in Weber 1946).

Figure 3.1 In a famous speech to students in Munich in 1919, Max Weber agreed with the view of Leon Trotsky, pictured here, that the modern state is based on violence. *Source: Sueddeutsche Zeitung Photo / Alamy Stock Photo*

Weber added an important qualification, though, when he noted that the state claims a monopoly on the *legitimate* use of violence. The authority of the modern state isn't based on force alone; it also depends on the consent or at least acquiescence of the people it governs. In democracies, constitutions, elections, and legislatures help to legitimize the state by protecting citizens from the capricious or tyrannical use of the state's power, giving citizens an opportunity to select their political leaders and the people's representatives a chance to debate how the state's power ought to be used. As we'll discuss in Chapter 5, authoritarian regimes also seek legitimacy, although it's a different sort of legitimacy from that of democratic regimes.

3.3 THE GROWTH OF THE STATE

LEARNING OUTCOMES

After reading Section 3.3, you'll be able to:

- Describe how the scope of the state has changed over the past 200 years
- Summarize the relationship between war and state building
- Explain how modern welfare states differ from earlier forms of states.

Just as it's hard for someone who grew up in a country with a reasonably well-functioning state to imagine what it's like to live in a country without one, it's hard for us who live now to grasp how the scope of the state—what states *do*—has changed over the past two centuries. Until the nineteenth century, most states were relatively small military and legal organizations that waged wars and upheld laws, and ordinary people were only vaguely aware of the central state and its institutions. Today, by contrast, most people interact with state officials regularly, since states provide a much wider range of services that people rely on throughout their lives.

Let's begin by considering Figure 3.2, which uses historical evidence on average central-government taxes between 1830 and 2010 to describe the size of the state in economic terms. These data are not available for all countries, so Figure 3.2 only describes tax revenues in western Europe, North and South America, and a few states in the Asia-Pacific region, such as Australia, Japan, and New Zealand (Argentina, Australia, Austria, Belgium, Bolivia, Brazil, Canada, Chile, Colombia, Denmark, Ecuador, Finland, France, Germany, Ireland, Italy, Japan, Mexico, Netherlands, New Zealand, Norway, Paraguay, Peru, Portugal, Spain, Sweden, Switzerland, the United Kingdom, the United States, Uruguay, and Venezuela). As the figure shows, the twenty-first-century state is on average four times larger than the nineteenth-century state, in terms of its share of the national economy—and that's actually a low estimate of how much the whole public sector of the economy has grown over this period, for Figure 3.2 does not include taxes at the local or regional levels of government, which often account for a large share of total taxation.

We see in Figure 3.2 that the largest jumps in central-government taxation occurred during and after the First World War (1914–1918) and the Second World War (1939–1945). Because of

Figure 3.2 Central-government tax revenues, as a percentage of the gross domestic product (a measure of the size of the economy), increased fourfold in the Americas, Europe, and the Asia-Pacific between the early nineteenth century and today. *Source: Author's own work, based on data from Andersson, Per and Thomas Brambor. 2019. 'Financing the State: Government Tax Revenue from 1800 to 2012. Version 2.0'. Lund: Lund University.*

these sorts of patterns in data on government revenues, many scholars of comparative politics believe that there is a relationship between state building and war. This idea is known as the 'bellicist theory of the state', after the Latin word for war, *bellum*. According to the bellicist theory, international rivalry has been one of the drivers of the increasing strength and scope of states since the early modern period in the sixteenth, seventeenth, and eighteenth centuries (see especially Tilly 1992). Even the rise of the welfare state, which doesn't seem very warlike, can be explained in part by the need for soldiers who are sufficiently fit and educated to fight and the need for social programmes for veterans and widows after wars (see, for example, Skocpol 1992).

But the bellicist theory applies mainly to states in Europe. Outside of that continent, state building has often been shaped by other forces, such as colonialism and trade (Centeno, Kohli, and Yashar 2017; Mazzuca 2021). The fact that many modern states in the Global South were created after decolonization has complicated state building, since the borders of the new states were often drawn by colonial overlords before independence, without paying much attention to the people who actually lived in the affected areas. If you take a look at any of the world maps in this book, you will note that many of the country borders in Africa are straight lines. There are no straight country borders in Europe.

Until the nineteenth century, a large proportion of government revenue was spent on the military, but in the course of the nineteenth century, governments began to spend more on domestic public services. One example is the police. It's easy to think that the police have always been around, but they haven't. The first modern civilian police force, the London Metropolitan Police, was established as late as 1829. Its famous 'bobbies'—a slang word for police officers—are named after the government minister behind the 1829 police reform, Robert Peel. Before the nineteenth century, what we now think of as police work was either not done at all or done by other officials at the local, regional, and national levels. Today, there are police forces in every country in the world, and the police perform fairly similar tasks across countries. Along with the military, the police are the embodiment of the state monopoly on violence we discussed in Section 3.2.

Another important example is education. The first time in their lives that most people come into immediate contact with the state, broadly defined, is their first day of school. But schools haven't been around for ever either, at least not for ordinary people outside social and economic elites. The first country in the world that made primary schooling compulsory for all children was Prussia in the late eighteenth century (Prussia was the largest among the several states that later became Germany). It took many decades, even centuries, for most countries in the world to provide basic education for all. But they do now. We see this in Figure 3.3, which uses data from Lee and Lee (2016) to describe the proportion of all children who have been enrolled in primary schools in different world regions since 1820. Only recently, in the 2000s, have enrolment rates approached 100 per cent in all regions. Secondary and tertiary education began to expand much later than primary education, and major differences remain between the main regions of the world (Figure 3.4).

The creation of a modern police force and a national education system were two important events during the rapid state-building process that occurred in Japan in the nineteenth century. You can read more about the transformation of the Japanese state in that period in Case Study 3.1.

Figure 3.3 By the early 2000s, most children attended primary schools in all major world regions. The acronym 'MENA' refers to the Middle East and North Africa. *Source: Author's own work, based on data courtesy of Lee, Jong-Wha and Hanol Lee. 2016. 'Human Capital in the Long Run'.* Journal of Development Economics 122

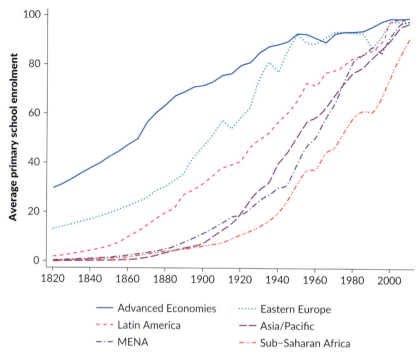

Figure 3.4 Secondary and tertiary education expanded later than primary education, and major differences remain between the main world regions. *Source: Author's own work based on data from Lee, Jong-Wha and Hanol Lee. 2016. 'Human Capital in the Long Run'.* Journal of Development Economics.

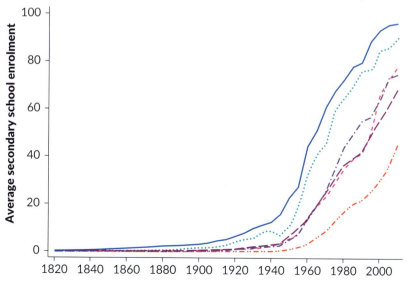

Figure 3.4 (Continued)

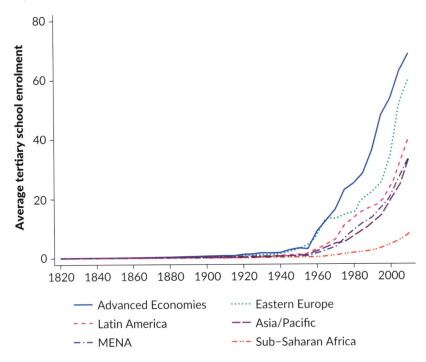

> **CASE STUDY 3.1**
> State building in Japan

How were states made, and how did they become strong? One of the most famous examples of state building in the modern world is the transformation of Japan from a feudal society with low GDP per capita in the middle of the nineteenth century to a powerful, modern state in the late nineteenth and early twentieth centuries. This is known as the Meiji Restoration, as the transformation occurred during the reign of Emperor Meiji (1867–1912) (Figure 3.5).

Ever since the early seventeenth century, Japan had been governed by the shogun, a military commander, and by the country's feudal lords. That old political system was known as the Tokugawa Shogunate, after the leading noble family in Japan at the time. In January 1868, the last shogun was ousted in a *coup d'état*. Power was restored to the emperor and, indirectly, to groups of political reformers with whom the emperor was associated. Those groups wished to turn Japan into a modern nation state and increase Japan's military power.

Within a few years, the new government had abolished the old self-governing feudal domains and replaced them with prefectures (regional administrative districts) that were governed directly from the capital, as in France and in Japan's neighbour China. Within the central government, a system of examinations for civil servants was introduced, giving Japan a more professional bureaucracy. Meanwhile, the Meiji reformers sought inspiration from other countries about how to put in place new policies, following the emperor's declaration in April 1868 that under his new government, 'knowledge shall be sought throughout the world' (Beasley 1990, 56). Missions were sent abroad to learn of the governments and policies of other countries, and foreign experts were brought to Japan to help reform Japanese institutions, laws, and government policies. Japan reformed its police force,

Figure 3.5 During the 45-year reign of Emperor Meiji (1867–1912), the Japanese state was transformed from a feudal, decentralized political structure to a modern, industrialized, and effective state. *Source: The Elisha Whittelsey Collection, The Elisha Whittelsey Fund, 1986, courtesy of the Metropolitan Museum of Art*

its public-health policies, and, importantly, its education system, which was brought under the control of the central government and made to resemble school systems in western Europe.

One of the things we learn from the example of the Meiji Restoration is that great changes in state power are often the result of a confluence of domestic and international factors. The domestic political changes that preceded the Meiji Restoration were related to changes in Japan's international environment. The Meiji reformers were concerned that Japan wouldn't be able to compete with other countries, or even survive as an independent state, if it didn't reform its political system.

A second lesson from the Meiji Restoration is that state building often leads to conflict. There were numerous rebellions in the early years of the Meiji period. The reforms of the education system were especially controversial. When the Meiji government decided to create a new, centralized school system, many Japanese people preferred to keep their old local schools and temple schools, and the new state schools were sometimes burned down (Platt 2004).

The third lesson from the history of modern Japan is that there is no simple and straightforward relationship between the strength of the state and the nature of the political regime. Although Japan did not become a democracy until after the Second World War, in the late nineteenth and early twentieth centuries, the Japanese political system was gradually becoming more democratic: there was a functioning constitution that constrained the emperor's power, and there were competitive elections through which different groups in society could make themselves heard by supporting different political parties. But by the 1930s, when Japan was allying with Adolf Hitler's national-socialist government in Germany, the military establishment had become highly influential in politics and the country had become more authoritarian. A stronger state does not necessarily mean that a country becomes more democratic, nor does it mean the opposite—there are many ways to govern a strong state.

In the wealthy states in Europe and the Americas, the creation of broad-based public services such as policing, education, and public health was a nineteenth-century phenomenon (Ansell and Lindvall 2021). In the late nineteenth and early twentieth centuries, states in Europe and the Americas also began to redistribute much of the money that their citizens earned through social insurances against the loss of income due to sickness, unemployment, or old age. Such social insurances are the hallmark of what is called the **welfare state**. A welfare state is a state that's responsible not only for things like the military, infrastructure, and the legal system, but also for the economic and social well-being of individual citizens and families. Social-insurance programmes and other welfare-state programmes vary a great deal in their generosity and coverage—that is, how many people get to enjoy the benefits—but basic social insurances are ubiquitous in the world today. For example, there are only a handful countries in the world that don't have at least a rudimentary pension system for citizens who are too old to work.

The increasing scope of the state raises many important research questions.

1. Why do modern states provide so many services for their citizens? In the short to medium term, governments and legislatures have historically adopted different sorts of policies, for reasons that we'll come back to in Chapter 15 on public policymaking, including interests, ideas, institutions, international influences, and even the idiosyncratic views of individual political leaders. In the long term, however, all states, regardless of the ideological orientations of their governments, collect more taxes, provide more services, and redistribute more income today than, say, 100 or 200 years ago. There is something about the social, economic, and political conditions during this long period that explains the increasing scope of the state. We have already mentioned the importance of international rivalry and the two world wars. Two other social and economic forces that have probably contributed to the changing role of the state are industrialization and urbanization, which have removed most people from the rural communities in which they used to live and made them demand more services and protection from their governments.

2. What consequences does the changing role of the state have for political conflicts? As we noted in the introduction to this chapter, political leaders, parties, and interest groups seek power and influence within the state since they want to use its resources for their own ends and purposes. This means that when states start to do things—and develop the capacity for doing those things—the nature of the political conflicts in society changes. As we'll discuss in Chapter 11, for example, one of the most important groups of parties in Europe in the twentieth century, the Christian Democratic parties, emerged because of conflicts over education in the nineteenth century, as lay Catholics protested against the introduction of national, secular education systems by liberal governments (Kalyvas 1996). In the twenty-first century, the rise of green parties and radical-right parties can also be explained, in part, by underlying changes in what states do.

3. This brings us to a third question: how is the scope of the state changing today, and how will it change in the future? Contemporary states are much more concerned with the protection of the natural environment than states in earlier historical periods were. The establishment of the first national parks in the nineteenth century was the state's first foray into the domain of environmental policy. Today, the natural environment has become a major concern all over the world, which has led some scholars to talk of the rise of a 'green state' (Eckersley 2004). We can only guess what the rise of artificial intelligence will mean for the changing role of the state in the future.

In Research Prompt 3.1, we consider processes of state building in today's world.

> **RESEARCH PROMPT 3.1**
> State building today

In Case Study 3.1, we studied state building in Japan in the last third of the nineteenth century, during the so-called Meiji Restoration. This was a remarkably rapid process, which is widely regarded as a paradigmatic example of the transition from an early modern to a modern state.

Are there parts of the world today where political leaders are trying to put in place the basic institutions and policies associated with a modern state? Identify at least two contemporary examples and analyse the challenges and successes faced by political leaders in these state-building efforts. One type of example you may want to consider is countries that have gone through war or a foreign occupation, such as Afghanistan, Iraq, or Bosnia. A second example is new countries that have emerged as a large country split into several smaller states, such as the Baltic states in Europe or the former Soviet republics in central Asia after the collapse of the Soviet Union in the early 1990s. A third, very different type of example is where an organization claims sovereignty over a territory that has previously been controlled by another state, such as the Gaza Strip or the West Bank in Palestine.

In your analysis, consider the following questions:

- What historical, social, and economic factors are influencing state-building efforts in these countries?
- How are political leaders addressing issues such as public administration, economic development, and the provision of public services?
- What roles do foreign governments and international organizations play in the state-building process?

Finally, consider what lessons can be drawn from the experiences of the two countries you have selected.

3.4 STATE CAPACITY

LEARNING OUTCOMES

After reading Section 3.4, you'll be able to:
- Define state capacity
- Evaluate different measures of state capacity
- Study the variation in state capacity within countries and over time.

In Section 3.3, we discussed what states are and what they do. In this section, we'll discuss a different but related question: what states *can* do. Scholars of comparative politics often refer to the ability of states to get things done as 'state capacity'. A little more formally, state capacity can be defined as 'the capacity of the state . . . to implement . . . political decisions' (Mann 1984, 189), the 'institutional capability of the state to carry out various policies' (Besley and Persson 2011, 6), 'the ability of state leaders to use the agencies of the state to get people in the society to do what they want them to do' (Migdal 1988, xiii), or the 'degree of control that state agents exercise over persons, activities, and resources within their government's territorial jurisdiction' (McAdam, Tarrow, and Tilly 2001, 78). Note that the last of these four definitions explicitly refers to the state's territoriality, which, as we discussed in Section 3.2, is a key part of the definition of the modern state.

To be more concrete, a state has high state capacity if public officials (that is, those who work for the state) are able to accomplish important things such as maintaining order, settling disputes, and carrying out the government's policies. Most scholars today agree that variations in state capacity help to explain many important social, economic, and political outcomes—including economic development (Besley and Persson 2011) and civil war (Fearon and Laitin 2003)—but it's a difficult thing to measure, for being *able* to do something doesn't always mean actually *doing it*. For example, some modern states collect more taxes than others, but it's entirely possible, even likely, that many of the states that have low taxes would have been able to collect more of them if their governments had wanted—they just chose not to. For example, public social spending as a percentage of GDP is approximately four times higher in Sweden than in Singapore, but both of those countries have high state capacity, so the difference in outcomes is most likely a result of political choices made by the Swedish and Singaporean governments.

Nonetheless, scholars and international political organizations such as the World Bank have in recent years sought to develop empirical indicators of state capacity that allow for international comparisons. Figure 3.6 is based on one such indicator: an estimate of 'government effectiveness' that has been developed by the World Bank. The idea of the World Bank's government-effectiveness indicator is to capture several different aspects of how the political system works, including the quality of public services, the quality of the bureaucracy, the competence of civil servants, how independent public officials are from political pressures, and whether the government is able to sustain its policies over time. This indicator is therefore meant to combine evidence on many of the things we have discussed in this chapter in a single number (although we need to keep in mind that the World Bank's main job is to promote economic development, so its government-effectiveness indicator is primarily meant to be applied to economic problems).

When we study this map, we see that government effectiveness is closely related to economic development. The prosperous democracies in western Europe, North America, and Oceania aren't just rich; they also have strong states with high levels of state capacity. In those countries, reasonably effective and professional bureaucrats and civil servants provide a wide range of public services, governments are generally able to adopt and implement broad-based public policies, and people have reason to be fairly confident that those policies will be carried out in practice.

The close relationship between state capacity and economic prosperity is clearly not a coincidence, but the explanation is far from obvious. Do some states function well and effectively because they are rich? Or are some countries rich because their states function well and effectively? Or is there some third, underlying factor that explains both state capacity and prosperity, such as geography, religion, culture, or historical experience? You'll recall our discussion of causality in Chapter 2: correlation is not causation, so when we observe that two things go together, that's only the beginning of the analysis, not the end. When it comes to the relationship between state capacity and prosperity, the truth is probably quite messy. Sometimes state capacity has simply come with increasing wealth. At other times, countries have promoted economic development and made themselves richer by investing in state capacity. That's what Japan did when it changed its political system in the late nineteenth century to encourage economic modernization (see Case Study 3.1). And sometimes fortuitous historical circumstances or other cultural and social factors have contributed to a strengthening of state capacity and rising living standards simultaneously.

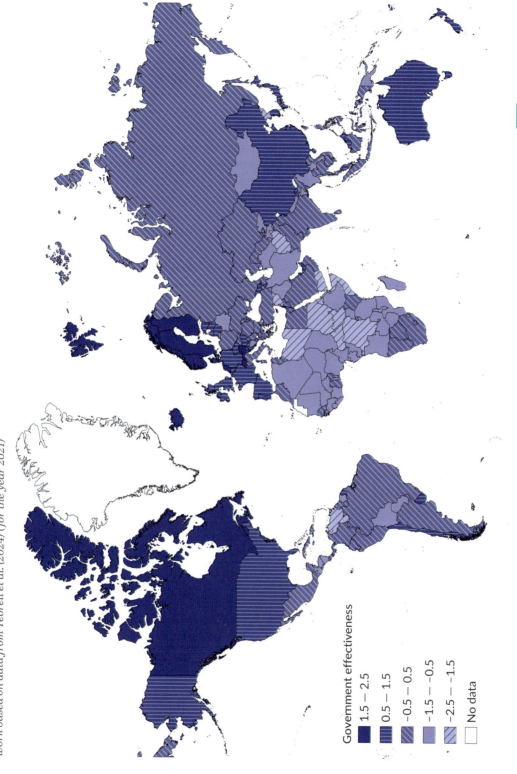

Figure 3.6 Judging by the World Bank's measure of 'government effectiveness', state capacity varies greatly around the world. *Source: Author's own work based on data from Teorell et al. (2024) (for the year 2021)*

In parts of the world that have lower state capacity, public services are of lower quality, governments are often unable to adopt broad-based public policies, and even if they do, people have good reasons to doubt that the policies will in fact be carried out effectively. In addition to these direct effects on the quality of public services and the implementation of public policies, low state capacity has powerful indirect effects on how political conflicts are resolved in a society, for if public policies aren't implemented effectively, democratic elections lose some of their meaning, and people look for alternative ways of making their voices heard. For example, Cornell and Grimes (2015) show in a comparative study of Latin America and the Caribbean that disruptive political protests are more frequent in countries that lack strong, professional bureaucratic institutions.

So far, we have concentrated on differences between countries, such as the country-level data on government effectiveness that we examined in Figure 3.6, but state capacity can also vary greatly *within* countries. Indeed, much of the cutting-edge comparative-politics work on state capacity in the 2010s and 2020s has been concerned with exactly this problem (Harbers and Steele 2020). For example, Soifer (2015) examines the reach of the state historically in a selection of Latin American countries and demonstrates that they varied widely in their ability to carry out public policies throughout their territories, and Harbers (2015) demonstrates that fiscal capacity (the government's ability to collect taxes) varies greatly within national territories today. Within some contemporary states, state authorities are so weak in parts of the country that the state's monopoly on violence is challenged by criminal gangs and other armed, organized groups. Please turn to Case Study 3.2, where we'll examine how Mexico is facing serious challenges from organized criminal gangs in many parts of its territory.

CASE STUDY 3.2
Gangs and the state in Mexico

Starting in the 1980s, Colombian cocaine manufacturers and distributors began to rely on Mexican gangs to transport narcotics northwards, into the United States. Those gangs already had a history of trafficking other narcotics, such as methamphetamine and heroin. In the 2000s and 2010s, the conflicts between the gangs and the Mexican state intensified, as did the conflicts among the various gangs. They have caused many tens of thousands of deaths in Mexico since the 1990s.

In parts of Mexico, the criminal cartels are so powerful that the state has effectively ceased to function, either because of fear or because of corrupt entanglements between the cartels and state officials, or because of both. One police chief in the city of Ciudad Juárez commented that when crimes were committed,

> There was no professional investigation; no bad investigation either. There just wasn't any investigation. When crimes happened, police would hide in our offices. (Sam Quinones, 'Once the World's Most Dangerous City, Juárez Returns to Life', *National Geographic*, June 2016)

Because of these developments, both domestic and international observers have concluded that the Mexican government has lost control over parts of its territory. Indeed, the *Washington*

Post reported in 2020 that a classified report from the Central Intelligence Agency estimated that 'drug-trafficking groups had gained effective control over about 20 per cent of Mexico' ('Violent Criminal Groups Are Eroding Mexico's Authority and Claiming More Territory', *Washington Post*, 29 October 2020).

Representatives of the Mexican government have disputed this view. For example, in 2009, Felipe Calderón, Mexico's president in 2006–2012, responded to the United States' concerns that Mexico might become a failed state:

> To say that Mexico is a failed state is absolutely false. I have not lost any part, any single point, of the Mexican territory. . . . [I]n Mexico, all the territory is in the hands of the Mexican authorities. (BBC News, Mexico rejects US drugs warning, 27 February 2009)

It would be wrong to characterize Mexico as a failed state that is comparable to countries with ongoing involvement in wars and very low GDP per capita, such as Afghanistan in Asia and Somalia in Africa. The truth is more complicated and more interesting: Mexico has become an example of how an otherwise prosperous and reasonably well-functioning state can lose control over pockets of its territory. It is also an example of how the state's 'monopoly of violence' can be challenged by private organizations. Beginning in the 1990s, Mexico's powerful cartels, which used to rely on protection from corrupt officials and politicians, have formed their own private, well-armed militias to protect their criminal operations. The rise in violence in Mexico in the 1990s, 2000s, and 2010s is a result of conflicts between the criminal militias, the military, and the police, and, especially, conflicts among the militias.

In the 2010s, in another turn of events, farmers, business owners, and other residents in parts of Mexico, especially in the state of Michoacán, formed organizations known as *autodefensas* to protect citizens from the gangs, since they did not trust the military and the police to maintain order. As one magazine article observed,

> Armed groups of ordinary citizens have set up security checkpoints, disarmed and chased away police they considered ineffective, and even organized ambitious manhunts to apprehend or kill suspected criminal bosses. (Alan Taylor, 'Mexico's Vigilantes', *The Atlantic*, 13 May 2014)

The Mexican government responded by sending the military and the police to Michoacán, but they eventually decided against disarming *autodefensas* and instead sought to turn the vigilante groups into a form of rural police.

There are times when the state ceases to function altogether. The government in the capital can no longer control its territory. The centre cannot hold. The authority of the state breaks down completely. The laws cease to have meaning, since there's no one there to uphold and enforce them. Organizations other than the state—such as warbands, private armies, and criminal syndicates—claim to control large parts of the country. In these circumstances, we speak of 'failed states' or 'state collapse'. The most common cause of state failure is war, and especially civil war, which is a war within one state as opposed to a war among different states. The close relationship between state failure and violence isn't surprising. As you learned in Section 3.2, many scholars agree with Max Weber's view that the state can be defined as an organization that successfully claims a monopoly over legitimate violence in a given territory. This definition suggests that widespread violence in a territory is the clearest sign that the state has, in a sense, ceased to function. In Chapter 1, we made the point that one of the purposes of political institutions is to change the nature of conflicts from 'fights' into 'games' or 'debates'. When different groups in society cease to resolve conflicts through formal political procedures and instead use brute force to get what they want, political institutions cease to perform this function. In that sense, most other political institutions depend on a functioning state.

3.5 STATES AND NATIONS

LEARNING OUTCOMES

After reading Section 3.5, you'll be able to:
- Define nations and nationalism
- Summarize some of the main theories of the origins of nation states
- Identify contemporary challenges to the idea of the nation.

We often think of the state as an organization that is meant for a particular group of people who share a common history, speak the same language, and share certain cultural characteristics. What we have here is the idea of the *nation state*: the claim that each people has—or ought to have—a state, and, conversely, that each state is, or ought to be, associated with a people.

The idea of the nation state is expressed clearly in the first two articles of the French constitution from 1958. Article 1 lays out some of the basic political principles on which the French state is founded: it's meant to be an 'indivisible, secular, democratic and social' republic that treats all citizens as equal before the law, has a decentralized organization, and promotes 'equal access by women and men to elective offices'. Article 2 has a different sort of message. It says that the 'language of the Republic shall be French', that France's emblem is the 'blue, white and red tricolour flag', and that its national anthem is 'La Marseillaise'. In other words, after defining the political principles on which the French republic is founded, the constitution goes on to explain that the French people have a shared language and shared national symbols—the flag and the national anthem—that are associated with the country's history.

There are many other examples of how the idea of the state has become tied up with the idea of a national community with a shared history, language, and culture. Indeed, the idea of the nation state is so pervasive in the modern world that many people simply take it for granted and assume that the nation state is the only natural form of political organization. But it isn't. Nationalism is in fact a fairly new idea, which began to spread across the world in the nineteenth century, after the Great Revolution in France in 1789–1799. There is broad agreement among political scientists, sociologists, and historians that nations, as we know them today, are historical constructs that began to emerge in that period (for an overview of nations and nationalism, see Mylonas and Tudor 2023).

As the political scientist Benedict Anderson (1983) puts it, a nation is an 'imagined' community, not a form of community that comes naturally. It was made possible by the modern economic, social, and political forces of industrialization, urbanization, the spread of communication technologies, and the creation of country-wide primary education systems for all citizens (see Section 3.3). Before the nineteenth century, most people in the world lived in small, agrarian communities, didn't venture far from where they were born, and knew little about the larger political community around them. Their identities weren't national: they were rooted in their local community (and perhaps also in a set of religious beliefs that were shared in a *wider* community than that of a single state). Indeed, scholars such as Gellner (1983) have argued that when it first emerged in Europe, the main purpose of nationalism was to serve the needs of an industrial economy, in which people become disconnected from local communities and instead develop a sense of belonging to a wider national community.

Nationalism became an even more powerful political force in the twentieth century, as other, older forms of political organization disappeared. The end of the First World War resulted in the fall of several great empires—the Austrian, the German, the Russian, and the Turkish—and as the old empires were dissolved, many new nation states emerged in Europe. In the period between the two world wars, fascism—an aggressive, violent form of nationalism—became one of the most influential political ideologies in Europe and elsewhere, and fascist movements took power in many countries, most notably in Italy in the 1920s and Germany in the 1930s.

Then, in the middle of the twentieth century, the most important political movement around the world was decolonization—the dissolution of vast colonial empires that had been dominated by European states such as Belgium, France, the Netherlands, Portugal, and the United Kingdom. Decolonization was inspired by ideas of nationalism and national self-determination. Groups fighting for independence were typically motivated by the idea that as a people distinct from their colonial masters, they ought to decide their own fate. The language of nationalism was used to challenge colonial power, and the new governments that were formed after countries became independent from the European colonial empires often understood themselves in nationalist terms.

Nationalism continues to be a powerful political force in today's world. Perhaps the clearest example of this is the decades-long struggle between Israel and the organizations that represent the Palestinian people who dwelled in the territory that is now Israel before the late 1940s. The idea behind the creation of Israel was that the Jewish people ought to have a state of their own. This idea is known as Zionism, and it began to spread in Europe in the nineteenth century. It is closely related to other national movements that also emerged and grew stronger in that same period. But the Palestinian organizations are *also* motivated by nationalism. The charter of Fatah, the Palestinian organization that controls much of the West Bank, states that Fatah is 'a *national*, revolutionary movement' (my emphasis).

In the last few decades, nationalism has become an increasingly important ideology among political parties in the wealthy democracies in Europe, North America, and Oceania. As we'll discuss in Chapter 11, new nationalist right-wing parties have emerged in most of Europe's democracies since the 1980s, and many of them have grown to become large and influential parties in their countries, including Front National (today Rassemblement National) in France, the True Finns in Finland, and the Alternative für Deutschland in Germany.

To sum up, then, although nations are 'imagined' communities and the idea of the nation state is quite new—emerging and spreading over the past 200 years or so—nationalism remains an exceptionally influential and powerful idea. The idea of the modern state and to some extent also the modern idea of democracy are tied up with the idea of a national community and, at times, with nationalism—the belief that each nation ought to have a state and each state ought to serve one particular nation, or people. Like many other ideas in politics, the ideas of the nation, the nation state, and nationalism can have very different sorts of consequences. On the one hand, ideas of national sovereignty and self-determination have inspired liberation movements and pro-democracy groups. On the other hand, the same sorts of ideas have led to inter-state wars, civil wars, sectarian conflicts, and the repression of ethnic, linguistic, and religious minorities.

In today's world, the idea of the nation state is challenged both by increasing migration and by the emergence of powerful inter-state organizations such as the European Union, which promote the idea that people have, or ought to have, political loyalties that go beyond national borders. Many scholars believe that the rise of nationalist parties and the increasing salience of nationalist ideologies is in part a response to these social, economic, and political trends in contemporary societies.

3.6 CONCLUSION

We have learned in this chapter that the state isn't something we can take for granted and that states around the world are very different from each other. Some are large, some are small. Some are strong, some are weak. Some are resilient and stable, some are fragile or have even broken down altogether. When we look back, we find that states have changed greatly over time. Some 200 years ago, even the strongest states in the world provided few services for their citizens. They were largely military and legal organizations, nothing like the large, functionally differentiated states we see today.

We'll now move on to the question of how states are *governed*. We'll begin, in Chapters 4 and 5, with the basic question of whether political leaders are elected by and responsible to the people (which is the hallmark of democracy) or whether they're only responsive to some smaller group (which is the defining quality of an authoritarian state). In the chapters that follow, we'll consider many other institutions that matter greatly for how states are governed and organized. Everything we've learned about modern states in this chapter is relevant to those discussions. For example, in Chapters 4 and 5, we'll be learning about *coups d'état*, which is when a small group of conspirators remove the leaders of a country and establish a new government. That word literally means 'stroke against the state', so there can be no *coup* without an *état*—and that's just one of many connections we'll find between state building and the development of political regimes such as democracy and authoritarianism.

SUMMARY

- The modern world is divided into approximately 200 states, which are organizations that claim a monopoly on violence within a particular territory.
- We need to understand what states are and do since the main goal of political leaders, parties, and interest groups is to control or influence the central state institutions.

- Modern states are large and powerful organizations that provide a wide range of services for their citizens, redistribute income and wealth within the population, and collect taxes that can correspond to as much as 50 per cent of GDP.
- Some 200 years ago, states were very different: they were smaller military-legal organizations that provided very few of the public services that most people today take for granted.
- State capacity—the ability of public officials to carry out the policies a country's political leaders have adopted—varies greatly between countries, and has changed greatly over time.
- People can also experience the state very differently *within* countries—in many parts of the world, the presence of the state varies a lot within the government's territorial jurisdiction.
- Approximately two centuries ago, in the wake of the French Revolution, the idea of the state became fused with the idea of the nation—the notion that all those who dwell in a country belong together, form a community, and have a shared identity.
- Nationalism—the idea that each nation ought to have a state of its own—has shaped and continues to shape the modern world: it has led to numerous bloody wars, but historically, it has also been associated with national liberation and the introduction of democracy.

STUDY QUESTIONS

1. About a hundred years ago, Max Weber famously defined a state as an organization that claims a monopoly over the legitimate use of violence. Having read about how states have changed over the decades and centuries, and how states vary across the world today, do you think that Weber's definition captures the essential properties of the state, or are there things you'd like to add to it (or to take out of it)?
2. In Case Study 3.1 about Japan, you learned how that country reorganized its political institutions some 100–150 years ago, building an effective, centralized state and turning itself into a regional power with a modern, industrial economy. As you look around the world today, are there countries that are undergoing similar processes of state building—or was Japan's experience unique?

FURTHER READING

Kimberly J. Morgan and Ann Shola Orloff, *The Many Hands of the State* (2017).
  Contains numerous case studies of different aspects of states and statehood.

Harris Mylonas and Maya Tudor, *Varieties of Nationalism* (2023).
  Reviews the political-science literature on nations and nationalism and assesses nationalism's political consequences.

Max Weber, 'Politics as a Vocation' (1919, reprinted in Weber 1946).
  Provides a classic definition of the state and is quite frankly a must-read for all students of politics.

CHAPTER 4
DEMOCRACY

CHAPTER GUIDE

4.1 Introduction
4.2 Rule by the People
4.3 Democracy around the World
4.4 Democratization
4.5 Democracy's Effects

4.6 Conclusion
Summary
Study Questions
Further Reading

4.1 INTRODUCTION

Approximately half of the countries in the world are democracies. Every few years, elections are held, and the people have an opportunity to replace their political leaders. In authoritarian political systems, the people don't have this power. Political leaders therefore answer to some smaller group, such as the wealthy, the military, or a political party. There may be elections, but they don't decide the distribution of power in the country. Before the nineteenth century, almost all states in human history were authoritarian (although the modern word 'authoritarianism' wasn't in use back then). Indeed, 200 years ago, most rulers were kings—or, occasionally, queens—who had *inherited* their power. Monarchs typically only shared power, if at all, with a small elite of administrators, aristocrats, and members of the clergy. In this chapter, we will explore the main differences between democracies and authoritarian states and study the history of democracy.

Scholars of comparative politics use the term 'regime' to describe the rules that decide who controls a country's central political institutions. O'Donnell (2001, 14) defines regimes as the 'patterns, formal or informal and explicit or implicit, that determine the channels of access to principal governmental positions'. There's an important connection between the concept of a political regime and the concept of the state, for access to 'governmental positions' means having power over the state apparatus. As we just learned in Chapter 3, the state is a uniquely important and powerful organization, and those who control the government can use the state's power for their own ends. That's why the choice between democracy and authoritarianism is so important. In a democracy, the power of the state cannot be used against the interests of the people, at least not in the long run. An authoritarian regime isn't constrained in this way.

In Section 4.2, we'll discuss the meaning of the term 'democracy'. The word 'democracy' has many different meanings in ordinary language, but scholars of comparative politics usually have something quite specific in mind when they study the differences between democratic and authoritarian systems. In Section 4.3, we'll examine the distribution of democratic regimes in the world today. We touched upon this topic in Chapter 1. Now that we come back to it a second time, we'll pay more attention to the methodological problem of how to measure democracy. In Section 4.4, we'll study the main drivers of democratization—when, how, and why authoritarian states become democratic. In Section 4.5, finally, we'll learn about the effects of democracy and authoritarianism on important outcomes such as economic development, political violence, and social equality.

4.2 RULE BY THE PEOPLE

LEARNING OUTCOMES

After reading Section 4.2, you'll be able to:

- Define democracy
- Summarize some of the basic problems in democratic theory
- Distinguish between different forms of democracy.

The word **democracy** literally means 'rule by the people'. The word's origins are Greek, and its history goes back 2,500 years to the city state of Athens. *Demos*, in ancient Greek, meant 'people', or 'the common people', and *kratía* meant 'power' or 'rule'. Democracy means something very different to us than it did to the ancients, but modern definitions of democracy continue to flow from the word's literal meaning of rule by the people.

In political systems that are not democratic, a smaller group controls the state, dominating all others. There are many names for non-democratic regimes, including 'dictatorship', 'autocracy', and 'authoritarianism'. These three terms are used more or less interchangeably in contemporary scholarship. The word 'dictatorship' goes back to the ancient Roman constitution's provisions for handing over power to a single individual, a 'dictator'. The word 'autocracy' literally means 'self-rule', which again implies that one person controls the state. Since there are many non-democratic regimes that don't put power in the hands of a single individual, we will refer to non-democratic political systems as **authoritarian** in this book. It means that the people have to bow to the authority of the powerful; they don't have the final say.

But the simple idea of democracy as rule by the people leaves a lot of questions unanswered. What does it mean for the people to *rule*? Who *are* the people in the first place? And what do they rule *over*? By answering these three questions, we can develop more precise ideas of what democracy means. They are central to **democratic theory**, which is the part of political theory that examines the idea of democracy, distinguishes between its different varieties, and assesses the arguments for and against letting the people rule.

4.2.1 What does it mean for the people to rule?

There are two ways for the people to rule: directly or indirectly. Direct democracy means that the people themselves decide important political questions. Referendums, such as the Brexit referendum in the United Kingdom in 2016, are an example of direct democracy in action. Indirect democracy means that the people elect representatives, and then those representatives adopt laws, impose taxes, control the government, and make all other important political decisions. Every democratic state in the world today practises **representative democracy**, although a few, such as Switzerland, also hold frequent referendums. When we discuss how democratic systems work, we will concentrate on representative democracies. That's why we opened this chapter with the simple observation that in democracies, the people have the opportunity, through recurring elections, to replace their political leaders.

The two most important decision making institutions in modern states are legislatures, or parliaments, and executives, or governments. In all modern democracies, the people elect the members of the legislature. Under presidentialism, the people also elect the head of government. Under parliamentarism, the head of government isn't directly elected, but answers to the legislature, which is. (A few democracies combine presidentialism and parliamentarism into a mixed system known as semi-presidentialism, but let's save that for Chapter 8, in which you'll learn more about legislatures and executives.)

To assess whether a modern state is democratic, we must begin by asking two questions, given the centrality of legislatures and executives.

- Are there free and fair elections in which most people can vote?
  Elections are 'free' when political parties and candidates are allowed to run without interference from the government. They are 'fair' when the votes are counted accurately and the electoral process isn't biased in favour of some parties or candidates. 'Most people' usually means all adult citizens.
- Are all those who have political power in the state either directly elected or ultimately accountable to an elected, representative body, such as the legislature?

In his book *Polyarchy* (1971), which is a major source of inspiration for the modern empirical literature on democracy, the political scientist Robert Dahl set up two basic criteria for a reasonably democratic system: 'participation' and 'contestation'. Participation means that people are able to participate in politics. Contestation means that there is a real 'contest' for political power. By answering the two questions we've just discussed, we can assess whether a political system meets these basic criteria.

Both questions are important. It's not enough that people have people the right to vote if the government isn't accountable to the people or the people's representatives. The German Empire (1871–1918) is an example of a political system in which a large proportion of the population—adult men—had the right to vote in the legislative elections, but the emperor chose the head of government, the chancellor, who wasn't accountable to the legislature.

Most theories of democracy ask for more than this. They argue that the concept of democracy includes other rights and freedoms, beyond the right to vote, such as freedom of speech, freedom of assembly, and freedom of association. In this view, if citizens can't organize freely, convene safely, and speak openly about politics, elections become an empty ritual. As we will soon see, many empirical measures of democracy therefore include indicators of such basic civic rights. Some empirical measures also include the rule of law—the idea that political leaders must be bound by legal rules and that all citizens must be equal before the law. We will consider the relationship between politics and the law in more detail in Chapter 9.

Some theories of democracy go even further. They say that democracy isn't just about choosing political leaders—it's an ongoing process through which a society learns about itself, develops new ideas, and reaches a broader consensus about matters of common interest. They're known as **deliberative** theories of democracy (from the verb 'deliberate', which means to reason carefully). Sometimes when we study democracy, we're interested in these other aspects of democratic government, and not only, or even primarily, in elections and accountability.

4.2.2 Who are the people?

We now have a clearer sense of what it can mean for the people to rule. But let's take a step back. Who are the people in the first place? Citizens of established democracies sometimes forget how important that question is, since they live in parts of the world where adults have had the right to vote for many decades, ethnic and religious relations are relatively peaceful, and rules of citizenship are well defined and broadly accepted. As we discussed in Chapter 3, the definition of 'the people' is often contested.

Because democracy means that the people rule, who gets to be a part of the people becomes a political issue of first importance. It isn't only about drawing the line between one people and another, but also about which groups within the people should have the right to participate in politics.

One of the most important political changes in the world over the past 130 years is that before the 1890s, women didn't have the right to vote anywhere, but they now have the right to vote in almost every country. In 1893, New Zealand became the first independent state to extend the right to vote to women. The struggle for female **suffrage** has been one of the defining political conflicts of the nineteenth and twentieth centuries. Figure 4.1 offers a concrete example of how the women's movement in the United Kingdom expressed itself politically in the early twentieth century. Across the face of a coin depicting King Edward VII, one of the principal symbols of the state's power, suffragette activists have stamped the words 'Votes for women'. Women in the United Kingdom finally got the right to vote in 1918, but they only got the same rights as men a decade later, in 1928.

Political philosophers have long sought to clarify the principles that *should* apply when defining who constitutes 'the people' in a political sense, a concept for which scholars sometimes rely on the Latin word for people, *demos*. One common view is that the people ought to include all those who are permanently resident in a country and subject to its laws, with the understanding that extending the right to vote to children isn't usually required for a country to be considered democratic.

However, the straightforward idea that those who are affected by a government's decisions ought to have a say in who governs raises many difficult philosophical and practical questions. In an increasingly interconnected world, where decisions made in one country can have powerful effects in other countries, it isn't so clear who is affected by a government's laws and policies and who isn't. We'll come back to the implications of this interconnectedness in Chapter 15.

4.2.3 What do the people rule over?

The third question—what do the people rule *over*?—may seem a little abstract, but it is crucial. In both comparative politics in particular and political science in general, democracy is almost always understood to mean that the people rule the *state*. It is not necessary for other parts of society to be governed by the people.

Figure 4.1 British women who fought for the right to vote in the early twentieth century were known as suffragettes. In one famous campaign, the suffragettes defaced coins by stamping 'Votes for women' across them. *Source: Heritage Image Partnership Ltd / Alamy Stock Photo*

Consider the distribution of economic power in the world today. Most countries have capitalist economic systems, which means that those who own private companies have a lot of power—they get to appoint the managers of the companies they own, who in turn make many important decisions about investments, hiring, and operations. According to most theories of democracy, countries with capitalist systems can still be considered democratic. Investors and corporate managers wield great power, but not over the state itself.

According to most standard definitions, what the people's representatives *do* with their power—which policies they adopt—also has no bearing on whether a country counts as democratic. The exception is when elected politicians undermine or abolish democracy itself, as the German parliament did on 23 March 1933, when it adopted the Enabling Act, which granted supreme power to Adolf Hitler, the leader of the National Socialist Party.

In other words, a country in which the political leaders are elected in free and fair elections and the government is responsible either to the legislature or to the people is usually considered democratic even if the government wastes money, treats people unfairly, lets the environment come to harm, or makes other ill-considered political choices. Scholars of comparative politics usually think of democracy as a procedure for selecting political leaders and making decisions. It doesn't guarantee that the leaders are worth the people's trust or that they make good use of the power they've been granted, though it may contribute to those outcomes.

4.3 DEMOCRACY AROUND THE WORLD

LEARNING OUTCOMES

After reading Section 4.3, you'll be able to:
- Identify states that are usually considered democratic
- Evaluate different approaches to measuring democracy.

Let's move from theory to practice. In this section, we'll examine the state of democracy in the world of the early 2020s. We will rely on two empirical measures that are widely used in comparative politics today: a dichotomous indicator of democracy compiled by Boix, Miller, and Rosato (2013), which we discussed briefly in Chapter 1, and a gradual measure of democracy compiled by the Varieties of Democracy Project (Coppedge et al. 2024).

As we use these data to explore the variety of political regimes around the world, we'll take some time to consider the methodological problems scholars have had to overcome to collect evidence about democracy and authoritarianism. There is broad agreement among scholars of comparative politics on many of the basic conceptual issues in democratic theory that we discussed in Section 4.2. For example, few scholars would dispute that democracy requires free, fair, and inclusive elections and a government that is directly or indirectly accountable to the people. But scholars nevertheless disagree on what sorts of evidence we should gather and analyse when we assess political regimes.

In Chapter 1, we studied a map that distinguished between democracies and authoritarian states in the world in 2020 (Figure 1.1). It relied on an indicator of democracy that was originally compiled by Boix, Miller, and Rosato (2013). When we first studied this map, we noted that the world's democracies seem to be concentrated in the Americas, Europe, southern Africa, Oceania, and a few large states in Asia. We also drew some preliminary conclusions about other important outcomes that are correlated with democracy. For example, with some important exceptions—such as the oil-rich states around the Persian Gulf—democracies tend to have higher GDP per capita than authoritarian states.

There are other patterns in the data that may occur to you. For instance, the proportion of democracies is much lower in regions of the world that were colonized by European powers until the middle of the twentieth century than in Europe itself or the Americas, where most countries gained independence from European colonizers in the eighteenth and nineteenth centuries. It has proven more difficult to establish durable democratic regimes in countries that remained colonies until the twentieth century. Europe's colonial powers didn't govern their dominions in Africa and Asia in ways that supported a smooth transition to stable democratic rule after independence.

Now, let's take a look at the map in Figure 4.2, which describes the level of democracy around the world in 2023 with the help of a different measure of democracy than the one proposed by Boix, Miller, and Rosato (2013). This map relies on data on 'polyarchy' that were compiled by the team behind the Varieties of Democracy project (Coppedge et al. 2024)—a large research programme that involves scholars and experts from all over the world. Like Boix, Miller, and Rosato, the V-Dem project bases its measure of democracy on the theoretical work of Robert Dahl more than 50 years ago (see especially Dahl 1971).

The regional patterns we saw in Figure 1.1 stand out on this map, too. We see that the level of democracy is comparatively high in Europe, the Americas, southern Africa, Oceania, and in Asian countries such as Japan and South Korea. The most authoritarian states in the world, according to the V-Dem measure, are in eastern Asia (China and North Korea are two examples), central Asia (Afghanistan), the Middle East (Qatar and Saudi Arabia), and Africa (Eritrea).

But we see the world a little differently when we examine the map in Figure 4.2 from when we looked at the map in Figure 1.1. According to the V-Dem measure, there are major differences in the quality of democracy among countries that were categorized as democratic by Boix, Miller, and Rosato (2013). There are also major differences among countries that Boix, Miller, and Rosato (2013) categorize as *non*-democratic. Some are highly authoritarian. Others occupy a range of democracy in between the most democratic and the most authoritarian states.

One explanation of these differences is that the V-Dem measure is updated to 2023 whereas the Boix, Miller, and Rosato measure is only updated to 2020. In some countries, things happened between 2020 and 2023 that changed the assessment of the quality of democracy. For example, the V-Dem project categorized Tunisia as significantly more democratic in 2020 than in 2023, which explains one important difference between the two maps.

But the main explanation is that Boix, Miller, and Rosato (2013) have proposed a dichotomous indicator of democracy that can only take two values, democratic or authoritarian, whereas the measure developed by the V-Dem project is gradual and can take many values between highly democratic and highly authoritarian. There is an important debate about whether we ought to think of democracy as a matter of kind, categorizing countries as either democratic or authoritarian (dichotomous measures), or as a matter of degree, characterizing countries as more or less democratic (gradual measures). There are good arguments on both sides. Those who favour dichotomous indicators argue that either a country lives up to the designation 'democracy' or it doesn't. Those who favour gradual measures believe there are important differences within these two broad categories and argue that empirical measures of democracy should take this variation seriously.

Another key difference between the data presented in Figure 1.1 and Figure 4.2 lies in the underlying concepts of democracy that inform the two measures. The first measure is narrower and only takes into account a few basic questions about the administration of elections and the accountability of the government:

- The executive is directly or indirectly elected in popular elections and is responsible either directly to voters or to a legislature.
- The legislature (or the executive if elected directly) is chosen in free and fair elections.
- A majority of adult men has the right to vote.

(Boix, Miller, and Rosato 2013, 1530)

Note that Boix, Miller, and Rosato (2013) originally decided to count some countries as democratic in earlier historical periods even if women didn't have the right to vote. This is because they developed their indicator of democracy to study the development of political regimes from the year 1800 onwards, and for much of the nineteenth century, the main political question wasn't whether voting rights should be extended to women, but whether they should be extended to the working class. This decision by Boix, Miller, and Rosato (2013) doesn't matter for the map in Figure 1.1, since

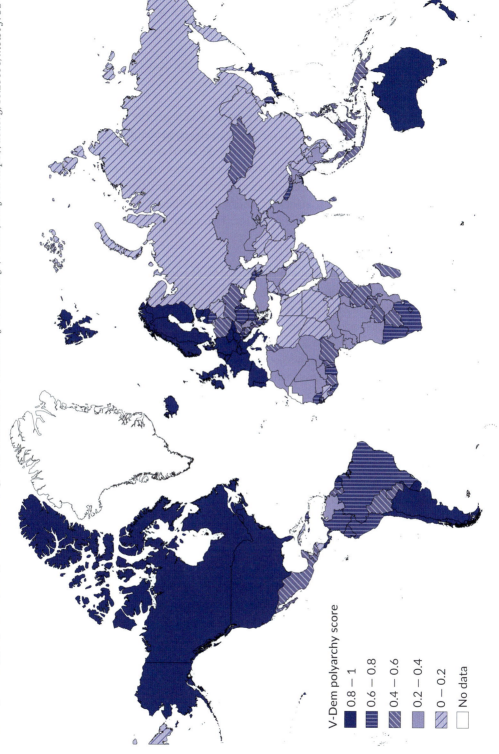

Figure 4.2 A gradual measure of democracy offers a more nuanced view of the state of democracy in the world. *Source: Author's own work, based on data from Coppedge et al. (2024), "V-Dem Country–Year Dataset v14" Varieties of Democracy (V-Dem) Project. https://doi.org/10.23696/mcwt-fr58*

women had the right to vote in almost all countries in 2020, but it does matter when describing the evolution of political regimes over time. In Section 4.4, we'll therefore use a newer version of Boix, Miller, and Rosato's measure, which requires that a majority of adult men *and women* have the right to vote.

The V-Dem project's measure of polyarchy (or electoral democracy) is based on a broader concept of democracy that includes additional elements:

> The electoral principle of democracy seeks to embody the core value of making rulers responsive to citizens, achieved through electoral competition for the electorate's approval under circumstances when suffrage is extensive; political and civil society organizations can operate freely; elections are clean and not marred by fraud or systematic irregularities; and elections affect the composition of the chief executive of the country. In between elections, there is freedom of expression and an independent media capable of presenting alternative views on matters of political relevance. (Coppedge et al. 2024)

A third methodological difference concerns how the data were collected. The V-Dem project's polyarchy measure relies mainly on an **expert survey**. The scholars behind the project sought the opinions of experts worldwide on the political institutions of individual countries. They then used statistical methods to derive a democracy score based on these assessments. Some scholars only trust measures that are based on evidence of observable events, such as actual transfers of power (see, for example, Alvarez et al. 1996). Other scholars, such as the V-Dem team, believe that objective measures may overlook important facts that experts can provide insights into.

Table 4.1 summarizes the main differences between the measures of democracy that scholars of comparative politics rely on.

Although the maps in Figure 4.2 and Figure 1.1 are broadly similar, different approaches to measuring democracy can lead to diverging assessments of the state of democracy in individual countries. As you may have noticed, for example, there are two countries in central Europe that are categorized as democratic in Figure 1.1, but are ranked as significantly less democratic than their democratic neighbours in Figure 4.2: Hungary and Poland. We'll consider one of those countries in Case Study 5.2 in the next chapter.

Table 4.1 Measuring democracy

Types of measure	Main trade-off
Dichotomous or gradual?	Should we make a sharp distinction between democracy and authoritarianism or is democracy a matter of degree?
Narrow or broad?	Should we keep definitions of democracy as narrow as possible, for maximum clarity, or should we include many different criteria, acknowledging the complexity of the concept?
Objective or subjective?	Should we base our measures of democracy only on objectively verifiable information, to avoid making subjective judgments, or should we rely on experts, to benefit from their knowledge?

4.4 DEMOCRATIZATION

LEARNING OUTCOMES

After reading Section 4.4, you'll be able to:
- Describe the three big waves of democratization
- Explain which economic, social, and political conditions are most conducive to democratization.

The maps we studied in Section 4.3 are like snapshots, in that they describe the distribution of political regimes in the world at a particular point in time (specifically, we looked at maps representing the years 2020 and 2023). But political regimes are always changing, and sometimes they change a lot. In this section, we'll learn how states have gone from authoritarianism to democracy—or become more democratic over time—which is a process known as **democratization**. We'll also learn about the main causes of democratization. In Chapter 5, we'll study the opposite process, which is known as a **democratic breakdown** or a **reversal of democracy**.

4.4.1 Three waves of democracy

We use the same word for rule by the people that the Greeks used 2,500 years ago, but democracy meant something very different to the ancient Greeks than it means today (Veyne 1983). It would therefore be a mistake to think of the history of democracy as one single, continuous process that began in antiquity. Modern democracy, which is based on the idea of representative government and the practice of regular elections, began to emerge in the eighteenth and nineteenth centuries. Since then, representative democracy has spread across the world, but it hasn't spread evenly, or at a constant rate. Indeed, there have been times when the share of democracies among the world's states has decreased, not increased.

To see this, turn to Figure 4.3, which uses the dichotomous indicator of democracy that we discussed in Chapter 1 to describe the percentage of democracies among sovereign states since the year 1800. The figure plots both the original version of the Boix, Miller, and Rosato (2013) indicator, which only requires that more than half of adult men have the right to vote, and the newer version of the indicator that includes female suffrage, too. There are three things we need to keep in mind when we study this graph.

1. It only includes sovereign states, so some of the changes in the graph are a result of new countries being created or becoming independent (or, in a few cases, losing their independence).
2. As we discussed in Section 4.3, the Boix, Miller, and Rosato (2013) indicator of democracy simply distinguishes between countries that are democratic and countries that are not. What we're learning from the graph is therefore how many of the sovereign states in the world that met certain basic criteria of democracy.
3. The word 'basic' here reflects the fact that Boix, Miller, and Rosato (2013) set a low bar for democracy. Most people today would not count a country as democratic if only slightly more than half of all adults had the right to vote.

What stands out most clearly in Figure 4.3 are the three major 'waves' of democratization in the modern era, first described by Huntington (1991). The first wave began in the middle of the

Figure 4.3 There have been three big waves of democracy since the early nineteenth century. Author's own work based on data from Boix, Miller, and Rosato (2013), courtesy of 'A Complete Dataset of Political Regimes, 1800–2007' by Carles Boix, Matthew Miller, and Sebastian Rosato.

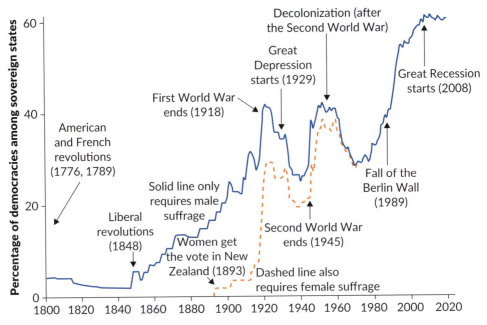

nineteenth century and ended around 1920. The second began in 1945 and ended a few years later. The third wave began in the 1970s, became more powerful in the early 1990s, and came to an end around 2010. In the 1920s–1930s and 1960s–1970s, the two first waves of democracy receded, and the proportion of democracies decreased. We'll have more to say about these periods in Chapter 5.

Figure 4.3 also identifies a few historical events that have played a major role in the modern history of democracy. The first two events are the American and French Revolutions in the final third of the eighteenth century. They resulted in new written constitutions that were at least partially democratic (although we must keep in mind that women didn't have the right to vote, the United States still allowed slavery, and France's democratic reforms were soon reversed).

The next events identified in the graph are the revolutions in Europe in 1848–1849. In many European countries, those revolutions failed, but most scholars believe they contributed to democratic reforms in the long run.

Towards the end of the nineteenth century, we see that countries began to grant women the right to vote, starting with New Zealand in 1893. The dashed line describes the percentage of democracies in the world if we include female suffrage among the basic requirements of democracy. There are still three waves, but the first wave starts much later.

We also see in the graph that the end of the First World War resulted in the creation of many new democracies following the break-up of Europe's empires and the formation of new independent states. But a few years into the 1920s, the long first wave of democratization came to an end.

After the Second World War, there was a new wave of democratization around the world. This was the period in which Germany and Japan became stable democracies after their defeats in the

Second World War. Unlike Germany, Japan had not been democratic before—it had regular elections and a functioning party system in the early twentieth century, but its monarchical regime became increasingly authoritarian in the 1930s.

Another important development in the decades after the war was decolonization—the formation of new independent states in parts of the world that had previously been controlled by European powers such as Belgium, France, the Netherlands, Portugal, and the United Kingdom. In some cases, such as India, decolonization resulted in the creation of a democratic regime. In many other cases, the new independent states that emerged in the second half of the twentieth century didn't develop into durable democracies.

The long third wave of democracy began in the 1970s, when the southern European states Portugal, Greece, and Spain democratized. It picked up strength with the restoration of democracy in the large South American states Argentina and Brazil in the 1980s, and it really took off after the fall of the Berlin Wall in 1989 (see Figure 4.4) and the end of the Cold War in the early 1990s. This was a period when Russia and many of the old allies of the Soviet Union adopted democratic constitutions. But the third wave of democratization wasn't destined to last forever, and it seems to have come to an end in the 2010s.

Before we go on to analyse the main explanations of democratization, let's consider an alternative graph that gives us a slightly different version of the history of democracy. Figure 4.5 uses the gradual V-Dem measure of 'polyarchy' instead of the dichotomous measure we relied on in Figure 4.3. The V-Dem measure is broader than the Boix, Miller, and Rosato (2013) measure since it encompasses evidence about freedom of organization, freedom of expression, and the

Figure 4.4 The fall of the Berlin Wall in 1989 was an important event during the third wave of democratization. *Source: Agencja Fotograficzna Caro / Alamy Stock Photo*

Figure 4.5 When using a gradual measure of democracy, the three big waves are still visible. *Source: Author's own work, based on data from Coppedge et al. (2024), "V-Dem Country–Year Dataset v14" Varieties of Democracy (V-Dem) Project. https://doi.org/10.23696/mcwt-fr58*

independence of the media, not just the right to vote, the administration of the elections, and the accountability of the government.

There are at least two important differences between Figure 4.5 and Figure 4.3 that warrant attention. First of all, in Figure 4.5, which treats democracy as a matter of degree, not kind, the first long wave of democratization in the nineteenth and early twentieth centuries appears to start earlier than in Figure 4.3. The reason is that the V-Dem project's polyarchy measure is influenced by gradual liberalizing reforms within authoritarian regimes in the first half of the nineteenth century. Second, according to the V-Dem measure, democracy began to recede in the world in the late 2010s, but according to Boix, Miller, and Rosato's dichotomous indicator, the share of democracies remained stable at least until 2020.

4.4.2 Economic development and the growth of the state

The rise of democracy is one of the most significant global political transformations of the past two centuries. Scholars of comparative politics are therefore eager to explain democratization—that is, to identify factors that make a transition from authoritarianism to democracy more likely (if we think of democracy as a matter of kind) or that are associated with higher levels of democracy (if we think of democracy as a matter of degree) (Teorell 2010).

As we learned from Figure 4.3 and Figure 4.5, representative democracy began to emerge in the eighteenth and nineteenth centuries and spread across the world during the twentieth and early twenty-first centuries. This historical period was characterized by rapid economic growth, a transition from a largely agricultural to an industrial and increasingly service-based economy, urbanization, and, as we learned in Chapter 3, the expansion of primary education, rising literacy rates, and the expansion of secondary and tertiary education.

Because of this confluence of events, many scholars believe that economic growth, industrialization, urbanization, rising levels of education, and increasing literacy might be conducive to democracy. This is known as the modernization theory, and it goes back at least to the work of Lipset (1959) more than sixty years ago.

The central idea of modernization theory is that economic growth and social modernization lead to democratization since people expect more from their governments when they become wealthier, move to the cities, and get educated. Conversely, scholars have long argued that democracy has arrived more slowly in agrarian economies, especially where land ownership has been more unevenly distributed among the population (as Barrington Moore argued in his famous book *Social Origins of Dictatorship and Democracy*, 1966). Inglehart and Welzel (2010) have developed a modern version of modernization theory in which modernization leads to major changes in cultural values, which in turn contribute to democratization.

Other scholars have instead emphasized the importance of the growing scope and power of the state itself. One idea behind this theory is that democracy cannot function without effective public administration (although the state must not become so strong that political leaders can dominate civil society, as argued by Acemoglu and Robinson (2019)). Rising levels of taxation also force political leaders to give citizens more of a say in how the country is run. One of the explanations for the 'curse of oil' that we discussed in Chapter 1 is that income from natural resources can make governments less dependent on ordinary citizens.

4.4.3 Crises, parties, and social movements

In addition to these long-term structural economic, social, and political conditions, we need to consider short-term factors that explain the timing and onset of democratization. The state of the economy is one such factor. All types of regime become more vulnerable in an economic downturn, so democratization becomes more likely if the economy is shrinking. Another factor is war. As we saw in Figure 4.3, many countries adopted democracy after the First and Second World Wars, and the same pattern can be observed in the aftermath of wars more generally. For example, democratization in France during the Third Republic (1870–1940) was a result of the defeat of the Second Empire in the Franco-Prussian War of 1870–1871.

From our discussion so far, it might seem as if democratization happens either because of impersonal social, economic, and political forces or because of major events such as economic downturns and wars. But the efforts of political parties, social movements, and individual men and women also matter. For example, if the opposition parties in an authoritarian state can lay aside their differences and work together for democratic reforms, democratization becomes more likely.

Social movements can also contribute to democratization. For example, it is unlikely that the extension of the right to vote to women during the twentieth century would have happened without the efforts of women's movements such as the British suffragettes. The extension of the right to vote to women often coincided with the extension of voting rights to working-class men, and political alliances between the women's movement and the labour movement were crucial in many countries in the early twentieth century (Teele 2018).

Finally, scholars have long noted that many episodes of democratization are preceded by political conflicts within authoritarian regimes. This argument follows Skocpol (1979), who emphasized the importance of intra-regime conflicts for the success of revolutionary movements.

4.4.4 The international environment

Developments in the international system also matter greatly for the likelihood of democratization. As we saw in Figure 4.3, the end of the Cold War in the early 1990s was associated with a big increase in the number of democracies in the world. As the Soviet Union no longer sought to exercise control over countries in eastern Europe, many countries in this region adopted democratic constitutions and began to conduct free and fair elections. So, for a while, did Russia itself, but the Russian government reverted to authoritarianism during the presidency of Vladimir Putin in the 2000s.

To learn more about the importance of the international environment for democratization, turn to Case Study 4.1, which examines the transition to democracy in the West African state of Benin in the 1990s and 2000s. Benin has reverted to authoritarianism in recent years, but it was long regarded as one of the most successful cases of democratization in Africa after the Cold War.

CASE STUDY 4.1
Democratization in Benin

Benin—a small country in West Africa that borders on Togo in the west, Nigeria in the east, and Burkina Faso and Niger in the north—was an authoritarian regime between the early 1960s and the late 1980s. Its government was dominated by the military and by a single political party, the Revolutionary Party of the People of Benin. At the beginning of the 1990s, however, Benin made a transition to democracy, and it remained democratic until the late 2010s. The case of Benin illustrates many of the ideas about democratization that we have discussed in this section.

First of all, the process of democratization began with an economic crisis, which by the end of 1988 led to social unrest and mass protests against Benin's authoritarian leaders. This suggests that both economic events and the mobilization of a reform movement contributed to democratization.

The case of Benin also demonstrates the importance of the interaction between domestic factors and developments in the international system. As shown by Gazibo (2005), the timing of the collapse of Benin's authoritarian regime favoured democracy, for by the early 1990s, many international donors were conditioning their foreign aid on democratic reforms. Benin's neighbour Niger—which found itself in a similar economic and political situation in the early 1990s—chose not to negotiate with foreign donors about restructuring the country's economy. But Benin's leaders did, which allowed them to secure a sustained flow of financial aid, facilitating the transition to a democratic regime.

As Gazibo (2005, 79) explains, 'The result was an astonishing economic recovery in Benin by 1993. This economic performance translated into a relatively peaceful political climate that was favourable, in turn, to democratic consolidation.' By contrast, the economic crisis in Niger deepened, complicating democratic reforms, and Niger experienced two military coups in 1996 and 1999. Whereas Benin remained a functioning democracy for almost 30 years between the early 1990s and the late 2010s, Niger went back and forth between democracy and authoritarianism throughout this period.

In recent years, however, Benin's president, Patrice Talon, has used the power of his office to undermine democracy by using the police and the judiciary to further his political goals, exercising control over the media, and persecuting opposition parties. Today, Benin is best categorized as a hybrid, electoral-authoritarian regime (see Chapter 5).

4.5 DEMOCRACY'S EFFECTS

LEARNING OUTCOMES
After reading Section 4.5, you'll be able to:
- Summarize how democracy influences important economic, social, and political outcomes
- Explain the theory of the democratic peace
- Describe the relationship between democracy and political equality.

As we discussed in Chapter 1, scholars of comparative politics keep coming back to two basic questions about political systems—where they come from, and what effects they have. Having studied the main causes of democratization, we will now consider the effects of democracy on other important economic, social, and political outcomes. Does democracy make a difference?

This a difficult question to answer. As we discussed in Chapter 1, economic development and democracy are highly correlated—most countries with high levels of GDP per capita are democracies and most countries with low levels of GDP per capita are authoritarian states. But it's very hard to determine if democracy leads to growth, if growth leads to democracy—or if both democracy and growth are results of a third factor. One factor that is likely to contribute to both economic development and democratization is social trust—a widespread belief that most people can be trusted—which is something that varies greatly among countries. Social trust tends to increase economic efficiency by reducing the costs of doing business, but it can also sustain democracy by mitigating political conflicts. Another factor that may contribute to both economic development and democratization is education. Many scholars believe that rising levels of education have contributed to democratic reforms, but they have also contributed to economic growth by making people more productive.

However, most studies suggest that on average, democracy tends to have a positive effect on economic development. A recent meta-analysis by Colagrossi, Rossignoli, and Maggioni (2020) found a small, positive effect of democracy on economic growth, and Acemoglu et al. (2019, 50) found that although GDP per capita often declines just before a period of democratization, 25 years after a permanent transition to democracy, GDP per capita is about 20 per cent higher than it would be otherwise.

Democracy also appears to be associated with a higher likelihood of peace among countries. This pattern is known as the democratic peace. Although there are many examples of democracies that have gone to war against authoritarian states, there are almost no examples of democracies waging war against other democracies. The idea that representative governments are unlikely to go to war against each other goes back to the work of the eighteenth-century German philosopher Immanuel Kant, whom we encountered in Chapter 1, and his famous book *Perpetual Peace* (1795).

Research Prompt 4.1 will deepen your understanding of the relationship between democracy and war.

>
>
> **RESEARCH PROMPT 4.1**
> War, peace, and political regimes
>
> Please consult the website of the Uppsala Conflict Data Program (https://ucdp.uu.se). This data-collection programme compiles information about armed conflicts around the world and estimates the number of deaths in those conflicts. Consider the role played by democracy and authoritarianism by learning about the regimes of the countries that are currently involved in inter-state wars (between countries) and civil wars (within countries). Do you find any examples of wars between democracies? Do you find any examples of democracies that are engaged in domestic armed conflicts with groups within their territories? What do you infer about the relationship between political regimes and large-scale political violence?

There are other types of violence that seem to be less common in democracies than in authoritarian states. For example, Davenport and Armstrong (2004) find that democracy is associated with less political repression and fewer violations of human rights than authoritarianism. This capacity of democracy for resolving political conflicts peacefully is perhaps its most enduring accomplishment. For example, Przeworski (2010) has argued that democracy is the best form of government since it provides 'a framework within which somewhat equal, somewhat effective, and somewhat free people can struggle peacefully'. 'Somewhat' may not sound like much, but it is—political history is replete with violence among political adversaries, so an institution that helps us contain violence must be regarded as enormously beneficial.

However, whereas having an established democracy reduces the risk of violent conflicts, the process of *democratization* is often fraught with danger. To learn more about this problem, turn to Case Study 4.2, which examines the fate of democracy in Myanmar.

>
>
> **CASE STUDY 4.2**
> The rise and fall of democracy in Myanmar
>
> In 1948, Myanmar, then called Burma, became independent from Britain. Fourteen years later, in 1962, a Cold War military *coup d'état* put an end to Burma's short history of parliamentary democracy. For almost 50 years thereafter, a military regime controlled the country. There was a pro-democracy movement, but it was treated harshly by Myanmar's military government. For example, the woman who rose to become the democracy movement's leader, Aung San Suu Kyi, was forced to live under house arrest during much of the 1990s and 2000s (Egreteau 2016; David and Holliday 2018).
>
> In the late 2000s, as a result of mounting international pressure, Myanmar's military regime agreed to hold elections. The first elections, in 2010, were boycotted by the pro-democracy National League for Democracy, but in 2015, the party, led by Aung San Suu Kyi, won a majority of the seats in both chambers of Myanmar's parliament.
>
> The first lesson we learn from the example of Myanmar—and from the example of Benin, which we considered earlier—is that transitions from authoritarianism to democracy are often the result of a combination of international events and domestic factors such as an active pro-democracy movement.
>
> The second lesson is that even if free elections are held and a pro-democratic party wins, it can be difficult to assess whether a country effectively meets the criteria of democratic government,
>
>

something that recalls our discussion of problems of measurement in Section 4.3. The military remained a powerful force in Myanmarese politics after the National League for Democracy won the elections, so the country's political regime had both democratic and authoritarian elements.

For decades, Myanmar's government has been harassing and persecuting a predominantly Muslim minority—the Rohingya people—that lives in the western part of the country. In 2017–2018, during Myanmar's democratic period, much of the Rohingya population was driven out of the country. Many foreign observers had hoped that Aung San Suu Kyi would speak out against the persecution of the Rohingyas, but she did not.

This brings us to the third lesson one might draw from Myanmar's experiment with democracy. Research in comparative politics suggests that the escalation of violence in Myanmar during its period of democratization in the 2010s wasn't a coincidence. Although democracy is generally a system in which 'we don't kill each other', as the political scientist Adam Przeworski has put it, nationalist and sectarian violence is fairly common during *democratization*—the process of introducing and establishing democracy in a country. In his book *The Dark Side of Democracy* (2005), Mann argues that ethnic and sectarian violence during democratization is a common historical pattern (see also Snyder 2000).

There is also a fourth lesson from Myanmar. Young democracies are especially vulnerable to coups and other attempts to abolish democratic control. On 1 February 2021, a few years into Myanmar's second experiment with democracy, there was another military coup, and Aung San Suu Kyi, the democratically elected head of government, was again placed under house arrest. We will come back to the problem of democratic reversals in Chapter 5.

We end this section by noting that many powerful arguments for democracy centre around its intrinsic value, not its effects on other things we care about. Most importantly, democracy is the only form of government that is consistent with the principle of political equality—the idea that as humans, we are of equal worth and should enjoy equal rights and responsibilities. In this view, we ought to choose democracy over other forms of government since it's the only regime that treats us as equals (Beitz 1989; Dahl 1998).

4.6 CONCLUSION

The choice between democracy and authoritarianism is the most fundamental choice a country makes about how to govern itself. Are there regular, free, and fair elections in which the voters have the chance to replace their leaders? Or do those leaders answer to a smaller group, such as the wealthy, the military, or a political party? This is what the choice between democracy and authoritarianism comes down to.

It's a choice that is closely related to one of the main themes of this book: how societies deal with conflict. Responding to the question of what we can realistically expect from democracy, Adam Przeworski once said, 'Democracy is a system that keeps us from killing each other', adding that this is 'good enough' (cited in Munck and Snyder 2007, 475). In Chapter 1, we distinguished between three types of conflict: 'fights', 'games', and 'debates'. The main benefit of democracy is that it transforms political conflicts from 'fights' into 'games' and 'debates', while respecting basic principles of political equality. It recognizes that as humans, we will always disagree, but shows that we can handle those disagreements in ways that uphold the idea that no individual or group is inherently worth more than others.

In the next chapter, we will to turn to the parts of the world that are *not* democratic: we're going to learn how authoritarian systems work.

SUMMARY

- In democracies, there are free and fair elections in which the people have a chance to replace their political leaders.
- In authoritarian states, political leaders are responsive to some smaller group, such as the wealthy, the military, or a political party.
- Some measures of democracy are dichotomous, whereas others are gradual, and some measures are narrow, concentrating on a few important institutions, whereas others are broader and more complex.
- Democracy is most firmly rooted in the Americas, in western and central Europe, and in Oceania, but there are also many established democracies in Africa and Asia.
- There have been three big waves of democratization in the world since the beginning of the nineteenth century.
- Democratization is influenced by long-run socioeconomic changes, sudden events such as economic downturns and wars, parties and social movements, and the international environment.
- It is difficult to estimate the effects of democracy on other social, economic, and political outcomes, but on average, democracy seems to make societies more prosperous and peaceful.
- Democracy is the only form of government that lives up to the ideal of political equality—the idea that no individual or group should dominate others.

STUDY QUESTIONS

1. On the one hand, the word 'democracy' refers to a political ideal—we can imagine a fully democratic society in which everyone is treated equally and has equal opportunities to influence the political process. On the other hand, it refers to a type of political regime that is actually practised in many parts of the world. Should we measure actual democracies against our vision of an ideal democracy or are we really talking about two different things when we talk of the democratic ideal and democracy in practice?
2. One of the key differences between the democracy scores that scholars of comparative politics typically rely on is that some of them are stripped-down and simple whereas others are more complex and take many different aspects of democracy into account. Which approach makes most sense to you?

FURTHER READING

Ruth Collier, *Pathways to Democracy* (1999).
  Conducts a case-by-case analysis of transitions to democracy in Europe and Latin America.

Robert Dahl, *On Democracy* (1998).
  Examines the history, theory, and practice of democracy.

Adam Przeworski, *Democracy and the Limits of Self-Government* (2010).
  Develops a realistic analysis of what democracy can and cannot accomplish.

CHAPTER 5
AUTHORITARIANISM

CHAPTER GUIDE

5.1 Introduction
5.2 Varieties of Authoritarianism
5.3 Hybrid Regimes
5.4 How Democracies Die
5.5 How Authoritarian Systems Work

5.6 Conclusion
Summary
Study Questions
Further Reading

5.1 INTRODUCTION

In Chapter 4, we examined the differences between democracy and authoritarianism, learned which countries in the world are democratic, studied the three waves of democracy since the beginning of the nineteenth century, and analysed the causes and consequences of democratization. In this chapter, we'll concentrate on authoritarian states: we'll identify the main differences among them and learn how their institutions work.

Democracy means that political power flows from the people. Of course, in modern, representative democracies, the people don't actually make laws, adopt public policies, and govern the day-to-day operations of the state. Professional politicians and public officials do all those things. But every so often, the people have a chance of removing their political leaders and replacing them with others. That's what democracy means in practice in today's world.

So where does power flow from in an authoritarian state? If the people cannot replace the country's political leaders—well, then, who can? The answer to that question varies among authoritarian states. Political power may reside in a political party, such as the Chinese Communist Party, a family, such as the royal House of Saud in Saudi Arabia, or the clergy, as in the theocracy of Iran. Power may also reside in some other group, a single individual, or indeed a combination of groups, organizations, and individuals.

We'll discuss these important differences among authoritarian states in Section 5.2. In Section 5.3, we'll examine a category of authoritarian regimes that scholars of comparative politics refer to as 'hybrid' or 'electoral-authoritarian'. They are regimes in which the government organizes elections, allows other parties to compete, and purports to respect democratic values and institutions, but ensures it stays in office by harassing the opposition, monopolizing the mass media, or rigging the elections. Hybrid regimes have become much more common since the end of the Cold War in the early 1990s. In Section 5.4, we'll examine the main explanations for democratic reversals: why democratic regimes sometimes revert to non-democratic forms of government. In Section 5.5, finally, we'll learn more about how institutions and organizations such as electoral rules, legislatures, and political parties work in contemporary authoritarian regimes. We'll discuss those institutions in more depth in Chapters 7, 8, and 11; in this chapter, we'll study them in the context of authoritarian politics.

5.2 VARIETIES OF AUTHORITARIANISM

LEARNING OUTCOMES

After reading Section 5.2, you'll be able to:

- Distinguish between different types of authoritarianism
- Identify examples of each type among contemporary authoritarian regimes.

There are many ways to distinguish between authoritarian regimes. One approach is to separate the most authoritarian states from the least authoritarian. We are already familiar with this approach: the 'gradual' measures of democracy we discussed in Chapter 4 let us distinguish between closed authoritarian regimes and regimes that meet some but not all of the requirements of democracy. Another approach is to categorize the ideologies of the ruling elites. This is the idea behind labels such as 'communist dictatorship' and 'fascist dictatorship'. In this section, we will follow a third approach, which begins with the question 'If the people don't have power, who does?' In modern scholarship, this approach is associated most closely with the work of Geddes (1999) and Geddes, Wright, and Frantz, (2014, 2018), who have proposed a widely used categorization of authoritarian regimes.

Geddes (1999) originally distinguished between three authoritarian regime types—military regimes, single-party regimes, and personalist regimes—and then went on to examine combinations of those pure types. More recently, Geddes, Wright, and Frantz have expanded the typology also to include non-democratic monarchies (note that there are democratic monarchies, especially in Europe, where the monarch remains the head of state but has little or no political power). They also refer to 'dominant-party' regimes instead of single-party regimes, broadening this category by including countries in which one party effectively controls the state, even if other parties are allowed.

Let's take a moment to examine the main differences between the pure types in the scheme proposed by Geddes and her co-authors:

1. Military regimes
2. Dominant-party regimes
3. Personalist regimes
4. Monarchies.

In **military regimes**, officers from the armed forces control the state, either openly or behind the scenes. Military regimes were especially common at the height of the Cold War in the 1960s and 1970s. Today, one example of a military regime is Myanmar, where a group of military officers took power in a *coup d'état* on 1 February 2021, after a period of democratic rule (see Case Study 4.2). Thailand is another military dictatorship on the western side of the mainland part of South-East Asia. Both Thailand and Myanmar have changed their political regimes several times since independence, which is an example of how much more prone to change military dictatorships are than one-party states or monarchies (see Section 5.5).

In **dominant-party regimes**, there is only one significant political party and it controls the state. During the Cold War, the communist states were dominant-party regimes. Many of them were allied with the Soviet Union, which was controlled by the Communist Party of the Soviet Union. The world's second-largest country by population, China, remains a dominant-party regime under the leadership of the Chinese Communist Party. Other dominant-party regimes are Laos, North Korea, and Vietnam in Asia and Ethiopia and Mozambique in Africa.

You can read more about the structure of the Chinese political system in Case Study 5.1. Its formal political institutions resemble those of most other countries—there is a legislature, an executive, and a judiciary, as in almost all other states. But the Chinese Communist Party's own parallel organizations overlap with those of the legislature, the executive, and the judiciary, allowing the party to maintain effective control. This institutional parallelism between state and party is typical of single-party regimes. It also characterized the fascist regimes in Europe in the 1920s and 1930s, such as Germany and Italy. The **theocracy** of Iran—in which the clergy rule—has a lot in common with dominant-party regimes. There are elections that determine the composition of the legislature and who becomes president, but just as the Chinese Communist Party effectively controls the legislature, the executive, and the judiciary in China, the clergy effectively controls political institutions in Iran.

CASE STUDY 5.1
One-party rule in China

At first glance, the formal political institutions in China resemble those of many other countries around the world. For example, as the country's legislature, the National People's Congress is formally the highest organ of state power, with the authority to amend the constitution and supervise the other branches of government. It is made up of around 3,000 delegates, who are elected by provincial political bodies. The president is the head of state and serves as the chairman of the National People's Congress. The premier is the head of government and leads the State Council, which is responsible for public administration and the formulation of public policies. The State Council drafts new legislation, which is reviewed and amended by the National People's Congress and its Standing Committee before being adopted.

But, typically for a single-party system, China's formal political institutions are ultimately controlled by the Communist Party. Heilmann (2016) therefore refers to the Communist Party as the 'sovereign of the state' (2016, 61). The preamble to China's constitution establishes the power of the Communist Party as a basic characteristic of the country's political system, stating that 'The socialist system is the fundamental system of the People's Republic of China' and that 'Leadership by the Communist Party of China is the defining feature of socialism with Chinese characteristics'. In other words, the constitution does not envision that any other party could control the state. Only the Communist Party can.

Between the 1980s and the 2000s, the Communist Party loosened its grip on the private lives of Chinese citizens and liberalized the economy by adopting market-friendly policies. Foreign observers interpreted these late-twentieth and early-twenty-first-century reforms as a 'grand bargain' by which citizens got more freedom and a chance to increase their income while letting the Communist Party maintain control over the political system (Dickson 2016, 28). To facilitate these liberalizing reforms, the state and the Communist Party became more distinct, and the country's legislative, executive, and judiciary branches of government got more well-defined roles (Heilmann 2016, 73).

But the Communist Party's institutions and offices continue to overlap with those of the state at all levels of government, and, as recent political developments have shown, the party effectively remains the sole source of political power. Under the rule of Xi Jinping—who rose to power in 2012—many of the political changes that were adopted in the 1980s, 1990s, and 2000s were rolled back. The removal of term limits for the office of the president in 2018, allowing Xi Jinping to remain in office, marked the end of China's era of reform.

In **personalist regimes**, political power doesn't reside in a structured organization such as a group of military officers (as in military regimes) or a political party (as in dominant-party regimes). It instead depends on a single individual who dominates the political system. Muammar al-Gaddafi, dictator of Libya in 1969–2011, was an example of a personalist political leader, as was Hugo Chavez, president of Venezuela in 1999–2013. It's also possible to categorize leaders such as Vladimir Putin of Russia and even Xi Jinping of China as leaders with personalist ambitions. As we discussed in Case Study 5.1, Xi Jinping rose through the ranks of the Chinese Communist Party, but he then amassed more and more personal power. In many personalist regimes, public policies are highly unpredictable since they depend on the whims of one man, or—much more rarely—one woman. Personalist authoritarian leaders have become more common in the twenty-first century (see, for example, Kendall-Taylor, Frantz, and Wright 2016).

In authoritarian **monarchies**, finally, there is a head of state who has inherited his or her position—a king, queen, emperor, or empress—and who controls the government, or at least has significant political powers.

Historically, monarchy has been the most common of all forms of government. In the seventeenth and eighteenth centuries, for example, most independent states in the world were governed by monarchs. Today, the authoritarian monarchies in the world are concentrated around the Persian Gulf, with Saudi Arabia, long ruled by the kings and princes of the Saud family, being the best-known example. But there are also authoritarian monarchies in Jordan and Morocco and in Eswatini, a small country that borders South Africa. Unlike monarchs in these authoritarian states, the kings and queens in Europe's constitutional monarchies have given up their claims to political power and only perform ceremonial functions.

One possible counter-argument to treating monarchies as a unique regime type is that it can also be seen as a version of the personalist type. Just as in a personalist regime, political power in an authoritarian monarchy is concentrated in a single individual. The argument *for* treating monarchies as a distinct type is that the source of the monarch's authority is different from that of a personalist ruler. The sociologist Max Weber, about whom we read in Chapter 3, distinguished between 'traditional' and 'charismatic' claims to political legitimacy (Weber 1978 [1921]). Traditional authority is based on custom and tradition, whereas charismatic authority is based on the leader's personal qualities. Monarchies rely on the former; personalist regimes rely on the latter. By contrast, democracies rely mainly on the third form of authority identified by Weber: the 'rational-legal' type, which is based on formal rules and procedures.

The categorization of authoritarian regimes as military, dominant-party, personalist, and monarchical provides us with a helpful taxonomy, but it's important to keep in mind that military, dominant-party, personalist, and monarchical regimes are 'ideal types'—that is, they are stylized models of how authoritarian regimes can be organized. Real-world authoritarian regimes are often best understood as a mix of these different ideal types.

Some scholars, notably Svolik (2012), have argued that it would best to move away from the idea of 'types' of authoritarian regime altogether. He suggests that we ought to think of the influence of the military in politics as a variable that is relevant for *all* authoritarian regimes (instead of separating military regimes from other types of authoritarianism), just as the autonomy and power of an individual leader can be seen as a variable that is relevant for all authoritarian regimes (instead of separating personalism from other types).

5.3 HYBRID REGIMES

LEARNING OUTCOMES

After reading Section 5.3, you'll be able to:
- Describe the rise of hybrid regimes
- Distinguish hybrid regimes from democracies.

It used to be simple to distinguish authoritarianism from democracy. In the past, authoritarian rulers typically didn't claim to be democratic—and even if they did, they used labels such as 'people's democracy' or 'democratic dictatorship' that distinguished their regimes from representative democracy.

Historically, monarchs usually haven't claimed to have a mandate from the people. They've claimed to have a mandate from God, which is why the formal title of a contemporary monarch such as King Charles III of the United Kingdom of Great Britain and Northern Ireland includes the phrase 'by the Grace of God'.

In the first half of the twentieth century, fascist leaders such as Benito Mussolini in Italy and Adolf Hitler in Germany were openly contemptuous of democratic institutions. For example, Adolf Hitler claimed in a speech in Berlin in 1941 that 'the . . . National Socialist Revolution has defeated democracy'. The communist authoritarian regimes that emerged during the twentieth century often referred to themselves as 'people's democracies', but it was clear to all that the communist party controlled the state, as the Chinese Communist Party controls China today.

In the second half of the twentieth century, many military dictatorships emerged. When they took power, military leaders often said they intended to restore political power to civilian institutions, but it was clear that they didn't recognize the legitimacy of their political opponents. For example, in an interview in *Time Magazine* a few weeks after the *coup d'état* in Chile in September 1973, the new leader Augusto Pinochet (see Figure 5.1) declared that the time for party politics was over. 'We don't want politics', he said. 'The only party now is the Chilean party, and its members are all Chileans'. Authoritarian leaders often speak of the people in this abstract sense—they claim to know the people's will, but they don't let actual people speak for themselves in free and fair elections.

Today, it's not so simple anymore to recognize authoritarian regimes. In the aftermath of the Cold War and the third wave of democratization that we learned about in Chapter 4, the idea of democracy has become so widely accepted in all parts of the world that very few political leaders openly oppose it, and in approximately half of all authoritarian states, the ruling party or leader runs for office, allows competition from other parties, and declares their support for democratic values and institutions.

But they don't give the opposition a fair chance. They rig the elections, harass the other parties, and use their influence over the bureaucracy, the judiciary, and the media to overcome dissent and dominate public opinion. The transformation of Russia from a flawed but functioning multi-party democracy in the 1990s into an increasingly violent and repressive regime under Vladimir Putin in the 2010s is an example of this sort of process. There are still elections in Russia, but the government uses its power over the media, the courts, and other key institutions to keep challengers at bay, in combination with attacks on opposition politicians and critical journalists to suppress dissent (see, for example, Lewis 2020).

Scholars of comparative politics refer to regimes that appear democratic on the surface but are actually authoritarian as 'competitive authoritarian' (Levitsky and Way 2010), 'electoral-

Figure 5.1 Augusto Pinochet (in the centre of the photo) declared in 1973 that the time for party politics was over. He is pictured here in 1974 with the then-president of Argentina, Juan Perón (on the right).
Source: Keystone Press / Alamy Stock Photo

authoritarian' (Schedler 2002), or 'hybrid' regimes (Diamond 2002). Levitsky and Way defined such regimes as follows:

> In competitive authoritarian regimes, formal democratic institutions are widely viewed as the principal means of obtaining and exercising political authority. Incumbents violate those rules so often and to such an extent, however, that the regime fails to meet conventional minimum standards for democracy. (Levitsky and Way 2010, 52)

This raises the question if we should think of hybrid regimes as their own type of authoritarianism, alongside military, dominant-party, personalist, and monarchical regimes, which are the main types we discussed in Section 5.2. There is no agreement among scholars on this point. On the one hand, the observation that 'formal democratic institutions are widely viewed as the principal means of obtaining and exercising political authority', as Levitsky and Way put it, suggests that hybrid regimes are qualitatively different from other types of authoritarianism. Following this logic, Hadenius and Teorell (2007) and Wahman, Teorell, and Hadenius (2013) have developed an indicator of authoritarian regime types that distinguishes between military, single-party, and monarchist authoritarian regimes, like Geddes, Wright, and Frantz (2014), but then adds 'multiparty authoritarian' regimes as a separate category, which corresponds roughly to hybrid regimes. On the other hand, it's possible for military, personalist, and monarchical regimes to hold multiparty elections, and many of them do, so there is also an argument for saying that all authoritarian regimes—regardless of their type—can be more or less hybrid.

Although the contemporary scholarly literature on electoral authoritarianism has concentrated on the rise of hybrid regimes since the end of the Cold War, this is not actually a new phenomenon. As pointed out by Gandhi and Lust-Okar (2009, 404), the political system in France during the Second Empire (1851–1870) was an electoral-authoritarian system. Zeldin (1958) showed long ago in his analysis of Napoleon III's regime that the French emperor used elections he knew he would win to mobilize support for his government—just as authoritarian leaders in hybrid regimes today use rigged elections to legitimize theirs.

One of the consequences of the rise of hybrid regimes is that the categorization of individual countries as either democratic or authoritarian has become politically contested. In the European Union, the democratic credentials of two member states, Poland and Hungary, have long been questioned. In 2018, the European Parliament initiated a so-called Article 7 procedure (referring to Article 7 of the Treaty on European Union) to determine if Hungary's rights within the Union ought to be suspended for this reason. Case Study 5.2 discusses the evolution of the Hungarian political system during the 2010s, identifying a series of events that led European Union lawmakers to ask if Hungary had crossed the line between democracy and authoritarianism.

CASE STUDY 5.2
The fate of democracy in Hungary

The European Union requires its member states to have democratic constitutions. In the 2010s, there were mounting concerns within the European Union about political developments in Hungary. International democracy observers such as the Freedom House organization and the V-Dem project no longer categorize Hungary as a democracy. For example, in 2024, Freedom House categorized Hungary as 'partly free' and as a 'transitional or hybrid regime'.

But it's not straightforward to determine precisely when and how Hungary crossed the threshold between democracy and authoritarianism, making Hungary an illustrative example of the challenges scholars of comparative politics are facing when they study regime transitions. Let's consider a timeline of political events in Hungary between 2010 and 2020 (the main sources for the timeline are Ágh 2016, Bozóki and Hegedűs 2018, Haglund, Schulze, and Vangelov 2022, and Kornai 2015).

2010   The party Fidesz, led by Viktor Orbán, wins a landslide victory in Hungary's parliamentary election.

2011   The parliament approves a new constitution, which removes institutional checks on the power of the government. The parliament also approves a new law that redraws electoral boundaries, reduces the number of seats in parliament by 50 per cent, advantaging Fidesz, and creates a new National Media Authority, increasing the government's control over the media. The media law is later amended due to international pressure.

2012   The retirement age for judges is lowered from 70 to 62, forcing many judges to retire.

2013   The parliament approves an amendment to the 2011 constitution that reduces the independence of Hungary's Constitutional Court.

2014   International election monitors argue that biased media coverage and restrictive campaign rules give an unfair advantage to Fidesz in parliamentary elections this year.

2016   Hungary's largest independent newspaper, *Népszabadság* (Liberty of the People), is shut down. *Népszabadság*'s owners, the company Mediaworks, cite financial difficulties as the reason for this decision, but many sources report that the government is involved (see, for example, 'Newspaper Closes in Hungary, and Hungarians See Government's Hand', *New York Times*, 11 October 2016).

2017   The parliament passes a law requiring non-governmental organizations to register as 'foreign' organizations if they accept funding from other countries. The independent Central European University later announces it will move most of its operations to Vienna.

2019   The parliament passes a new law that raises fines and other penalties for lawmakers whose actions are deemed 'disruptive', and prohibits independent legislators from caucusing with the party groups in the parliament.

2020   During the Covid-19 pandemic, the parliament passes the Authorization Act, which confers sweeping emergency powers to the executive (those powers are revoked by parliament during the summer). The parliament also creates a new crime, 'scaremongering', making the dissemination of allegedly false or distorted information during a state of emergency a criminal offence. Meanwhile, public funding for political parties is cut in a manner that disproportionately harms opposition parties.

2022   The European Parliament adopts its Resolution of 15 September 2022 on the proposal for a Council decision determining, pursuant to Article 7(1) of the Treaty on European Union, the existence of a clear risk of a serious breach by Hungary of the values on which the Union is founded.

In a speech in 2014, Viktor Orbán, the leader of Fidesz, said he was opposed to the idea of 'liberal' democracy and that 'the new state that we are constructing in Hungary is an illiberal state, a non-liberal state'. He also suggested that the economic success of authoritarian regimes such as China called for a reassessment of democratic government.

So by the early 2020s, the European Parliament had adopted a resolution that said it no longer regards Hungary as a full democracy. If you agree, at which point between 2010 and 2022 would you say Hungary ceased to be a democracy and turned into an authoritarian state?

As this example shows, it is often difficult for scholars, political commentators, journalists, or other observers to determine if a regime should be categorized as a democracy or as an electoral-authoritarian system. While transitions from democracy to military or one-party regimes have typically been associated with dramatic events such as *coups d'état*, revolutions, or foreign occupations, transitions from democracy to electoral authoritarianism are often creeping and diffuse. In Research Prompt 5.1, we will examine a few more borderline cases when it comes to distinguishing between democracy and authoritarianism.

RESEARCH PROMPT 5.1
Categorizing hybrid regimes

As discussed in this section, one reason it's difficult to categorize countries as democracies, electoral-authoritarian regimes, or closed authoritarian regimes is that regime changes are often creeping and diffuse. To think more about this boundary-drawing problem, try to find out more about what happened in the three recent transitions from democracy to 'electoral autocracy' according to the team behind the Varieties of Democracy project: El Salvador, Nigeria, and Tunisia, which were categorized as democracies in 2020 but as 'electoral autocracies' in 2021. Do you agree that these countries were authoritarian states in 2021? If so, do you also agree that they were democracies in 2020? What events do you think might explain the recategorization of these three countries in Africa and Central America?

5.4 HOW DEMOCRACIES DIE

LEARNING OUTCOMES
After reading Section 5.4, you'll be able to:
- Describe the main periods in which many of the world's democracies have died
- Distinguish between different types of democratic reversal
- Identify factors that contribute to the downfall of democratic regimes.

Figure 4.3 in Chapter 4 described the three major waves of democratization that began in the middle of the nineteenth century, after the Second World War, and in the middle of the 1970s. In Section 4.4, we took that figure as our starting point for a discussion of factors that contribute to democratization. But there were also two periods in the twentieth century in which many countries reverted from democracy to authoritarianism. The first of these periods began in the early

1920s and continued until the Second World War. The second began in the late 1950s and continued until the middle of the 1970s. We'll take these two periods as starting points for a discussion of how democracies die.

5.4.1 Incumbent takeovers and *coups d'état*

The start of the first major period of democratic decline in the twentieth century is often associated with Benito Mussolini's March on Rome in 1922, which resulted in the formation of a fascist government in Italy and, over the next few years, the creation of a fascist dictatorship. In the 1930s, in the wake of the Great Depression—a major economic crisis—Italy was followed by other European countries, most importantly Germany. Germany's first democratic regime, the Weimar Republic, ended in 1933 with the rise to power of Adolf Hitler's National Socialist Party. No elections were held in Germany between 1933 and 1949.

What both of these regime changes have in common is that they were initiated by the incumbent government, not from the outside. Consider Germany. In January 1933, the German president, Paul von Hindenburg, appointed Adolf Hitler chancellor. This appointment was made according to the rules that were laid down in the German constitution, so the fact that Hitler became chancellor was not in itself a regime change. But then Hitler's government went on to use its newly won power to change the German political system during the spring of 1933. It organized flawed elections on 5 March, increasing the National Socialist Party's share of the vote, and then, on 24 March, it made the parliament adopt new legislation, the Enabling Act (*Ermächtigungsgesetz*), that effectively gave Hitler dictatorial powers. This type of regime transformation from within can be called a 'self-coup' or an incumbent takeover. The government, having risen to power legally, uses the power of its office to change the political regime.

In the decades after the Second World War, the fate of democracy was heavily influenced by the Cold War rivalry between the two post-war superpowers, the United States and the Soviet Union. In Germany and Japan, which became allies of the United States, the end of the war led to the establishment of parliamentary democracy. Among the allies of the Soviet Union, the prospects for democratization were more bleak. This became clear in the late 1940s and 1950s, when democracy movements were quashed in countries such as Czechoslovakia, Hungary, and Poland (see Figure 5.2).

But the period of democratic decline in the 1950s, 1960s, and 1970s is mainly associated with a series of *coups d'état* that destroyed many democracies in Latin America, Africa, and Asia in the middle of the Cold War. The term *coup d'état* comes from the French and literally means 'strike against the state' (*coup* means 'blow' or 'strike', and *état* means 'state'). In a *coup d'état*, conspirators within the state force out the incumbent government and take over central political institutions. One of the defining events of the second period of democratic decline in the twentieth century was the coup in Chile on 11 September 1973, which brought a group of military officers to power and destroyed Chile's decades-old democracy. *Coups d'état* have occurred throughout the nineteenth, twentieth, and twenty-first centuries, but they were an especially common form of regime change at the height of the Cold War (Djuve, Knutsen, and Wig 2020, 941).

Most transitions from democracy to authoritarianism are the result of either incumbent takeovers or coups (Svolik 2015). However, it's also possible for both coups and incumbent takeovers to result in transitions from authoritarianism to democracy or transitions from one type of authoritarianism to another. Indeed, Marinov and Goemans (2014) show that in the twenty-first century, coups have often led to democratization—at least indirectly, after a transitional period.

Figure 5.2 In 1956, Soviet troops quashed a revolt against the communist regime in Hungary. *Source: Nagy Gyula / Wikimedia Commons CC BY-SA 3.0*

Incumbent takeovers and coups can be distinguished from two other types of regime change, which are more common during periods of democratization than during democratic reversals.

Transitions to democracy sometimes begin in civil society, as people who are not part of the elite mobilize against the government. We can call this type of regime change an uprising, or, if it results in more profound changes to the regime, a revolution. Democratization in the United States and France started with the American and French revolutions, which began in the 1760s and 1770s (the American) and the 1780s (the French). They resulted in a fundamental transformation of the political regimes of the United States, which formed as a result of the American Revolution, and France, where many of the institutions of the *ancien régime* (the Old Regime) were destroyed. But revolutions aren't just an eighteenth- and nineteenth-century phenomenon. In the twentieth and twenty-first centuries, communist revolutions transformed the political systems of Russia and China in 1917 and 1949, an Islamic revolution transformed the political system of Iran in 1979, and, more recently, a popular uprising, the 'Jasmine Revolution', brought about the democratization of Tunisia at the beginning of the so-called Arab Spring in 2010–2011. As these examples show, revolutions do not always lead to democratization, but they sometimes do.

A fourth type of regime change results from foreign interventions and inter-state wars. The introduction of parliamentary democracy in Germany and Japan after the Second World War provides two clear examples. But there are also more recent examples, including the adoption of a new constitution in Iraq after the invasion of that country by the United States, Britain, and their allies in 2003. Like revolutions, foreign interventions rarely result in transitions from democracy to authoritarianism, although there are exceptions.

To sum up: in an incumbent takeover, the regime change begins within the *government itself*; in a *coup d'état*, the regime change begins within the *state* but outside the government; in a popular uprising or revolution, the regime change begins in *civil society*; and in a foreign intervention or inter-state war, the regime change is brought about by one or more *foreign powers*. As we have seen, most democratic reversals are associated with the first two types of regime change. Democratizations can be associated with all four types.

5.4.2 Explaining transitions to authoritarianism

The first question we ask when we analyse the likelihood of a transition from democracy to authoritarianism should always be this: Do all of the major political parties and interest groups believe they benefit from resolving political conflicts through democratic elections, or do they have reason to think they might be better off trying to undermine or destroy democracy and take power for themselves?

One factor that influences these trade-offs is political institutions. For example, if the party in power is free to fill government agencies with its own supporters and loyalists, this raises the stakes in politics, giving parties and interest groups a strong incentive to seek political power by any means. Another institution that many scholars believe poses risks for democratic stability is presidentialism—that is, having a directly elected president instead of having a head of government who is responsible to the legislature (see Chapter 8). The idea behind this theory is that presidential systems can be deadlocked by conflicts between the legislature and the president, and the president can use their individual mandate from the voters to justify taking power into their own hands, circumventing the legislature (Linz 1990).

If we move beyond such strategic calculations and consider the role of norms and values, we can add new layers to the analysis of the trade-offs that parties and interest groups face. In countries that remain democratic for a long time, people grow accustomed to resolving conflicts within the bounds of democratic institutions and stop considering the alternative of undermining or destroying those institutions. It is worth noting that in the first reverse wave of democracy in the 1920s and 1930s, all the old democracies in Europe and Latin America survived. The countries in which democracy broke down had all democratized after the First World War (Cornell, Møller, and Skaaning 2020). This is true for the 2010s and 2020s as well. As we discussed in Section 5.2, there were widespread concerns in the European Union in this period about the stability of the democratic systems of Hungary and Poland, both of which democratized in the 1990s, in the third wave of democracy. There are fewer concerns about the stability of democratic institutions in European states that have been democratic for longer.

Political commentators often begin the analysis with a different question from the one we've posed here: they don't ask whether the major political parties and interest groups accept that political conflicts need to be resolved within democratic institutions, but whether ordinary people support the idea of democracy. In other words, they look for the causes of democratic stability at the mass level, not at the elite level. Comparative analyses of past democratic breakdowns suggest this is the wrong approach. In her book *Ordinary People in Extraordinary Times*, Nancy Bermeo

(2003) shows that there is little evidence that democratic breakdowns in the past have been preceded by a loss of faith in democratic values among ordinary men and women. The causes of democratic breakdowns should probably be sought in the interactions of political parties and interest groups at the elite level, not in the general population.

Several of the types of factors that contribute to democratization, and which we discussed in Section 4.4, can also contribute to democratic reversals. For example, the international environment after the end of the Cold War seems to have been especially favourable for transitions to democracy, but the international environment can also have the opposite effect. That was the case at the height of the Cold War, when the superpowers often intervened in countries that were strategically important in the geopolitical struggle between East and West and encouraged conspirators to undertake coups. It is well documented, for example, that the United States supported the *coup d'état* against the democratically elected government in Guatemala in 1954, and a few years before that, in 1948, the Soviet Union supported a coup against the democratically elected government of Czechoslovakia.

One of the most consistent findings in empirical analyses of democratic breakdowns is that democracies are vulnerable during economic crises. The explanation for this result is most likely that in an economic downturn, it becomes more difficult to resolve conflicts between different parties and groups. This is an especially important factor in new democracies, which have typically been brought about by diverse coalitions of parties and groups and which don't yet have entrenched democratic norms that sustain democracy in hard times.

5.5 HOW AUTHORITARIAN SYSTEMS WORK

LEARNING OUTCOMES

After reading Section 5.5, you'll be able to:

- Analyse the challenges that authoritarian rulers face
- Study the role of political institutions in authoritarian regimes
- Distinguish between stable and unstable dictatorships.

We will conclude this chapter by discussing the inner workings of authoritarian regimes. We will begin by discussing the main challenges that authoritarian rulers face. Then we'll examine the role of political institutions and organizations such as electoral systems, legislatures, and political parties in authoritarian systems. Finally, we will analyse the relationship between the types of authoritarianism that we learned about in Section 5.2 and the longevity of authoritarian regimes.

A basic driving force in the politics of authoritarian regimes is the need for rulers to fend off threats to their power and authority. As Svolik (2012) has pointed out, authoritarian rulers face two distinct types of threat. One comes from outside the regime—that is, from the people over whom the authoritarian government rules. Svolik calls this 'the problem of authoritarian control'. The other comes from within the regime—that is, from other members of the country's governing elite. Svolik calls this 'the problem of authoritarian power sharing'.

The Arab Spring—the democratic movement that emerged in North Africa and the Middle East in the early 2010s (see Figure 5.3)—is an example of a failure of authoritarian control. By all accounts, the democracy movement came as a surprise to the region's authoritarian leaders. In Tunisia, the Arab Spring led to a transition to democracy. In Syria, it led to a drawn-out civil war.

The deposition of the Soviet leader Nikita Khrushchev in October 1964—when Khrushchev was removed by other members of the party leadership on his return from a holiday in Georgia—is a well-known historical example of a failure of authoritarian power sharing. Khrushchev was outmanoeuvred by other members of the Soviet elite, led by the future leader of the country, Leonid Brezhnev, and was removed from the leadership, but this did not mean that the regime itself was weakened (Khrushchev's loss of control within the regime did not lead to a loss of control for the regime).

There is a growing scholarly literature in comparative politics on how authoritarian rulers try to solve these challenges and hold on to the power they have. Paying attention to the problems of authoritarian control and authoritarian power sharing is particularly helpful when we seek to explain which functions institutions such as electoral systems, legislatures and political parties have in authoritarian regimes.

When we examine those institutions in detail in Chapters 7, 8, and 11, we will mainly be discussing their role in democracies. Elections give the people a chance to replace their political leaders. Legislatures make laws, control the state budget, and exercise oversight over the government. Political parties compete with each other for power over the state. In most authoritarian states,

Figure 5.3 In the early 2010s, a major movement for democracy unexpectedly emerged in North Africa and the Middle East, beginning in Tunisia. *Source: FETHI BELAID/AFP via Getty Images*

the people cannot replace their political leaders, the government won't be bound by the legislature and there is no real competition for power. This raises the question why they even have elections, legislatures, and often also multiple parties. In the past, scholars of comparative politics often assumed that most political institutions in authoritarian states were mere façades, serving no other purpose than legitimizing the current leadership.

Modern scholarship takes a different view. Elections in authoritarian regimes are not merely ceremonial, but serve the vital purpose of anticipating and fending off potential threats to the regime—that is, of helping authoritarian leaders solve the problems of authoritarian control and authoritarian power sharing. They can help leaders manage the relationships between different groups within the regime, sharing political power among members of the elite. They can be used to identify political leaders at the local and regional levels who perform well with the voters and who are therefore candidates for higher office. They can be used to co-opt and buy off members of opposition parties. Finally, big electoral wins for the ruling party can become propaganda victories for the governing elite and scare off potential challengers (Gandhi and Lust-Okar 2009).

Similarly, in a recent study of the role of legislatures under authoritarianism, Gandhi, Noble, and Svolik (2020, 1362) dispute the idea that authoritarian legislatures are a mere façade, arguing that 'genuine politics . . . takes place within authoritarian legislatures and during the legislative stage of policymaking'. The notion that authoritarian legislatures are 'merely ceremonial institutions . . . is, at best, a caricature'. There are important similarities between authoritarian and democratic legislatures, especially when it comes to their internal organization and procedural rules and how the legislators behave. The theories scholars have developed to analyse legislative politics in democracies, and that we'll discuss in Chapter 8, can therefore also be used to analyse legislative politics under authoritarianism. But there are also important differences, which again have to do with the two main problems authoritarian leaders have to solve. For example, legislatures in authoritarian states have a more top-down relationship with the voters than legislatures in democracies, using their political power to build support for the regime and extracting information that the authoritarian elite can use to avert threats to their authority. Meanwhile, they are more subservient to the executive and normally don't exercise much oversight over the government.

Political parties can also serve useful functions for an authoritarian ruler. Most importantly, when an authoritarian government is dependent on the support of a broader coalition of regime supporters, allowing the members of that broader group to organize themselves in one or more political parties facilitates bargaining between the government and the groups it depends on, and reassures the supporters of the regime that they have a stake in the future of the country. This type of argument helps explain the longevity of both dominant-party and multi-party authoritarian regimes compared with, for instance, military dictatorships (Magaloni 2008).

This brings us to another important strand of the literature on the inner workings of authoritarian regimes, which is concerned with the *stability* of different types of authoritarian system. Based on their categorization of authoritarian systems as military, dominant-party, personalist, and monarchical, Geddes, Wright, and Frantz (2014) have studied when and how these different types of regimes come to an end, and they find that there are major differences between the main forms. Monarchies are the most stable, with the likelihood of breakdown being just 2 per cent per year. They are followed by dominant-party regimes (3 per cent per year) and personalist regimes (7 per cent per year), with military regimes being by far the least stable of all the forms of authoritarian government (13 per cent per year). The scholarship on political institutions and parties in authoritarian regimes that we have examined in this section helps explain these patterns. If authoritarian regimes could survive by only using repression, violence, and propaganda to fend off external threats to the country's leaders, nothing would stop military regimes from doing so. But institutions matter in authoritarian states, just as they do in democracies.

5.6 CONCLUSION

There are more than 8 billion people in the world, and roughly half of them live under authoritarianism. As scholars of comparative politics, we therefore need to understand how authoritarian regimes differ from each other, how authoritarian political systems work, and what consequences arise as a result of the differences among authoritarian regimes.

In this chapter, we have discussed different ways of distinguishing between the main types of authoritarian regime, concentrating on how power is distributed between different individuals and groups, such as military officers, kings, party organizations, and individual political leaders. We have taken a tour around the world and tried to identify the main differences between authoritarian regimes in the Americas, Europe, Africa, and Asia. We have studied how and why democratic systems are replaced by authoritarian systems, and we've learned about the different forms that such regime transitions can take, including *coups d'état* and incumbent takeovers. Finally, we have discussed the functions of basic political institutions and organizations such as elections, legislatures, and political parties in authoritarian regimes, as compared with democratic regimes, finding both similarities and differences.

We will study those institutions in more detail in Chapter 7, which is concerned with electoral systems, Chapter 8, which is concerned with legislatures and executives, and Chapter 11, which is concerned with political parties. First, however, we will learn about the important institution of federalism.

SUMMARY

- One way of categorizing authoritarian regimes is by identifying the groups that control the government. Scholars of comparative politics often distinguish between military regimes, dominant-party regimes, monarchies, and personalist regimes.
- Another approach is to distinguish between authoritarian regimes that allow at least some opposition parties to run in elections and closed authoritarian regimes that don't tolerate any opposition at all. Hybrid, electoral-authoritarian regimes have become much more common since the 1980s, and most authoritarian regimes today are electoral-authoritarian.
- It can be difficult to distinguish between electoral-authoritarian regimes and democracies, and scholars disagree on how to categorize countries, including large and powerful countries such as India.
- Both in Africa and the Middle East and in Asia, there is a wide variety of authoritarian regime types.
- Democracies break down when powerful groups in society decide that they are better off trying to attain control over the government without competing in elections.

- Democracies are vulnerable during economic crises.
- Some of the major debates in comparative politics today are concerned with how authoritarian regimes work, including what rulers do to stay in power and what functions institutions and organizations such as elections, legislatures, and political parties have in authoritarian systems.
- Monarchies and dominant-party regimes are more stable than military, personalist, and electoral-authoritarian regimes, since the ruling family or the ruling party is less vulnerable to conflicts within the elite.

STUDY QUESTIONS

1. In the chapter, we've discussed two different ways of categorizing authoritarian regimes: by identifying the groups that control the government (a military junta, a political party, etc.) or by distinguishing between regimes that allow opposition parties to compete in elections and regimes that don't. Do you think hybrid regimes ought to be seen as an additional category alongside, for example, military and dominant-party regimes, or do you think it's better to treat the degree of competition within an authoritarian regime as a separate question that's relevant across regimes, no matter what the dominant group is?

2. As we discussed in Section 5.5, some of the major debates in comparative politics are concerned with what's happening inside authoritarian regimes, including what techniques rulers use to stay in power and how institutions such as elections and legislatures work. Going back to our discussion of research methods in Chapter 2, can you think of some of the main challenges involved in studying the inner workings of authoritarian systems?

FURTHER READING

Nancy Bermeo, *Ordinary People in Extraordinary Times* (2003).
   Examines the role played by ordinary citizens in political crises, demonstrating that elites have usually been responsible for democracy's downfall.

Barbara Geddes, Joseph Wright, and Erica Frantz, *How Dictatorships Work* (2018).
   Describes differences among authoritarian systems, explains why authoritarian states are governed differently, and analyses transitions between different types of democratic and authoritarian regimes.

Jennifer Gandhi, Ben Noble, and Milan Svolik, 'Legislatures and Legislative Politics without Democracy' (2020).
   Introduction to a recent journal issue that asks what authoritarian legislatures and legislators actually do and why dictatorships even have legislatures in the first place.

Steven Levitsky and Daniel Ziblatt, *How Democracies Die* (2018).
   Draws historical lessons concerning the threats to contemporary democracies, especially the United States.

CHAPTER 6
FEDERALISM

CHAPTER GUIDE

6.1 Introduction
6.2 The Meaning of Federalism
6.3 Federal and Unitary States around the World
6.4 The Origins of Federalism
6.5 Federalism's Effects
6.6 Conclusion
Summary
Study Questions
Further Reading

6.1 INTRODUCTION

As we discussed in Chapter 1, the world's states are organized very differently. Most states are *unitary*, which means that political power is concentrated at the national level. But some states are *federal*, which means that political power is divided between the national government and regional governments, with each level of government being responsible for some things but not others.

The differences between unitary and federal states are an old and important topic in comparative politics. Scholars have long tried to explain why the world's states are structured so differently and how federalism shapes political conflicts and influences public policies, compared with states that aren't federal. We will explore the origins and effects of federalism in this chapter, but we will also examine the allocation of responsibilities between central, regional, and local authorities within all states, for the simple distinction between unitary and federal states isn't enough to describe the relationship between different levels of government across states. To understand the territorial organization of the state, we need nuanced measures of the responsibilities of different levels of government for different areas of politics and public policy.

Section 6.2 defines federalism and gives concrete examples of how federal states are organized. Section 6.3 examines the distribution of federal and unitary states in the world and examines data on the autonomy of sub-national governments across all types of state. Section 6.4 discusses the origins and causes of federalism. Section 6.5 discusses its effects.

6.2 THE MEANING OF FEDERALISM

LEARNING OUTCOMES

After reading Section 6.2, you'll be able to:
- Define federalism
- Analyse the responsibilities of national, regional, and local governments in federal constitutions.

Most of the states in the world are **unitary**, which means that political power is concentrated at the national level of government. But about 25 countries, including some of the world's largest and most powerful states, are organized differently: they are **federal**, which means that political power is divided between the national government and sub-national governments (which are sometimes, a little confusingly, called 'states'—a word we also use, as in Chapter 3, to refer to the political organization of entire countries).

We briefly discussed the differences between unitary and federal states in Section 1.3, where we studied the examples of Egypt and Ethiopia. We'll now take a step back and address the conceptual question of what the word 'federalism' means. It goes back to a Latin term, *foedus*, that means 'league' or 'alliance', so we know that a federation is a union of some sort. But *what* sort?

According to one useful definition that was proposed by the American political scientist William Riker (1975, 101),

> Federalism is a political organization in which the activities of government are divided between regional governments and a central government in such a way that each kind of government has some activities on which it makes final decisions.

Other scholars have defined federalism a little differently, but Riker's definition is especially instructive since it has three important ideas built into it. Let's discuss each in turn.

6.2.1 Power is shared between central and regional governments

A federal state is made up of several different regions, each region has its own government, and the regional governments have the power to act autonomously: they don't just do the central government's bidding.

The regions that make up federal states can be called different things. For example, they're known as *Bundesländer*—or just *Länder* (lands)—in Germany, cantons in Switzerland, emirates in the United Arab Emirates, provinces in Argentina and Canada, regions and communities in Belgium, and states in Australia, Brazil, India, and the United States. But the idea is the same: the regions are political units in their own right within the country's larger, federal structure. Figure 6.1 shows how two federal countries, Brazil and the United Arab Emirates, are divided into 'states' and 'emirates', respectively.

6.2.2 Central and regional governments have distinct powers

The second idea that's built into Riker's definition of federalism is that both the central government and the regional governments make 'final decisions' on at least some matters. In other words, there are some things regional governments can do without being overridden by the national government, and there are some things the central government can do without consulting the regional governments.

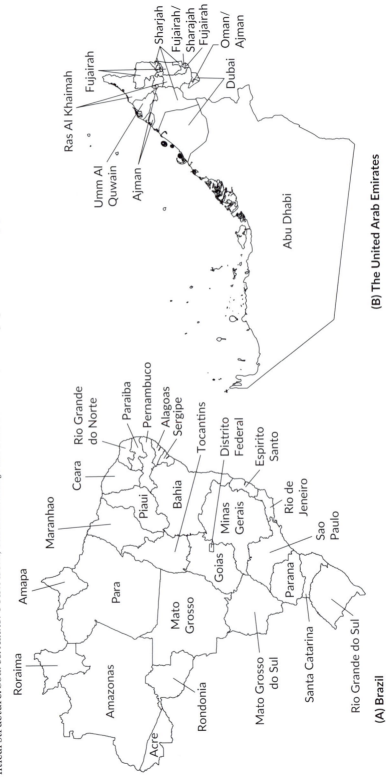

Figure 6.1 Federal states such as Brazil and the United Arab Emirates consist of regions with their own governments that coexist within a larger political structure. *Source: Author's own work, based on data from GeoBoundaries, courtesy of William & Mary geoLab*

That's why federalism is not the same thing as decentralization. Decentralization simply means that political decisions are made by a lower level of government rather than a higher one, and that can happen in both unitary and federal states. Indeed, many non-federal countries, especially in Europe, are highly decentralized in the sense that local and regional authorities provide a lot of services and make many decisions that affect people's lives. But in unitary states, local and regional authorities only have this power as long as the national government lets them. Put differently, in unitary states, political decisions are sometimes made by local and regional officials because the national government thinks it's a good idea to make those decisions closer to the citizens who are affected by them. In federal states, the constitution dictates that there are issues that belong to regional governments—no matter what the national government thinks.

6.2.3 Federal states are organized differently

A third idea that's built into the definition of federalism is that although federal states have some things in common—such as the idea that each level of government has the final word on at least some matters—they can nevertheless be organized very differently to one another. All the definition says is that each level of government makes final decisions on *some* issues: it doesn't say which issues belong where, nor does it say that the central government and regional governments need to be balanced in some way. In principle, it's possible to imagine a federal state in which regional governments do only one thing, or, conversely, in which the central government does only one thing.

The allocation of responsibilities between the central government and regional governments varies quite a lot among the federal states in the world. Some federal constitutions, such as that of the United States, merely list all the powers of the central government. For example, Article I, Section 9 of the US constitution provides that the national legislature—the Congress—has the power to 'establish Post Offices and post Roads' and 'punish Piracies and Felonies committed on the high Seas'. The understanding is that powers that are not listed are left to the states. Other federal constitutions instead list the powers of each level of government separately. For example, the Indian constitution lists the powers of the national government (this is known as the 'Union List'), the powers of the sub-national, state governments (the 'State List'), and areas in which both the national government and the state governments can be involved (the 'Concurrent List'). Research Prompt 6.1 will deepen your understanding of the variation in approaches among federal constitutions by helping you compare the powers accorded to national and regional governments in India and Nigeria, as they're set out in the constitutions of these two countries.

RESEARCH PROMPT 6.1
Federalism in India and Nigeria

India and Nigeria are both populous federal countries (indeed, India is the world's most populous country and Nigeria is Africa's most populous country). It is interesting to compare the powers of their central and regional governments, as set out in their constitutions.

India is divided into 28 states and 8 'union territories' (territories that are directly controlled by the central government). Nigeria, on the other hand, has 36 states and just one 'federal capital territory'. The responsibilities allocated to the national government and the states are set out in both countries' constitutions, and exploring these responsibilities gives us a sense of the variety of political arrangements in federal countries.

1. Download Schedule 7 of India's constitution from the website of India's Ministry of External Affairs. For the responsibilities of the national government, see the 'Union List'. For the responsibilities of the states, see the 'State List'. For the shared responsibilities, see the 'Concurrent List'. Identify one important responsibility of the national government, one important responsibility of the states, and one important shared responsibility, and try to explain why those three powers were allocated in this manner.

2. Download the constitution of Nigeria from the International Centre for Nigerian Law. Consult Schedule 2. The responsibilities of the central government are set out in the 'Exclusive List' and the shared responsibilities are set out in the 'Concurrent List'. Identify three important differences between India and Nigeria.

What ultimately matters in a federal state, however, isn't just the text of the constitution but also how the responsibilities for different policies are allocated *in practice* between the national government and regional governments. These arrangements are often disputed and change over time. In the United States, for example, the meaning of the constitution's Article I, Section 9, which sets out the areas in which the Congress may legislate, has long been debated. One particularly important change occurred in the 1930s, when the United States Supreme Court first declared many of the economic and social policies of President Franklin D. Roosevelt to be unconstitutional but then reversed course. Since that time, the US constitution's 'Commerce Clause', which provides that 'The Congress shall have Power to regulate Commerce with foreign Nations, and among the several States, and with the Indian Tribes', has been taken to mean that the federal government has broad powers to regulate the economy.

6.3 FEDERAL AND UNITARY STATES AROUND THE WORLD

LEARNING OUTCOMES

After reading Section 6.3, you'll be able to:

- Identify the world's federal states
- Describe the level of autonomy of sub-national governments across states
- Summarize the structures of regional organizations such as the European Union and the African Union.

Now that we know what federalism means and how national and regional governments share power within federal states, we're ready to take a closer look at the world's federations. Figure 6.2 identifies all the federal states in the world and Table 6.1 lists them by name. The figure and the table identify all states that are listed as federal by the Forum of Federations, an organization that studies federal and decentralized forms of government, except for Cyprus, which has not yet implemented a federal constitution.

Two things stand out in Figure 6.2 and Table 6.1. First, only a small number of countries are federal. There are close to 200 independent states in the world, but the list of federal countries in Table 6.1 only comprises around 25. So most states are unitary, not federal. But second, the list of federal states includes seven of the world's largest and most influential countries: Argentina,

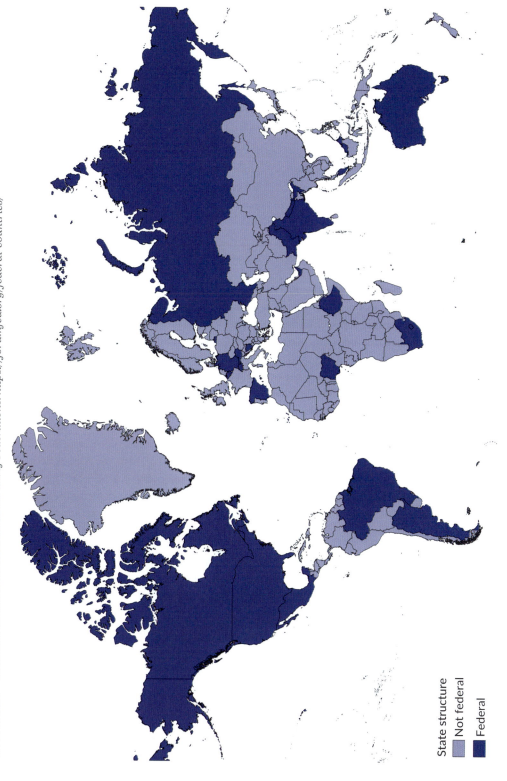

Figure 6.2 Although more countries are unitary than federal, the number that are widely recognized as federal includes some of the world's largest countries—and some of the smallest. *Source: Forum of Federations: https://forumfed.org/federal-countries/*

Table 6.1 Federal states in 2023

Africa	Americas	Asia	Europe	Oceania
Comoros	Argentina	India	Austria	Australia
Ethiopia	Brazil	Malaysia	Belgium	Micronesia
Nigeria	Canada	Nepal	Bosnia and Herzegovina	
South Africa	Mexico	Pakistan	Germany	
	Saint Kitts and Nevis	United Arab Emirates	Russia	
	United States		Spain	
			Switzerland	

Source: Forum of Federations: https://forumfed.org/federal-countries/

Australia, Brazil, Canada, India, Russia, and the United States. The main reason, as we'll discuss in Section 6.4, is that most of these large countries were formed when numerous smaller political units—independent states or former colonies—merged into a new, larger composite state.

It's a curious fact that some of the world's *smallest* countries are also federal: Comoros off the coast of East Africa, Saint Kitts and Nevis in the Caribbean, and Micronesia in Oceania. But they're hard to see in Figure 6.2, since they're so small (Saint Kitts and Nevis occupies two small volcanic islands that have a combined population of approximately 50,000). These are all island nations, which rely on federalism to manage the relationships between the different islands.

Figure 6.2 and Table 6.1 categorize countries as either federal or not federal, but, as we discussed in Section 6.2, the relative power of the regional governments varies a lot among the federal states. The same can be said about formally unitary states: in some of them, the regions have a lot of political authority; in others, regional governments are non-existent or at least largely irrelevant. Table 6.2 uses data on 'regional authority' from Hooghe et al. (2016) to describe the authority of the regional level in a large group of countries at two points in time. We learn several important things from this table.

1. The federal states (with the names in bold in the table) allocate much more authority to the regional level of government, *on average*, than unitary states, exactly as one might expect given that the constitutions of federal states provide that power is divided between the central government and regional governments.

2. There is a lot of variation among both unitary and federal states, and there are several unitary states in which regional governments exercise a great deal of authority. The way to think about this is that although the power of regional governments isn't guaranteed in the constitution in unitary states, the regional level can still have a lot of importance in practice.

3. More countries have increased the authority of regional governments than decreased it since the middle of the nineteenth century, both among unitary and among federal states. This suggests that to understand politics in modern states, we increasingly need to pay attention to the regional level of government and not just to the competition for and exercise of political power at the national level.

Table 6.2 The authority of regional governments in 1968 and 2018

Country	1968	2018	Country	1968	2018
Albania		2.0	**Germany**	34.5	37.7
Argentina	9.5	24.5	Greece	1.0	9.0
Australia	23.0	25.5	Guatemala	1.0	1.0
Austria	21.0	23.0	Guyana	0.0	0.0
Bahamas		0.0	Haiti	1.0	5.5
Bangladesh		19.0	Honduras	1.0	1.0
Barbados	0.0	0.0	Hungary		8.1
Belgium	16.0	33.9	Iceland	0.0	0.0
Belize		0.0	**India**	16.9	35.6
Bhutan	0.0	0.0	Indonesia	11.7	20.8
Bolivia	5.5	12.5	Ireland	0.0	11.0
Bosnia and Herzegovina		36.3	Israel	2.0	2.0
Brazil	8.9	21.8	Italy	10.3	26.0
Brunei		0.0	Jamaica	0.0	0.0
Bulgaria		2.0	Japan	10.9	18.1
Cambodia	4.0	5.0	Kosovo		0.0
Canada	27.6	27.8	Laos	0.0	1.0
Chile	1.0	6.0	Latvia		4.0
China	3.0	15.6	Lithuania		2.0
Colombia	8.5	15.0	Luxembourg	0.0	0.0
Costa Rica	1.0	0.1	Malaysia	22.1	21.5
Croatia		9.6	Malta	0.0	0.0
Cuba	1.0	5.0	**Mexico**	14.5	21.4
Cyprus	1.0	1.0	Mongolia		4.5
Czech Republic		12.3	Montenegro		0.0
Denmark	7.5	7.3	Myanmar	2.0	12.9
Dominican Republic	3.6	3.6	Nepal	8.5	19.5
East Timor		0.0	Netherlands	15.9	17.5
Ecuador	9.5	9.8	New Zealand	3.3	11.0
El Salvador	1.0	2.1	Nicaragua	1.0	4.5
Estonia		0.0	North-Macedonia		4.3
Finland	1.1	7.1	Norway	6.2	12.1
France	8.3	21.9	Pakistan	13.5	28.7

(*Continued*)

Table 6.2 (Continued)

Country	1968	2018	Country	1968	2018
Panama	1.1	5.4	Sri Lanka	1.0	11.0
Papua New Guinea		8.7	Suriname		0.0
Paraguay	1.0	8.1	Sweden	20.0	12.0
Peru	6.0	22.1	**Switzerland**	24.5	26.5
Philippines	8.0	11.1	Taiwan	7.4	11.0
Poland		11.3	Thailand	3.0	4.0
Portugal	2.0	9.5	Trinidad and Tobago	0.1	0.5
Romania		10.1	Turkey	6.0	8.8
Russia		21.9	Ukraine		7.1
Serbia		7.4	United Kingdom	10.4	9.6
Singapore	0.0	0.0	**United States**	29.6	29.6
Slovakia		8.8	Uruguay	9.0	12.0
Slovenia		3.2	**Venezuela**	10.7	6.1
South Korea	1.0	13.2	Vietnam	4.0	8.0
Spain	3.1	35.6			

Source: Data from Hooghe, Liesbet, Gary Marks, Arjan H. Schakel, Sandra Chapman-Osterkatz, Sara Niedzwiecki, and Sarah Shair-Rosenfield. 2016. Measuring Regional Authority. Volume I. A Postfunctionalist Theory of Governance. Oxford: Oxford University Press.

Our discussion so far has focused on individual states, but one part of the world, Europe, is also becoming more federal in another sense. Over the course of the late twentieth and early twenty-first centuries, the member states of the European Union have created a new form of federal system that now encompasses much of western, central, and eastern Europe (see Figure 6.3). Today's European Union, with its 27 member states, is the result of an historical process that began with the creation of the European Coal and Steel Community, with six member states, in the 1950s (Case Study 6.1).

CASE STUDY 6.1
The European Union

The question of whether the European Union (EU) ought to be seen as a federal system is much debated among scholars, in addition to being politically controversial. Many experts believe it's wrong to call the EU a federal system, especially a federal *state*, since it lacks many of the powers that the central level of government has in the federal states shown and listed in Figure 6.2 and Table 6.1. For example, the EU doesn't have the power to collect taxes, which makes it dependent on financial contributions from its member states, and there is no European army.

→

But let's go back to the definition of federalism we discussed in Section 6.2. Riker's definition only says that in a federal political organization, 'the activities of government are divided' so that 'each kind of government has some activities on which it makes final decisions'—it doesn't say which activities belong where. By that definition, the EU is quite clearly a federal organization, as there are several policy areas, especially in the economic domain, in which 'final decisions' are made by the EU, not national governments. Trade policy is one important example of the EU's 'exclusive competencies' (a legal term referring to areas in which only the EU has the power to act), and in the 19 countries that use the euro as their currency, monetary policy is the exclusive competency of the European Central Bank.

Indeed, many of the political leaders who were involved in creating the EU were inspired by federalist ideas (Burgess 2000). For example, when the French foreign minister Robert Schuman proposed the Coal and Steel Community in 1950, he said that 'instituting a new High Authority, whose decisions will bind France, Germany and other member countries', would 'lead to the realization of the first concrete foundation of a European federation indispensable to the preservation of peace'. For these and other reasons, scholars such as Larsen (2021), who compares the EU with the old German Confederation and pre-Civil-War United States, see the history of the EU as a part of the long history of federalism.

Figure 6.3 The European Union has 27 member states. *Source: Kolja21 / Wikimedia Commons (CC BY 3.0)*

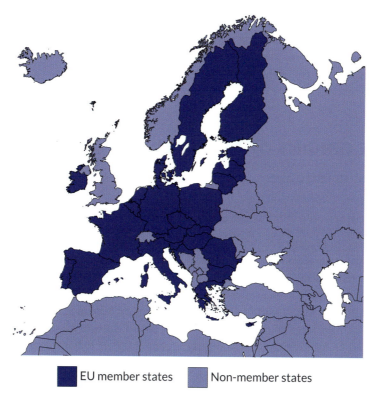

The form of continent-wide regional institution building exemplified by the European Union has come further in Europe than in other parts of the world. So far, other regional organizations, such as the Association of Southeast Asian Nations (ASEAN) and South America's Southern Common Market (Mercosur, El Mercado Común del Sur), typically limit their activities to trade agreements and looser forms of inter-governmental cooperation and economic exchange.

But there is a long tradition of regional cooperation in Africa that's associated with ideas about federalism and a pan-African ambition of creating a United States of Africa, which stems from the period in the middle of the twentieth century when most states in Africa gained independence from Europe's colonial powers. The idea of creating an African federal system was influential within the first inter-governmental organization on the continent: the Organization of African Unity (OAU), founded in 1963. It has also been influential within the most important international organization in Africa today: the African Union (AU), which replaced the older OAU in the early 2000s. Although regional collaboration in Africa is neither as broad nor as deep as in Europe—which means that the AU is far from a federal system—the AU is an important organization that has promoted cooperation around security, human rights, and public health (Tieku 2013, 2018). There is also a smaller regional organization in eastern Africa that has federal ambitions. We consider that organization in Research Prompt 6.2.

> **RESEARCH PROMPT 6.2**
> The East African Community
>
> The East African Community is a regional organization with six partner states: Burundi, Kenya, Rwanda, South Sudan, Tanzania, and Uganda. The long-term goal of the East African Community is to create a political federation. Visit the website of the East African Community and read about its plans. Then look for newspaper coverage of the negotiations between the six states and try to find out why the plans for a new federal system haven't yet come to fruition.

6.4 THE ORIGINS OF FEDERALISM

LEARNING OUTCOME

After reading Section 6.4, you'll be able to:
- Explain how federal institutions emerged in different countries.

As we discussed in Chapter 1, scholars of comparative politics keep coming back to two basic types of question: why are political systems so different, and how do those differences matter for people's lives? In this section, we will consider the origins of federal institutions and examine the main pathways to federalism. In Section 6.5, we will learn about federalism's effects.

Most federal states in the world today were formed when several smaller states or colonies merged into a single, large country. In those cases, federalism was a way of bringing the earlier states or colonies together while preserving some of their independence and autonomy.

But there are also a few federal states that were once unitary. In those cases, governments have typically put in place federal institutions to mitigate domestic political conflicts—either conflicts between different regions or conflicts between the central government and the regions, or some of the regions.

Germany is a good example of the first of these two paths to federalism—a federal state that was formed through the merging of smaller states or colonies to create a single country. Until the 1860s, what we now think of as Germany was a patchwork of smaller states known as the German Confederation. The Confederation was a loose form of cooperation between many of the German-speaking countries in Europe, forming a group that preceded the German Empire. As you can see, in Figure 6.4 the borders of the modern *Bundesländer*, or states, in the current Federal Republic of Germany often correspond to the borders of the independent countries that once existed in the north-western part of the old German Confederation. Germany was not the only country that was formed in Europe in the nineteenth century; so was Italy. One of the reasons Germany

Figure 6.4 The borders of Germany's *Bundesländer* often correspond to the borders of smaller states that existed before German unification in the 1870s. This map shows modern-day Germany overlaid with the German Confederation (1815–1866), with shared borders shown in bold. *Source: German Confederation: Ziegelbrenner / Wikimedia Commons (CC BY-SA 3.0) (https://commons.wikimedia.org/wiki/File:Deutscher_Bund.svg); modern-day Germany: Author's own work based on data from https://data.humdata.org/dataset/whosonfirst-data-admin-deu (OCHA CC BY 4.0)*

developed into a federation but Italy didn't is that the states that made up Germany were more evenly matched in terms of their strength and political organization at the founding of the two countries (see Ziblatt 2008).

The United States is another example of a federal state that was established when smaller states or colonies were merged. It formed when 13 British colonies in North America rebelled against Great Britain in the 1770s. And the United States isn't the only country that chose federalism when it gained independence from Great Britain or the United Kingdom—so did Canada, Nigeria, India, Pakistan, and Australia. South Africa is another former colony that has since become a federal state, but its path to federalism was a little more complicated: federalism was considered and rejected when South Africa became independent at the beginning of the twentieth century, but the country's current constitution, adopted after the end of the racist system of *apartheid*, is effectively federal.

Federalism in Argentina, Brazil, and Mexico can also be traced back to when those countries became independent, although they became independent from Spain, not Great Britain or the United Kingdom. There used to be more federal countries in Central and South America, but they have since disintegrated into several smaller states. One example is the Central American Federation, which existed in 1823–1840 and fell apart after a civil war in the 1830s. It covered an area that corresponds to present-day Costa Rica, El Salvador, Guatemala, Honduras, Nicaragua, and parts of Mexico.

There are other federal countries that have a very different history: they were once unitary states but adopted federalism as a means of mitigating conflicts between regions, between ethnic groups, or between the central government and a few regions that sought autonomy or even independence. One example is Ethiopia. The formerly unitary country adopted a new federal constitution in the 1990s with the intention of mitigating conflicts between its ethnic groups. But there are many other examples of states that have adopted federalism more recently to mitigate conflicts between regions, including European countries such as Belgium and Spain. We could even add to this list the United Kingdom. Although the United Kingdom doesn't have a federal constitution, it resembles a federation since many powers were devolved to Northern Ireland, Scotland, and Wales in the 1990s and 2000s. We'll come back to the relationship between federalism and regional conflicts in Section 6.5.

6.5 FEDERALISM'S EFFECTS

LEARNING OUTCOMES

After reading Section 6.5, you'll be able to:

- Analyse the relationships between federalism and other political institutions
- Describe some of federalism's political effects
- Give examples of how federalism has been used for peacebuilding.

Now we know what federalism is, how federal countries are structured, which countries in the world are federal, and how they turned out that way. In this section, we'll explore federalism's effects. As we've discussed throughout this book, scholars of comparative politics don't just want to figure out where institutions come from and how they work; they also want to understand how institutions shape political conflicts and people's lives.

6.5.1 Policymaking in federal states

The key thing to understand about a federal system, as the political scientist Pablo Beramendi reminds us in a useful overview of the topic (2007, 754), is that

> As opposed to unions or unitary states, federations and confederations show an architecture of government with dual structures, driven by a process of bargaining between a number of constituent units and a centre.

It's that 'process of bargaining' we'll concentrate on in this section. We already know that federations have 'dual structures' since that's an element of the definition of federalism we discussed in Section 6.2.

In unitary states, politics is mainly about what happens at the centre: the elections to the national legislature and the formation of the central government decide who has power in the state, and public policies are negotiated and put in motion in the country's capital. That's not how things work in federal states. Some policies are negotiated and put in motion in the national capital, but some are negotiated in regional capitals, and some are negotiated between the national government and the regional governments. National political leaders cannot go it alone: they must always pay attention to what regional decision makers are doing.

One key aspect of the relationship between the central government and the states in a federal system concerns public finances, specifically how much tax the central government and the states collect and how much money each level of government spends on public services and other government programmes.

The central government's share of public spending is on average much lower in federal states than in unitary states, but there is a lot of variation within both groups of countries. In some unitary states, spending by local and regional governments in fact represents a larger share of total government spending than in most federal states.

6.5.2 The relationship between federalism and other institutions

Federalism usually comes with other institutions that protect the interests of the regional governments vis-à-vis the central government. One such institution is a constitutional court or supreme court that has the power of **judicial review** (see Chapter 9). This means that courts have the authority to review decisions made by politicians—both at the central level and at the regional level—and to determine whether those decisions are in conflict with the constitution or with other legislation. Courts play a more significant political role in federal states than in unitary states, since they're often called in to resolve disputes between different levels of government (or indeed between different regional governments).

Another institution that is more common in federal states than in unitary states is bicameralism (see Chapter 8): in most federal states, the legislature has two chambers, with one chamber representing the regional governments. Of all the federal countries in Figure 6.2 and Table 6.1, only the island nations of Comoros, Micronesia, and Saint Kitts and Nevis have unicameral legislatures. All the others have bicameral legislatures, save for the United Arab Emirates, which is a federation of monarchies and doesn't have a legislature in the commonly understood sense of the word (its Federal National Council is merely an advisory body). The chamber that represents the interests of the regions in federal legislatures is often called the 'senate', such as the United States Senate (in which the 50 states have two senators each), but it can have other names, such as Germany's Bundesrat.

Because of the nature of federalism and the presence of institutions that protect the interests of regional governments, policymaking is usually a more complicated affair in federations than it is in unitary states. Since political powers are divided between the national government and regional governments, any policy initiative that involves both levels of government requires complex negotiations between national decision makers and regional ones. For example, if the government would like to reform the labour market, but some things, such as labour law, are the national government's responsibility while other things, such as employment services, are regional responsibilities, it's more complicated to reform the labour market than it would have been otherwise (Lindvall 2017, Chapter 3).

Another effect of federalism—and a key difference between federal states and unitary states—is that federalism leads to competition between a country's regions. Supporters of federalism believe this competition is a good thing since it encourages innovation, experimentation, and learning, and gives regional governments incentives to pursue good policies in order to avoid falling behind other regions. Critics of federalism worry that competition between regions undermines national solidarity and renders countries unable to address common problems (see, for example, Gerring and Thacker 2010).

6.5.3 Federalism can reduce conflict within countries

The last consequence of federalism that we'll consider is in some ways the most important: while federalism can increase competition between regions, it can also help to mitigate deep and sometimes violent conflicts within a country. As we discussed in Section 6.3, most federal states have been formed through the merging of several smaller states or colonies. But some federal countries adopted federal constitutions because they were looking for a way to reduce conflicts within their existing territories. They hoped that giving regions more autonomy would reduce tensions and hold the country together.

There are several examples in western Europe of this path to federalism. One is Belgium, which underwent a gradual process of decentralization in the twentieth century, before becoming formally federal in 1993. Belgium is divided between a Flemish-speaking part in the north and a French-speaking part in the south, and the purpose of the new federal constitution was to mitigate conflicts between those two communities. Spain has also become a de facto federal state after granting autonomy to two regions that have long sought independence: the Basque Country in the north and Catalonia in the north-east.

Federalism is sometimes also the direct result of civil wars. Bosnia and Herzegovina, the subject of Case Study 6.2, is one example. Ethiopia, with its specific ethnicity-based form of federalism, is another (see Chapter 1).

CASE STUDY 6.2
War and federalism in Bosnia and Herzegovina

In the early 1990s, after the fall of the Berlin Wall in 1989, the republic of Yugoslavia disintegrated, resulting in the creation of several new states along the eastern coast of the Adriatic Sea: Bosnia and Herzegovina, Croatia, Montenegro, North Macedonia, Serbia, Slovenia, and later Kosovo (not all countries recognize Kosovo as an independent state, since Serbia claims Kosovo is a part of Serbia). The break-up of Yugoslavia resulted in a war within Bosnia and Herzegovina, a country with three large ethnic groups: Bosniaks, Croats, and Serbs. After an international intervention, that war ended with a peace agreement, the Dayton Accord, in 1995.

Among many other provisions, the Dayton Accord decided that Bosnia would be a federal republic, to give each different ethnic group some measure of autonomy. The Bosnian state that emerged has a complicated federal structure (see Figure 6.5). Despite containing three ethnic

Figure 6.5 After the Bosnian War in the 1990s, a complicated federal structure was put in place in Bosnia and Herzegovina to give different ethnic groups some autonomy. This map shows the Dayton Agreement line, the Federation of Bosnia and Herzegovina, and the Republika Srpska within the Republic of Bosnia and Herzegovina. *Source: Library of Congress, Geography and Map Division*

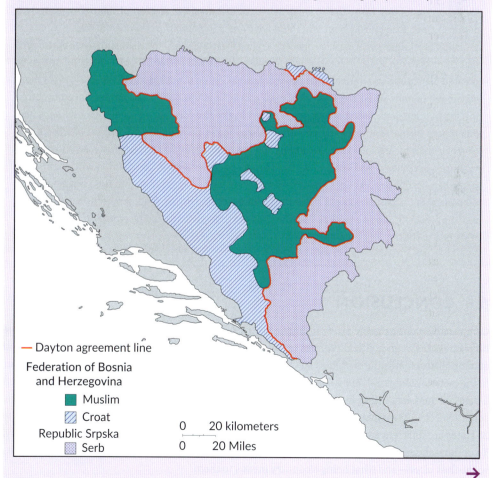

groups, the state is made up of just two political 'entities': the Federation of Bosnia and Herzegovina, which is where most Bosniaks and Croats reside, and the Republic of Srpska, in which most of the Serb population of the country reside. Each of these entities has a separate constitution. One of them, the Federation of Bosnia and Herzegovina, is *itself* a federation, consisting of ten 'cantons'.

There are numerous power-sharing arrangements at all levels of government. At the federal level, each of the three major ethnic groups is directly represented in the executive and has veto rights; there is a minority veto in the parliament; and in the second chamber, the House of Peoples, each ethnic group has equal representation and the quorum rules imply that policy changes require some support from within in each group. Following constitutional changes adopted in 2002, the governments of the federal entities and the cantonal governments within Bosnia and Herzegovina must include representation of Bosniaks, Croats, and Serbs.

These power-sharing arrangements and Bosnia and Herzegovina's particular form of federalism reflect a compromise between the country's ethnic communities (Gromes 2010, 356–360). The Bosniak political parties, which represent the largest ethnic group, preferred a majoritarian, unitary democracy with first-past-the-post elections. Many Serbs prefer partition and independence for Republika Srpska. Many Croats, meanwhile, believe that the division of the country into two entities fails to take into account that there are three peoples in the country, not two.

The political situation in Bosnia and Herzegovina illustrates both the risks and the opportunities that come with relying on federal arrangements in a post-war society. On the one hand, the complicated constitutional arrangements make policymaking slow and arduous—especially since there have been periods when the Bosniak, Croat, and Serb ethno-nationalist parties have boycotted the federal decision making structures outlined in the Dayton Accord. The emphasis on ethnic differences in the politics of the country has also made permanent the division of Bosnia and Herzegovina's society into separate groups. On the other hand, war has not resumed and political violence has declined. As Gromes (2010, 354) argues, 'federalism in conjunction with a consociational democracy, peacekeeping troops, and the prospect of integration into the European Union brought about a partial success of peace-building'. Although the federal system hasn't worked well, he argues, 'it seems plausible that Bosnia and Herzegovina would be worse off with a unitary state or a partition'.

6.6 CONCLUSION

Comparative politics is the study of how countries are governed. That's why we learn about the differences between political regimes (a topic we've covered in the previous three chapters) and about political institutions such as electoral rules, legislatures, and executives (topics we'll cover in the next few chapters). But we must also keep in mind that *what it means to be a country* is itself a political question. Either for historical reasons or because of political conflicts in our own time, some 25 of the 193 member states of the United Nations are federations, not unitary states. Those 25 states are different sorts of countries from the remaining 168, and they're governed differently. To understand how countries are governed, we must first understand how they became countries in the first place—and what being a country means to them.

One of this book's main themes is the relationship between institutions and conflict. Scholars of comparative politics try to understand how conflicts in different societies around the world are channelled, shaped, mitigated, resolved, or intensified by political institutions. This theme has been present throughout this chapter on federal and unitary states. As we discussed in Sections 6.4 and 6.5, federalism is often a *consequence* of conflicts between regions and between the regions and the central government. Indeed, federalism is sometimes put in place for the direct purpose of building peace in countries affected by war after the cessation of hostilities. But federalism also *shapes* political conflicts. In federal states, the powers of the national government and of regional governments are always contested, as federalism adds a layer of territorial competition to all the other conflicts that can exist in a society.

The themes we have discussed in this chapter are closely related to many themes that are discussed elsewhere in the book. The chapter deals with the structure and territorial organization of the state, and therefore complements our earlier discussion of the state in Chapter 3. But it also anticipates several of the coming chapters, for, as we discussed in Section 6.5, federalism tends to come with other institutions, such as bicameral legislatures (Chapter 8) and powerful high courts (Chapter 9). Political parties (Chapter 11) and other political associations (Chapter 13) also tend to organize themselves differently in different types of states.

SUMMARY

- There are approximately 25 federal states in the world.
- In federal states, political power is divided between the national government and regional governments.
- The structure of federal states varies, as does the allocation of responsibilities between different levels of government.
- The European Union is a continent-spanning federal system, but it lacks many of the powers commonly associated with sovereign states.
- Some countries have been federal ever since they were founded through the merging of several smaller states; other countries adopted federalism to deal with divisive conflicts or the aftermath of war.
- Federalism often comes with other institutions, such as bicameralism and a strong constitutional court or supreme court.
- Policymaking in a federation typically involves negotiations and coordination across several levels of government.
- In post-conflict societies, federalism may promote peace, but it can also lead to a deadlocked political system.

STUDY QUESTIONS

1. On the whole, is the world becoming more federal?
2. There are many examples of federations that have ceased to exist, including the Central African Federation, the Federal Republic of Central America, the Czech and Slovak Federative

Republic, the union of Malaysia and Singapore (now two separate countries), and the United States of Colombia. Based on what you've learned in this chapter, why might federations, once formed, be dissolved?

FURTHER READING

Pablo Beramendi, 'Federalism' (2007).
  Reviews the theoretical and empirical literature on federalism.

Nancy Bermeo, 'A New Look at Federalism: The Import of Institutions' (2002).
  Analyses the role of federal institutions in post-conflict societies.

John Loughlin, John Kincaid, and Wilfried Swenden (eds.), *Routledge Handbook of Regionalism and Federalism* (2013).
  Gives a broad overview of regionalism and federalism and contains numerous country studies.

CHAPTER 7
ELECTORAL SYSTEMS

CHAPTER GUIDE

7.1 Introduction
7.2 Majoritarian, Proportional, and Mixed Systems
7.3 Characteristics of Electoral Systems
7.4 Electoral Systems around the World
7.5 Elections and Representation
7.6 Conclusion
Summary
Study Questions
Further Reading

7.1 INTRODUCTION

As we discussed in Chapter 4, all modern democracies are *representative*: apart from the occasional referendum, important political decisions aren't made directly by the people; they're made by the people's elected representatives. The power of the people is manifested through elections. This makes the electoral system—the rules that govern how elections are conducted—an especially important institution in modern states. Indeed, many scholars believe that the main differences between the world's democracies go back to their electoral systems, because they shape the party system. The distinction between majoritarian and proportional systems is especially important. Countries with proportional electoral systems tend to have a greater number of viable political parties than countries with majoritarian electoral systems.

The word 'election' comes from the Latin word *eligere*, which means 'to pick out', so we know that holding an election means choosing some people over others. But there are many ways to make such a choice. In this chapter, we'll explore the main types of electoral system, find out where those different systems are used, learn how they emerged, and study how they've changed through history. We will also consider the relationship between elections and political representation—that is, how different groups of people are represented in legislatures and other important institutions. In Chapter 12, we'll learn about how voters choose between the parties and candidates that compete for their votes.

As we learned in Chapter 5, elections don't have the same sorts of political effects under authoritarianism as they do under democracy, for either the elections aren't free and fair or the country's actual leaders aren't elected. In authoritarian states, elections often serve mainly to strengthen the legitimacy of the regime by mobilizing support for the country's rulers. But elections can also encourage opposition parties to mobilize and opposition groups to work together, which may make a transition to democracy more likely. In this chapter, we'll concentrate on the origins and effects of electoral systems in democratic regimes, but many of the things you'll learn about how electoral systems are structured are relevant for authoritarian regimes as well.

7.2 MAJORITARIAN, PROPORTIONAL, AND MIXED SYSTEMS

LEARNING OUTCOMES
After reading Section 7.2, you'll be able to:
- Define the main characteristics of an electoral system
- Distinguish between majoritarian, proportional, and mixed systems.

There are very few countries that don't hold any elections at all. To be more specific, the only countries in the world in which no national legislative elections were held between 2010 and 2019 are China, Eritrea, Qatar, Saudi Arabia, Somalia, South Sudan, and Yemen. These countries also count among the world's most authoritarian states (see Chapter 5). China and Eritrea are dominant-party regimes. Qatar and Saudi Arabia are absolute monarchies. Somalia, South Sudan, and Yemen are sometimes categorized as failed states (see Chapter 3).

The term **electoral system** refers to the rules that govern how elections are conducted. As we'll learn in this chapter, no two countries have identical electoral systems, since electoral systems can vary in many different ways. Three characteristics of electoral systems stand out as being particularly important.

1. Elections are typically conducted in particular geographical areas, which are known as **electoral districts**. One especially important characteristic of the electoral system is how many representatives are elected from each district. The technical term for that number is **district magnitude**.
2. When the voters vote, they do so by handing in a paper ballot or transmitting a digital ballot via a computer at the polling station or online. What is on that ballot is another important characteristic of the electoral system. The technical term here is **ballot structure**.
3. When all the votes have been cast, there needs to be a method of translating those votes into 'seats' in the legislature (that is, places in the parliament or in some other political assembly). The technical term for that method is the **electoral formula**.

We'll discuss these three characteristics in more detail in the next section, but first, let's take a moment to discuss how they are combined in the two main types of electoral system, the **majoritarian** and the **proportional**.

In a typical majoritarian system, each electoral district elects one single representative, which means that district magnitude is 1, the voters simply pick a candidate from a list of candidates on the ballot, and the electoral formula is called **first past the post**: the candidate who gets the most votes wins the election in that district. Since the candidate in a first-past-the-post system who gets the most votes wins the election even if that candidate doesn't actually get a majority, the term plurality voting is sometimes preferred to 'majority voting', reserving the latter term for systems with run-off elections between the top two candidates, as in France, or systems in which voters get to rank the candidates, as in Australia. In a system with run-off elections, if no candidate gets more than 50 per cent of the votes in the election, a follow-up election is held, where only the top two candidates are eligible. Systems in which the voters get to rank the candidates are known as preferential- or alternative-voting systems. The effects are similar to having run-off elections without the need for actually having a second round.

In a typical proportional system, on the other hand, each district elects several representatives, so the average district magnitude (how many representatives are elected from an electoral district) is greater than 1, sometimes much greater. The voters normally choose among lists of candidates that are proposed by political parties—party lists—and not among individuals. Finally, the electoral formula can be one of several methods that allocate seats more or less proportionally. This means that each political party's share of the seats in the legislature is approximately the same as its share of the votes—so if a party gets 10 per cent of the vote, it gets approximately 10 per cent of the seats.

Many countries have electoral systems that don't fit into either of these two main categories. For example, there are majoritarian systems with an average district magnitude that is greater than 1 and there are proportional systems where the voters are able to choose among individual politicians, not just parties. Moreover, some electoral systems are mixed: they combine majoritarian and proportional elements. Both Germany and New Zealand (which you will read about in Case Study 7.2) are examples of mixed electoral systems.

But it can nevertheless be helpful to separate electoral systems into two or three main types, since majoritarian and proportional systems are so different from each other. Indeed, many scholars believe that the choice between majoritarian elections and proportional elections is so important that we should think of democracies as coming in two types: the more majoritarian ones and the more proportional ones. For example, Bingham Powell, in his book *Elections as Instruments of Democracy* (2000), distinguishes between the majoritarian and the proportional 'visions' of democracy, and Arend Lijphart, in his book *Patterns of Democracy* (2012), distinguishes between 'majoritarian' and 'consensus' democracies, and both of them regard the electoral system as fundamental.

7.3 CHARACTERISTICS OF ELECTORAL SYSTEMS

LEARNING OUTCOMES

After reading Section 7.3, you'll be able to:
- Explain how the main elements of electoral systems work
- Compare the electoral systems of different countries
- Analyse the consequences of different electoral rules.

Let us now examine the three main characteristics of electoral systems in detail, beginning with the number of candidates who are elected from each electoral district.

7.3.1 The size of the electoral districts

As we saw in Section 7.2, electoral districts are the geographical areas in which elections are conducted. The key distinction to remember here relates to the number of representatives who are elected from each district. Districts that elect one single representative are known as single-member districts. Districts that elect more than one representative are known as multi-member districts. The choice between single-member districts and multi-member districts is highly consequential. In single-member districts, there can only be one winner, which means that one party must win and all others must lose. In systems with multi-member districts, each district typically elects a more diverse group of representatives.

In countries with single-member districts, the electoral map typically looks something like the map of the 2022 election to the House of Representatives in the United States (Figure 7.1). Each congressional district pictured on that map is represented by one single individual, who represents one particular party—the Democratic or the Republican Party. The fact that there are only two competitive parties in the United States is a consequence of the majoritarian electoral system, especially the system of single-member districts. As we'll discuss in more detail in Section 7.5, there are typically fewer parties in systems with single-member districts than in systems with multi-member districts. Incidentally, while it may look as if the map is completely dominated by the Republican Party, that party in fact only won the 2022 election narrowly. The explanation for the map's appearance is that the Democratic Party is much stronger in the cities (where people live close to each other and the electoral districts are geographically smaller) than in the countryside and in smaller towns (where people live further apart and the electoral districts are geographically larger).

In countries with *multi-member districts*, all or most districts elect several representatives, not a single representative. Each part of the country is therefore represented by several people, who may well represent several different parties (in fact, they typically do). Keeping the size of the legislature constant, the total number of districts is smaller in a country with multi-member districts than in a country with single-member districts. For example, in 2024, there were 650 members of parliament in the United Kingdom, with each member representing one district; if the United Kingdom changed its electoral system and created multi-member districts with an average district magnitude of, say, 26, there would be 25 electoral districts (since 25 × 26 = 650).

The districts in a country with multi-member districts often elect different numbers of representatives. Take a look at the map of Türkiye in Figure 7.2. The map shows how many members of Türkiye's parliament were elected from each electoral district in the Türk parliamentary election in the spring of 2023. Note that many of the rural districts in the larger, Asian part of Türkiye (everything but the five top-left districts on the map) elected only one or two members of parliament each. By contrast, the district magnitude in the electoral districts in Istanbul—Europe's largest city, located in the north-western part of the country—was approximately 30.

There are countries that aren't divided into electoral districts at all, which means that the whole country acts as one district, and the district magnitude is equal to the number of seats in the legislature. This is the case for elections to Israel's parliament, the Knesset, and the lower house of the Dutch parliament, *Tweede Kamer der Staten-Generaal*. We can think of this type of arrangement

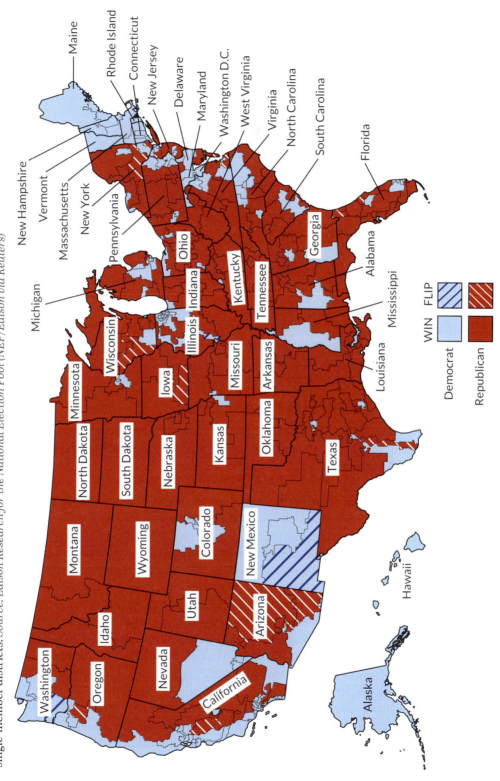

Figure 7.1 The results of the 2022 election to the House of Representatives. Elections to the United States Congress are held every two years in 435 single-member districts. *Source: Edison Research for the National Election Pool (NEP/Edison via Reuters)*

Figure 7.2 Türkiye is divided into 87 electoral districts, each of which elects between one and 36 members of parliament (the figures on the map refer to the number of members of parliament elected from each district). *Source: MapsandMP / Wikimedia Commons (CC BY-SA 4.0)*

as a pure form of proportional representation in which there is no geographical linkage between members of the legislature and particular parts of the country, and national issues therefore tend to take precedence over local ones.

7.3.2 What the ballots look like

The second important characteristic of the electoral system is the *ballot structure*: what the electoral ballots actually look like and, more generally, what sort of choice each voter is asked to make when participating in the election.

In countries with majoritarian or plurality elections in single-member districts, voters typically get to choose from a list of names: each party nominates one candidate in each district, and then each voter selects one of the nominated candidates. Since a president is a single individual, this is how presidents are typically chosen. Figure 7.3 is a picture of a ballot from a presidential election in the United States, in which the voters were asked to pick among candidates for president and vice president. Incidentally, the picture is of the infamous 'butterfly ballot', which benefited the Republican candidate George W. Bush in the exceptionally close presidential election in the United States in 2000. Bush won narrowly in Florida, where this ballot was used, and it's widely believed that the design of the ballot misled many voters who wished to vote for the Democratic candidate Al Gore into voting for the conservative candidate Pat Buchanan, since the hole voters were supposed to punch to vote for Pat Buchanan was the second one from the top and Al Gore's name was second from the top in the left-hand column of names (Wand et al. 2001).

But there are also countries with single-member districts in which the ballots list *parties*, not individual candidates—even if each party is in fact represented by one individual in each district. Botswana, one of the most stable democracies in Africa, is such a country. As Figure 7.4 shows, on ballots in Botswana, the voters choose between parties, not individual people.

This 'parties, not people' approach also applies in most countries with multi-member districts and proportional electoral rules. In such countries, the voters typically don't choose among individual candidates; they are asked to choose among the parties, each party having put together a

Figure 7.3 The infamous 'Butterfly Ballot' was used in Palm Beach County in Florida in the presidential election in the United States in 2000. *Source: Wikimedia Commons (public domain)*

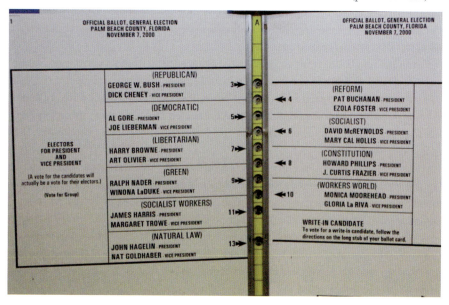

Figure 7.4 Unlike in many other countries with single-member districts, the ballots in Botswana list the names of parties, not the names of individual candidates. *Source: MONIRUL BHUIYAN / Getty Images*

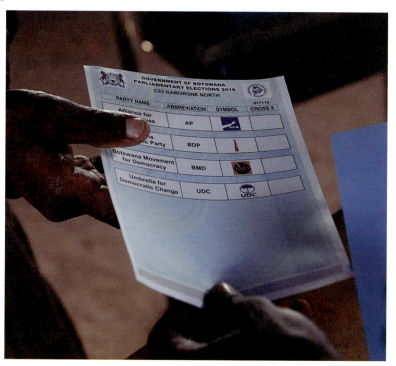

list of candidates who run in each district. If the only choice the voters have is between lists that were compiled by the parties, the system is called *closed-list*, since the voters cannot alter the lists of people the parties have drawn up. If the voters can influence the choice of individual candidates after picking a party—by removing names, adding names, or indicating a preference for a particular candidate—the system is called *open-list*.

For an example of a ballot from an open-list system, see the (remarkably large) Dutch ballot in Figure 7.5. The Netherlands has one of the world's most proportional electoral systems, so there are many competitive parties in Dutch politics. Even so, if the voters were only allowed to choose among parties, there wouldn't be a need for such a large ballot as the one in Figure 7.5, but since the voters are also allowed to indicate preferences for particular candidates, the ballot has become very large indeed.

Finally, let's look at a ballot from a mixed electoral system. Figure 7.6 shows an example from Germany. In this country, each voter has two votes: one in a single-member-district election and one in a proportional, party-list election. The text at the top of the ballot reads 'You have two votes'. The single-member-district part of the election guarantees that each part of the country is represented by at least one member of parliament and voters can identify an individual politician as 'their' representative. The list-proportional part of the election guarantees a nationally proportional outcome. You can read about another mixed electoral system that is very similar to Germany's in Case Study 7.2 later in this chapter.

Figure 7.5 This exceptionally large ballot paper was used in the Dutch general election in 2017. *Source: 1Veertje / Wikimedia Commons (CC BY-SA 3.0)*

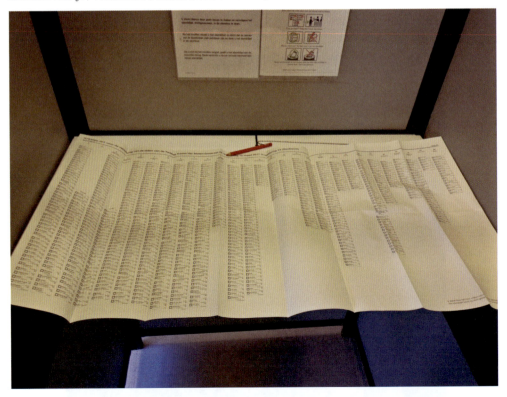

Figure 7.6 In German federal elections, each voter has two votes: one for a candidate in a single-member district and one for a party. *Source: Ulrich Baumgarten via Getty Images*

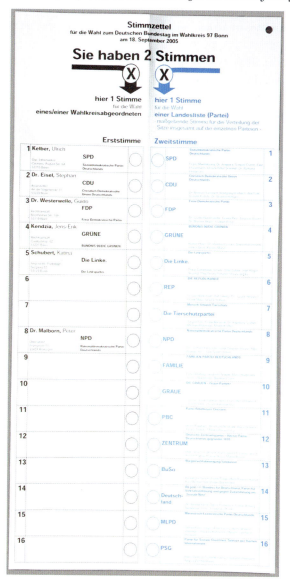

7.3.3 How the seats are allocated

The third main characteristic of the electoral system is the *electoral formula*: how the ballots that have been cast in the election are converted into seats in the legislature. The word 'seats' is used in this context since each member of a legislature typically has their own actual seat, but it also means something more abstract: a candidate wins a seat when he or she becomes a member of the legislative assembly.

In countries with single-member districts, the most common electoral formula is plurality voting, or *first past the post*: in each electoral district, the candidate who gets the most votes wins. That's how elections have long been conducted in the United Kingdom. It is also a method that is widely used among countries in Africa, Asia, North America, and Oceania that were once British colonies.

Although it's common, plurality voting isn't the only possible electoral formula in countries with single-member districts. The main alternative, as we discussed earlier, is majority voting. With majority voting, it isn't enough to get more votes than any other candidate: to win, you need more than 50 per cent of the votes. One way to guarantee such an outcome is having run-off elections between the top candidates in each district (unless one candidate won a majority of the votes in the first round). That is the system that is used in France. Another way to guarantee that one candidate gets a simple majority is alternative voting. Under this system, which is used in parliamentary elections in Australia, voters are asked to rank the candidates, not just pick their favourite, and then the votes for the less popular candidates are reallocated to other, more successful candidates until one candidate ends up with more than 50 per cent.

It's theoretically possible to use plurality and majority voting in systems with multi-member districts as well, but most countries with multi-member districts use more proportional methods for allocating the seats in the legislature. There are numerous such methods, which are typically named after the mathematicians who came up with them, notably the Belgian mathematician Victor D'Hondt (the D'Hondt method) and the French mathematician André Sainte-Laguë (the Sainte-Laguë method). These methods for allocating seats in the legislature are designed to bring about reasonably proportional outcomes, with each party's share of the seats corresponding to its share of the votes. But there are slight differences between them. The Sainte-Laguë method tends to lead to more proportional outcomes, overall, than the D'Hondt method. The D'Hondt method privileges larger parties.

Another rule that can be used to disadvantage small parties in countries with proportional elections is an *electoral threshold*: a rule about the minimum percentage of votes that a party needs to win any seats at all. The Netherlands, which we discussed in the context of ballot structures, has no electoral threshold, so a party can get into parliament even with just 0.67 per cent of the votes (100 per cent divided by the total number of seats in the lower chamber of the Dutch parliament, which is 150). Türkiye, which we discussed when considering the size of the electoral districts, has the highest threshold of any country with proportional elections: 10 per cent.

7.4 ELECTORAL SYSTEMS AROUND THE WORLD

LEARNING OUTCOMES

After reading Section 7.4, you'll be able to:
- Describe the distribution of electoral systems in the world
- Explain why countries have different electoral systems
- Analyse the causes of electoral-system reform.

We've seen that electoral systems differ from each other in many ways, and that it's possible to combine both single-member and multi-member electoral districts with different ballot structures (what the ballots look like) and different electoral formulas (how the votes are converted into seats). But as we discussed in Section 7.2, it is nevertheless possible to place almost all electoral systems in the world in one of three categories:

- Majoritarian systems, which have single-member districts and plurality or majority voting
- Proportional systems, which have multi-member districts, list voting, and some way of assuring that each party's share of the votes in the legislature corresponds to that party's share of the vote
- Mixed systems, which combine majoritarian and proportional elements.

In this section, we'll discuss the distribution of those three types of system in the world today, and how they've evolved over time.

7.4.1 Electoral systems today

Figure 7.7 illustrates the variety of electoral systems in the world today, using the three categories we've just discussed (majoritarian, proportional, mixed), as well as an 'other' category for a few countries in the Middle East that have special electoral arrangements that don't fit easily into the three main categories.

The map reveals several interesting patterns. Starting with the majoritarian systems, we can immediately see that majoritarian elections are common in former British colonies, including the United States and Canada in the Americas, Botswana, Ghana, Kenya, Sierra Leone, Tanzania, and Zambia in Africa, Bangladesh, India, Myanmar, and Pakistan in South Asia, and Australia in Oceania. But there are also numerous countries in which the adoption of majoritarian elections was not a consequence of a legacy of British colonialism. Among the examples are Belarus in Europe, Iran in the Middle East, Turkmenistan and Uzbekistan in central Asia, and several former French colonies in Africa.

Proportional elections are especially common in western Europe (although not in the United Kingdom and France, two of the most populous countries in the region) and in Latin America. As we'll soon see, many western European countries switched from majoritarian to proportional elections at the beginning of the last century. In Latin America, there was a more gradual shift to proportional representation during the twentieth century. The electoral system in Indonesia, the fourth country in the world by population size, is also proportional, as are the electoral systems of several African countries, including large states such as Algeria and South Africa.

Mixed electoral systems—which is a summary term for a range of methods that combine majoritarian and proportional rules, with some being more proportional than others—exist in all parts of the world and in different political regimes. In the Americas, there are mixed electoral systems in Bolivia, Ecuador, Mexico, and Venezuela. In Europe, there are mixed electoral systems in Germany and in several countries in eastern Europe, notably Ukraine, which is one of Europe's largest countries. In Asia, countries such as Japan and Thailand have mixed electoral systems. In Oceania, New Zealand does. Mixed electoral systems are especially common in the northern and central parts of Africa.

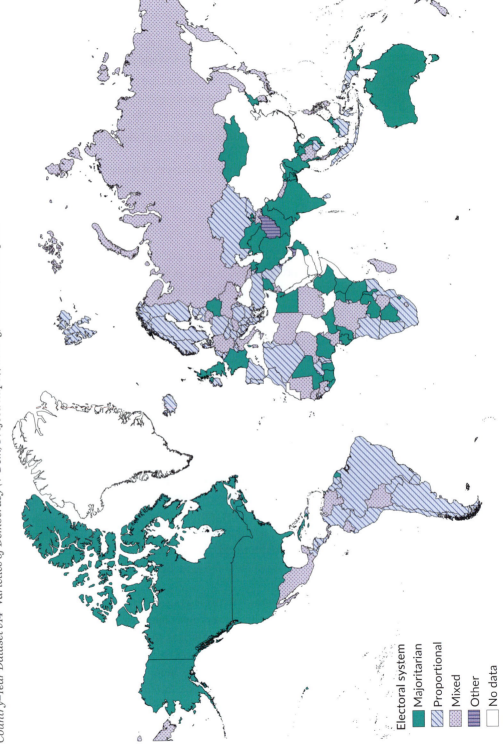

Figure 7.7 Electoral systems varied greatly around the world in 2023. *Source*: Author's own work, based on data from Coppedge et al. (2024), "V-Dem Country–Year Dataset v14" Varieties of Democracy (V-Dem) Project. https://doi.org/10.23696/mcwt-fr58

7.4.2 How different electoral systems emerged

Our discussion so far should have given you a rough idea of why particular electoral systems have emerged in different parts of the world. In this section we will explore their development in more detail. Figure 7.8 provides a useful starting point for such considerations, as it describes the proportion of majoritarian, proportional, and mixed electoral systems among the independent countries in western Europe, North and South America, and Oceania during the 200-year period between 1800 and 2000. (Regrettably, it's difficult to find global data on electoral systems that go this far back in time, which is why the data in the figure only cover selected parts of the world.)

Figure 7.8 describes the following broad trends when it comes to electoral systems in western Europe and in former western European colonies in Oceania and the Americas:

- Until the end of the nineteenth century, various forms of majoritarian elections (and indirect elections, which are combined with majoritarian elections here) were completely dominant.
- The major breakthrough for proportional elections was in the first two decades of the twentieth century.
- The share of countries with proportional elections increased again after the Second World War.
- The share of countries with majoritarian elections declined throughout the twentieth century.
- Mixed electoral systems have become increasing popular.

Figure 7.8 Over time, proportional and mixed electoral systems have become more common than majoritarian systems. *Source: Author's own work, based on the categorization of electoral systems in Colomer (2004). Colomer, Josep M., editor. 2004. The Handbook of Electoral System Choice. Basingstoke: Palgrave.*

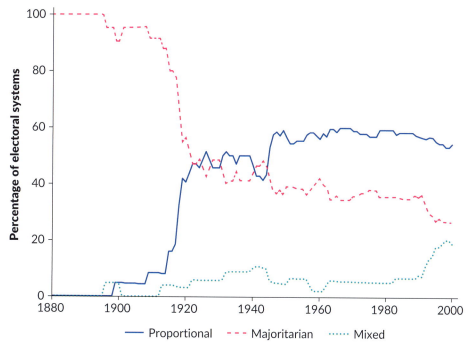

The first country in the world to introduce a proportional electoral system at the national level was Belgium in 1899. By that time, the idea of proportional elections had been debated among intellectuals and political leaders for more than a hundred years, but it took until the end of the nineteenth century for the idea to be tried out in practice. In the course of the twentieth century, proportional representation became significantly more popular than majoritarian elections. It spread especially quickly in the first quarter of the twentieth century—first in Europe, then in Latin America.

The shift to proportional elections in many countries in this period was often justified by ideas about the moral superiority of proportional elections that ensured the party composition of the legislature reflected the votes given in elections. However, when scholars of comparative politics have studied electoral reforms—who implemented them, and which countries did and didn't change their electoral rules—they have typically concluded that the main factor driving the changes was political expediency. In other words, reform was politically convenient to the people in power at the time.

The most widely accepted explanation for the shift to proportional representation in western Europe is that the conservative, Catholic, and liberal parties that were in power in most countries in the early twentieth century were concerned that socialist working-class parties would become completely dominant once workers got the right to vote. With proportional representation, the old right-wing parties would remain electorally viable even if the socialist parties grew stronger (Boix 1999). Similar motivations lay behind the more gradual shift to proportional representation in Latin America during the twentieth century (Wills-Otero 2009): across Latin America, proportional representation was introduced when previously dominant parties came under threat because of the emergence of new parties and the growth of the voting population. By adopting proportional representation, dominant parties safeguarded their future electoral viability. Chile is one example: proportional elections were introduced in 1925 after the vote share of the largest party had declined from 80 to 50 per cent, and universal male suffrage had been realized (Wills-Otero 2009, 43).

In Case Study 7.1, we will study the history of electoral-system reform in Papua New Guinea.

> **CASE STUDY 7.1**
> Papua New Guinea's alternative-vote system
>
> Papua New Guinea has been a democracy since 1964. Its single-chamber legislature consists of 111 members who serve for five years at a time. Of these, 89 are elected from open lists and 22 are chosen from the country's electoral provinces and districts.
>
> The politics of Papua New Guinea is strongly influenced by the country's ethnic divisions, and political mobilization has primarily been directed at clans and tribes and not been based on political issues. But this was not regarded as a major problem before Papua New Guinea gained independence from the United Kingdom in 1975, owing to the country's electoral system which gave voters the opportunity to rank the candidates (Reilly 2002, 164–165). This system incentivized and encouraged politicians in Papua New Guinea to seek electoral support beyond their own ethnic groups, either by campaigning for second-preference votes or by forming alliances with other

candidates and factions. Once elected, politicians owed loyalty and accountability to a diverse group of voters.

However, when the old electoral system was abolished after independence and replaced with a first-past-the-post system, politicians' incentives changed. Cooperation across ethnic groups declined, resulting in a 'retribalization' of politics. Without cooperative incentives in place, Papua New Guinea saw a rise in fractionalization and risk of violence, each reinforcing the other.

In response to this crisis, Papua New Guinea sought to return to an electoral system more closely resembling its old preferential-voting system. As a result, it implemented the limited-preferential-voting (LPV) system, which allows voters to rank their top three candidate choices. Election-related violence reportedly shrank from around 100 deaths after the 2002 election to a handful after the first LPV election in 2007.

Not only does the case of Papua New Guinea provide a powerful illustration of the crucial role institutions play in political interactions and outcomes; it also presents us with an opportunity to study how changing the rules of the game changed the behaviour and strategies of political elites as well as the relations between different groups.

The fact that political leaders often adopt reforms because of political expediency doesn't mean we should stop caring about principles or the moral justifications for different electoral rules. But we need to be realistic about the prospects for electoral-system reform. Political decisions are always made by those who are in power at the time, and those people are in power because they did well and got themselves elected under the *existing* electoral system. They are understandably going to be wary about changing a system that has allowed them to do well, regardless of how compelling the moral arguments for doing so might be. This is why political expediency matters.

It's also why big electoral-system reforms have historically been quite rare. Turn to Research Prompt 7.1 to learn why electoral-system reforms sometimes do happen nevertheless—and why they often don't.

RESEARCH PROMPT 7.1
Electoral-system reforms

As we've discussed in the main text, major electoral reforms have historically been quite rare, but there are examples. One is New Zealand, which, changed its electoral system in a big way in the 1990s (see Case Study 7.2). Another, more recent example is Iraq, which decided in 2019 to go from a proportional electoral system to a majoritarian one. The first election held under the new, majoritarian rules was the parliamentary election in 2021. Try to find out more about why Iraq decided to change its electoral system—and whether the reform had the intended consequences.

There have been several examples in recent years of countries, and parts of countries, that have held referendums on proposals about changing their electoral systems, but the proposals have been turned down by the voters. One example is the United Kingdom, which held a referendum on adopting a different electoral system in 2011. Another example is the Canadian province of British Columbia, which held a referendum on introducing proportional elections in 2018. These referendum campaigns give us an opportunity to study the arguments for and against electoral-system reform. Try to find out what the main messages were of the campaigns for and against changing the electoral system in at least one of these two cases.

7.5 ELECTIONS AND REPRESENTATION

LEARNING OUTCOMES

After reading Section 7.5, you'll be able to:

- Distinguish between different dimensions of political representation
- Explain how the electoral system can affect the number of viable parties
- Analyse the relationship between the electoral system, representation, and electoral turnout.

Electoral systems matter greatly for how different groups of citizens are represented in politics.

Before we discuss why this might be, let's stop for a moment to discuss what it means for citizens and groups of citizens to be 'represented'. One classic twentieth-century study of the idea of representation is Hanna Pitkin's book *The Concept of Representation* (1967). In her book, Pitkin argued that the concept of representation has at least four dimensions: *formalistic*, *symbolic*, *descriptive*, and *substantive* representation.

- Formalistic representation means that there is some procedure for appointing representatives (electoral systems are, of course, methods used for this purpose).
- Symbolic representation means that those who are represented actually *feel* represented: they think of their representatives as somehow standing in for them.
- Descriptive representation means that the representatives resemble those they represent (in terms of political opinions, social background, gender, etc.).
- Substantive representation, finally, means that the representatives act in the interest of those they represent.

The electoral system of a democracy influences all of these outcomes. Many scholars believe that descriptive representation increases symbolic and substantive representation, first because people are more likely to identify with their representatives if they feel that they are in some sense like them, and second, because politicians are more likely to act in the interests of the voters if they have things in common with them. There is therefore a lot of empirical research on representation that examines the relationship between the electoral system and different measures of descriptive representation. Most measures show proportional representation to be associated with more representative outcomes. See, for example, Figure 7.9, which shows the percentage of women in legislatures around the world in early 2021. The figure demonstrates a clear relationship between the electoral system and the representation of women: in countries with proportional

Figure 7.9 The share of women among the members of legislatures in democracies is highest in countries with proportional elections. *Source: Data on women in parliament from the Inter-Parliamentary Union, available on IPU Parline (https://data.ipu.org/women-ranking/) (C) IPU; data on electoral systems and democracy from Coppedge et al. (2024), "V-Dem Country–Year Dataset v11.1" Varieties of Democracy (V-Dem) Project. https://doi.org/10.23696/vdemds21*

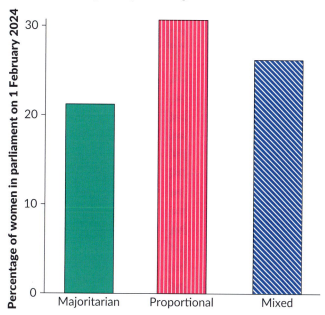

electoral systems, the proportion of women in legislatures is almost 10 percentage points higher than it is in countries with majoritarian electoral systems (with mixed systems falling somewhere in between).

As you know from Chapter 2, just because there is an empirical relationship between two things, we cannot conclude that there's a *causal* relationship—we don't know that one thing caused the other. In this case, however, there is relatively robust evidence in contemporary scholarship on democracies that electoral rules influence the political representation of women, although the effects vary depending on the social and political circumstances (Roberts, Seawright, and Cyr 2013, Salmond 2006, Golder et al. 2017, Skorge 2023).

It is rare for a democratic country to change its electoral system in a big way. Since the people in power have always done fairly well under the existing system—as previously mentioned, that's how they got themselves elected in the first place—they usually don't want to shake things up too much. When countries *do* reform their electoral systems, we should therefore pay close attention. These countries can teach us important things about the causes and consequences of electoral-system reforms.

On 6 November 1993, New Zealand held a referendum in which voters were asked whether they wanted to keep that country's old majoritarian electoral system—a first-past-the-post system with single-member districts—or replace it with a new, mixed system. The proposed new system was a mixed-member proportional system that was similar to Germany's (see Section 7.3). Figure 7.10 is a picture of a ballot paper from New Zealand. Under the new system, each voter would get two

Figure 7.10 This is the sample ballot that was included in the Electoral Act 1993, through which the new electoral system was enacted. *Source: New Zealand Ministry of Justice, Crown Copyright New Zealand*

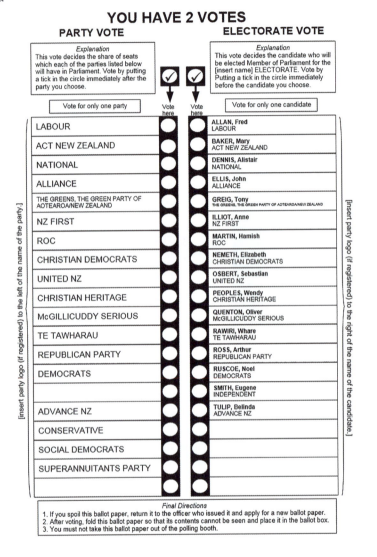

votes, one of which was for an individual candidate (the 'electorate' vote) and one of which was for a party (the 'party' vote). Each party's share of the total number of seats in the parliament in New Zealand's capital, Wellington, would then be decided by the 'party' vote, but which individuals actually got the seats would be decided by the 'electorate' vote. Candidates from the closed party lists filled the remaining seats once the single-member-district seats were filled. In the referendum, a majority supported the new mixed-member proportional system (54 per cent voted in favour). The new system was first used in the general election of 1996. In 2011, there was a new referendum on whether New Zealand should go back to a more majoritarian system, but 58 per cent voted to keep the system that had been introduced in 1993.

There were several reasons for the 1993 referendum, the most important being widespread disaffection with the old electoral system and low confidence in parliament among New Zealand voters. On two occasions in the late 1970s and early 1980s, the centre-left Labour Party had won more votes in the general election than the centre-right National Party, yet the National Party had won more seats due to the electoral system. There was therefore a lot of opposition to the earlier electoral system among more left-wing voters, but also across parties. In 1984, a government commission recommended the introduction of a mixed-member proportional system, and after a few further political twists and turns, the National Party held a referendum in 1992, which was followed by the binding referendum in 1993, in which the political parties promised to adopt the electoral system the voters wanted. The electoral-system reform in New Zealand is described and the referendum is analysed by Aimer and Miller (2002) and Riambau, Stillman, and Boe-Gibson (2021), and Jackson and McRobie (2019) analyse the referendum, the reasons why it happened, and its aftermath.

In Case Study 7.2, you can read more about what consequences the electoral-system reform in New Zealand had for political representation and for other important outcomes.

CASE STUDY 7.2
New Zealand's electoral-system reform

The immediate consequence of the electoral-system reform in New Zealand in the 1990s was that more parties got into the New Zealand parliament, just as political-science theories of electoral systems would have predicted. In the early 1990s, less than 70 per cent of the voters supported one of the two main parties—the Labour Party or the National Party—yet those parties controlled almost all of the seats in parliament. The reform meant that the smaller parties won many more seats in the election of 1996: the populist right-wing party New Zealand First won 17 (out of 120), the left-wing Alliance won 13 seats, and the right-wing liberal party ACT won 8. As a consequence, although the National Party leader Jim Bolger held on to power, his party needed to negotiate with New Zealand First before forming a new government. The elections in 2008 provided another example of the new electoral system's hospitality to smaller parties, as the Green Party won 6.7 per cent of the party vote and therefore got 9 seats in the parliament.

The electoral-system reform in New Zealand also tells us something about the consequences of the electoral system for political representation. Figure 7.11 shows the representation of women in New Zealand's parliament in all elections since 1931, when the first woman member was elected. As the figure shows, the proportion of women began increasing in the 1980s, as demands for electoral-system reform grew stronger, but there was a big jump between the 1993 and 1996 elections (the 1996 election being the first one in which the new electoral system was used).

Górecki and Pierzgalski (2023) have compared election outcomes and economic redistribution in New Zealand with a group of countries that did not change their electoral systems from majoritarian to proportional in the 1990s, as New Zealand did. Their goal was to test an idea proposed by Iversen and Soskice (2006), who argued that proportional electoral systems tend to favour parties on the left and therefore also income redistribution. The case of New Zealand supports Iversen and Soskice's idea: New Zealand has had more left-wing governments and more economic redistribution since the 1990s compared with what one might have expected if it had kept the old majoritarian system.

Figure 7.11 Female representation in New Zealand's parliament has increased greatly since 1931, when the first woman member was elected. *Source: Author's own work based on data from the parliament of New Zealand, Crown Copyright New Zealand*

The electoral system in New Zealand has an additional element that is worth noting. Ever since 1867, New Zealand's indigenous population, the Māori, have voted separately in general elections. Prior to the 1993 reform, there was a fixed number of seats for the Māori. Under the current system, the Māori can choose whether they want to vote in a general electoral district or in a special Māori district. At the time of writing, there are seven Māori parliamentary seats, but if a greater proportion of the Māori citizens—who make up more than 15 per cent of the population in New Zealand—chose to register in Māori-only districts, the number of Māori parliamentary seats would increase (Geddis 2006).

In addition to the representation of women, the electoral system also influences the representation of social classes, ethnic groups, groups with minority religious views, and groups with different political opinions.

The main reason for this is that the electoral system has both direct and indirect effects on the number of political parties that can get into the legislature. The idea that there is a close relationship between the electoral system and the number of viable parties, with more parties being elected where the electoral system is proportional, goes back to the work of the French political scientist Maurice Duverger in the 1940s and 1950s. **Duverger's Law** is the idea that majoritarian electoral rules tend to favour two-party systems, whereas proportional electoral rules typically lead to multi-party systems.

Duverger's Law is far from absolute: as we'll discuss in Chapter 11, there can be many parties in a majoritarian system too, if the smaller parties are concentrated in particular regions, and there can be only a few parties in a proportional system, if two or three parties manage to get the support of the most important groups in society. On average, however, there are fewer significant parties in majoritarian systems than there are in proportional systems.

The fact that there are fewer significant parties in majoritarian systems than there are in proportional systems typically means that in countries with majoritarian systems, a large group of voters doesn't sympathize with any of the main political parties. That is probably the explanation for another pattern that we observe when we compare countries with different electoral systems: electoral participation, or turnout, tends to be higher in countries with proportional elections. In those countries, a larger share of the electorate find a party that they sympathize or even identify with.

Table 7.1 lists the 20 democratic countries in the world that had the highest level of turnout in elections in 2019. As the table shows, most of the countries with very high turnout practise

Table 7.1 The 20 countries with the highest level of turnout in 2019

Country	Turnout (%)	Electoral system	Mandatory
Malta	92	Proportional	
Australia	92	Majoritarian	Yes
Uruguay	90	Proportional	Yes
Luxembourg	90	Proportional	Yes
Bolivia	88	Mixed	Yes
Belgium	88	Proportional	Yes
Seychelles	88	Mixed	
Sweden	87	Proportional	
Guinea-Bissau	85	Proportional	
Denmark	85	Proportional	
Sierra Leone	84	Majoritarian	
Sri Lanka	84	Proportional	
Botswana	83	Majoritarian	
Malaysia	82	Majoritarian	
Netherlands	82	Proportional	
Indonesia	82	Proportional	
Peru	82	Proportional	Yes
Iceland	81	Proportional	
Timor	81	Proportional	
São Tomé and Príncipe	81	Proportional	

Source: Data from Coppedge et al. (2024), "V-Dem Country-Year Dataset v14" Varieties of Democracy (V-Dem) Project. https://doi.org/10.23696/mcwt-fr58

compulsory voting. In other words, voting is mandatory for all or most voters. We also find that most of the countries in the list have proportional elections, suggesting that a proportional electoral system makes citizens more likely to participate in elections.

There are also a few majoritarian countries with high turnout on this list, and, as we discussed in Chapter 2, correlation is not causation: two things can go together without one of them being the cause of the other. However, there are strong reasons to believe that the electoral system does influence turnout. Many studies have sought to estimate the causal effect of electoral-system reforms on turnout by carefully studying countries that have changed their electoral systems. Those studies have typically found that such reforms have a positive effect on the proportion of eligible voters who actually vote (Eggers 2015; Cox, Fiva, and Smith 2016).

On balance, therefore, it seems that proportional representation makes political systems more representative. A wider range of opinions are represented within legislatures and within other elective assemblies, since more parties get in. Electoral turnout is higher because there are more people who feel that they have a reason to vote. Elected assemblies tend to better resemble the wider population because more women and members of other groups who have historically been underrepresented in politics—such as immigrants, members of ethnic and religious minorities, and members of the working class—are able to pursue a political career.

One common argument for electoral systems with single-member districts is that they clarify the connection between the representative and the voters: the voters are able to identify a single individual who represents them. One way to think about this argument, using Pitkin's concepts of different forms of representation, is that majoritarian electoral systems with single-member districts have an easy-to-understand form of symbolic and formalistic representation. Advocates of proportional representation argue, on the other hand, that majoritarian electoral systems with single-member districts are inferior when it comes to descriptive and substantive representation.

The other common argument for majoritarian elections is that they allow for stronger governments. We'll discuss that question in Chapter 15, which deals with political decision making in different political systems.

7.6 CONCLUSION

The electoral system has a profound effect on how the political system channels conflicts among different groups in society. In majoritarian systems, there are typically only a few strong parties (and sometimes only two, as in the United States), so there's a good chance that one party wins an absolute majority. This means that conflicts are resolved, at least temporarily, *on election day*. The voters get to choose between two teams of politicians that offer solutions to the country's problems, and then the party that wins the election gets to carry out its policies. This also clarifies who's responsible for the government's policies: a single, governing party. In proportional systems, conflicts are typically *not* resolved on election day. The voters have the opportunity to choose among many different parties, and then it's up to those parties, once elected, to negotiate with each other about public policies and, in parliamentary systems, about who should form a new government. In other words, elections in proportional systems are not meant to resolve social, economic, and political conflicts, right away—they're about appointing a group of political leaders who then go on to negotiate with each other over the next few years about how the country's problems should be addressed.

The main weaknesses of majoritarian and proportional elections are directly related to this essential difference in how the two systems channel conflicts. The main weakness of majoritarian elections is that they force the voters into a crude choice between two or at most a few alternatives. Many voters in majoritarian systems don't feel that either of the main parties speaks for them. They therefore lose confidence in the political system and may even refrain from voting. It may also take time for new social, economic, and political problems to get the attention they deserve, since it is exceptionally difficult, in majoritarian systems, for new parties to break through. The main weakness of proportional elections, on the other hand, is that the people's elected representatives may fail in their task of negotiating with each other about new policies and about who should form a government, and when they do, there is no mechanism for resolving conflicts in a satisfactory manner. Remaining unaddressed, social, economic, and political conflicts may then lead to what's sometimes called *gridlock* or *democratic paralysis*: a failure to act. We'll come back to these important issues in Chapter 15.

SUMMARY

- There are three main types of electoral system: majoritarian, proportional, and mixed.
- Electoral systems vary with respect to three main characteristics: district magnitude, ballot structure, and the electoral formula.
- Proportional elections are the most common type of electoral system, and mixed elections are the least common, but mixed systems have become more popular since the 1990s.
- In the nineteenth century, all countries had some form of majoritarian system, but in the first half of the twentieth century, proportional rules were adopted in many countries.
- There is a strong and robust relationship between the electoral system and the party system: countries with proportional systems typically have more parties in the legislature.
- Proportional and majoritarian electoral systems enhance different forms of political representation: majoritarian elections make it easier for voters to identify their representative; in proportional systems, a greater range of groups and opinions become represented in elected assemblies.
- Under proportional rules, minority groups are more easily represented; as we will discuss in Chapters 8 and 15, majoritarian rules have other advantages: they make it easier to form governments and hold those governments accountable.

STUDY QUESTIONS

1. Now that you've read the whole chapter, why do you think majoritarian elections have become so rare since the nineteenth century—and why do you think mixed electoral systems, such as that of Germany and that of New Zealand, have become increasingly popular in recent years?
2. Scholars of political behaviour have found that in many countries, large groups of voters vote 'strategically'—that is, they don't vote for the party they like best, but for some other party. What sorts of electoral rules do you think are most likely to encourage voters to vote strategically in this sense?

FURTHER READING

Bingham Powell, *Elections as Instruments of Democracy* **(2000) and Arend Lijphart,** *Patterns of Democracy* **(2012).**
Examine the fundamental role that electoral systems play in shaping modern representative democracies.

Gary Cox, *Making Votes Count* **(1997).**
Tries to find out how, exactly, electoral rules influence political outcomes.

Amel Ahmed, *Democracy and the Politics of Electoral System Choice* **(2012).**
Traces the origins of electoral systems in Belgium, France, the United Kingdom, and the United States.

CHAPTER 8

LEGISLATURES AND EXECUTIVES

CHAPTER GUIDE

8.1 Introduction
8.2 Parliamentarism and Presidentialism
8.3 Legislatures
8.4 Executives
8.5 The Relationship between the Legislature and the Executive

8.6 Conclusion
Summary
Study Questions
Further Reading

8.1 INTRODUCTION

This chapter is concerned with legislatures and executives. Legislatures make laws, take decisions about the national budget, hold the executive to account, and serve as a forum for debates about important political issues. Executives carry out public policies, govern state agencies, and represent the country in relations with other countries. The relationship between the legislature and the executive is called the 'form of government'. In parliamentary systems, the executive (or 'government') is responsible to the legislature (or 'parliament'). In presidential systems, it is not.

As we'll see in Chapter 9, 99 per cent of all written constitutions contain provisions about a legislature and 98 per cent contain provisions about a cabinet (the group of people who make up the executive) (Elkins and Ginsburg 2021, 334). Let's consider an example, to get a feel for how a state might organize these important institutions. In 1988, after almost 25 years of dictatorship, Brazil adopted a new, democratic constitution. Title IV, Chapter I, Section I provides that the legislative power in Brazil is exercised by the National Congress, which consists of two chambers: the Chamber of Deputies and the Federal Senate. Chapter I also outlines how the members of the Chamber of Deputies and the Federal Senate are elected, what powers they have, and what procedures they must follow when they take decisions. Title IV, Chapter II, Section I provides that the executive power in Brazil is vested in the president, who gets to appoint a group of ministers. Chapter II also explains how the president is elected, what powers the president has, and what powers the ministers have.

We could have picked any constitution, really. Almost all constitutions lay out detailed rules about the powers and decision making procedures of legislatures and executives. There's a reason for this: the organization of the legislature and the executive, and the relationship between them, have powerful effects on the distribution of power in a political system.

Section 8.2 analyses parliamentarism and presidentialism, the two main forms of government in the modern world. Section 8.3 explains what legislatures do and how they are organized. Section 8.4 discusses what executives do, how they're organized, and who serves in governments. Section 8.5, finally, discusses the formation and dissolution of governments in parliamentary systems and the relationship between the legislature and the executive in presidential systems.

8.2 PARLIAMENTARISM AND PRESIDENTIALISM

LEARNING OUTCOMES

After reading Section 8.2, you'll be able to:

- Distinguish between parliamentary, presidential, and semi-presidential forms of government
- Describe the forms of government of the largest democracies in the world
- Explain the origins of different forms of government.

Think back to Chapter 7, in which we examined electoral systems around the world. Most of the examples we discussed in that chapter concerned legislative elections. In other words, they involved elections to national legislative assemblies such as parliaments. But a few of the examples concerned presidential elections. In a presidential election, the voters don't elect the members of an assembly. They instead elect a single individual for the jobs of **head of government** and **head of state**. In other words, presidential elections aren't about the **legislature** at all—they're about the **executive**.

Here's the important thing: almost all countries hold legislative elections, but only some countries hold presidential elections. The reason is that in most states, the head of government—the person who leads the government—isn't directly elected. Those countries have **parliamentary** forms of government, which means that the head of government is appointed by, or at least responsible to, the parliament, and the head of government isn't the same person as the head of state (the person who holds the highest political office in a state and acts as its representative in relations with other states). In countries with semi-presidential forms of government, the third main category after parliamentarism and presidentialism, executive power is shared between the president and the head of government.

Like many other concepts in comparative politics, parliamentary, presidential, and semi-presidential systems are best seen as ideal types. There is a lot of variety within each group. However, the three concepts remain useful for understanding different forms of government around the world. In this section, we will focus on democratic regimes. It is also possible to distinguish between these systems in authoritarian regimes. As long as there is a legislature and an executive, we can use these concepts to analyse the relationship between them. However, under authoritarianism, either the legislature or the executive, or both, aren't accountable to the people.

8.2.1 The three main forms of government

More than half of all democracies in the world have parliamentary forms of government. In a parliamentary system, the legislature has the power to remove the head of government, usually through a procedure known as a **vote of no confidence**. We say that the head of government is 'responsible' to the parliament. In a parliamentary system, the head of government is almost never directly elected, and the head of state and the head of government are two different people. The head of government is usually called prime minister. The head of state might be a king or queen—as in Norway, Spain, or the United Kingdom—or, more often, a ceremonial president, as in Germany.

The main alternative to parliamentarism is **presidentialism**. In a presidential system, the legislature doesn't normally have the power to remove the head of government, the head of government is directly elected, and the offices of head of state and head of government are combined in one person. The only circumstance in which the legislature has the power to remove the president from office in a country with a presidential form of government is when the president has broken the law. In the United States, for example, the Congress has the authority to remove the president if the president is convicted in a so-called impeachment trial of having committed 'high crimes and misdemeanors' (see Article Two, Section 4 of the United States constitution).

The key difference between parliamentarism and presidentialism, then, is that in a parliamentary system, the parliament has the power to remove the head of government for purely political reasons—it just needs to declare that the government no longer has the parliament's confidence—but in a presidential system, the legislature can only remove the head of government in special circumstances.

Prime ministers in countries with parliamentary forms of government often step down voluntarily when they realize they no longer have the support of a majority in parliament. One example is the resignation of Mario Draghi as prime minister of Italy in the summer of 2022, after several parties left his government. Realizing that his position had become untenable, Draghi resigned. By contrast, presidents in presidential systems typically resist being removed from office. One example is the impeachment trial of Dilma Rousseff, who was president of Brazil in 2011–2016 (see Figure 8.1). Rousseff argued that the accusations against her were politically motivated and

Figure 8.1 Protesters in the streets of São Paulo called for the impeachment of President Rousseff.
Source: Will Rodrigues / Shutterstock

Figure 8.2 The key differences between parliamentary, presidential, and semi-presidential forms of government lie in the relationship between the legislature and the executive. *Source: Author's own work*

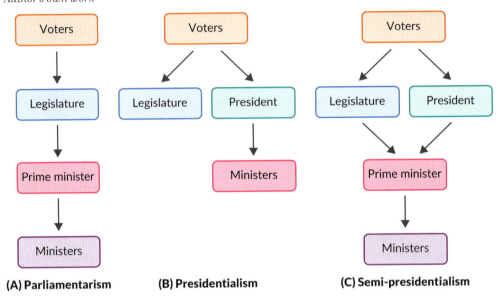

(A) Parliamentarism   (B) Presidentialism   (C) Semi-presidentialism

therefore tried to remain in office until the Senate voted to convict her of breaking Brazil's budget laws and removed her from office in August 2016.

There is also a third, mixed form of government, which is known as **semi-presidentialism**. In semi-presidential systems, such as France and many countries in central and eastern Europe, executive power is shared between the president, who cannot be removed by the parliament, and the prime minister, who can be. The president usually has more influence over foreign policy, and the prime minister usually has more influence over domestic policy.

Figure 8.2 describes schematically the main differences between parliamentary, presidential, and semi-presidential forms of government. Among democratic regimes, the key differences between the three types lie in how the people hand over power to their elected representatives and how those representatives in turn hand over power to other agents within the political system, such as government ministers. Strøm, Müller, and Bergman (2003) refer to this handing over of power as the 'chain of delegation'. In a parliamentary system, there is a unique chain of delegation that starts with the voters, who elect members of parliament, who then appoint a prime minister, who then appoints the other government ministers. In a presidential system, the voters delegate power separately to the legislature and to the executive—the president—which means that there are *two* chains of delegation. In a semi-presidential system, finally, there are initially two separate chains of delegation, as under presidentialism, but then the two chains come together again, for both the president and the legislature are involved in appointing the prime minister.

8.2.2 Forms of government around the world

Now that we've defined parliamentarism, presidentialism, and semi-presidentialism, we're ready to take a tour around the world and describe the forms of government of different countries. Figure 8.3 uses data from Anckar and Fredriksson (2019) to identify parliamentary,

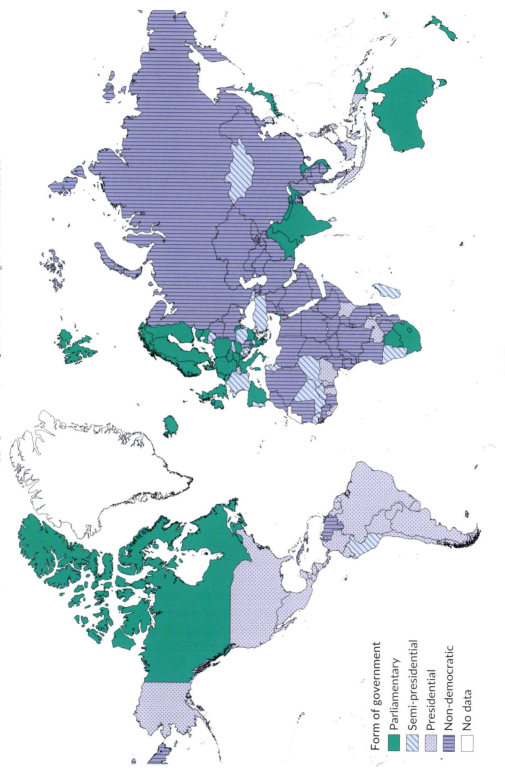

Figure 8.3 Presidentialism is most common in the Americas and parliamentarism is most common in Europe and Oceania; in Africa and Asia, we find a variety of political regimes. Source: Author's own work, based on data from Anckar, Carsten and Cecilia Fredriksson. 2019. 'Classifying Political Regimes 1800–2016'. European Political Science, Copyright © 2018, European Consortium for Political Research

presidential, and semi-presidential democratic regimes around the world in the year 2016 (the most recent year for which these data are available). The forms of government change very rarely, so for most countries, the information on the map is likely to remain up to date for many years or even decades. In a few countries, scholars disagree on how the form of government should be categorized. For example, Poland is sometimes categorized as a semi-presidential regime, since the president has extensive executive and legislative powers, although Anckar and Fredriksson categorize Poland as parliamentary. But most scholars agree on the broad patterns depicted in Figure 8.3.

Starting from the west and heading eastwards, the first thing we learn is that most democratic countries in the Americas have presidential forms of government. The exceptions are Barbados, Canada, Jamaica, and Trinidad and Tobago, which have parliamentary systems carried over from the days when they were British colonies, and Peru, which has a semi-presidential form of government. French Guiana is categorized as presidential since it remains a part of France.

In Europe, most countries have parliamentary systems, but several countries practise semi-presidentialism, including France, Portugal, Türkiye, and central and eastern European states such as Croatia, Romania, and Slovakia, which adopted semi-presidential constitutions after the end of communism in the early 1990s. Switzerland has an unusual collective executive, the Federal Council, in which the main political parties share power, which makes the form of government in Switzerland difficult to compare with any other political system.

Among the democratic states in Africa, we find parliamentary, semi-presidential, and presidential forms of government. Botswana and South Africa—also former British colonies—have parliamentary systems. The head of government and head of state of South Africa has the title of president but is appointed by parliament and isn't directly elected. Several countries in West Africa have semi-presidential forms of government, reflecting their history as former French colonies, whereas Kenya, Nigeria, and Zambia have presidential forms of government.

In Asia, India and Pakistan are both parliamentary, as are Bhutan, Japan, and Nepal, whereas South Korea and Indonesia have presidential forms of government. Finally, both Australia and New Zealand have been parliamentary since their independence from the United Kingdom more than a century ago.

These patterns give us some idea of the main historical explanations for why countries have different forms of government. Parliamentarism originally emerged in Europe in monarchies such as the United Kingdom and Sweden, as parliaments began to challenge the executive authority of kings and queens and insisted that they must have influence over the government. When parliamentarism was established, most of these countries weren't democratic, since the right to vote hadn't yet been extended to the working class or to women. Parliamentarism was therefore the result of power struggles within a more select social, economic, and political elite. Between the late nineteenth century and the middle of the twentieth, however, the idea of parliamentarism became closely intertwined with the idea of democracy across Europe.

In the Americas, presidentialism was usually adopted when the newly independent American states broke with their old colonial powers in the eighteenth and nineteenth centuries. The first president of the United States, George Washington, was elected in 1789, just after the new constitution was adopted, and the United States has remained a presidential republic ever since. In Central and South America, most states adopted presidentialism soon after becoming independent from Spain in the 1820s. Mexico was an empire in 1822–1823 but appointed its first president in 1824. Some Latin American states reverted back to monarchy later in the nineteenth century—as during the Second Mexican Empire in 1864–1867—but many of them have been presidential ever since independence. Brazil, however, was a monarchy for most of the nineteenth century after gaining independence from Portugal. The Brazilian Empire was only overthrown in a *coup d'état* in 1889. Today, as Figure 8.3 shows, almost all American states are presidential republics.

It is rare for countries to change from parliamentarism to presidentialism or from presidentialism to parliamentarism, just as it is rare for countries to change their electoral systems (see Chapter 7). One exception is France, which was effectively parliamentary during the Third Republic (1870–1940) and the Fourth Republic (1946–1958) but has been semi-presidential ever since the adoption of the constitution of the Fifth Republic in 1958.

8.2.3 How the form of government matters

Parliamentarism, presidentialism, and semi-presidentialism are the three main forms of government—or 'executive formats'—in today's world. Since countries adopted these different forms of government for complicated historical reasons, it is difficult to identify precisely what effects parliamentarism, presidentialism, and semi-presidentialism have on how political systems work. To do so, we would have to imagine what, say, Indonesia would be like if it had a parliamentary system instead of a presidential one, and that isn't easy to do. What we have here is yet another example of the basic problem of causality we discussed in Chapter 2.

We can say with confidence, however, that political processes tend to be very different in countries with different forms of government. Under parliamentarism, there is a mechanism for resolving profound conflicts between the parliament and the government, since the parliament can simply replace the head of government. Under presidentialism, there is no such mechanism. Using a term that we introduced in Chapter 2, this also means that presidentialism adds one 'veto player'—a person or institution that can block legislation and political decision making. In semi-presidential forms of government, political conflicts between the parliament and the president usually arise when the president and the prime minister represent different parties—a situation that is sometimes described by the French word *cohabitation*, which means 'living together'.

Because of these fundamental differences between parliamentary, presidential, and semi-presidential forms of government, scholars of comparative politics tend to ask different sorts of questions when they study countries with different executive formats. As we'll discuss in Section 8.5, many comparative studies of parliamentary systems are concerned with how governments are formed, how long governments survive, and why governments eventually fall. Comparative studies of presidential and semi-presidential forms of government are more often concerned with executive–legislative relations, or, in other words, with how presidents and legislators handle latent and manifest conflicts between the executive—the president—and the legislature.

8.3 LEGISLATURES

LEARNING OUTCOMES
After reading Section 8.3, you'll be able to:
- Explain what legislatures are and how they are organized
- Describe some of the main differences between legislatures around the world
- Summarize the activities of legislatures and how scholars of comparative politics study them.

The precursors of modern parliaments emerged in Europe many centuries ago, in the Middle Ages, as counterweights to the monarch. The king or, more rarely, the queen was expected to consult with the people's representatives before introducing new taxes and in some cases also before adopting new laws. In England, the idea that the monarch needed to seek consent before raising taxes has long been associated with the Magna Carta, an agreement in the Middle Ages between King John (1199–1216) and the English aristocracy and clergy about the limits of the king's power.

But the 'people' whom parliaments represented in medieval times, hundreds of years ago, were a select group of aristocrats, landowners, and clergymen. Much later, parliaments became more broadly representative of society, through a long and difficult process that involved civil wars, revolutions, and constitutional reforms. In the nineteenth and twentieth centuries, the suffrage was extended to the whole adult population in many countries, turning legislatures into democratic, representative institutions. That's also a period when many of the world's legislatures became permanent assemblies of professional politicians. In the past, parliaments met intermittently and infrequently; today, most legislatures are almost always in session.

8.3.1 What legislatures do

The first and most important function of **legislatures** is to make laws. That's what the word 'legislature' means: it goes back to the Latin term *legis lator*, 'proposer of laws'. Legislatures sometimes share the power to make laws with other institutions—in presidential systems, the president can usually block, or 'veto', legislation, at least temporarily, and in federal systems (which we learned about in Chapter 6), there are typically several layers of legislation that coexist at different levels of government. But in almost all countries in the world, the national legislature plays a central role in the process of making laws.

Another central function of legislatures is to make decisions about the state's incomes and expenditures: the national **budget**. In most countries, the executive prepares and proposes a budget bill, which the legislature then debates and approves. Legislatures have played this role for hundreds of years (as we just discussed, the first parliaments emerged in the medieval era in part to act as a check on the power of monarchs to raise taxes). Because of the expansion of the public sector and the role of government that we discussed in Chapter 3, many decisions about public spending are in practice made by executives or even by administrative agencies, but the ultimate power usually lies with the legislature.

In democratic systems, legislatures also exercise oversight over the executive. In parliamentary systems, this monitoring role is closely related to the parliament's central role in the government-formation process, and ultimately the parliament's power to dismiss the government (see Section 8.2). But legislatures also exercise oversight over the executive in most presidential systems. In the introduction to this chapter, we considered the example of Brazil. Article 49 of Brazil's constitution provides that the National Congress may 'examine each year the accounts rendered by the President of the Republic', 'consider the reports on the execution of Government plans', and 'supervise and control directly or through either of its Houses, the acts of the Executive Power' (that is, the president). Article 50 goes on to provide that the Chamber of Deputies and the Federal Senate 'may summon a Minister of State . . . to personally render information'.

A fourth, more general function of legislatures is as a forum of debates about important political issues. As you perhaps know, the word 'parliament' goes back to the French verb *parler*, which means 'to speak'. This function is closely related to the idea of the legislature as an elected body that represents the people. In Section 7.5, we discussed Hanna Pitkin's influential idea that the concept of representation has four dimensions: formalistic, symbolic, descriptive, and substantive representation. We can think of legislatures as being more or less representative in all these dimensions.

8.3.2 Where lawmakers meet

Although legislatures around the world perform similar functions—such as making laws, deciding on the state budget, monitoring the government, debating important political issues, and, more generally, representing the people—they're also different from each other in many ways. We can actually learn about a few of those differences by studying the buildings where the lawmakers meet, which are usually imposing structures in the centres of national capitals. Figure 8.4 uses the examples of the United Kingdom, France, Slovenia, and China to describe the four main types of seating arrangement in the principal chambers—or meeting halls—of national legislatures.

Perhaps the most famous parliamentary chamber in the world is the House of Commons in the Palace of Westminster in London. The first panel in Figure 8.4 describes the layout of its main chamber. When seen from the Strangers' Gallery, where visitors to the House of Commons can watch the proceedings, the government benches are on the left and the opposition benches are on the right, so the two sides face each other. This layout reflects the confrontational nature of politics in the United Kingdom, where party politics has long been dominated by two parties (the Conservatives and Labour for the past hundred years, the Conservatives and the Liberals before then).

The political scientist Arend Lijphart (2012)—whose theory of majoritarian and consensual democracies we discussed in Case Study 2.1 in Chapter 2—refers to the majoritarian, two-party form of democracy as the 'Westminster Model'. Several other member states of the Commonwealth have parliamentary chambers with a similar opposing-benches layout, including Botswana in Africa, Canada in North America, and Singapore in Asia (Botswana and Canada are democratic; Singapore is not).

But most parliaments don't look like the House of Commons. Most of them instead have a semicircular floor plan, such as that of Japan's National Diet in Tokyo in the second panel of Figure 8.4. This is a design that goes back to the French Revolution. Instead of facing each other, the members of the legislature face the speaker's rostrum, but the semicircular shape also allows members to address each other across the hall. In semicircular legislative chambers, as in opposing-benches chambers, the members often sit with other members representing the same party. But there are exceptions. For example, the members of the Norwegian and Swedish parliaments sit with members from other parties who represent the same part of the country. The idea behind this

Figure 8.4 'Opposing benches', 'semicircle', 'circle', and 'classroom' are the four main types of seating arrangement in legislative chambers around the world. *Source: https://parliamentbook.com/*

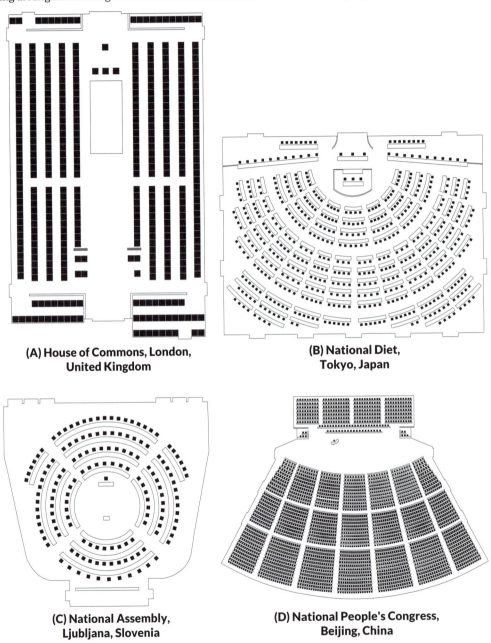

(A) House of Commons, London, United Kingdom

(B) National Diet, Tokyo, Japan

(C) National Assembly, Ljubljana, Slovenia

(D) National People's Congress, Beijing, China

alternative seating arrangement is to reduce partisan strife and emphasize the connections between the members of parliament and the geographical areas they represent.

There is also a mix of the two types of seating plan we've discussed so far: the 'horseshoe' shape (not illustrated in Figure 8.4). It has two opposing benches, like the House of Commons, but the benches are connected at one end. Australia's and South Africa's parliaments are two important examples. A fourth shape that is used in some contemporary parliamentary buildings is the circle. It is the most modern of all the layouts of legislative chambers. One example is the National Assembly in Slovenia (the third panel in Figure 8.4). The layout of Slovenia's parliamentary chamber is reminiscent of a large boardroom or conference room.

Finally, there are some legislatures that have a 'classroom' layout, which is more reminiscent of a theatre or a big auditorium at a university. Interestingly, this layout is uncommon in democracies—it's much more common in authoritarian states, in which communication in legislatures tends to be top-down, not back-and-forth. In authoritarian states, the proceedings of the legislature aren't necessarily meant to facilitate discussions among the members, but to give the country's leaders a chance to tell lawmakers what to do. The Great Hall of the People in Beijing, where China's National People's Congress convenes in March of each year, has classroom seating (see the fourth panel in Figure 8.4; we discussed the role of the National People's Congress in the Chinese political system in Case Study 5.1). So does the Russian parliament, the State Duma.

8.3.3 Unicameralism and bicameralism

Legislatures are old and important institutions, and the study of lawmaking assemblies has a long history in comparative politics. Scholars have asked many sorts of questions about the causes and consequences of differences in the organization of national legislatures. One of the key differences is that some legislatures are unicameral whereas others are bicameral. Just under 60 per cent of all legislatures have one single chamber, but just over 40 per cent are split into two chambers (or, in a few rare cases, more than two). The first group are called unicameral; the second, bicameral.

In a bicameral system, there can be different political majorities in the two chambers, and when that's the case, legislation requires complicated negotiations. Bicameral legislatures therefore often set up temporary or permanent committees that are meant to facilitate such negotiations, and legislation often involves broad compromises between—and within—the main political parties (Tsebelis and Money 1997).

Going back to our earlier discussion of the buildings and rooms where lawmakers convene, bicameral legislatures have separate halls for the two chambers. One example is the architect Oscar Niemeyer's famous building for Brazil's National Congress in Brasilia, with its separate halls for the Chamber of Deputies and the Federal Senate (see Figure 8.5).

Almost all federal states have bicameral legislatures, with one chamber that is directly elected and represents the whole country and one chamber that represents the interests of sub-national governments (which might be called states, provinces, or, in Germany, *Länder*). In many federal countries, including the United States, the two chambers are known as the 'House of Representatives' and the 'Senate'. In Germany, they're known as the *Bundestag* and the *Bundesrat*. Most non-federal, unitary states instead have unicameral legislatures, but a little more than a third of them are bicameral. In some cases—such as the United Kingdom with its House of Lords—the bicameral structure is a residue of old, pre-democratic political arrangements in which one chamber represented the aristocracy or the wealthy.

8.3.4 Committees, rules, parties, and debates

Scholars of politics have also studied many other important differences between legislatures around the world.

Figure 8.5 Bicameral legislatures such as Brazil's National Congress have separate halls for the two chambers—in Brasilia, the Senate meets in the northern part of the building and the larger Chamber of Deputies meets in the southern part. *Source: National Congress, Oscar Niemeyer, Brasilia, Brazil, 1960*

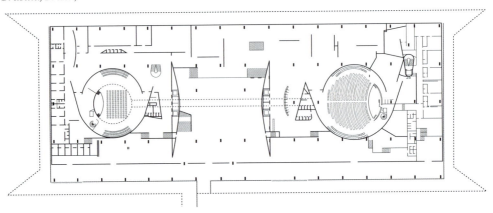

In many legislatures, the most important work is done not in the big meeting halls and parliamentary chambers that we have discussed so far, but in smaller rooms, where the standing **committees** meet. Committees are small groups of legislators that are tasked with reviewing particular types of legislation or performing specific functions such as monitoring and investigating the executive. Legislatures with strong committee systems are generally more powerful than legislatures without effective committees, since committees make the legislature less dependent on the government—through the committees, the parliament has its own organization for investigations and deliberations.

Legislatures have different rules about how the members vote, who is allowed to speak and for how long, in which order matters that come before the lawmakers are considered, and who is allowed to propose new legislation and introduce other proposals for the legislature's consideration. For example, Article 40 of the French constitution provides that private members' bills and amendments introduced by members of parliament are inadmissible 'where their enactment would result in either a diminution of public revenue or the creation or increase of any public expenditure', but the Scandinavian parliaments place no such limits on the right of members of parliament to introduce proposals about taxation and government expenditures. All these rules about voting procedures and the parliamentary agenda are consequential since they shape the political process and determine who has power and influence—and who hasn't.

There is a rich tradition of scholarship on how lawmakers behave when they vote. In some legislatures, such as the United States Congress, individual members have a lot of autonomy and do not necessarily vote with other members of their party. In other legislatures, including most parliaments in contemporary Europe, the political parties are so dominant that members of parliament effectively vote collectively as party groups. This happens when parties have effective methods of **party discipline**, which is a term that refers to the methods parties use to ensure their members vote with the party, maintaining party cohesion (Kam 2009). In some countries, such as the United

Kingdom, a leading politician known as the 'whip' is responsible for keeping each party's parliamentary group in line.

Finally, since the word 'parliament' stems from a verb that means 'to speak', it goes without saying that there's a lot of talk going on in parliaments and other legislatures. We can learn much about politics by studying parliamentary debates—who speaks, what they say, and how political discourse evolves. A lot of exciting work is currently being done in this area of comparative politics with the help of new research methods that allow scholars to analyse the minutes and protocols of legislative debates across decades, even centuries, to learn about things like the level of conflict within parliaments, the role of emotions in politics, and which political issues have been most important in different periods (see, for example, Bäck, Debus, and Fernandes 2021).

In Chapter 1, we discussed how political conflicts can take three different forms—'fights', 'games', and 'debates'—and we noted that political institutions can transform conflicts from fights to games or to debates. This is especially true for legislatures. They're an arena where sophisticated political 'games' are played, in which political leaders try to outmanoeuvre each other in a strategic and tactical contest for power. But they're also sites of 'debates', in which politicians try to put their ideas into words, shape political discourse, and engage with their opponents.

To learn more about the differences between national legislatures around the world, go to Research Prompt 8.1.

RESEARCH PROMPT 8.1
Legislative procedures

In this section, you've learned about some of the main ways in which legislatures differ from each other. We have discussed the differences between unicameralism and bicameralism, the role of committees, the rules and procedures concerning voting and the legislative agenda, party discipline, and political discourse in parliamentary debates. To learn more about these differences between national legislatures, go to the website of the Inter-Parliamentary Union, an international organization for national legislatures (www.ipu.org/national-parliaments), and pick any two legislatures on the interactive map you'll find there. Then consult the websites of the legislatures you've picked and study the differences between them. Here are a few questions you might ask:

1. Is the legislature unicameral or bicameral?
2. Who has the right to propose new legislation?
3. Are there standing committees and how are they organized?
4. How are votes carried out?
5. Are there rules of decorum that ensure members of the legislature are civil to each other?

What do you think explains those differences—and how do you think they might affect political debates and decision making in the two countries?

8.4 EXECUTIVES

LEARNING OUTCOMES

After reading Section 8.4, you'll be able to:
- Describe what executives are and do
- Summarize some of the main differences between governments around the world.

As we discussed in Section 8.3, a legislature is a group of people who make laws, decide on the state budget, monitor the executive, and debate political issues. By contrast, the government (members of the executive) is a group of people who carry out public policies, control government agencies, and represent the country in relations with other states. In most countries, this means that the legislature makes long-term decisions about legislation and economic priorities and public policies, whereas the executive enforces the laws, carries out the policies the legislature has decided, and runs the day-to-day operations of the state. In this section, we will discuss what executives are and learn about some of the main differences between governments around the world.

Executives are led by the head of government. In presidential systems, the head of government is almost always called 'president'. In parliamentary and semi-presidential systems, the head of government is known by many different names, such as *Kanzler* (chancellor) in Austria and Germany, *Taoiseach* (chief) in Ireland, and *Wazīr-ē-Āzam* (grand vizier) in Pakistan. But the English term 'prime minister' can be used generically for the head of government in all parliamentary systems.

In addition to the head of government, governments consist of ministers, who are usually responsible for specific areas of public policy, such as finances and economic affairs (the

Figure 8.6 *The average number of ministers in governments around the world has increased since the 1960s from 15 to just over 21. Source: Author's own work, based on data from Nyrup, Jacob and Stuart Bramwell. 2020. 'Who Governs?'* American Political Science Review

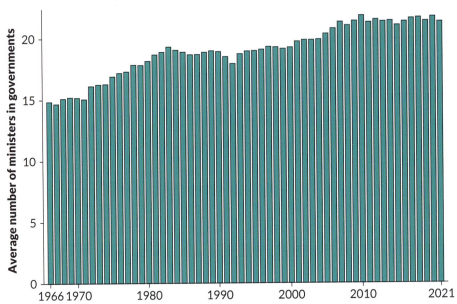

responsibility of the minister of finance or equivalent), foreign policy (the responsibility of the minister of foreign affairs or equivalent), or the environment (the responsibility of the minister of the environment or equivalent). Again, ministers are called different things in different countries, but the word 'minister' can be used as a generic term for a member of a government.

Government offices are usually divided into several executive departments, or ministries, each of which is led by a minister. Appointing the other ministers is one of the most important tasks of the head of government.

As Figure 8.6 shows, the average number of ministers in governments around the world has increased gradually from approximately 15 to over 21 between the middle of the 1960s and today, likely as a consequence of the increasing complexity of public policymaking over this period. But these averages hide a lot of variation between countries—there have been governments with only a handful of ministers and there have been governments with more than 50 ministers.

But those are not the only ways in which governments differ. Among other important differences that scholars of comparative politics have studied, we will concentrate on two: the difference between single-party governments and coalition governments and the differences between majority governments and minority governments.

Let's begin by considering Figure 8.7, which describes the average number of parties in governments in democracies between the middle of the 1960s and the early 2020s. As the graph shows, single-party governments and coalition governments were pretty evenly balanced until the late

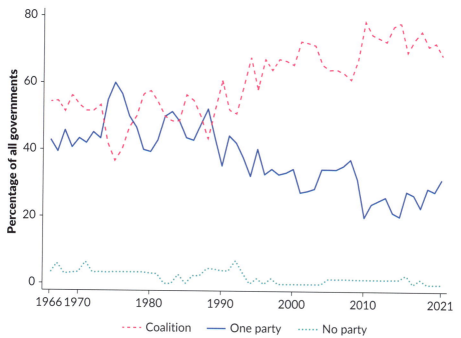

Figure 8.7 *The proportion of coalition governments among democracies has increased a lot since the 1980s. Source: Author's own work, based on data from Nyrup, Jacob and Stuart Bramwell. 2020. 'Who Governs?'* American Political Science Review

1980s, but since then the proportion of coalition governments has increased a lot—between 2010 and 2020, 70–80 per cent of all governments were coalitions, and only 20–30 per cent were single-party governments. There are many explanations for this pattern. One is that a larger share of democracies around the world have proportional or mixed electoral systems, not majoritarian electoral systems. As we saw in Chapter 7, proportional elections tend to increase the number of parties in the legislature, which in turn leads to more coalition governments since no party controls a sufficiently large share of the seats in parliament to form a government on its own. A second explanation is that party-system fragmentation—that is, the number of parties—has tended to increase in most democracies over recent decades, including in countries that have not changed their electoral system (see Chapter 11).

One might think that coalition governments would be rare in presidential systems, since the executive is more independent of the legislature when the head of government—the president—is elected separately. But coalition governments are actually quite common in presidential systems as well, particularly in Latin America. As we'll discuss more in Section 8.5, presidents often offer seats in government to other parties to increase the likelihood of getting legislation through the legislature, or, using a more technical term we'll say more about later, to improve executive–legislative relations.

Figure 8.7 also shows that a small share of governments in democracies have no parties in them. The reason is that parliaments and presidents sometimes appoint **technocratic** governments, which aren't made up of politicians but of civil servants and other experts without party affiliations. Such governments are especially common during economic crises.

Turning from governments in democracies to governments in authoritarian states, Figure 8.8 shows that no-party governments are much more common among authoritarian states than they are among democracies—approximately 20 per cent of all governments in authoritarian states aren't made up of political parties. But they're not predominant: in authoritarian states, too, governments are typically made up of one or more parties. When it comes to the mix of single-party and coalition governments, we see that coalition governments have long been less common among authoritarian states than among democracies, but over time, the share of coalition governments has grown from around 10 per cent in the 1960s, 1970s, and 1980s to over 40 per cent in the 2010s and early 2020s. This trend tracks the rise of hybrid regimes since the end of the Cold War. As we discussed in Chapter 5, hybrid regimes are non-democratic but tolerate some political competition, and Figure 8.8 demonstrates that this applies to the composition of governments too, not just elections and legislatures.

The distinction between single-party governments and coalition governments, or 'multi-party governments', isn't just of academic interest. Different sorts of governments also tend to pursue different policies. For example, there is a lot of research suggesting that coalition governments are associated with higher levels of public spending than single-party governments (Bawn and Rosenbluth 2006). Other differences between single-party governments and coalition governments are more debated among scholars. For example, as we'll discuss in Chapter 15, many scholars believe that coalition governments are more likely to end up in political 'deadlocks' or 'stalemates' since the parties tend to block each other, but other studies suggest that there are circumstances in which coalition governments are better able to take decisive action than single-party governments.

Figure 8.8 In authoritarian states, as in democracies, coalition governments have become much more common since the 1980s. *Source: Nyrup, Jacob and Stuart Bramwell. 2020. 'Who Governs?' American Political Science Review*

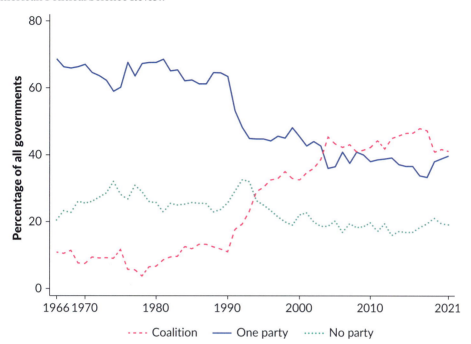

It is also important to understand the distinction between majority governments and minority governments. A majority government is made up of a party or a group of parties that together represent a majority in the legislature. A minority government is made up of a party or a group of parties that don't. Both single-party governments and coalition governments can be either majority or minority governments, so there are four possible combinations: single-party majority governments, single-party minority governments, coalition majority governments and coalition minority governments.

In parliamentary systems, governments have difficulty remaining in power if they are opposed by a majority in the parliament, so it's a little surprising that minority governments exist at all, but they're in fact quite common. One of the explanations that scholars have offered is that in some political systems, large parties close to the ideological centre of the party system have a strong bargaining position, since either the parties to their left or the parties to their right, or both, prefer them to alternative governments (assuming that the left–right dimension is the main ideological dimension). In these circumstances, centrist parties can have the opportunity to govern alone even if they don't control a majority of the seats in parliament. Another explanation is that countries are more likely to have minority governments if they have strong legislative institutions which allow parties that are not in government to influence policy from their position in the legislature (see especially Strøm 1990).

8.5 THE RELATIONSHIP BETWEEN THE LEGISLATURE AND THE EXECUTIVE

LEARNING OUTCOMES

After reading Section 8.5, you'll be able to:
- Describe how governments are formed in parliamentary systems
- Explain which factors affect how long a government lasts
- Analyse executive–legislative relations in presidential systems.

So far in this chapter, we've discussed the main forms of government around the world (Section 8.2), what legislatures are and do (Section 8.3), and what executives are and how they are organized (Section 8.4). In this section, we'll discuss the relationship *between* legislatures and executives in parliamentary and presidential regimes. As we noted at the beginning of the chapter, this relationship matters greatly for how political conflicts are resolved in modern political systems.

8.5.1 Parliamentary systems: how governments are born and die

The defining characteristic of a parliamentary democracy is that the parliament can force the government to resign. The prime minister and the government don't have a direct mandate from the people, which means that they depend on the support of parliament to form the government, to hold on to power, and to govern effectively. Because this confidence relationship between the parliament and the government is so central to how parliamentary systems work, the political history of countries with parliamentary forms of government is often told in terms of the 'birth', 'life', and 'death' of successive governments. Scholars of comparative politics have therefore taken a great interest in how new governments form—and how long they manage to stay in power.

As we discussed in Section 8.2, there are many types of government: some have a majority in parliament, some don't, and some are made up of a single party whereas others are made up of a coalition of parties. In Europe, which is the continent on which parliamentary systems are most common, the United Kingdom is an example of a country in which most governments tend to be single-party majority cabinets, due to that country's electoral system, which means that party politics revolves around the competition between two large parties, the Conservatives and Labour. But this is in fact a rare outcome in Europe. In most European countries, there are more than two parties that are large enough to influence government formation, so most governments are either coalitions between ideologically dissimilar parties (which is common in continental European countries such as Germany) or minority governments (which are especially common in Scandinavia), or both.

Beyond the electoral system and the party system, several factors have been found to influence the composition of governments in parliamentary and semi-presidential systems (see Schleiter 2020).

- The sizes of the parties matter. Larger parties are more likely to form governments.
- Ideological similarities also matter. Parties are more likely to form governments with other parties that are close to them ideologically.

- Political institutions play an important role. For example, minority governments are more likely to form if the parties in the parliament don't have to declare their active support for a new government in a so-called investiture vote.
- History also matters. Parties are more likely to form governments with other parties that they have a history of working with in the past.

Another important question is *how long it takes* to form a government. When a single party wins a majority of the seats in parliament, that party can typically form a single-party government very quickly, but when several parties need to find an agreement on whether they're going to govern together, it usually takes longer. Exactly how long it takes depends on how complex the situation is—how many parties are involved, for instance—and how compatible the parties are. In some cases, it can take a very long time to form a government in a parliamentary system. You can read about an important example of a drawn-out government-formation process in Case Study 8.1. This is a central problem in contemporary European politics, for it's taking longer and longer to form governments in parliamentary democracies with many parties. Between the 1970s and the 1990s, government formation in western European democracies took about a month on average. Between the late 1990s and the late 2010s, it took two months (Bergman, Bäck, and Hellström 2021, 691–692).

CASE STUDY 8.1
When it takes a long time to form a government

The longest government-formation process ever at the national level in a democratic system occurred in Belgium in 2010–2011. It took 541 days—almost a year and a half—to form a government after the Belgian parliamentary election of 2010. Drawn-out government-formation processes are common in Belgium (Van Aelst and Louwerse 2014, 480), but a year and a half is a very long time even by Belgian standards. (The formation of an executive in Northern Ireland in 2022–2024 took even longer, but it involved a sub-national government, not a national one.)

The underlying explanation for the difficulty of forming governments in Belgium is that the Belgian party system is unusually fragmented and diverse, since there are parallel party systems in Belgium's two main regions, the Dutch-speaking Flanders and the French-speaking Wallonia. The political parties aren't just divided by ideology but also by language—there are two Christian democratic parties, two social democratic parties, and so on—and voters in Flanders and voters in Wallonia have very different views on Belgium's federal structure, with the Dutch-speaking voters in Flanders seeking more autonomy, or even full independence, whereas the French-speaking voters in Wallonia favour a stronger central government.

After the parliamentary election in 2007, it took 196 days to form a government, which was already a lot, and in the years that followed, there were recurring conflicts within the governing coalition, leading to an early election in 2010. But the election didn't resolve the situation, since it resulted in an even more fragmented parliament and made the separatist Nieuw-Vlaamse Alliantie the largest party in the Flemish region. The negotiations about forming a new government therefore soon resulted in a stalemate and in a crisis of trust among Belgium's major parties (Abts, Dmitriy, and Marc 2012, 452).

> Almost one year after the election, Nieuw-Vlaamse Alliantie left the negotiations. The remaining parties soon agreed on the issue of federalism, but the negotiations were further delayed by remaining disagreements among the parties about economic and social policy, since the new government would include socialist, liberal, and conservative parties. In the end, a new government was formed on 6 December 2011, but this only happened once international investors began to lose trust in the strength of the Belgian economy and the European Commission threatened sanctions against Belgium (Hooghe 2012, 136).
>
> What happened in Belgium in 2010, then, was that many of the factors that cause drawn-out government-formation processes coincided. The party system was highly fragmented, so a large number of parties had to come to an agreement before a government could be formed. Those parties disagreed strongly with each other on many issues. And the conflicts between the parties were multi-dimensional—they didn't just involve left-right issues such as economic and social policy but also the structure of the Belgian federal state itself.

Many governments survive until the next scheduled election, but there are many ways for governments to end prematurely. They may lose a vote of no confidence, which is when the opposition parties call for the government to resign, or a **confidence vote**, which is when the government declares it will resign if it fails to win the legislature's support for its policies. They may also call early elections. Finally, they may be forced to resign because one or more governing parties leave the government or because of irreconcilable differences among or within the governing parties.

There are numerous factors that help to explain why some governments are less likely to survive than others. Some of those factors have to do with the nature of the government itself. For example, majority governments tend to survive longer, on average, than minority governments, and single-party governments last longer than coalitions. Other important factors have to do with the political and economic environment. For example, governments are more vulnerable if there are big changes in public opinion, if they're embroiled in political scandals, or if there is an economic crisis or foreign-policy crisis.

8.5.2 Presidential systems: executive–legislative relations

In both parliamentary and presidential systems, legislative and executive power reside in different institutions, but to get things done, the legislature and the government must cooperate. Although the legislature usually has the power to make laws, new legislation is typically prepared in the government ministries, and the executive normally has a legislative agenda it would like the legislature to pass. Meanwhile, although the legislature usually has the power to decide about the state's incomes and expenditures, it's normally the executive that controls the government agencies and that prepares an annual budget bill that's sent to the legislature for approval.

In other words, in most states, both the legislature and the executive are involved when important political decisions are to be made. This complex process, which is known as **executive–legislative relations**, is an important factor in modern politics.

Since the government's survival in a parliamentary system ultimately depends on the parliament, conflicts between the executive and the legislature can only go so far in parliamentary systems. If the conflicts become deep enough, the government will simply have to resign and be replaced by a new government, since the parliament always has the power to remove the government if it so desires. Somewhat paradoxically, however, once a government has been formed in a parliamentary system, the government is often able to control the legislative agenda—either because it controls a majority of the seats in the parliament or because it's able to engineer political deals that ensure its policies are adopted by the parliament.

In presidential systems, the legislature usually plays a more independent role in the political decision making process, since the legislature and the executive are more independent of each other. But the president nevertheless depends on the legislature to pass new legislation and approve the president's appointments to important public offices. Executive–legislative relations are therefore an acute problem in presidential systems—especially since it is entirely possible for the president to represent one party and the majority in the legislature to represent other parties, which means that there is a greater potential for conflict between the legislature and the executive than in a parliamentary system.

How executive–legislative relations play out in practice in presidential systems depends on the structure of the party system and on the proportion of the seats in the legislature that are held by the president's own party. It also depends on the powers of the president under the constitution. For instance, in some presidential systems, presidents have the authority to rule by decree or to issue executive orders that let them pass some of their policies without consulting the legislature. Moreover, there are numerous techniques that presidents can use to manage their relationships with the legislature, such as appointing leading politicians from other parties to posts within the government to signal the president's willingness to compromise with political opponents. To read about executive–legislative relations in Brazil in the 2010s, see Case Study 8.2.

CASE STUDY 8.2
Executive–legislative relations in Brazil

In Section 8.2, we discussed the impeachment of the socialist president of Brazil, Dilma Rousseff, in 2016. In this case study, we'll discuss the relationship between the president and the legislature in Brazil in the years leading up to the 2016 impeachment trial.

To get their bills passed, presidents in Brazil typically build broad coalition governments to improve cooperation between the president's party and the other parties in the legislature the National Congress (Darrieux 2019). This strategy had worked relatively smoothly under Dilma Rousseff's predecessor, Lula da Silva, whose two terms in office were characterized by broad legislative and electoral support for the president's policies (Nunes 2021, 227) (Lula returned to power in Brazil in 2023 after winning the 2022 presidential election). This was also a period of high economic growth, which made it easier for the president to reach compromises with the National Congress. The political capital built up during the prosperous Lula period paved the way for Lula's chief of staff, Rousseff, to become the next president, but Rousseff's time in office turned out to be less successful than Lula's.

One reason was the increasingly fragmented party system. By 2015, Brazil's legislature had 28 parties (Macaulay 2017, 135), and Rousseff found herself with a governing coalition of 10 different parties with varying ideological positions along the left–right scale (Darrieux 2019, 11). But Rousseff also governed differently. According to Nunes (2021, 230), 'The [Rousseff] government's view that the executive branch was above the legislative branch, together with the lack of a seasoned political negotiator, contributed to deteriorating relations with Congress and created a power vacuum within the legislative branch'. Rousseff also departed from the norm of nominating representatives from allied parties to ministerial positions, leading to discontent and dissatisfaction in the Congress.

After narrowly winning the election in 2015, Rousseff and her party opted for an all-or-nothing political strategy, trying to take control of key positions within the Chamber of Deputies, but they failed (Nunes 2021, 232). Having made many enemies in the legislature, Rousseff's government was obstructed by the Congress, which blocked many of the president's bills, aggravating Brazil's growing economic problems. The tension between Rousseff and her antagonists in the Congress finally culminated in the impeachment trial in 2016.

8.6 CONCLUSION

In this chapter, we have examined two of the most important political institutions in modern states: legislatures and executives. In most countries, whether they're democratic or not, the legislature plays a central role in political decision making by adopting laws and approving the state budget, whereas the executive supervises and controls the government agencies that conduct the day-to-day operations of the state. It is essential for scholars of comparative politics to understand how legislatures and executives are organized. It is also essential to understand the interaction between them: the parliament's power to make and break governments in parliamentary systems and the complex bargaining between the president and the legislature in presidential systems. In the previous chapter, we learned about how elections are conducted. In this chapter, we have concentrated on what members of the legislature and members of the government do with their power once they are elected or appointed.

In Section 8.4, we learned that executives are responsible for proposing new policies to the legislature and for carrying out those policies once the lawmakers have given their approval. But most of the practical work involved in implementing the executive's policies isn't actually done by the government ministers, who are, after all, only a small group of some 15–20 individuals. The practical work is instead done by government agencies that are staffed by unelected public officials who work in public administration. We are going to learn more about government agencies and public administration in Chapter 10, but first we're going to learn about the importance of constitutional rules and the role of courts of law in different political systems.

SUMMARY

- In parliamentary systems, the government depends on the parliament for its survival; in presidential systems, the head of government—the president—is elected separately and doesn't depend on the legislature.
- Most countries adopted either parliamentarism or presidentialism or the mixed form of semi-presidentialism when they democratized, or earlier, though some have changed their forms of government numerous times.
- The relationship between the legislature and the executive shapes political conflicts in modern states.
- Legislatures adopt laws, decide on the state budget, exercise oversight over the executive, and debate important political issues.
- There are numerous important differences between national legislatures, such as the number of chambers (some have two, most have only one), the strength of the legislative committees, and the level of party discipline and cohesion.
- Governments are groups of ministers that supervise and control government agencies and prepare legislation and budget proposals for the legislature's consideration.
- More and more governments are coalitions of several parties, and more and more ministers are women, though men are still in the majority.
- In parliamentary systems, a key political issue is which government can be formed and its chances of survival.
- In presidential systems, where the legislature typically cannot force the executive to resign, a key political issue is whether the president and the legislature can work together to adopt new policies—a process known as 'executive–legislative relations'.

STUDY QUESTIONS

1. In this chapter, you've learned about the three main forms of government in the world—parliamentarism, presidentialism, and semi-presidentialism. In Chapter 7, you learned about different types of electoral system—proportional, majoritarian, and mixed. Different forms of government can coexist with different types of electoral system. For example, in Latin America, presidentialism coexists with proportional electoral systems, whereas the United States combines a presidential system with majoritarian elections, and within Europe, parliamentarism and semi-presidentialism combine with different types of electoral system in different countries—for example, the United Kingdom, Germany, and the Scandinavian countries are all parliamentary, but the United Kingdom has a majoritarian electoral system, Germany has a mixed system, and the Scandinavian states have proportional systems. Now that you've learned both about electoral systems and about legislatures and executives what consequences do you think these different combinations have?

2. In both presidential and parliamentary systems, the executive depends on the legislative assembly to implement its policies. However, while executive–legislative conflicts can only go so far in parliamentary systems before the government is replaced, executive–legislative conflicts in presidential systems cannot always be resolved in this way—the president is elected by and responsible to the people and may also have some room to rule by decree without

even consulting the legislature. Against this background, what do you think are the main advantages and disadvantages of parliamentary and presidential systems? In their article 'Are Parliamentary Systems Better?' Gerring, Thacker, and Moreno (2009) argue that parliamentarism is simply . . . better. Do you agree?

FURTHER READING

Kaare Strøm, Wolfgang C. Müller, and Torbjörn Bergman, *Delegation and Accountability in Parliamentary Democracies* (2003).
Develops the idea of the 'chain of delegation' in parliamentary and presidential democracies.

Shane Martin, Thomas Saalfeld, and Kaare W. Strøm, *The Oxford Handbook of Legislative Studies* (2014).
Provides an overview of comparative-politics research on how legislatures work.

Rudy B. Andeweg et al., *The Oxford Handbook of Political Executives* (2020).
Does the same for executives.

CHAPTER 9

CONSTITUTIONS AND COURTS

CHAPTER GUIDE

9.1 Introduction
9.2 Constitutions
9.3 High Courts
9.4 Judicial Independence
9.5 Judicial Review

9.6 Conclusion
Summary
Study Questions
Further Reading

9.1 INTRODUCTION

There is a close relationship between politics and the law. As we just learned in Chapter 8, legislatures make law, as is evident from the literal meaning of the name we have for them, 'proposers of laws'. But at least in democracies, legislatures and executives are also *bound* by the law. Their place in the political system is defined by the constitution, which sets out the basic rules of politics, and independent courts uphold, interpret, and apply the constitution and the laws.

Section 9.2 is concerned with constitutions. We have already mentioned constitutions several times in this book. For example, in Chapter 6, we discussed the provisions on federalism in India's and Nigeria's constitutions, and in Chapter 8, we noted that almost all constitutions provide for a legislature and an executive. In this chapter, we'll learn more about the history of written constitutions and discuss what they tell us about the nature of modern politics.

In Section 9.3, we'll study constitutional courts and supreme courts, which are high courts at the apex of national legal systems. We'll also become familiar with an important debate in democratic theory about the role of constitutions and high courts as safeguards of democratic institutions and civic and human rights.

Section 9.4 examines the relationship between political leaders and the courts across democratic and authoritarian political regimes. We'll study the extent of judicial independence—the right of the courts to interpret and apply the laws without political interference—in different countries. Judicial independence is widely regarded as a prerequisite of democratic government.

Section 9.5, finally, studies the practice of judicial review, which is the power of the courts to declare laws or policies unconstitutional or illegal. Because of the system of judicial review, some of

9.2 CONSTITUTIONS

LEARNING OUTCOMES

After reading Section 2.2, you'll be able to:
- Summarize the history of constitutions
- Describe the contents of a typical constitution
- Assess the effects of written constitutions on political outcomes.

A constitution is a set of rules by which a state is governed. Most states in the world have a codified, written constitution that has a special legal and political status and is superior to ordinary laws. A few states, such as the United Kingdom, do not have a codified constitution. There is a constitution in the United Kingdom, but it's made up of numerous laws, traditions, treaties, and judicial opinions that together represent the constitutional order of the state; it's not set out in a single document.

One of the most striking differences between national constitutions concerns their age. Table 9.1, which relies on data from the Comparative Constitutions Project (Elkins and Ginsburg 2022), lists the year in which the current 'constitutional order' was established in almost all states in the world. The only states not listed in the table are countries without codified constitutions, such as the United Kingdom and San Marino (a small country on the outskirts of Rimini in eastern Italy, San Marino is sometimes cited as having the world's oldest written constitution, since some of the laws that make up its constitution were adopted at the beginning of the seventeenth century, but the bulk of its constitution is unwritten). For the purposes of these data, constitutional amendments don't count as the establishment of a new constitutional order; only major constitutional reforms do. For example, the United States has amended its constitution 27 times since 1789, but according to the criteria set by the Comparative Constitutions Project, the current constitutional order in the United States dates back to 1789, when the original constitution went into effect.

As Table 9.1 shows, some countries have very old constitutions, dating back to when the countries were founded. For example, the Netherlands became independent from France in 1813 and Belgium became independent from the Netherlands in 1830. But most countries adopted their current constitutions fairly recently. The adoption of new constitutions is often associated with major international or domestic events, such as the recreation of the Austrian and German states after Germany's defeat in the Second World War and the collapse of the French Fourth Republic in 1958, during the war in Algeria. However, constitutions can also be replaced peacefully and gradually, as Denmark and Sweden did when they adopted their current constitutions in 1953 and 1974.

Figure 9.1 makes it easier to see the age distribution of the world's constitutions. As the figure reveals, more than 40 per cent of all constitutions are between 20 and 40 years old. This is largely a consequence of the third wave of democratization, which picked up pace in the 1990s (see Chapter 4). After the fall of the Berlin Wall and the dissolution of the Soviet Union, many new countries were created, and many older countries adopted new, democratic constitutions.

The age of a country's constitution isn't merely of interest to historians and legal scholars. There is an important trade-off here: keeping an old constitution in place can make a country's politics

Table 9.1 The age of the constitution varies among countries

Country	Year	Country	Year	Country	Year	Country	Year
United States	1789	Botswana	1966	El Salvador	1983	Ghana	1992
Netherlands	1814	Mauritius	1968	Argentina	1983	Estonia	1992
Norway	1814	Nauru	1968	St. K. & Nevis	1983	Paraguay	1992
Belgium	1831	UAE	1971	Guin. Bissau	1984	Djibouti	1992
New Zealand	1852	Cameroon	1972	Guatemala	1985	Lithuania	1992
Canada	1867	North Korea	1972	Uruguay	1985	Kuwait	1992
Luxembourg	1868	Panama	1972	Liberia	1986	Vietnam	1992
Tonga	1875	Bahamas	1973	Tuvalu	1986	Slovakia	1992
Australia	1901	Sweden	1974	Bangladesh	1986	Cambodia	1993
Mexico	1917	São Tomé & P.	1975	Nicaragua	1987	Andorra	1993
Liechtenstein	1921	P. New Guinea	1975	Philippines	1987	Seychelles	1993
Lebanon	1926	Greece	1975	Haiti	1987	Peru	1993
Ireland	1937	T. and Tobago	1976	Suriname	1987	Czechia	1993
Iceland	1944	Portugal	1976	Brazil	1988	Lesotho	1993
Austria	1945	Tanzania	1977	Benin	1990	Russia	1993
Japan	1946	Dominica	1978	Namibia	1990	Malawi	1994
Taiwan	1947	Micronesia	1978	Burkina Faso	1991	Tajikistan	1994
Italy	1947	Saint Lucia	1978	Bulgaria	1991	Abkhazia	1994
South Korea	1948	Sri Lanka	1978	Slovenia	1991	Moldova	1994
India	1949	Spain	1978	Colombia	1991	Ethiopia	1994
Germany	1949	Solomon Isl.	1978	Zambia	1991	Belarus	1994
Costa Rica	1949	St. V. & Gren.	1979	Croatia	1991	Georgia	1995
Jordan	1952	Marshall Isl.	1979	Gabon	1991	Kazakhstan	1995
Denmark	1953	Iran	1979	Romania	1991	Uganda	1995
Malaysia	1957	Kiribati	1979	Yemen	1991	Armenia	1995
France	1958	Chile	1980	Latvia	1991	Bosnia and H.	1995
Israel	1958	Guyana	1980	Laos	1991	Azerbaijan	1995
Brunei	1959	Vanuatu	1980	Mauritania	1991	South Africa	1996
Indonesia	1959	Cape Verde	1980	N. Macedonia	1991	Sierra Leone	1996
Cyprus	1960	Ant. and Barb.	1981	Eq. Guinea	1991	Ukraine	1996
Monaco	1962	Palau	1981	Grenada	1991	Gambia	1996
Jamaica	1962	Belize	1981	Mongolia	1992	Oman	1996
Samoa	1962	Honduras	1982	Uzbekistan	1992	Poland	1997
Singapore	1963	China	1982	Saudi Arabia	1992	Eritrea	1997
Barbados	1966	Türkiye	1982	Togo	1992	Albania	1998

(Continued)

Table 9.1 (Continued)

Country	Year	Country	Year	Country	Year	Country	Year
Nigeria	1999	Iraq	2005	Madagascar	2010	C. African Rep.	2016
Finland	1999	DR Congo	2005	Hungary	2011	Côte d'Ivoire	2016
Venezuela	1999	Serbia	2006	Morocco	2011	Thailand	2017
Switzerland	1999	Montenegro	2007	South Sudan	2011	Burundi	2018
Senegal	2001	Kosovo	2008	Libya	2011	Chad	2018
South Ossetia	2001	Ecuador	2008	Somalia	2012	Comoros	2018
Pakistan	2002	Myanmar	2008	Syria	2012	Sudan	2019
Timor	2002	Maldives	2008	Fiji	2013	Cuba	2019
Bahrain	2002	Bhutan	2008	Zimbabwe	2013	Algeria	2020
Qatar	2003	Turkmenistan	2008	Egypt	2014	Guinea	2020
Rwanda	2003	Bolivia	2009	Tunisia	2014	Mali	2020
Afghanistan	2004	Kenya	2010	Dom. Rep.	2015	Kyrgyz Rep.	2021
Mozambique	2004	Niger	2010	Congo	2015	Malta	2021
Eswatini	2005	Angola	2010	Nepal	2015		

Source: Elkins, Zachary and Tom Ginsburg, 2022. 'Characteristics of National Constitutions, Version 4.0'. Comparative Constitutions Project. Last modified: 24 October 2022. Available at comparativeconstitutionsproject.org. CC BY 4.0.

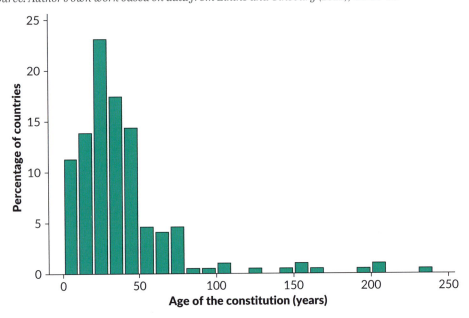

Figure 9.1 Most constitutions are only a few decades old, but some are much older.

Source: Author's own work based on data from Elkins and Ginsburg (2022), CC BY 4.0

more stable, predictable, and ordered, but it can also keep legislatures and executives from adapting the political system to changing circumstances. Consider the United States, which has an old constitution that is difficult to amend. The United States Supreme Court, which interprets and applies the constitution, must often answer difficult questions about how centuries-old constitutional provisions apply to contemporary problems. In recent years, the US Supreme Court has had to decide whether the Fourth Amendment's prohibition against 'unreasonable searches and seizures', adopted more than 230 years ago, makes it unconstitutional for the police to access a suspect's mobile phone when they make an arrest (*Riley* v. *California*, 573 US 373 (2014)) or ask phone companies for location data without a warrant (*Carpenter* v. *United States*, 585 US 138 (2018)).

Table 9.2 lists a few things that almost all constitutions have mentioned during the past two centuries. The list tells us a lot about what modern states have paid attention to when they've set up their political institutions. Throughout the modern period, states have existed in an international system in which they trade and make treaties with other states. They also exist in a world that draws boundaries between states, so rules of citizenship are important. As we learned in Chapter 8, legislatures and executives are key political institutions in nearly all states, and so is the office of head of state (who is typically either a president or a monarch). The governance of the armed forces is an important concern since the military epitomizes the state's monopoly on violence, which we discussed in Chapter 3. As we discussed in Chapter 6, most states have a territorial organization that distinguishes between the national government and sub-national governments. Finally, most constitutions contain provisions on the procedures to be followed if future generations wish to change or amend them.

But constitutions have also changed a lot over this long period. Many things that are mentioned in almost all constitutions today were almost never mentioned in eighteenth- and nineteenth-century constitutions. Figure 9.2 describes the percentage of all constitutions that (a) declare that

Table 9.2 Things almost all constitutions have mentioned since 1789

Topic	Percentage of constitutions	
	Before 1900	2000–2020
International trade	100	100
The legislature	98	99
Citizenship	97	98
The cabinet (executive)	93	98
Selection of head of state	93	98
The military	98	92
International treaties	95	90
Constitutional amendments	89	98
Sub-national governments	92	86

Source: Elkins, Zachary and Tom Ginsburg, 2022. 'Characteristics of National Constitutions, Version 4.0'. Comparative Constitutions Project. Last modified: 24 October 2022. Available at comparativeconstitutionsproject.org.

Figure 9.2 Constitutions increasingly declare that states are democratic, protect and regulate political parties, and prohibit various forms of discrimination. *Source: Based on data from Elkins, Zachary and Tom Ginsburg. 'What Can We Learn from Written Constitutions?' © 2021 Annual Review of Political Science*

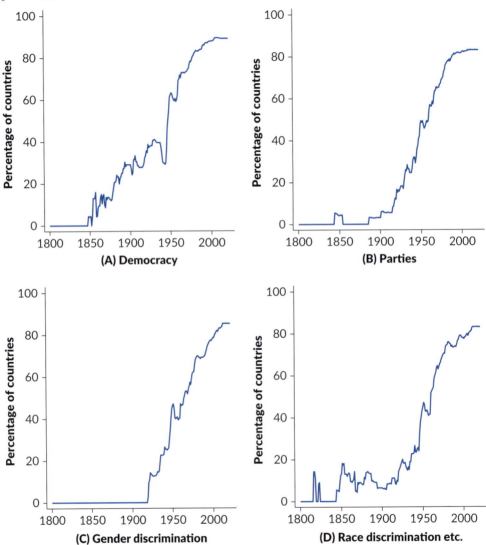

a state is democratic, (b) mention political parties (by protecting them, regulating their activities, or both), (c) prohibit gender discrimination, or (d) prohibit discrimination on the basis of nationality, country of origin, race, membership of a tribe or clan, or other demographic characteristics. As the figure shows, older constitutions had almost nothing to say about any of these things. Today, 80 to 90 per cent of all constitutions do.

Like Table 9.2, Figure 9.2 tells an important story about how countries have organized their political systems. The top-left panel demonstrates that the idea of democracy has spread across the world. Today, almost all countries say they're democratic (although we know from Chapter 4 that only about half of them are, according to the measures commonly used by scholars of comparative politics). The top-right panel demonstrates that whereas political parties were hardly mentioned in nineteenth-century constitutions, they're now seen as essential political organizations in most states (we'll say more about constitutional provisions on parties in Chapter 11). The two bottom panels show that the protection of specific groups in society against discrimination is included in most modern constitutions, but it was hardly mentioned in nineteenth-century constitutions (in fact, gender discrimination wasn't mentioned at all before the twentieth century, which, as we saw in Chapter 4, was when the women's movement began to make inroads into political systems).

The fact that almost all written constitutions mention democracy, even though only half of all countries meet the basic criteria of democracy that we discussed in Chapter 4, raises the question of whether written constitutions reflect how states are actually governed or merely how they wish to be perceived. We cannot take constitutional provisions at face value; we need to determine if they are applied in practice and if political leaders respect them.

For instance, the constitution of the Soviet Union that was adopted by the Congress of Soviets in 1936 was highly democratic on paper, purporting to protect a wide range of rights and liberties. But in the two years that followed its adoption, the leaders of the Communist Party of the Soviet Union persecuted and killed hundreds of thousands of the party's own members during the Great Terror. This example should make us think twice before interpreting constitutions literally.

However, the charts in Figure 9.2 do tell us something important about what states aspire to when they write their constitutions and the image they wish to project to their citizens and to the world.

In Case Study 9.1, we will continue our discussion of the effects of constitutional provisions by examining constitutional reforms in Zimbabwe in the 2000s.

CASE STUDY 9.1
Constitutional reform in Zimbabwe

The Republic of Zimbabwe was created in 1980 following the end of the white settler state of Rhodesia and British colonial rule. Its constitution was based on the so-called Lancaster House Agreement between the government of the United Kingdom, the government of the short-lived state Zimbabwe-Rhodesia, and the Patriotic Front, which was led by Robert Mugabe and Joshua Nkomo (see Figure 9.3). The Lancaster House Agreement gave Zimbabwe a parliamentary constitution with a prime minister, a ceremonial president, a bicameral legislature, and an independent legal system (Dzinesa 2012, 2).

The Lancaster House constitution remained in place for over 30 years, but it was amended 19 times, consolidating the power of the dominant party ZANU–PF (Zimbabwe African National Union–Patriotic Front). For example, Amendment 7, adopted in 1987, increased the power of the president and abolished the office of prime minister. Over time, the president, Robert Mugabe, was given the authority to appoint senators, dissolve parliament, remove a member of parliament who left their party, and appoint and dismiss judges, commissioners, security chiefs, and other high officials (Dzinesa 2012).

Figure 9.3 Robert Mugabe (left) and Joshua Nkomo (right) led the Patriotic Front in Zimbabwe.
Source: Keystone Press / Alamy Stock Photo

In the late 1990s, civil society organizations opposing the concentration of power in the president began advocating for constitutional reform through an umbrella organization known as the National Constitutional Assembly. Recognizing the Assembly's broad support, the government formed its own Constitutional Commission, but the proposed constitution still granted extensive powers to the president. It was rejected in a 2000 referendum.

By the end of the 2000s, the Movement for Democratic Change (MDC), which emerged from the 'no' campaign in the 2000 constitutional referendum, had grown strong enough to challenge ZANU-PF's dominance. In 2008, a power-sharing agreement allowed Robert Mugabe to remain president while the leader of MDC, Morgan Tsvangirai, became prime minister. This agreement served as the de facto constitution until the old constitution was replaced entirely in 2013. The 2013 constitution, a result of negotiations between ZANU-PF and MDC, was approved in a referendum and remains in effect today.

Compared with the revised Lancaster House constitution, the 2013 constitution has constrained the power of the executive and of the dominant party ZANU. It introduced presidential term limits, established a mixed electoral system, and tasked an independent Electoral Commission with running elections to reduce political violence and limit electoral misconduct. However,

ZANU has largely maintained its grip on Zimbabwe's political system. As noted by Sachikonye (2013), although the 2013 constitution established numerous autonomous institutions, it did not guarantee their funding and de facto independence. Consequently, 'the Zimbabwe Electoral Commission, the Zimbabwe Human Rights Commission and the Zimbabwe Media Commission have been starved of the resources, rendering them ineffective and depriving them of credibility' (Sachikonye 2013, 184).

We learn several things from Zimbabwe's decades-long process of constitutional reform.

1. When a new state establishes its constitution, it can become a battleground for the political parties, especially if it was drafted during a period of colonial rule or dictatorship.

2. Dominant political parties can amend, change, or circumvent the constitution for their own political ends, as Zimbabwe's ZANU-PF did under both the Lancaster House constitution and the 2013 constitution.

3. However, the fight for constitutional reform can contribute to political mobilization. In Zimbabwe, the broad coalition that opposed the constitutional reform in 2000 led to the formation of an opposition party that could challenge the previously dominant party. We will see a similar pattern in Case Study 13.2, which examines the movement for constitutional reform in Chile in the 2020s.

9.3 HIGH COURTS

LEARNING OUTCOMES

After reading Section 9.3, you'll be able to:
- Describe the role of courts in national political systems
- Distinguish between different types of high court
- Analyse the composition of judges on high courts.

We all have a rough idea of what **courts** of law are and what they do. They hold trials for those who are accused of crimes, and they adjudicate civil disputes involving contracts, inheritances, and divorces.

But courts are also a part of the political system. We will study two of their functions in the next two sections. In Section 9.4, we'll examine how courts act as a check on legislatures and executives, constraining political leaders by interpreting and applying the law independently, without taking instructions from people in power. In Section 9.5, we'll learn more about political systems where judges have the power of judicial review—the right to declare laws and policies unconstitutional or unlawful.

First, however, we will study the courts at the apex of national judicial systems. These courts are usually known as Supreme Courts, Constitutional Courts, or Courts of Cassation (*cours de cassation*) in France and many former French colonies. We can use the term **high court** for courts at the

Figure 9.4 National high courts are often housed in impressive buildings, exemplified by these court buildings in Israel and Germany. *Source: A: Seth Aronstam / Shutterstock; B: Hadrian / Shutterstock*

(A) Supreme Court, Israel

(B) Federal Constitutional Court, Germany

top of the judicial hierarchy in a country (some high courts are actually called High Court, such as the High Court of Australia).

High courts come in two main forms. Some of them are **appellate courts**, which means that they hear cases that have already been tried in lower courts and that have been appealed to the high court. Most of the courts bearing the name 'Supreme Court' are of this type. One example is the Supreme Court of Israel, which is pictured in the left-hand panel of Figure 9.4, and which was the focus of intense political conflicts and protests in Israel in the early 2020s.

The other main type is **constitutional courts**. Not surprisingly, they are often named 'Constitutional Court'. Constitutional courts are not part of the country's system of appellate courts and do not normally hear cases that have already been heard by other courts. Instead, they perform special functions that are defined by the constitution. For example, constitutional courts often have the power to review the constitutionality and legality of new legislation before it takes effect, which is a power that appellate courts don't have, since they only try cases that have made their way through the regular court system. One example of a constitutional court is Germany's Federal Constitutional Court, the *Bundesverfassungsgericht*, which is depicted in the right-hand panel of Figure 9.4.

In addition to the broader questions of judicial independence and judicial review that we'll discuss in the next two sections, scholars of comparative politics have examined the organization of high courts and how high courts decide cases. For example, one important difference between the high courts of the United States and the European Union—the Supreme Court of the United States and the Court of Justice of the European Union—is that the justices on the US Supreme Court issue dissenting opinions that reveal the differences between the justices, but the judges on the Court of Justice of the European Union do not.

Comparativists have also studied the appointment procedures for judges and analysed the composition of high courts. Figure 9.5, which relies on data from a major project on women on high courts around the world (Escobar-Lemmon et al. 2021), shows that between 1970 and 2012, the percentage of women on high courts around the world increased from almost 0 to just over 20 per cent. Incidentally, or perhaps not incidentally, the global average for women in legislatures in 2012 was also just over 20 per cent.

Figure 9.5 The proportion of women on high courts has increased over time, but remained below one third in all regions in 2010. *Source: Escobar-Lemmon, Maria C., Valerie J. Hoekstra, Alice J. Kang, and Miki Caul Kittilson. 2021. Reimagining the Judiciary: Women's Representation on High Courts Worldwide. Oxford: Oxford University Press.*

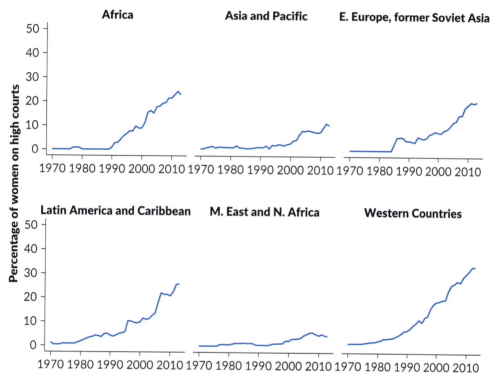

9.4 JUDICIAL INDEPENDENCE

LEARNING OUTCOMES

After reading Section 9.4, you'll be able to:
- Define judicial independence
- Analyse the role of the judiciary in maintaining democratic rule.

In this section, we're going to examine the independence of the judiciary from political interference. **Judicial independence** requires that two conditions are met. First, judges must be free to decide cases on the basis of their own interpretation of the law without undue influence from the government or other powerful institutions or groups. Second, the decisions they make must be allowed to take effect—that is, the opinions of the courts must actually influence how cases are eventually resolved (Ríos-Figueroa and Staton 2014, 107).

The most important consequence of judicial independence is that it can keep the government from using its authority arbitrarily, capriciously, or tyrannically. Where the judiciary is independent, the legislature can write general laws and the executive can issue general directives, but how those laws and directives are applied in individual cases isn't ultimately up to the government and its agencies, but to courts of law.

For an extreme historical example of unchecked, arbitrary government power, consider the so-called *lettres de cachet* ('letters of the seal') that the French king sometimes issued before the Great Revolution. By putting an order in a *lettre de cachet*, the king could act as he pleased against political opponents without asking for a court order and without even specifying which law his enemies were supposed to have broken. In a system with an independent judiciary, people in power cannot unleash the power of the state against their enemies in this manner.

In modern democracies, the importance of the courts becomes especially apparent when they decide cases that involve electoral procedures or other political processes that are central to the fairness of the elections. An independent judiciary can help safeguard fair elections by stopping leaders from harassing their opponents, punishing their critics, or manipulating the voting process. In Research Prompt 9.1, we'll analyse concrete examples of how law courts have overseen recent elections.

> **RESEARCH PROMPT 9.1**
> Courts and elections
>
> Law courts are often asked to resolve disputes over the administration of elections. For example, after the presidential election in the United States in November 2020, the incumbent president Donald Trump and groups associated with the president filed 63 different lawsuits that questioned the integrity of the election. The courts decided against President Trump in all these cases, and later heard cases where Trump himself was accused of interfering with the 2020 election. These cases remained unresolved at the time of the 2024 election.
>
> Consult an election website—such as Adam Carr's Election Archive, which is run by an Australian volunteer—and find out which countries have held national elections in the last few months. Then consult a reputable newspaper to learn if there were any court cases in connection with these elections. Do you observe any differences across countries when it comes to the ability of the courts to resolve disputes over electoral procedures?

Figure 9.6 describes the level of judicial independence in different countries around the world, using data from the Varieties of Democracy project that concern the highest court in each country (that is, the types of court we discussed in Section 9.3).

The first thing that stands out when we examine this map and compare it with other maps we've seen in this book is the close empirical relationship between judicial independence and democracy. The political dependence of the courts in authoritarian states such as China and Russia is striking. There are differences among democratic states, as the map also reveals, but they are on the whole small in comparison with the big differences between democratic states and authoritarian states.

The evidence in this map strongly suggests that having independent judges is important for the maintenance of democratic rule. As we discussed in Chapter 5, another piece of evidence supporting this view is that when political leaders with authoritarian tendencies consolidate their power and suppress opposition parties, the legal system often becomes a key battleground in the struggle over democracy.

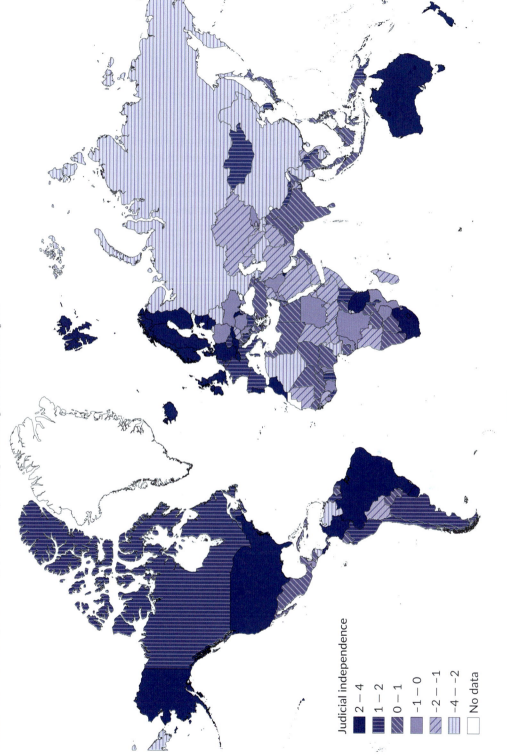

Figure 9.6 Judicial independence around the world. *Source:* Author's own work, based on data from Coppedge et al. (2024), "V-Dem Country-Year Dataset v14" Varieties of Democracy (V-Dem) Project. https://doi.org/10.23696/mcwt-fr58

9.5 JUDICIAL REVIEW

LEARNING OUTCOMES

After reading Section 9.5, you'll be able to:

- Define judicial review
- Describe how courts have resolved important political conflicts
- Explain the strategic interaction between judges and politicians.

In many modern states, courts have the right of judicial review—the right to declare laws and executive decisions unconstitutional—and frequently exercise this right.

Judicial review is not the same thing as judicial independence. As we discussed in Section 9.4, judicial independence means that the courts are free to apply the law without political interference. Judicial review, on the other hand, means that the courts have the power to declare the laws themselves unconstitutional. In other words, the courts can go beyond deciding individual cases and challenge the authority of the legislature and the executive directly.

Judicial independence is a prerequisite of democracy. Judicial review is not. There are well-functioning, established democracies in which the courts don't have this power or by tradition use it very sparingly. Finland and Switzerland are two examples.

As we noted in Chapter 6, courts are more likely to have and to use the right of judicial review in federal states. The reason is that they are often asked to resolve disputes between different levels of government. When political power is divided between the national government and sub-national governments, there is more room for the courts to challenge the legislature and the executive than in systems where power is concentrated at the national level. Similarly, in presidential systems, courts have more influence over public outcomes under divided government than under unified government (divided government means that the president and the majority in the legislature represent different parties, whereas unified government means they represent the same party). Again, courts have more room for manoeuvre when the power of legislatures and executives is more fragmented and contested.

These examples from federal and presidential systems illustrate the broader point that in countries where courts have the power to declare laws and government directives unconstitutional, public policy can develop into a complicated strategic game between the legislature, the executive, and the judiciary. Courts are different from legislatures and executives since they have no direct way of enforcing their decisions. Legislatures typically have power over the state's budget and the executive controls government agencies, including the police and the military. Courts have power over neither 'the purse' (the budget) nor 'the sword' (the coercive apparatus of the state); they can merely say what the law is. But when the courts are unlikely to be overridden by the legislature or the executive because of political divisions, they can act more autonomously (Vanberg 2015).

When there are political conflicts within political parties or between political parties in coalition governments, or across different chambers of the legislature, political leaders may deliberately draft vague laws and issue ambiguous government directives. This strategic choice leaves the courts with the responsibility to interpret and apply those laws and directives in practice. Many scholars of comparative politics believe that courts have become more influential in politics over time (see, for example, Tate and Vallinder 1995). The strategic choices of legislatures and executives to leave certain important political matters to the courts have contributed to this process of 'judicialization'.

One of the consequences of putting in place a system of judicial review is that controversial political issues are often decided in the courts, not by the people's elected representatives in legislatures and executives. For a discussion of how high courts around the world have addressed the controversial political issue of abortion, see Case Study 9.2.

CASE STUDY 9.2
High courts and abortion

A woman's right to have an abortion is a divisive political issue in many countries. All states in the world regulate abortions in some way—by prohibiting late abortions, for instance—but the rules vary greatly among countries. In some parts of the world, there are no restrictions on abortions in the first trimester, and abortions are provided in public hospitals at no cost to the pregnant woman. In other countries, all abortions are banned.

But those are not the only differences we see among countries when it comes to how governments have handled this issue. Another difference concerns the *source* of the rules that govern abortion in different states. In some countries, the rules on abortion are laid down in laws that were adopted by the legislature. The United Kingdom is one example: the current rules on abortion were put in place by the parliament in the late 1960s, through the Abortion Act 1967. In other countries, by contrast, the rules on abortion have been made by high courts. The United States is the best-known example. Abortions were illegal in many parts of the United States until the Supreme Court case *Roe* v. *Wade* in 1973, which made abortion legal throughout the country during the first two trimesters of pregnancy. The Supreme Court, not the Congress or the state legislatures, made the decision to legalize abortion. In 2022, the Supreme Court overruled its earlier decision and handed power back to the individual states, which immediately led to abortion becoming illegal across large swaths of the United States.

In this case study, we'll discuss two other recent cases of how high courts have redefined abortion law: Mexico and Germany.

Mexico has long had restrictive abortion laws, but in September 2021, the Mexican Supreme Court determined that it is contrary to Mexico's constitution to punish a woman for having an abortion. The argument the judges made was that a woman has an unconditional right to autonomy in a secular state. The court also noted that making abortion a crime disproportionately affects poorer women. Although the Supreme Court decision affected only one state, Coahuila, it was widely expected that it would lead to the legalization of abortion in all parts of Mexico.

In the case of Germany, the most important decision on abortion by the Federal Constitutional Court, or *Bundesverfassungsgericht*, was made in the 1970s, just like the US Supreme Court's decision in *Roe* v. *Wade*. The centre-left government at the time had passed a law that reformed abortion legislation by allowing women to choose if they wanted to go through with the pregnancy within the first 12 weeks. The conservative opposition parties and *Land* governments appealed to the Constitutional Court. In 1975, the court declared the new law unconstitutional since it didn't recognize the foetus's right to life (Kommers 1994, 4–10). But it also left room for politicians to permit abortions in certain circumstances.

After the country's reunification in 1990, the court brought up abortion once more, since the formerly communist eastern part of Germany had more permissive laws on a woman's right to choose, but the Constitutional Court made a similar argument as in 1975 (Kommers 1994, 10–25). Much more recently, the Constitutional Court has addressed another topic related to abortions: a ban on advertising abortions, which was challenged by a doctor who wished to say on her website that she offers abortions (Kottasová 2021).

We'll end by briefly considering another European case, Poland, where abortion has also come up in court cases in recent years. In the cases of Mexico and Germany, as we have seen, legislation became more permissive or remained quite permissive. The Polish Constitutional Court, however, has ruled that the existing laws on abortion are *too* permissive. This decision has resulted in a ban on abortions in practice, even though there is no law explicitly banning them.

9.6 CONCLUSION

In this chapter, we have studied the relationship between a country's political decision making bodies, such as the legislature and the executive, and its legal institutions, such as the constitution and the courts.

Most countries in the world have a written constitution that sets out the basic rules of politics, but constitutions were adopted at different times and contain different sorts of provisions. We noted that in some countries, there is a high court that is tasked with interpreting and applying the constitution. In other countries, the legislature itself is ultimately the arbiter of what the constitution says.

The right of the courts to interpret and apply the country's laws without political interference as it decides cases is widely regarded as an important precondition of democratic government. In some countries, high courts also have the power to declare laws unconstitutional, overriding decisions made by the legislature and the executive. Consequently, courts have sometimes had to decide for themselves how societies ought to confront controversial issues such as a woman's right to have an abortion.

Whether courts have this overtly political role or not, they are an important part of the political system, since they often decide cases that have major consequences for how public policies are implemented in practice. Another type of organization that influences the implementation of public policies—with profound consequences for the daily lives of ordinary people—is public administrative agencies. They are the topic of Chapter 10.

SUMMARY

- Most states in the world have a written constitution that sets out the basic rules of politics, but what's written in the constitution varies greatly among countries.
- Some countries change their constitutions rarely, whereas other countries change them often to adapt them to changing circumstances.
- High courts have an important function in the judicial system as the ultimate arbiters of how the law should be interpreted and applied.

- Well-functioning democratic states typically have an independent judicial system with courts that are free to decide cases in accordance with their own interpretation of the law.
- Many other states lack judicial independence, which means that courts of law often decide cases in accordance with the wishes of political leaders.
- In countries where courts have the right of judicial review, controversial political issues are often decided in the courts, not by legislatures and executives.
- Where courts have this power, politics can take the form of a strategic game between the judiciary, the legislature, and the executive.

STUDY QUESTIONS

1. In previous chapters, we have sometimes referred to the texts of national constitutions to describe differences among states and give meaning to concepts such as 'federalism' and 'legislature'. Having read this chapter, do you think we ought to take constitutions seriously in this way, or do they say too little about how power is exercised in practice?
2. Many scholars of comparative politics believe that the political power of courts has increased greatly over time in many countries. Some scholars even use the term 'juristocracy'—rule by judges—for the consequences of this process (Hirschl 2007). Having read this chapter, do you agree that judiciaries have on the whole become more powerful—and how does politics change when they do?

FURTHER READING

Gregory A. Caldeira, R. Daniel Kelemen, and Keith E. Whittington (eds.), *The Oxford Handbook of Law and Politics* (2008).
  Discusses the role of the judiciary in modern states, especially democracies.

Zachary Elkins and Tom Ginsburg, 'What Can We Learn from Written Constitutions?' (2021).
  Provides an overview of what's written in national constitutions and discusses whether written constitutions accurately describe how political systems work.

Maria C. Escobar-Lemmon, Valerie J. Hoekstra, Alice J. Kang, and Miki Caul Kittilson, *Reimagining the Judiciary* (2021).
  Analyses the representation of women on high courts around the world.

CHAPTER 10

PUBLIC ADMINISTRATION

CHAPTER GUIDE

10.1 Introduction
10.2 The Need for Public Administration
10.3 Public Administration around the World
10.4 Corruption
10.5 Delegation, Democracy, and Technocracy
10.6 Conclusion
Summary
Study Questions
Further Reading

10.1 INTRODUCTION

In the last few chapters, we have studied institutions such as electoral systems, legislatures and executives, and high courts. Those are the things many people think of when they hear the word 'politics'. There's an election. A government is formed. The government proposes new policies. The legislature makes laws and decides how much to tax and spend. In countries where judges have the right of judicial review, high courts may be asked to determine if the government and the legislature have acted constitutionally. End of story.

Except it isn't the end of the story. Many political decisions that have profound effects on people's lives aren't made by government ministers, members of the legislature, or judges on high courts—they're made by officials who work in public administration. Those officials are employed by administrative agencies at the national, regional, and local levels that carry out the day-to-day operations of the state.

Implementing public policies isn't merely a technical matter. If it were, we could think of public administration as a sort of machine that turns policies and laws into decisions in individual cases in a neutral and predictable manner. But government agencies make all sorts of consequential political decisions when they carry out their work, since political decision makers cannot specify in every detail how policies ought to be implemented. This leaves a lot of room for interpretations made by administrative officials. Government agencies therefore wield great power. Public officials are also involved in the development of new public policies, since politicians depend on their expertise when they write new laws and take new policy initiatives. As Krause (1999) puts it, public administration is a 'two-way street'.

In Section 10.2, we'll begin by exploring why public administration is necessary—that is, why political leaders depend on bureaucrats to carry out their policies. The need for public administration has increased greatly over time because of the increasing scope of the modern state that we discussed in Chapter 3. This holds for all states, but in Section 10.3, we'll learn that both the organization of government agencies and the relationship between politicians and public officials vary greatly among countries. In Section 10.4, we'll examine one of the main problems in public administration, and in political systems generally—corruption, which is the misuse of public office for private gain. Finally, in Section 10.5, we'll study policy domains in which governments in many democracies have delegated a lot of power to autonomous government agencies. This delegation raises important questions about the role experts in public administration should play in modern democratic states.

10.2 THE NEED FOR PUBLIC ADMINISTRATION

LEARNING OUTCOMES

After reading Section 10.2, you'll be able to:
- Explain the origins of modern public administration
- Analyse the relationship between politicians and public officials.

We use the term **public administration** for the activity of carrying out the government's policies and managing the day-to-day operations of the state. We use the term **government agencies** for the administrative organizations that do this work. Government agencies are staffed mainly by non-elected public officials. The words 'bureaucracy', 'the bureaucracy', and 'officials' are sometimes used to refer to public administration, government agencies, and public officials. But the term 'bureaucracy'—which literally means 'rule by offices'—also refers to one particular model of public administration, which emerged in Europe in the nineteenth century. To avoid confusion, we will therefore stick to the more generic terms.

The creation of permanent and specialized government agencies for the collection of taxes and the implementation of public policies was an important phase in the long process of state formation we discussed in Chapter 3. It happened gradually, not suddenly. About 1,200 years ago, Imperial China became the first state in the world to introduce a system of examinations for those who wished to work in public administration. In medieval times, a few countries in Europe created permanent institutions for tax collection and the administration of justice. Somewhat later, in the early modern period (around 1500–1800), several European states began to organize more specialized administrative departments, some of which still exist today (for an overview, see Vogler 2023).

One alternative to having permanent government agencies is to outsource administration to private individuals or companies. A historical example of this is the practice of 'tax farming', where individuals or companies paid a fee for the right to collect taxes from the residents of a specific area. Another alternative is that each political leader comes into office with their own group of advisers and helpers. This was also a common historical practice. Both models have become less viable in modern states, which provide many services requiring significant manpower and expertise.

In Europe, the German sociologist Max Weber is often credited with developing the first comprehensive theory of public administration. For Weber (1978 [1921]), a 'bureaucracy' is a particular form of administrative organization that is defined by hierarchy, general rules that govern the organization's activities, and, importantly, staffing practices that ensure officials are hired on the basis of their training and skills, not on the basis of other considerations, such as their political loyalties. People who pursue a career in the bureaucracy can expect success and advancement on the basis of their employment record and their service. Weber expected that bureaucracy would displace all other forms of public administration since he deemed that it is exceptionally effective. As we'll see in Section 10.3, however, national systems of public administration today can be categorized as more or less 'Weberian', which suggests that although Weber's theory still has a lot to say about how public administration works, the bureaucratic model hasn't displaced all others.

Politicians delegate authority to unelected public officials because it's impossible for them to anticipate all the questions that might arise when a law is enacted or a policy is implemented. But when they do, they give up some of their power. Scholars of public administration sometimes use the term **principal–agent problem** to describe the trade-off that politicians face when they task public officials with carrying out their policies.

Principal–agent theory examines the relationship between someone who has power to begin with—such as, in this case, a politician—and someone to whom they grant power—such as, in this case, a public official. A principal–agent problem is when the principal and the agent can have different interests, which may lead the agent to use the authority that's been given to them to do things the principal might not have wanted and could not anticipate. Politicians in modern states typically do not have the time, the knowledge, or the administrative resources that are necessary to carry out their policies. Principal–agent problems are therefore ubiquitous in modern politics. In the context of the relationship between politicians and public officials, they can lead to problems such as shirking (when officials don't make an effort to work towards the goals the government has set for them), sabotage (when officials actively undermine the ambitions of the politicians), or drift (when officials deviate over time from the policy the government expected them to pursue). A key factor here is that officials normally know much more about the specifics of the policies they're carrying out and the environment in which the policy is being implemented.

Principal–agent models have been used to analyse other important political relationships in modern politics. One is the relationship between parliaments and governments in parliamentary systems, where the parliament can be seen as the principal and the government as the agent (see Chapter 8). A second is the relationship between voters and politicians in democracies. Here, the voters are the principals and the politicians are the agents (see Chapter 12). But the principal–agent model is especially helpful when it comes to understanding the relationship between politicians and public officials, since the principal–agent problem that politicians face is so concrete—they want things done, but they rely on others to do them.

Because it's often difficult for political decision makers to anticipate all the decisions public officials will have to make when they carry out their policies, legislatures and governments often write laws and issue directives that are formulated in general, or even sweeping, terms. They then let government agencies—or, in some cases, the courts (Chapter 9)—work out the details. This practice, which is often a practical necessity, has raised important constitutional and legal issues in many countries around the world. We will study those issues in Research Prompt 10.1.

> **RESEARCH PROMPT 10.1**
> Politicians, public officials, or courts?

On 17 January 2024, the Supreme Court of the United States heard oral arguments in the case *Loper Bright Enterprises* v. *Raimondo*, which was brought by a group of fishermen who objected to the National Marine Fisheries Service's policy of having the fishermen pay the salaries of the federal inspectors who sometimes accompany them on their fishing trips to ensure they follow the regulations issued by the agency (see Figure 10.1). The fishermen complained that no law explicitly authorized the National Marine Fisheries Service to force the fishermen to pay for the inspections, and that the agency couldn't impose this fee on its own accord. The government argued, contrary to the fishermen's view, that the National Marine Fisheries Service needed room for manoeuvre when deciding how best to enact the laws and carry out the government's policies. The court ultimately decided in favour of the fishermen.

This case raises important questions about the relationship between politicians, public officials, citizens, and the courts (the fishermen asked the Supreme Court to overturn its decision in a much earlier case, *Chevron* v. *Natural Resources Defense Council*, in which the court stated that it would

Figure 10.1 In *Loper Bright Enterprises* v. *Raimondo*, the United States Supreme Court ruled that fishermen could not be forced to pay the salaries of Marine Fisheries Service inspectors accompanying them on fishing trips. *Source: David Kay / Shutterstock*

defer to government agencies when they made decisions about how to interpret laws and regulations in their area of expertise).

1. All oral arguments of the Supreme Court of the United States are available as audio files via the research project Oyez (www.oyez.org). Listen to the oral argument in the case of *Loper Bright Enterprises* v. *Raimondo* and summarize the main arguments for and against the plaintiffs' view that a government agency should not have the right to impose costs on them without the explicit authorization of the United States Congress.

2. In the United States, a system in which the courts of law have the right to judicial review, these sorts of issues are often resolved in the courts. But fishing is a big industry in many countries around the world, and the relationship between fishermen and public authorities that exercise oversight over fishing is almost always fraught. Choose a country other than the United States, find out which public agency is responsible for monitoring fishing, and try to find out if the legislature has regulated the activities of that agency in detail or if the agency has a lot of leeway when carrying out its duties. What similarities and differences do you find between the United States and the country you have chosen?

10.3 PUBLIC ADMINISTRATION AROUND THE WORLD

LEARNING OUTCOMES

After reading Section 10.3, you'll be able to:
- Distinguish between different types of administrative institution
- Compare the relationship between politicians and officials in different countries.

As we discussed in Section 10.2, the growth of public administration and the proliferation of government agencies is a process that is common to most parts of the world, and it is perhaps a necessary consequence of the increasing scope of government that we learned about in Chapter 3. But there isn't one single model of public administration in today's world. Indeed, countries vary greatly on at least two dimensions. First of all, public agencies are organized very differently, especially when it comes to how officials are recruited. Second, the nature of the relationship between politicians and public officials varies greatly among countries. In this section, we will explore these key differences.

10.3.1 Careers in public administration

We will begin with the question how public officials are recruited and how government agencies are organized. One way of thinking about how public administration varies among countries is to treat Weber's description of an ideal bureaucracy as a model against which actual bureaucracies can be measured, to see which bureaucracies are most 'Weberian' (see, for example, Evans and Rauch 1999). That sort of comparison is made in Figure 10.2, which is based on data from Nistotskaya et al. (2021).

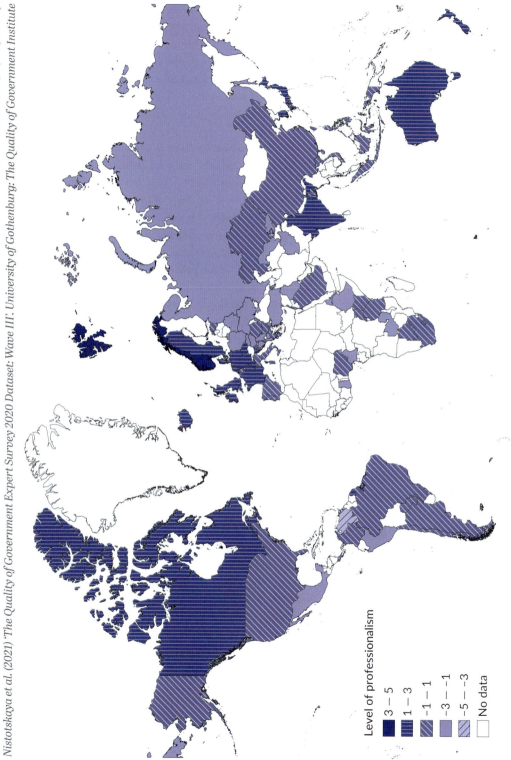

Figure 10.2 Public administration is more 'professional' in some countries than others. Source: Author's own work, based on survey of experts by Nistotskaya et al. (2021) 'The Quality of Government Expert Survey 2020 Dataset: Wave III'. University of Gothenburg: The Quality of Government Institute

The scholars who collected these data compiled information about three aspects of public administration that are related to Weber's concept of bureaucracy—merit-based recruitment (that is, whether those who work in public administration are hired based on their training, qualifications, and experience), the absence of patronage (patronage means that those who work in public administration are hired based on their political or personal affiliations), and job security (which means that those who work in public administration cannot be fired arbitrarily). The map is based on a combined measure of 'professionalism' that develops one single score from these three different indicators.

In a 'Weberian' bureaucracy, a job in public administration is something you get because of training, skills, and experience, and you're not fired arbitrarily for political or other reasons. As Figure 10.2 shows, government agencies are the most 'Weberian' in western Europe north of the Alps, Oceania, Japan, South Korea, and Canada. In other parts of the world, national systems of public administration lie further from Weber's model of bureaucracy. This is either because, in those states, political connections and loyalties are more likely to win somebody a job in public administration than training and other formal qualifications, or because personal connections and networks play an important role. A system in which political connections play an important role is sometimes called a 'spoils' system, since important positions in public administration are treated as 'spoils of war' that the winner of the election is free to distribute among their supporters. Systems in which personal connections are more important can be called 'patronage-based' or 'clientelistic', reflecting the fact that networks between patrons and clients determine access to jobs in public administration (see Chapters 11 and 15), or 'patrimonial' if family ties decide who gets a job and who doesn't.

10.3.2 Politicization

The evidence in Figure 10.2 concerns the nature of public administration *as such*, concentrating on what it's like to get a job and work in government agencies. Let us now consider another way of comparing administrative politics in different countries, which emphasizes the *relationship between officials and politicians*.

These differences among countries can be clearly seen at the top levels of public administration. In a few small western European democracies, the only one in a government ministry who loses their job when there's a change in government is the government minister her- or himself. Everyone else is a civil servant who isn't appointed for political reasons and who pursues a career as a professional administrator. In other countries—most countries, in fact—both the central state administration and lower levels of administration are highly politicized, in the sense that a lot of people lose their jobs when there's an election or a new leader comes to power. That sort of system is typically based on the idea that a new government can only get its job done if it can rely on administrative agencies to be loyal to its political ambitions and ideas. In some countries, including a democracy such as the United States, the president uses appointments to positions in public administration to reward his or her supporters for their loyalty.

In a recent review of the literature on public administration the political scientists Carl Dahlström and Victor Lapuente (2022) argue that it's helpful to compare the relationship between officials and politicians along two separate dimensions. They call the first dimension 'accountability vs. autonomy'. Accountability means that officials answer directly to the politicians and the politicians have means of influencing their decisions; autonomy means that officials and government agencies are free to use their own judgement and decision making procedures. The second dimension is 'law vs. management', where law means that officials are expected to follow predetermined rules, whereas management means that officials are expected to be more service-oriented, putting less emphasis on following rules and more emphasis on getting a good outcome.

On the basis of these distinctions, Dahlström and Lapuente (2022) present a two-dimensional model of different relationships between officials and politicians (Figure 10.3). In the classical Weberian model, officials are expected to follow predetermined rules but have a lot of autonomy from politicians when it comes to interpreting and applying those rules. This model is especially common in continental European countries such as Germany and in East Asia. In the 'legalistic' model, officials are also law- and rules-based, but have less autonomy from their political masters. This is a model that's more prevalent in southern Europe. In the 'populistic' model, rules are less important and officials care more about the outcomes they achieve, but the level of political control is high. Dahlström and Lapuente (2022) explain that this model was common historically in the Americas, both North and South. The fourth and final model is the 'liberal' type in which officials are service- and outcome-oriented, but autonomous from the political leaders. This model is common in, for example, northern Europe and New Zealand.

To see how the relationship between public officials and politicians can affect important political outcomes, see Case Study 10.1.

Figure 10.3 Four types of public administration. *Source: Dahlström, Carl and Victor Lapuente. 2022. 'Comparative Bureaucratic Politics'. Copyright ©2022 by Annual Reviews. (CC BY 4.0)*

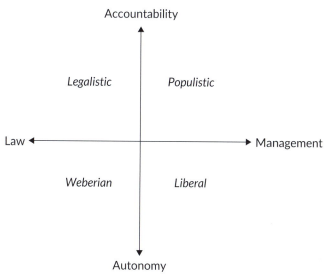

CASE STUDY 10.1
Officials, politicians, and Covid-19

Towards the end of 2019 and at the beginning of 2020, a dangerous new virus began to spread over the world, causing a disease called Covid-19 (Coronavirus Disease 2019). The epidemic started in China but it soon reached Europe and the Middle East and then got to other parts of the world.

When the new virus emerged, most countries in the world put in place public health policies that they hoped would slow down the spread of Covid-19. Many countries opted for restrictive policies that prohibited people from moving about, gathering, and interacting with others—to prevent the transmission of the virus—and people were sometimes confined to their homes to prevent the spread of the virus in the population.

But there were important differences between countries. On a global level, political regimes and varying levels of state capacity help to explain much of this variation, but intriguing differences remain between countries that are seemingly very similar. To explain those differences, we need to take into account the structure of public administration and the relationship between officials and politicians. Public health policies require a lot of expertise, so the influence of public health agencies is potentially very significant.

Let's consider the cases of Denmark and Sweden. Denmark was one of the first countries in Europe to put in place regulations that required people to work from their homes, closed restaurants and bars, and kept children at home instead of letting them go to school. Denmark thus instituted a 'lockdown' to prevent the spread of the virus. Neighbouring Sweden, on the other hand, was one of the most liberal countries in Europe, relying mainly on voluntary recommendations and guidelines (see Figure 10.4).

Figure 10.4 In Sweden during the Covid-19 pandemic, safety measures were mostly voluntary, and less restrictive than in Denmark and other countries. The sign reads '2 metres: Keep your distance both in water and on land'. *Source: Jeppe Gustafsson / Shutterstock*

> In both Denmark and Sweden, there was a social democratic government at the time of the pandemic, but the relationship between the political decision makers in the government and the experts in the public health authorities varied greatly between the two countries. In Denmark, the government quickly determined—contrary to the advice of the country's public health authority—that it was essential to take action to prevent the spread of the virus, and the key decisions were taken inside the central government offices. In Sweden, by contrast, the government played a less active role, leaving much of the decision making to the national public health authority, which believed that the social costs of a lockdown exceeded the public health benefits for the population.
>
> The pros and cons of each country's approach to the pandemic remain debated in both Denmark and Sweden. What's interesting to us in the context of this chapter, however, is *why* the Danish and the Swedish approaches were so different. According to a study commissioned by the Danish parliament, the role of the bureaucracy is an important part of the explanation. First of all, Sweden has a long tradition of autonomous bureaucratic authorities, trusting them to implement laws and government policies according to their own best judgement. In a broader comparative perspective, Denmark also has an autonomous bureaucracy, but the relationship between officials and politicians is closer than it is in Sweden. Second, whereas Denmark has several public agencies that advise the government on public health policy, Sweden has only one. Since the Danish government got more varied advice from the different agencies, how to respond to Covid-19 became a politically salient issue earlier in that country.

10.4 CORRUPTION

LEARNING OUTCOMES

After reading Section 10.4, you'll be able to:
- Define corruption
- Describe how corruption varies among countries
- Explain why some countries are more corrupt than others.

One of the reasons that we ought to take an interest in how government agencies are organized, how public officials are recruited, and what the relationship between public officials and politicians is like is that all these factors influence the risk of **corruption** in a society. Often defined as 'the misuse of public office for private gain', corruption means that politicians and public officials use their power and influence to benefit themselves, their families, or some other narrowly defined group, either by taking bribes or in other ways.

We have already come across the problem of corruption in Chapter 2, where we discussed how to measure the extent of this important phenomenon. Most people in the world live in countries with widespread corruption, and the experience of doing so greatly influences how they think about politics. In countries with low levels of corruption, people tend to think that political leaders act in the public's interest and that public officials by and large do what they can to carry out the government's policies and uphold the law. In countries with high levels of corruption, things are very different: it can be easy for people to think that both political leaders and public officials act in their own interest, or in the interest of some smaller group, and not in the interest of all citizens.

For these reasons, corruption is associated with many bad things, including low levels of social trust, low economic growth, and low-quality public services. During the war between Russia and Ukraine that followed the full-scale invasion of Ukraine by Russia in 2022, both Ukraine's political leaders and foreign donors were concerned about the effects of corruption on the country's war effort—before the war, Ukraine was widely regarded as one of the most corrupt countries in Europe (see, for example, 'Ukrainians understand corruption can kill: Kyiv takes on an old enemy', *The Guardian*, 19 September 2023).

Consider Figure 10.5, which uses data from the organization Transparency International to identify countries in the world whose officials are highly corrupt and countries that control corruption more effectively. As the map shows, the level of corruption varies greatly among countries. Scholars of comparative politics try to explain why this is. They also try to understand the economic, social, and political effects that corruption has around the world.

If you compare the map in Figure 10.5 with the map in Figure 4.2, you will find that high levels of democracy don't always come with low levels of corruption. In other words, democracy and corruption are not particularly highly correlated. There are democratic countries with quite a lot of corruption, as in many parts of Latin America, and there are strongly authoritarian countries with low levels of corruption, such as Singapore in South-East Asia.

The weak correlation between democracy and corruption has at least two important implications. First of all, it tells us something about how political scientists use the word 'democracy'. As we discussed in Chapter 4, the word 'democracy' is often used in everyday conversation in the broad sense of 'a good, well-ordered society', but political scientists typically use the word in a much narrower sense. For political scientists, and especially for scholars of comparative politics, democracy is a method of appointing political leaders and making political decisions, and it is entirely possible for a democracy to have bad leaders who make bad decisions. The second implication of the weak correlation between democracy and corruption is that it reaffirms a point we've made earlier: formal political institutions cannot be studied in isolation. Democracy means something else to the people of a country in which political leaders and state officials are corrupt than it means to the people of a country in which most leaders and officials can be trusted.

One drawback with the widely used definition of corruption as the misuse of public office for private gain is that the term 'misuse' also needs defining, and what constitutes misuse or abuse in some national or historical contexts may not be regarded in that way in other contexts. But that can also be seen as a strength of the definition, since it can be adapted to different circumstances. Among the more specific forms that corruption can take are bribery (when someone pays a politician or public official to influence their decision making), embezzlement (when politicians or public officials steal money that is meant for public projects), and nepotism (when politicians or public officials make decisions that are favourable to their friends, families, or extended families).

Rothstein and Teorell (2008) have argued that the opposite of corruption is when political decision makers and officials are *impartial* in applying the laws and carrying out government policies, or, more specifically, that '[w]hen implementing laws and policies, government officials shall not take anything about the case/citizen into consideration that is not beforehand stipulated in the law or policy' (187). The idea behind this definition is that laws and policies may themselves be

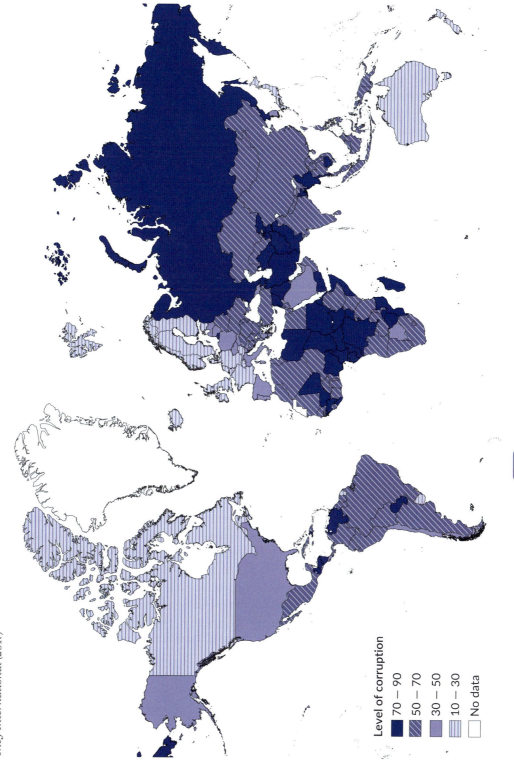

Figure 10.5 Corruption around the world in 2018. *Source: Author's own work based on data from Teorell et al. (2024), relying on data from Transparency International (2017)*

partial, in that they benefit some people and not others (for example, some people may qualify for unemployment assistance while others don't)—that's politics—but once they're adopted, government ministers, public officials, and other decision makers must be guided only by the law or policy itself and not by other considerations. In this view, impartial, transparent, and predictable courts, government agencies, and other institutions that uphold the law and carry out public policies represent the ideal of good government, whereas corruption represents bad government.

Scholars ask many different sorts of questions about corruption. One concerns the variety of corrupt practices. Distinctions are often made between **petty corruption**, which involves day-to-day, small-scale corrupt activities such as officials accepting bribes to provide public services, **grand corruption**, which involves corrupt activities on a large scale, such as multi-million-dollar bribes to politicians and public officials by corporations that wish to secure public contracts, and **systemic corruption**, which is when corrupt practices are so endemic in a society that it has become normalized and affects almost everyone.

This brings us to the second type of question scholars ask about corruption: where it comes from. One important finding is that once corruption has become widespread in a society, it is very difficult to get rid of it. What we have here is a classic **collective-action problem**: though most people are worse off because of corruption, as long as everyone thinks everyone else is corrupt, no one has an incentive to act in the public interest. Major reforms of public administration that put a premium on recruiting the most highly qualified candidates seem to be able to bring down corruption—but in countries with systemic corruption, governments are unlikely to undertake such reforms.

One important finding from contemporary research on corruption and the quality of public administration around the world is that there may be pockets of well-functioning public agencies within political systems that are otherwise corrupt and functioning poorly. We'll explore two examples of this in Case Study 10.2.

CASE STUDY 10.2
Public administration in Brazil and Africa

As we discussed in Chapter 3, an important literature in comparative politics argues that the presence and power of the state varies across national territories. Relatedly, there is an important literature in comparative public administration which argues that the quality of government agencies varies greatly within states, including the prevalence of corruption. For example, Gingerich (2013) has shown that differences in capacity among government agencies are often greater *within* countries than *between* countries. If we compare two countries, A and B, and find that the public administration in country A works better, on average, than the public administration in country B, we will nevertheless often find that many individual agencies in country B work better than many individual agencies in country A.

This finding is echoed in a recent study of government agencies in Brazil by Bersch et al. (2017). The authors of this study analysed data from 326,000 civil servants across 95 major federal agencies. They found that the central state administration in Brazil is highly diverse, with agencies varying greatly in capacity and autonomy. As the authors put it, there are 'islands of excellence' within the Brazilian state, including the foreign ministry and the central bank. But there are also many poorly functioning agencies such as the ministry of sports and several agencies involved in infrastructure development.

Importantly, the authors find that lower capacity and autonomy are associated with a higher level of corruption. This may suggest that addressing corruption—which is relatively high in Brazil (see Figure 10.5)—requires enhancing agency capacity and reducing interference from politicians in the day-to-day operations of the state.

Brazil is not the only state in which scholars have found such 'islands of excellence' among national administrative agencies. The case studies of Ghana, Kenya, Rwanda, Uganda, and Zambia in the recent book *Pockets of Effectiveness and the Politics of State Building and Development in Africa* (Hickey 2023) show that despite the difficult political context in Africa, there are parts of these five states that have worked remarkably effectively. The authors refer to this phenomenon as 'pockets of bureaucratic effectiveness'. But the five case studies also find that the performance of the administrative agencies of Ghana, Kenya, Rwanda, Uganda, and Zambia has varied greatly over time. The authors attribute these changes to underlying political factors: during periods when power has been highly dispersed among political parties, their factions, and other groups, government agencies have been more vulnerable to political pressures that have kept them from pursuing their missions effectively.

But interestingly, severing politics and administration completely does not appear to have been a successful strategy. For example, Abdulai (2023) finds that in Ghana, 'every period of good performance . . . involved leaders who combined technocratic expertise with political loyalty', which 'earned them the political protection required to adopt often unconventional organizational practices . . . and to push through difficult reforms'. He concludes that pockets of effectiveness gain organizational autonomy not by isolating themselves from politics, but by cultivating strong political relations and bargaining with the country's rulers.

10.5 DELEGATION, DEMOCRACY, AND TECHNOCRACY

LEARNING OUTCOMES

After reading Section 10.5, you'll be able to:

- Account for the delegation of political power to independent experts in different countries in the world
- Assess contemporary debates about technocracy.

Section 10.3 emphasized some of the advantages of having an independent bureaucracy. But in a democracy, the power of government agencies must also be contained. Public officials are not elected and therefore lack the democratic legitimacy that elected politicians enjoy. After all, democracy means that the voters can remove their political leaders from office, but in most countries, officials cannot be removed in this way.

Nevertheless, there has been a trend in recent decades of giving more power to government agencies. This has happened because governments have delegated more and more responsibilities to experts, whom they have authorized to conduct policy in certain domains. This process has gone furthest in economic policy. A few decades ago it was normal for central banks, which are tasked with conducting monetary policy and safeguarding the payments system, to take instructions from legislatures and executives. Today, central banks are autonomous in most parts of the world. Within the European Union, competition policy—rules designed to ensure fair competition among companies from different EU member states—has also been delegated to expert agencies.

There are critics who argue that this sort of delegation can go too far. They claim that the increasing power of officials and experts has led to **technocracy**, which means government by those who have technical knowledge and skills as opposed to government by the people, which is the hallmark of democracy.

In Chapter 9, we discussed the political power and influence of courts and judges around the world, noting that many scholars believe courts have become more powerful over time. Some scholars even use the term 'juristocracy', rule by judges, to refer to political systems in which many political issues are decided by unelected jurists, not elected politicians. The idea of 'technocracy' is similar. Many scholars believe that unelected officials who are experts on the policy areas they manage have become increasingly powerful over time, which is a challenge to established ideas of how democracies ought to work, since the idea of democracy is that elected politicians should resolve the main political conflicts in society. For example, Caramani (2017) has argued that in today's world, the established party model of representative democracy is squeezed between technocracy and populism (see Chapter 11), with technocrats claiming that governments should simply do what experts tell them to and populists claiming that they know what the people really need.

Legislatures and executives delegate important policymaking competencies to central banks and other public authorities because they hope that handing over certain problems to independent decision makers will lead to better outcomes (Majone 1998). But when they do this, they also lose control over important policy instruments. Striking the right balance between listening to experts and letting elected politicians try to resolve conflicts in society is an increasingly important issue in today's world.

10.6 CONCLUSION

In this chapter, we have examined differences in public administration among countries. We began in Section 10.2 by discussing why public administration is necessary—that is, why political leaders cannot govern countries, regions, and localities on their own, but depend on public officials to carry out their policies. The need for public officials has increased greatly over the past century because of the increasing scope of the modern state. States provide many services for their citizens and enforce many rules that regulate both economic and social life, and all those functions are performed by public officials.

While this holds for states generally, we learned in Section 10.3 that both the nature of public administration and the relationship between politicians and public officials vary greatly among countries. We studied evidence suggesting that public administration is much more professionalized in some countries than others, and we learned that public officials and political decision makers are at arm's length from each other in some states but closely intertwined in others. In Section 10.4, we examined one of the main problems in public administration—and in political systems generally—across the world today: corruption, or the misuse of public office for private gain.

In Section 10.5, finally, we learned about contemporary debates on technocracy, which is rule by experts. In some policy domains, notably monetary policy, governments in many countries have delegated a lot of power to autonomous government agencies. These trends raise important questions about what the relationship between politicians and public officials ought to be like in modern democratic systems.

This chapter concludes the part of the book that is concerned with the central political institutions in modern states: federalism, electoral systems, legislatures, executives, constitutions, high courts, and government agencies. In the next chapter, we're going to learn about organizations that are not part of the state itself, but that seek power over the central institutions of the state by winning seats in the legislature and forming or participating in the government—political parties.

SUMMARY

- Government agencies carry out the government's policies and run the day-to-day operations of the state.
- Politicians must delegate authority to public officials, since they lack the time, expertise, and administrative resources that are necessary for implementing public policies.
- But they give up something when they do: public officials and government agencies may have interests that differ from those of their political masters.
- In many countries, public administration is highly politicized: public-sector jobs usually go to people with the right connections and personal loyalties.
- In other countries, however, government agencies are professional organizations.
- There are countries in which top public officials are dependent on political decision makers and follow their instructions; in other countries, there is more of an arm's-length relationship between political leaders and civil servants and other officials.
- Corruption—the misuse of public office for private gain—is a widespread problem but also varies greatly among countries.
- Once corruption has become established and become 'systemic', it is very difficult to get rid of.
- The proper role of experts in democracies is a much-debated issue in the world today.

STUDY QUESTIONS

1. Is it possible to distinguish between making public policies and carrying them out?
2. In a democracy, political responsiveness requires that governments are able to carry out the policies they ran on in the election. This means that governments need to be able to control public administration. But if public agencies become too politicized, there can be harmful consequences. Having read this chapter, how do you think political systems ought to strike the right balance between the effectiveness of the government and the autonomy and integrity of government agencies and the public officials who work for them?

FURTHER READING

Joel Aberbach, Robert D. Putnam, and Bert Rockman, *Bureaucrats and Politicians in Western Democracies* (1981).
  Analyses the roles of officials and politicians on the basis of hundreds of interviews in seven countries.

Eri Bertsou and Daniele Caramani, *The Technocratic Challenge to Democracy* (2020).
  Examines different forms of technocracy and the relationship between technocracy and democracy.

Carl Dahlström and Victor Lapuente, 'Dimensions of Bureaucratic Politics' (2022).
  Develops four different models of the relationship between politicians and public officials.

CHAPTER 11

POLITICAL PARTIES

CHAPTER GUIDE

11.1 Introduction
11.2 What Political Parties Do
11.3 How Parties Are Organized
11.4 Party Families
11.5 Party Systems

11.6 Conclusion
Summary
Study Questions
Further Reading

11.1 INTRODUCTION

Parties are the most important political organizations in modern states. Politics revolves around parties in democracies, where parties, and the candidates they put forward, compete with one another in free and fair elections. As we discussed in Chapter 5, politics also revolves around parties in many authoritarian regimes. In one-party states such as China, a single ruling party controls the government. In electoral-authoritarian, hybrid regimes, there are multi-party elections—as in democracies—but the ruling party uses its power over the state and the media to harass, weaken, and defeat its rivals.

So far in this book, we've learned about the nature of the state (Chapter 3), democratic and authoritarian regimes (Chapters 4–5), and important institutions such as electoral rules, legislatures, executives, high courts, and administrative agencies (Chapters 7–10). Political parties can influence all of these things. They seek power within the state. They can build, prop up, and overthrow both democratic and authoritarian regimes. They compete in elections, populate legislatures and executives, and often exert influence over both public administration and the courts. Consequently, parties aren't just worth learning about in their own right—we also understand states, regimes, and institutions better when we observe what political parties do with them.

Section 11.2 explains what political parties are, what they do, and how they differ from each other. Section 11.3 discusses how parties are organized internally. Section 11.4 describes some of the main families of political parties and the social groups they represent. Section 11.5 studies the relationships among the political parties, which scholars of comparative politics call the 'party system'.

11.2 WHAT POLITICAL PARTIES DO

LEARNING OUTCOMES

After reading Section 11.2, you'll be able to:
- Define political parties
- Describe the roles parties perform in different political systems
- Distinguish between different strategies of political parties.

11.2.1 Defining parties

The word 'party' stems from a Latin verb that means 'to divide'. As the word's original meaning suggests, the concept of **political parties** is closely related to the idea that societies are divided into distinct groups, with conflicting interests and ideals: a party represents a 'part' of society. But there are many other types of organization that also do this, including interest groups such as trade unions and environmental associations, which we'll study in Chapter 13. To define political parties more precisely, we need to ask ourselves what sets parties apart from all other organizations.

The answer is that political parties try to control the state apparatus by winning seats in the legislature, participating in the government, or both. In his book *Parties and Party Systems*, the Italian political scientist Giovanni Sartori (1976, 64) defined a political party as 'any political group that presents at elections, and is capable of placing through elections, candidates for public office'. In another twentieth-century classic, *An Economic Theory of Democracy*, Anthony Downs (1957, 24) defined a political party as 'a coalition of men seeking to control the governing apparatus by legal means'. (Downs is using 'men' in an old-fashioned sense here, and means 'people', not exclusively males.)

These definitions are a little too restrictive for our purposes, since Sartori and Downs were primarily interested in democracies. We'll want to discuss the role of political parties in authoritarian states, including one-party states that don't organize elections at all and hybrid regimes in which the elections are rigged. But Sartori's and Downs's crisp definitions get to the heart of the matter: political parties seek to control the state. There are many organizations that try to influence public policies indirectly—with methods such as lobbying, propaganda, and protests—but there is only one type of organization that seeks political power directly, and that is political parties.

11.2.2 The role of parties

Since the concept of political parties is associated with the idea that societies are divided into groups with different interests and ideals, many philosophers and political leaders before the twentieth century feared that parties would aggravate social conflicts. For example, James Madison, who was one of the authors of the famous political treatise *The Federalist Papers* and later became the fourth president of the United States, was very concerned about what he called 'factions', which he defined as 'citizens . . . who are united and actuated by some common impulse of passion, or of interest, adverse to the rights of other citizens, or to the permanent and aggregate interests of the community'. According to Madison, factions pose a grave threat to representative democratic institutions: 'The friend of popular governments never finds himself so much alarmed for their character and fate, as when he contemplates their propensity to this dangerous vice', Madison wrote (Federalist 10, Hamilton, Madison, and Jay 2003 [1787–1788]).

That's not how most of us think of parties today. Indeed, contemporary scholarship on representative democracies suggests that parties perform several important functions in modern democracies (see, for example, Rosenblum 2008, Kölln 2015, and Rosenbluth and Shapiro 2018):

1. They recruit candidates for high office.
2. They offer the voters clear alternatives on election day by presenting contrasting policy platforms.
3. They help make politics more predictable and politicians more accountable.
4. More generally, they channel conflicts in society so they can be worked out within the political system.

Many national constitutions recognize that political parties contribute to making democracy work. For example, the French constitution, which was adopted in 1958, states that 'parties and groups shall contribute to the exercise of suffrage' and 'shall be formed and carry on their activities freely'. It also guarantees 'the equitable participation of political parties and groups in the democratic life of the Nation'. Germany's constitution declares, similarly, that political parties 'shall participate in the formation of the political will of the people'. But the German Basic Law of 1949 also treats parties with some caution, since a political party, the National Socialists, became powerful enough in the 1930s to disregard and destroy Germany's first democratic constitution, the Weimar Republic, bringing an end to democracy. The current German constitution therefore states that the internal organization of political parties 'must conform to democratic principles' and authorizes the Federal Constitutional Court to ban political parties that 'seek to undermine or abolish the free democratic basic order'. A third, more recent example is the constitution of South Africa, which was adopted in the 1990s, a few years after the end of the racist apartheid system and the enfranchisement of the Black population. In South Africa's constitution, the words 'party' and 'parties' appear 142 times. Many of those provisions concern the representation of minority parties in various committees and other political bodies, guaranteeing them a voice in the political system even if they are not in the majority.

In authoritarian regimes, political parties perform very different functions than in democracies. As we saw in Case Study 5.1, the Communist Party of China effectively controls the Chinese political system. Interestingly, the text of China's constitution says absolutely nothing about political parties. But its preamble—its introduction—does. It describes the role that the Communist Party has played for the success of China's 'socialist cause' and goes on to explain that the Communist Party of China leads 'a broad patriotic united front which is composed of the democratic parties and people's organizations and which embraces all socialist working people, all builders of socialism, all patriots who support socialism, and all patriots who stand for the reunification of the motherland'. It also predicts that the 'multi-party cooperation and political consultation led by the Communist Party of China will exist and develop for a long time to come'. This language is typical of a one-party state. There may be different 'parties and people's organizations', but they're all led by the ruling party under the banner of national unity.

The key thing to understand about political parties in modern representative democracies is that they're active both inside the central institutions of the state, such as the legislature and the executive, and in wider society. In the legislature and the executive, they engage with other parties and with the public officials who carry out the government's policies. In wider society, they engage with members, activists, voters, interest groups, and voluntary associations. Because of this dual role, parties are able to mediate between the state and society, representing the interests and opinions of different social groups within the political system. Scholars sometimes use the term linkage to describe this mediating role of political parties in a democratic political system (Dalton, Farrell, and McAllister 2011). For a stylized graphical description of the role of parties in representative democracies, see Figure 11.1. As we'll discuss in Section 11.3, the dual role of political parties is also reflected in their organizational structures: most parties exist as organizations both within the legislature and in civil society alongside other associations and groups.

When new parties emerge, they often form outside formal political institutions and then work their way inside them, unless they formed as the result of a splinter or merger of existing parties. To learn more about how the largest political party in the world today—Bharatiya Janata Party in India—won a majority in the lower house of India's parliament, the Lok Sabha, see Case Study 11.1.

Figure 11.1 In democracies, political parties mediate between the state and society by linking citizens to the governing apparatus of the state. *Source: Author's own work*

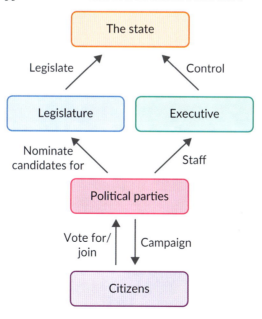

CASE STUDY 11.1
BJP, the world's largest political party

Bharatiya Janata Party—the Indian People's Party, commonly known as BJP—is the world's largest political party in terms of members (see Figure 11.2). For many decades after India became independent from the United Kingdom in the late 1940s, Indian politics was dominated by the left-of-centre Congress Party, but in the twenty-first century, BJP became India's largest party, and its leader Narendra Modi became prime minister in 2014.

BJP's path to power is an example of how a party that emerged from a social movement developed into a dominant political force. As we'll discuss in Section 11.4, BJP also exemplifies one of the main ideological tendencies of our time: right-wing populism. It is a nationalist political ideology that combines an appeal to conservatives with economic and social policies that appeal to middle-income voters. BJP's form of nationalism is known as Hindu nationalism, or Hindutva in Sanskrit and Hindi.

BJP emerged from Hindu nationalist movements that go back to the 1920s, such as the paramilitary organization Rashtriya Swayamsevak Sangh (RSS, the National Volunteers Organisation), which promotes a political identity based on Hinduism and which still exists today (Palshikar 2015; Manjari 2019). In 1951, the RSS evolved into the political party Bharatiya Jana Sangh, which in the 1970s became the main party in a coalition that was formed in opposition to the then-dominant Congress Party. This coalition—the Janata Coalition—won the elections of 1977. When it lost power again in 1980, Bharatiya Jana Sangh reorganized and got its current name, BJP. As

Figure 11.2 BJP supporters flying the party's flag during an election rally. *Source: Talukdar David / Shutterstock*

it grew stronger in the 1980s and 1990s, especially in Hindi-speaking parts of the country, BJP developed into India's main opposition party. In 2014, it won a majority in the lower house of India's parliament, the Lok Sabha, despite winning only 31 per cent of the vote (a result of India's majoritarian electoral system—see Chapter 7). In the following years, BJP also won power in 21 of India's 28 states, including the largest state, Uttar Pradesh.

Like other successful populist parties, BJP has managed to bring together groups that were previously on opposite sides in politics, including both secular Indians, religious Hindus, and Hindu nationalists. It also combines political appeals to low-income voters with appeals to conservatives, and it has broadened its base by becoming the 'principal carrier of conservatism in India' (Chhibber and Verma 2018, 234). Meanwhile, Narendra Modi is a popular politician who has used both mainstream and social media effectively to promote his party's message.

Religion is one of the main dividing lines in Indian politics, with the Congress Party representing secularism and BJP representing Hindu nationalism. BJP opposes secular conceptions of Indian national identity. The second-largest religion in India is Islam, and over the years, BJP has engaged in divisive political conflicts over religious sites, such as the sixteenth-century mosque in Ayodhya in Uttar Pradesh. In 1992, a Hindu nationalist mob destroyed the mosque, and this event was followed by riots that killed thousands.

When Narendra Modi first won the premiership in 2014, he emphasized economic issues such as economic development and jobs. In the party's next election campaign, however, Hindu nationalism was a dominant theme. BJP's programme emphasized populism, national security, and ethnic and religious issues (Jaffrelot and Verniers 2020, 161). After the election, BJP introduced legislation that denied India's Muslims equal citizenship (Ganguly 2020, 123). The Citizenship Amendment Act, adopted in 2019, expedited the conferral of citizenship on Buddhists, Christians, Jains, Hindus, Parsis and Sikhs—but excluded Muslims. Meanwhile, the government has 'flagrantly and callously disregarded the actions of Hindu vigilante groups' (Ganguly 2020, 124). In 2019, the BJP government removed the special status of the state Jammu and Kashmir, a contested Muslim-majority region bordering on Pakistan that had until then enjoyed a lot of autonomy.

11.2.3 Party strategies

So far in this section, we have discussed what sets political parties apart from other organizations and what roles parties perform in democratic systems. What intrigues scholars of comparative politics the most about political parties, however, is how varied they are, with respect to their political strategies, which we'll discuss in this section, with respect to their organizations, which we'll discuss in Section 11.3, and with respect to their ideologies and the groups that support them, which we'll discuss in Section 11.4.

Political parties have many different goals. By definition, parties put up candidates for public office, so they typically want to do well in elections, win seats in the legislature, and influence, participate in, or even form the government. But that's not all they want. Most parties also have particular policies they want to pursue—policies that they're associated with for historical reasons and that their members and activists care deeply about. All the while, parties need to take into account what other parties are up to, since elections, legislative bargaining, and governing force parties to act strategically with regard to both their opponents and their allies.

In an attempt to categorize the various goals that political parties pursue, Müller and Strøm (1999) have argued that parties balance three principal goals: **policy** (implementing the policies the party prefers), **office** (getting into government), and **votes** (doing well in elections). Note that getting many votes doesn't necessarily improve a party's chances of winning office. In multi-party systems, parties can only win office by collaborating with other parties, and winning many votes doesn't always mean that others will seek collaboration. Indeed, it can, in some circumstances, have the opposite effect.

It's often impossible for a party to achieve all these goals fully at the same time. For example, the policies a party's members and activists want may not be the policies pivotal voters want. Moreover, in countries with proportional elections and multi-party systems, votes don't necessarily improve a party's chances of winning office, and getting the party's policies through parliament typically requires compromises with others. So parties need to prioritize. Scholars of political parties have long sought to understand how different types of party have prioritized between different goals across countries and over time.

One key finding in the scholarly literature is that some parties tend to prioritize particular issues, such as immigration, the environment, or regional autonomy, whereas other parties have broader policy platforms and tend to care more about winning elections and forming governments. Meguid (2005) calls the first type of parties 'niche' parties, since they carve out a particular niche for themselves, and the second type of parties 'mainstream' parties. Niche parties have become more common over time, although some of them have later evolved into larger mainstream parties, as we'll discuss in Case Study 11.2, which is concerned with the German Greens.

Another important idea to keep in mind is the distinction between **programmatic** and **clientelistic** political parties. Programmatic and clientelistic politics are the two methods parties use when they appeal to their voters and supporters. Whereas programmatic parties compete by presenting the voters with coherent policy platforms, clientelistic parties compete by offering particular groups of voters material benefits in return for their votes (Stokes et al. 2013). Clientelistic politics is more common in countries with many low-income voters, since those voters often lack the economic and educational resources that are required to follow politics at the national level. But there are important elements of clientelism among parties in countries with higher incomes as well, just as there are important elements of programmatic policies among parties in countries with lower average incomes. Figure 11.3 uses data from the V-Dem project to describe the types of 'linkage'—clientelistic or programmatic—in different countries around the world in the early 2020s. We'll come back to the problem of clientelism in Chapter 15.

A third way to make sense of the differences between political parties is to study their organizational structures (Panebianco 1988). We'll discuss party organizations in Section 11.3. A fourth way to categorize parties is to examine their ideological orientations and the groups that support them. We'll discuss the differences between the main party families in the world in Section 11.4.

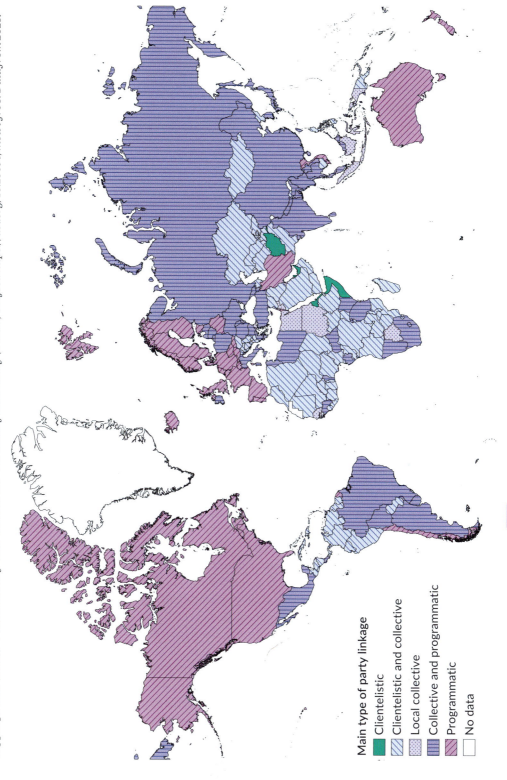

Figure 11.3 The types of linkage between parties and voters vary greatly across the world. 'Clientelistic' means that voters are rewarded with goods, cash, or jobs. 'Local collective' means that voters are rewarded with local collective goods such as wells, roads, and bridges. 'Programmatic' means that voters are mainly concerned about their party's positions on national policies and visions for society. *Source: Author's own work, based on data from Coppedge et al. (2024), "V-Dem Country–Year Dataset v14" Varieties of Democracy (V-Dem) Project. https://doi.org/10.23696/mcwt-fr58. Data from 2023.*

11.3 HOW PARTIES ARE ORGANIZED

LEARNING OUTCOMES

After reading Section 11.3, you'll be able to:
- Describe the history of modern political parties
- Distinguish between the main forms of party organization.

11.3.1 The origins of parties

As we discussed in Section 11.2, political parties have a dual role: they work within the central institutions of the state, such as the legislature and the executive, but they are also civil society organizations. It is this dual role that enables parties to mediate between the state and society. In Case Study 11.1, we learned about a party that emerged from civil society organizations—Bharatiya Janata Party in India. Those civil society organizations formed a party that entered parliament many years later; it now controls 240 of the 543 seats in the Lok Sabha, the lower house of India's parliament. In Case Study 11.2 in this section, we'll learn about another, very different party that also grew out of civil society organizations: Germany's Greens.

But there are many parties that did not begin as civil society organizations. In Europe and the Americas, modern political parties emerged within legislatures in the eighteenth and nineteenth centuries, as groups of like-minded legislators began to coordinate their work to increase their combined power and influence. These groups evolved into more permanent organizations within legislative assemblies, developed rules and procedures of their own, and set criteria for membership. Eventually they grew into reasonably stable associations that became associated with ideological labels that voters could recognize. The first party systems in western Europe and the Americas in the nineteenth century were almost always structured around a liberal party on the left and a conservative party on the right. Since few people could vote back then, all parties represented relatively privileged, wealthy groups.

New parties that were founded outside parliaments emerged in Europe towards the end of the nineteenth century. Most of them were left-wing, socialist parties that represented citizens who didn't yet have the right to vote—industrial workers in towns and cities and agricultural workers in rural areas. But some of the new parties were religious and had formed because of divisive conflicts between the state and the church. The new parties that emerged around the beginning of the twentieth century had a very different sort of organization from liberal and conservative parties. Being founded outside elite political institutions, they were first and foremost mass-based civil society organizations. The French political scientist Maurice Duverger argued in his book *Political Parties* (1951) that since the socialist parties were so successful in the early twentieth century, liberal and conservative parties had to develop broad-based membership organizations of their own to keep up. When the working class won the right to vote as a result of major suffrage reforms in the early twentieth century, the socialist parties became integrated into countries' political systems and had to adapt their organizations to their new status as major players within the political system. From then on, most of the major parties in the American and European democracies have existed both within legislatures and as civil society organizations. The main exceptions are modern, personalist parties that are dominated by their leaders. For example, the Dutch party VVD has only one member, the party leader Geert Wilders.

In many countries that became independent from European colonial powers during the twentieth century, one or more of the principal political parties emerged from the anti-colonial movements that worked towards independence and the creation of a new state. One example is the dominant party in Zimbabwe, ZANU-PF, which we discussed in Case Study 9.1 in Chapter 9. Other prominent examples are the dominant party in Algeria, FLN (*Front de libération nationale*, or National Liberation Front) and the dominant party in India before the rise of BJP, the Indian National Congress (on the role of the Congress Party in India's process of state building and democratization since independence, see Tudor (2013)). A related example is the dominant party in South Africa, the ANC (the African National Congress), although the ANC did not work towards independence but the abolition of the racist apartheid system in South Africa. The three biggest political parties in Ireland—Fianna Fáil, Sinn Féin, and Fine Gael—also trace their origins to the Irish independence movement and the Irish Civil War in the 1920s.

11.3.2 Party organizations

The dual role of parties is normally reflected in their organizations. Most parties have a parliamentary office that coordinates the party's legislative activities and that is separate from the central party office, which runs election campaigns and develops the party's long-term policies. In addition to the central party office, which is typically located in the country's capital, most political parties also have a territorial organization that mirrors the territorial organization of the country, with regional branches in larger cities and provinces, and local branches in towns and municipalities.

But party organizations also vary greatly over time, between countries, and between different types of party.

1. In some parties, party members have a say in how the party is run and in setting its political priorities; in other parties, party leaders effectively control the party organization. In other words, some parties are more **internally democratic** than others. On average, ordinary party members have more of a say in high-income countries with high levels of social trust. Smaller parties are typically more internally democratic than larger parties (Bolin et al. 2017).

2. Political parties are **financed** from different types of source, including members' fees, donations from corporations and interest organizations, and public funding. Party funding varies systematically across countries and across different types of party. Costa Lobo and Razzuoli (2017) demonstrate empirically that voters in countries with more public funding for parties perceive the parties as more responsive to their wishes, presumably because the voters are less concerned that parties follow the wishes of donors and lobby groups.

3. Partly as a consequence of these differences in party democracy and party finances, political parties have access to different sorts of **organizational resources**. For example, some parties have a large staff of professional policy analysts and communication specialists, while others don't. As we'll discuss in Chapter 14, changes in the media environment have put pressure on parties to reform their organizations. So has intensified cooperation within international organizations such as the European Union (see Chapter 6).

To study these sorts of differences between countries, over time, and between types of party in more detail, turn to Research Prompt 11.1.

> **RESEARCH PROMPT 11.1**
> Understanding party organizations
>
> Political parties can be structured very differently. The online Political Party Database (www.politicalpartydb.org) provides up-to-date information about the organizations of political parties in more than 50 democratic states, including examples from all continents. The data were compiled for Webb, Poguntke, and Scarrow (2017), a recent comparative study of party organizations.
>
> One of the resources you can find in the Political Party Database is an archive of party statutes—that is, the rules that govern the inner workings of political parties. Choose two of the countries in the database (keeping in mind that you need to understand their languages) and then choose two parties in each country, one older and one younger. Study the statutory rules concerning the relationship between the party leader, the central party organization, and the party congress, which is usually where the members have a chance to push for changes in party policy. Do you observe any differences in rules that lead you to assess that some parties are more democratic than others? Are there differences between the two countries you picked? And are younger parties more democratic than older parties or vice versa?

11.4 PARTY FAMILIES

LEARNING OUTCOMES

After reading Section 11.4, you'll be able to:
- Compare the main party families around the world
- Examine the relationship between political parties and the social groups they represent.

11.4.1 From left to right

So far in this chapter, we have defined political parties, examined the roles parties play in different political systems, explained how parties are organized, and compared the strength of parties across countries. In this section, we'll discuss some of the most important families of parties. Those families are defined by their ideological orientations—that is, what sorts of goals they strive for and what policies they have in mind for reaching those goals—and by the composition of the social groups that have historically supported them.

Mapping families of parties worldwide is no easy task, for scholarship on parties has evolved on a regional basis, and there is no common conceptual framework that can be used to categorize parties across regions. Scholars of Latin American politics have developed detailed analyses of parties in Latin America, scholars of European politics have developed detailed analyses of parties in Europe, and so on. In fact, there are important differences *within* the main world regions that scholars of comparative politics have only just begun to understand. For example, among eastern European states, the conflict between groups seeking a closer association with the European Union and groups opposing this westward orientation has often overshadowed other political conflicts—most dramatically in Ukraine in the 2010s, the period that led up to the full-scale war between Ukraine and Russia that began in 2022.

That said, there is one ideological dimension in politics that exists in most parts of the world: the left–right dimension, which in the twentieth century became an economic dimension that involved issues related to redistribution and the role of the state in the economy. The use of the terms 'left' and 'right' to describe basic political orientations goes back to the French Revolution (1789–1799). When the French legislature met during the revolutionary period, its most radical members sat on the left. That's why we associate the word 'left' with radicalism. At that time, being left wing meant opposing the church and the monarchy, whereas being right wing meant defending those institutions. Beginning in the late nineteenth century, the terms 'left' and 'right' began to take on different meanings, since political conflicts were increasingly concerned with the economy rather than the cultural and constitutional issues that had mattered most in the past.

In the parts of the world where the economic left–right dimension structures party competition, the largest parties on the left are typically centre-left social democratic parties. To the left, they often have more radical left wing parties (which are in many cases successor parties to communist parties that split from the social democrats after the Russian Revolution in 1917). Left-wing parties are defined primarily by their economic programmes. Representing lower-income and middle-income working-class voters, they typically want to redistribute wealth from the rich to the poor, and they want a large welfare state paid for by taxes. In economically prosperous regions such as western Europe, social democratic parties have in recent decades begun to attract wealthier middle-class voters, and they are no longer as closely associated with the working class as they once were (Gingrich and Häusermann 2015).

In the middle of the left–right scale, we find centrist liberal and socially conservative parties. Liberal parties are one of the oldest party families. Historically, they represented business owners and professionals such as doctors and lawyers, whereas conservative parties represented landowners and the aristocracy. Towards the end of the nineteenth century, liberal parties embraced democracy and sought to build support among a broader middle-class electorate. Ideologically centrist parties have allied sometimes with the left and sometimes with the right. Many populist radical-right parties, which we'll discuss later, are also centrist—or at least ambivalent—on economic issues, as are green parties, though they tend to be further left.

Furthest right on economic issues we find conservative and right-wing liberal parties. Right-wing parties are usually backed by business interests and high-income earners and tend to favour low taxes and oppose economic redistribution. Figure 11.4 describes the proportion of heads of government that have been centre-left, centrist, and right-wing on economic issues in a sample of approximately 30 countries in Europe, the Americas, and the Asia-Pacific region between 1870 and the early 2010s.

We learn at least three important things from this figure.

1. Right-wing parties have been remarkably successful—at least when it comes to reaching the highest pinnacles of power—throughout the period under study.

2. Centrist, especially liberal, parties were the main challengers to conservative, right-wing parties in the nineteenth century and at the beginning of the twentieth, but in the inter-war period and after the Second World War, social democratic, left-wing parties became the main challengers.

3. The fortunes of left-wing, centrist, and right-wing parties have fluctuated over time. Since the data that are used in the figure concern the ideological orientation of the head of government, this pattern depends on both changing electoral behaviour (Chapter 12) and changing patterns of government formation (Chapter 8).

Figure 11.4 The political power of left, centre, and right parties has fluctuated over the years. *Source: Author's own work based on data from Brambor, Thomas, Johannes Lindvall, Ann-Ida Gyllenspetz, and Annika Stjernquist. 2024. 'The Ideology of Heads of Government, 1870–2023'. Version 2.0. Department of Political Science, University of Gothenburg.*

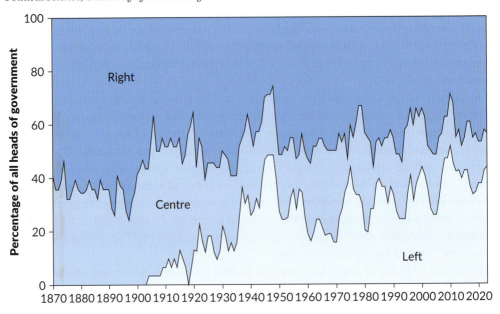

11.4.2 Religion, regions, and the environment

It is often convenient to sort political parties from left to right, especially when we analyse politics in the Americas, western Europe, and the Asia-Pacific region, where economic left–right conflicts have long structured the competition between the main political groups. But there are many other types of conflict that structure party competition—both in these three regions and elsewhere.

One group of parties that is hard to place on the economic left–right scale are religious parties, which include Christian democratic parties in Europe and Latin America and Muslim parties such as Türkiye's ruling party, AKP, in the Middle East (see Figure 11.5). In several continental European countries, including the largest western European country, Germany, the Christian democrats have long been the dominant party on the centre-right and the right. Europe's Christian democratic parties are successors to confessional parties and movements in the nineteenth century that sought to protect the church from the secular reforms that were favoured by the liberal parties of that era (Kalyvas 1996). Only later did they orient themselves to the right in economic terms.

In many countries, politics is defined not only by conflicts between economic and religious groups, but also by conflicts between regions. Regional parties are sometimes on the left and sometimes on the right; what they have in common is their support for regional autonomy and perhaps even independence. Two examples of left-wing regional parties are the Scottish National Party in the United Kingdom and Bloc Québécois in the French-speaking parts of Canada. The Lega Nord, in Italy, is an example of a right-wing regional party: formed in 1989, it seeks autonomy and independence for the northern part of Italy. In many countries, regional parties have grown in number and importance in recent decades.

Figure 11.5 AKP in Türkiye is an example of a religious party. *Source: Alexandros Michailidis / Shutterstock*

Green parties are another fast-growing family of parties. They have formed not because of conflicts of interest between social classes, religious groups, or regions, but because of the rise of the environmental movement towards the end of the twentieth century. The first green party that entered a national parliament was the German Green Party. Although the defining characteristic of green parties is their concern for the environment, they have increasingly come to represent particular social and economic groups, notably educated voters who live in cities and work in the service sector. You can read more about the German Green Party in Case Study 11.2.

CASE STUDY 11.2
Germany's Green Party

Germany's Green Party, *Die Grünen*, was founded in 1980. It grew out of a network of environmental organizations. In the parliamentary elections in 1983, the Greens won 5.6 per cent of the vote and gained 28 seats in the German parliament, the Bundestag. This was a big surprise, since Germany was widely regarded as having one of western Europe's most stable party systems. In 1987, the Greens increased their vote share to 8.3 per cent, and they hovered between 7.3 and 10.7 per cent during the 1990s, 2000s, and 2010s, after merging with their two eastern German sister parties in the years following German unification in 1990. In 1998, the Greens joined a coalition government led by the Social Democrats.

In the parliamentary election in 2021, the Greens increased their vote share to almost 15 per cent (see Figure 11.6). In the years leading up to that election, the opinion polls even had the Greens as Germany's second-largest party, but the Social Democrats rallied in the election campaign and overtook both the Greens and the Christian democratic CDU/CSU.

→ The history of Germany's Green Party is thus one of remarkable success. Over a period of four decades, the Greens have established themselves as one of the strongest parties in the country. They have also been politically successful in that many of their signature policies have been adopted by the other German parties. For example, Germany is phasing out nuclear power, which was a key item on the Green Party's political agenda.

But the electoral and political success of the Greens has come with internal strife. The party was long divided between a more radical wing, commonly known as the Fundamentalists (or *Fundis*), and a more moderate wing, known as the Realists (*Realos*). The conflict between these two factions concerned important matters of policy, with the *Fundis* being more deeply committed to the ecologism and pacifism of the civil society organizations from which the party emerged. But the conflict also concerned the party's organization and strategy. The Fundamentalists were committed to principles of participatory, grassroots democracy, which complicated cooperation with other parties.

Over time, the Realists marginalized the Fundamentalists, especially between 1998 and 2005, when the Greens governed Germany together with the Social Democrats. The party's organization is now more similar to that of other parties, and it has moderated its political programme to become a more viable coalition partner and to appeal to new groups of voters among Germany's middle class. In the contemporary German party system, the Greens are supported by many moderate voters who dislike the two previously dominant parties—the Social Democrats and the Christian Democrats—and who believe the other small parties are either too far to the left (The Left, *Die Linke*) or too far to the right (the increasingly market-liberal Free Democratic Party and the radical-right populist Alternative for Germany, *Alternative für Deutschland*).

Figure 11.6 The German Green Party's election results since 1980. *Source: Author's own work, based on data from the Parlgov project (https://parlgov.org/); Döring, Holger, Alexandra Quaas, Maike Hesse, and Philip Manow. 2023. Parliaments and Governments Database (ParlGov): Information on Parties, Elections and Cabinets in Established Democracies. Development Version.*

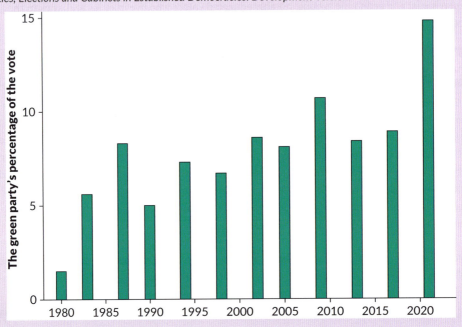

11.4.3 The rise of populism

The fastest-growing party family in the world today consists of what are known as populist radical-right parties. 'Populism' is a term with many different meanings in contemporary scholarship. It can refer to parties with a certain style of political communication and messaging, to parties that see themselves as challengers to the established parties in a political system, and to a set of policy priorities. But the term 'populism' itself is most closely associated with the claim that the most important conflict in society is between the people and an unprincipled, feckless, and corrupt political establishment. This is what sets populists apart from other parties. As we have discussed throughout this section, most political parties represent the views of particular groups in society, which are defined by economic interests, religion, language, or values. Populists claim they're different and say they represent the people—the true people—against political elites.

When it comes to the content of their policies, most populist radical-right parties run on a platform of nationalism, conservative social values, and centrist economic policies, arguing that nations are under threat from immigration, internationalization, and the decline of traditional values.

There are both left-wing and right-wing versions of populism, but in recent years the most successful populists in the world have been nationalist right-wing politicians such as Narendra Modi, India's prime minister since 2014 (see Case Study 11.1); Rodrigo Duterte, the president of the Philippines between 2016 and 2022; and Donald Trump, who was president of the United States between 2017 and 2021, and won the presidency again in 2024. Across Europe, anti-immigrant, right-wing populist parties have grown since the 1980s, and populist parties have either participated in governments or been included in the support coalitions of governments in most European states.

In many countries, the rise of populist parties and politicians from the 1980s and 1990s took established parties by surprise, since populism had not been a significant political force in living memory. But it shouldn't have come as a surprise, for populism has existed at least since the late nineteenth century. As Case Study 11.3 shows, populism has come and gone in different parts of the world throughout the history of modern representative democracy.

CASE STUDY 11.3
Populism then and now

Consider the following story. A famous man without much previous political experience quickly becomes one of his country's most popular politicians. His political ideas used to be vague and ambiguous, but now he's running for office with a populist and nationalist programme. Among his many supporters are both traditionally conservative voters and blue-collar workers who used to vote for a different party. His message is simple: 'I stand with the people against the hypocritical and corrupt establishment!' 'I'll create jobs!' 'I will restore our country's greatness!'

You may be guessing that this is a summary of the career of Donald Trump, who was president of the United States between 2017 and 2021, and won the presidency again in 2024. It could have been—everything fits—but it's also the story of the French general and politician Georges Boulanger (1837–1891), who almost won power in France in 1889.

Just like Trump, Boulanger mobilized both ideological conservatives and parts of the blue-collar working class, and Trump's election campaign in the United States in 2016 sounded like an echo of Boulanger's campaigns in France in the 1880s. 'Boulanger will defend you against foreign competition', said the 1888 programme of the Boulangist party. That sort of economic protectionism was an important theme in Donald Trump's campaign as well: 'We must protect our borders from the ravages of other countries making our products, stealing our companies and destroying our jobs', Donald Trump said in his 2017 inaugural address. Boulanger promised to rid France from what he called 'parasites'—by which he meant corrupt, established politicians who had betrayed the people—and he described himself as a champion of honesty and integrity. Nearly 130 years later, Trump called his opponent Hillary Clinton 'Crooked Hillary' and exclaimed 'Drain the Swamp!', promising that he would clean up Washington. Boulanger promised to restore France's glory after the humiliating loss to Germany in the Franco-Prussian War in the early 1870s, and he declared that 'everyone should once again be able to say with pride: I am French!' Donald Trump's main campaign slogan was 'Make America Great Again!' In 2024, Trump again ran on the slogan 'Make America Great Again' and won the presidency for a second time.

So populism isn't new. It has a long history—and not only in North America and Europe. Populism has been a major political force in Latin America ever since the Great Depression in the 1930s. A first wave of left-wing populism in Latin America around the Second World War was associated with leaders such as the Argentinian politician Juan Perón (president 1946–1955 and 1973–1974). It was followed by a right-wing populist wave in the 1980s and then by another left-wing populist wave in the 2000s (De la Torre 2017).

To study the ideological orientations of different parties in more detail, turn to Research Prompt 11.2.

RESEARCH PROMPT 11.2
Party programmes

Political parties typically adopt party platforms and manifestos that explain their views and present the policies they plan to adopt if they come to power. When scholars of comparative politics study political parties, they often consult these platforms and manifestos to learn about differences and similarities among parties in different countries. A major research project called the Comparative Manifestos Project—or, MARPOR, for Manifesto Research on Political Representation—has compiled party manifestos from numerous countries.

1. Go to the website of the Comparative Manifestos Project and register an account so you can access the materials (this is free). Choose a country whose language you can read, and read the introduction to the most recent manifestos from the two largest parties in the country you've selected. Do the two parties present themselves in a way that reminds you of the description of different party families you've just read?

2. Now compare parties that are from different countries but belong to the same party family. What differences do you see? How would you explain those differences?

11.5 PARTY SYSTEMS

LEARNING OUTCOMES

After reading Section 11.5, you'll be able to:
- Recognize different types of party system
- Understand why the party system is more than the sum of its parts
- Explain why party systems vary across countries.

To understand party politics, it isn't enough to learn what political parties are, how they're organized, what they want to accomplish, and which groups in society they represent. We also need to consider how parties interact with each other. As we've already discussed, the word 'party' is related to the word 'part': a party is an organization that represents one part of society, with other parties representing other parts. It is important for us to understand how all those different parts fit together.

What individual parties do often depends on the other parties they're competing or cooperating with. For example, a centre-left party is likely to behave very differently if there is a more radical party on its left flank than if it only needs to worry about its competitors to the right. Similarly, a conservative or religious party is likely to behave differently if it has a more radical right-wing competitor than if it merely has to worry about the parties in the centre and on the left. We need to understand not only the individual parties but also the *party system*. By characterizing the party system, we can make predictions about what political competition and political decision making are going to be like in a country.

11.5.1 Categorizing party systems

The first thing to do when categorizing party systems is to count the number of parties.

- *Two-party system*: a system in which only two parties can compete effectively for power
- *Multi-party system*: a system in which there are more than two parties that can compete effectively for power.
- *One-party system*: a system with only one party.

One complication is that parties are sometimes so small that they don't really matter politically. For this reason, scholars don't simply count the actual number of parties. They instead try to take into account the relative sizes of the parties or their roles in the system. One method, advocated by scholars such as Sartori, is to count only those parties that might join a government or that won't join a government but are big enough to influence how the other parties govern. Another method is to use a mathematical formula to adjust the count by considering the relative sizes of the parties. One popular measure of this kind is the 'effective number of parties' (Laakso and Taagepera 1979). It's equal to the actual number of parties if the parties are of the same size, but smaller than the actual number of parties if they're not.

For an example of why it's important to dig deeper and not merely count the number of parties, consider the parliaments in Switzerland and the United Kingdom. In 2022, there were 11 parties in the National Council in Switzerland and 11 parties in the House of Commons in the United Kingdom (although the members of one party, Sinn Féin, chose not to be seated since they

Table 11.1 Parties in the British and Swiss parliaments in 2022

Switzerland	United Kingdom
The Centre	Alba Party
Evangelical People's Party	Alliance Party
FDP. The Liberals	Conservative Party
Federal Democratic Union	Democratic Unionist Party
Green Liberal Party	Green Party
Green Party	Labour Party
Social Democratic Party	Liberal Democrats
solidaritéS	Plaid Cymru
Swiss Party of Labour	Scottish National Party
Swiss People's Party	Sinn Féin
Ticino League	Social Democratic and Labour Party

don't recognize British sovereignty over Northern Ireland) (see Table 11.1). Judging from these numbers, it might appear as if the party systems in Switzerland and the United Kingdom are quite similar. But they could hardly be more different, and Figure 11.7 shows why.

The United Kingdom effectively has a two-party system, since there are two parties that are dominant across the country, the Labour Party on the left and the Conservatives on the right. The other parties are much smaller, so political competition in the United Kingdom is usually a matter of whether the Conservatives or the Labour Party will get a majority of the seats. There have been times when the Liberal Democrats have won enough votes to make a difference. For example, in the election of 2010, neither the Conservatives nor the Labour Party won a majority, which meant that the Conservatives had to turn to the Liberal Democrats and form a coalition government. But those are the exceptions: in most elections, due to the nature of the British electoral system, which we discussed in Chapter 7, one party does manage to win a majority of the seats.

Figure 11.7 In 2022, the British and Swiss parliaments had the same number of parties, but in the United Kingdom, one party controlled a majority of the seats. *Source: Based on Nick Mon / Wikimedia Commons*

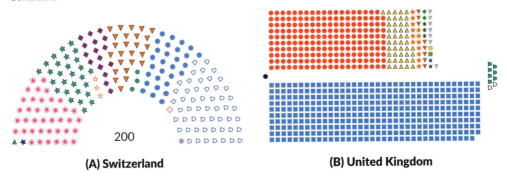

(A) Switzerland

(B) United Kingdom

In Switzerland, as in the United Kingdom, there are a few parties that are so small that they hardly matter politically. But as Figure 11.7 shows, there are several parties that are quite strong, including the right-wing populist Swiss People's Party, the Social Democrats, the Liberals, the Greens, and the center-right party Centre. Switzerland is a fragmented multi-party system, which means that no party is big enough to govern alone. In fact, as we mentioned in Chapter 8, Switzerland has a permanent coalition government that is made up of four of the parties in the parliament (the Centre, the Liberals, the Social Democrats, and the Swiss People's Party).

The number of parties, however you count it, isn't the only important characteristic of a party system. Another thing to consider is the range of political opinions that are represented.

- One way of measuring this range—going back to our discussion of party families in Section 11.4—is to consider which families of parties are represented in a country's party system.
- Another alternative is to develop a quantitative measure of ideological dispersion that says how far apart the party furthest to the left and the party furthest to the right are.
- A third alternative is to examine which ideological dimensions are relevant to consider when describing the main conflicts between the parties in the system.

11.5.2 The origins of party systems

As we discussed in Chapter 7, one of the main explanations for why countries have different party systems is the electoral system, which has both direct and indirect effects on the number of political parties that stand a chance of getting elected. As noted by Duverger in the 1950s, 'the simple-majority single-ballot system favours the two-party system', whereas 'proportional representation favours multi-partyism' (Duverger 1963, 239). Voters are reluctant to vote for parties that have no chance of winning, which hurts the chances of smaller parties in majoritarian systems with single-member districts. On average, there are therefore fewer parties in majoritarian systems than in proportional systems (Cox 1990).

But the electoral system is just one of several explanations for the fact that countries have such different party systems. The party system also depends on the structure of conflicts in society. Lipset and Rokkan (1967) showed that the party systems in western Europe were shaped by two great economic, social, and political revolutions that led to new conflicts in European societies (see Table 11.2). The two revolutions were the national revolution (the rise of nation states) and the industrial revolution (the transition from an agrarian to an industrial economy), and they generated four types of conflict. The national revolution resulted in centre–periphery conflicts between national capitals and more remote areas within each country as well as conflicts between the state and the church. The industrial revolution resulted in conflicts between rural (agrarian) and urban (industrial) areas and conflicts between business owners and workers. An in-depth explanation of

Table 11.2 The national and industrial revolutions shaped political conflicts in Europe

National revolution	Industrial revolution
Centre–periphery	Urban–rural
State–church	Business owners–workers

why countries have different party systems must take into account *both* the electoral rules and the structure of conflicts in society (Neto and Cox 1997).

Lipset and Rokkan's account applies mainly to western Europe, but in other world regions, there are other sorts of structural economic and social conflicts that explain the structure of party systems, notably conflicts between religious denominations and conflicts associated with the history of colonialism and decolonization.

The relationship between the electoral system and the party system isn't absolute. One of the reasons is that Duverger's Law—the idea that only the two largest parties are viable in a majoritarian system—holds mainly at the level of electoral districts, not in the country as a whole. This means that there may well be more than two parties in a country with majoritarian elections, as long as smaller parties are geographically concentrated. That's why the relatively small Northern Irish, Scottish, and Welsh parties in the United Kingdom are represented in parliament, even if the United Kingdom has a majoritarian electoral system, and that's why the regional Indian parties that we read about in Case Study 11.1 can get elected to India's parliament.

11.6 CONCLUSION

People have different economic interests, belong to different ethnic and linguistic groups, and follow different ideals. One of the key questions in politics is how all these differences and disagreements become expressed and how they are absorbed by the political system. In modern states, this depends crucially on political parties. That's why this chapter is devoted to political parties and to how the parties interact with each other in party systems. To understand modern politics, you need to understand how political parties work, what they do, and how they influence institutions, political competition, and policymaking.

Since political parties are a result of conflict—they emerge because societies consist of different groups with conflicting interests and ideals—many political philosophers and political leaders in the past saw parties as divisive and dangerous. And it's true: they can be. There are parties that have instigated political violence and incited civil strife. There are parties that have undermined and even destroyed the institutions that support constitutional, democratic regimes. But parties are also essential to modern representative government, since they offer voters clear alternatives on election day, vet candidates for high office, let voters hold politicians to account, and, more generally, help people make sense of politics. Perhaps future technological or social changes will one day render political parties obsolete. For now, though, modern politics is unthinkable without parties.

The next chapter is concerned with election campaigns and electoral behaviour. We won't leave the political parties behind, for parties are the first movers in modern elections, but now we'll study what happens when the parties meet the voters.

SUMMARY

- A party is an organization that tries to win seats in the legislature, control the government, or both.
- The first political parties emerged when legislators in parliaments began to cooperate with each other, but modern political parties are also a part of civil society.

- Most democratic constitutions recognize the important role of political parties.
- But most authoritarian states are also dominated by parties, especially hybrid regimes and one-party states.
- The structure of party organizations varies among parties and among countries.
- It's usually possible to sort political parties from left to right, but there are some parties, such as regional parties, that are more difficult to place.
- The party system is the way in which the political parties interact with each other.
- Party systems vary with respect to the number of parties and the range of political opinions within the system.

STUDY QUESTIONS

1. In the beginning of the chapter, we noted that political parties perform important functions in a democracy, such as recruiting candidates for high office and helping voters make informed choices between competing political alternatives. We also noted, however, that many political thinkers throughout history have viewed parties with suspicion, regarding them as potentially dangerous or divisive. Based on what you've learned in this chapter, do you think political parties today tend to strengthen or weaken democracy?

2. We have defined the party system as "the interactions among the parties within a political system." But is the party system more than the sum of its parts? In other words, is it enough to understand each individual party, or do we need to look at how the parties relate to each other to fully understand the system as a whole?

FURTHER READING

Catherine de Vries and Sara Hobolt, *Political Entrepreneurs: The Rise of Challenger Parties in Europe* (2020).
Studies how new parties in Europe have managed to challenge the older mainstream parties that once dominated political life on the continent.

Michael Freeden, Lyman Tower Sargent, and Marc Stears (eds.), *The Oxford Handbook of Political Ideologies* (2013).
Analyses the political ideologies that define modern parties.

Nancy Rosenblum, *On the Side of the Angels: An Appreciation of Political Parties* (2008).
Explains why political parties and partisanship are probably good for democracy.

Susan C. Stokes et al., *Brokers, Voters, and Clientelism* (2013).
Conducts an in-depth analysis of how clientelistic systems work.

CHAPTER 12

ELECTORAL BEHAVIOUR

CHAPTER GUIDE

12.1 Introduction
12.2 Studying Public Opinion
12.3 Why People Vote as They Do
12.4 Voter Turnout
12.5 The Structure of Public Opinion

12.6 Conclusion
Summary
Study Questions
Further Reading

12.1 INTRODUCTION

Until now, we have mainly studied politics at the elite level. We haven't paid close attention to how ordinary people form their political opinions, participate in politics, and decide for whom to vote. In this chapter, we'll study politics from the vantage point of ordinary citizens, not from the vantage point of political elites in legislatures, executives, courts, or government agencies. Section 12.2 discusses the methods scholars have used to study public opinion. Section 12.3 discusses how people form political opinions and decide which parties to support. Section 12.4 analyses differences in voter turnout across countries and over time. Finally, Section 12.5 studies how political opinions are distributed in the population and how the structure of public opinion influences important political outcomes.

Modern politics is mass politics. Before the modern period, politics and government were often reserved to a small elite of monarchs, noblemen, military officers, advisers, and clergy, with ordinary people having no influence in, and often no knowledge of, political affairs. One reason is that politics and government meant something very different 1,000, 500, or even 250 years ago, since the state and its institutions didn't reach very far into the lives of individuals, families, and local communities (Chapter 3). Things are different now. As we discussed in Chapter 1, the stakes are high in modern politics—politics can make the difference between life and death, or a good life and an extremely difficult one—and men and women around the world know this. Even in closed authoritarian states such as China, where the people don't have the same power to act on their political views as in a democracy, political leaders study public opinion carefully. In democracies, the power of the people to choose their leaders according to the policies they promise and deliver makes changes in public opinion very important. We will concentrate mainly on democratic regimes in this chapter.

As we observed in Chapter 11, political parties are both parts of the state (since they organize teams of politicians within central institutions such as the legislature and the executive) and parts of society (since they appeal to, mobilize, and represent groups of voters who have certain interests and values in common). In other words, when we moved from discussing legislatures, executives, courts, and government agencies in Chapters 8–10 to discussing parties in Chapter 11, we began to step outside the domain of formal political institutions and into the wider society around them. In this chapter, we venture further into society at large, and in the two chapters that follow, we'll keep doing so: in Chapter 13, we'll study the role of interest organizations and other forms of voluntary associations, and in Chapter 14, we'll learn about how old and new media influence political communication—that is, how people learn about politics and how political ideas are disseminated and spread.

12.2 STUDYING PUBLIC OPINION

LEARNING OUTCOMES

After reading Section 12.2, you'll be able to:
- Describe the methods scholars use to study public opinion and electoral behaviour
- Summarize the ecological-inference problem.

In democracies, who has power in the state ultimately depends on how people vote. Since the early days of modern democracy, political scholars have therefore developed methods that can be used to systematically analyse voting behaviour and the formation of political opinions.

The first empirical studies of public opinion and electoral behaviour relied on comparisons between different regions and localities. One early example is the French geographer André Siegfried's book *Tableau politique de la France de l'Ouest sous la Troisième République* (Political Table of Western France during the Third Republic), which examined geographical differences in voting in the French Third Republic (1870–1940), the first somewhat democratic regime in the history of France. Another early example is the Swedish political scientist Herbert Tingsten's book *Political Behaviour*, which used data on electoral outcomes in Swedish localities to study electoral behaviour during the first 15 years after *that* country's transition to democracy. One thing Tingsten paid close attention to was differences in voting behaviour between women and men, for in Sweden, unlike in France, women could vote in the 1920s and 1930s.

The main drawback of methods that rely on geographical differences in public opinion and electoral behaviour is that it's difficult to draw conclusions about the opinions and behaviour of *individuals* from comparisons between *places*. Let's say that both the rate of unemployment and the proportion of populist radical-right voters increase in a district. It seems natural to conclude that the unemployed are more likely to vote for the radical right, but it's entirely possible that support for the populist radical right has instead increased among voters who are *not* unemployed—as a result of the unemployment they see around them. (This is not a made-up example. Kurer (2020) shows that support for populist radical-right parties is strongest among workers who 'survive' in an occupation that is threatened by labour-market restructuring, not among those who actually lose their jobs.) Drawing conclusions about individuals from observations of groups is known as the **ecological-inference fallacy**.

Beginning in the inter-war period, and especially in the first decades after the Second World War, political scientists and sociologists who wanted to learn more about political opinions and electoral behaviour at the level of individuals instead began to rely on **surveys**—interview studies in which large samples of randomly selected voters are asked about their backgrounds, their political attitudes, and which parties they vote for. Starting in the 1950s, many countries have established recurring national elections studies. The first of these, the American National Election Studies, go back to the election of 1948. The national election studies have since been complemented by many other types of survey of political opinions and behaviours (Figure 12.1). Much of our knowledge of public opinion and electoral behaviour relies on evidence from these long series of data.

Even more recently, teams of scholars have created harmonized cross-country surveys such as the Europe-focused Eurobarometer (which goes back to 1973), the global World Values Survey (which goes back to 1981), the Latin-America-focused Latinobarómetro (which goes back to 1995), and the Africa-focused Afrobarometer (which goes back to 1999). These surveys enable students and scholars to conduct more systematic comparative research on public opinion and political behaviour across countries. We will examine some of those data in this chapter. Meanwhile, national election studies have begun to collaborate more closely with each other, which has enabled scholars to study public opinion and political behaviour in a comparative perspective, identifying similarities and differences among countries. For example, as we will see in Section 12.3, a long-standing concern among scholars of political behaviour has been to understand the relationship

Figure 12.1 Much of the political opinion data available to political scientists and sociologists comes from surveys of the public. This includes 'exit polls' outside polling stations, but the majority of the data comes from online, telephone, or postal surveys. *Source: Robert K. Chin / Alamy Stock Photo*

between social class and voting—that is, whether people in different social classes prefer different parties and vary in the extent to which they participate in politics. Advances in data-collection and research methodology have made it possible to compare the strength of this relationship across countries (see, for example, Evans 1999).

12.3 WHY PEOPLE VOTE AS THEY DO

LEARNING OUTCOMES

After reading Section 12.3, you'll be able to:
- Distinguish between different explanations of electoral behaviour
- Compare political behaviour across countries.

In Chapter 2, we discussed the main theoretical approaches in comparative politics, which we labelled rationalist, sociological, psychological, and institutional. Each type of theory has been used to explain how people form political opinions and decide for whom to vote.

12.3.1 Rationalist explanations

Rationalist explanations of electoral behaviour start from the assumption that when voters vote, they try to identify the party, or candidate, that will best represent their views, govern in their interests, or both.

In one version of the rationalist approach, elections provide an opportunity for political parties to present their ideas and for the voters to choose the party they like best. In this view, voters vote 'prospectively': they look to the future. A key example of this perspective is the spatial model of voting, which assumes that parties and voters can be positioned in an ideological space—along the left–right scale, for instance—allowing voters to choose the party closest to their own views. Empirical research on prospective voting examines how parties communicate their policies through programmes and election manifestos and how voters respond to them.

In another version of the rationalist approach to electoral behaviour, voters don't look forwards but backwards: they concentrate on what has happened since the last election and use their votes to punish the governing party if things have gone badly and reward it if things have gone well. This is known as the 'retrospective' model of voting. Most of the empirical literature on backward-looking, 'retrospective' voting is concerned with the relationship between electoral outcomes on the one hand and economic indicators such as growth, unemployment, and inflation on the other. The idea that governments lose votes in hard times is known as 'economic voting'. Scholars have consistently found an empirical relationship between economic downturns and voting against the government throughout the history of democracy and in many different parts of the world.

The retrospective-voting approach is associated with the 'accountability' model of representative democracy, which emphasizes that elections give voters a chance to hold politicians to account. The prospective-voting approach, on the other hand, is associated with the 'mandate' model, which emphasizes that elections give voters a chance to pick politicians they think will pursue good policies in the future (Przeworski, Stokes, and Manin 1999).

In Chapter 10, we discussed the usefulness of principal–agent models when analysing the relationship between politicians and public officials. In that context, politicians (the principals) delegate power to public officials (the agents), hoping that the officials will carry out their policies according to their wishes. Principal–agent models can be used to analyse the relationship between voters and politicians, too. In this context, the voters, not the politicians, are the principals. On election day, they hand over their power to the politicians, in the hope that they will adopt policies that are in the voters' interests. The accountability model and the mandate model present two different perspectives on this relationship.

12.3.2 Sociological explanations

Not all theories of voting assume, as rationalist theories do, that voters actively try to figure out which party will bring them the most benefits. Indeed, a lot of work on electoral behaviour is based on the very different idea that people's vote choices are best explained by sociological factors such as their jobs, their education, where they live, and where they grew up. In this view, people's political attitudes—including their attitudes to the political parties—are shaped by enduring loyalties and habits that come with their backgrounds, experiences, and positions in society. Class voting, which we discussed in Section 12.2, is often explained in this way, although it can also be explained with the help of other models, including rationalist ones.

Class is but one of several social categorizations that help to explain political behaviour. In recent years, many scholars have argued that education has become an increasingly important dividing line in society, noting that voters with and without a university education tend to have very different political outlooks. For example, support for Green parties is much higher among well-educated voters than among voters who have lower levels of education, but the opposite is true for right-wing populist parties (Ivarsflaten and Stubager 2012; Cavaille and Marshall 2019). It seems that attending university has a powerful socializing effect on people's political opinions (Stubager 2008). There are even those who argue that conflicts between educational groups have become comparable to the historical conflicts over class and religion that we learned about in Chapter 11 (Bovens and Wille 2017). Other scholars maintain that education matters mainly because of its connection to the labour market and people's incomes, which makes it difficult to distinguish between the effects of education, jobs, and economic inequality.

Sociological explanations can also help to account for why men and women vote differently, as we will discuss in Case Study 12.1.

CASE STUDY 12.1
The changing gender gap

One of the most important findings in comparative research on how people vote concerns the differences between women and men. In most countries, women used to be less likely than men to vote for parties on the left and more likely to vote for conservative parties. This pattern is known as the 'old gender gap'. One of the main explanations is that women have traditionally been more religious than men. Another explanation is that women didn't enter the labour market on a large scale until the end of the twentieth century.

More recently, however, a 'modern gender gap' has emerged. In most high-income countries with democratic institutions, women are today more likely to vote for parties on the left than men, and less likely to vote for right-wing parties, especially radical-right parties. There are several plausible explanations for the modern gender gap, including women's higher educational attainment and remaining wage disparities between employed women and men. In the United States, the modern gender gap emerged in the 1980s. Other democracies followed in the ensuing decades (Inglehart and Norris 2000). In the United Kingdom, it took much longer for women to move over to the left, but recent evidence suggests that a modern gender gap emerged in the United Kingdom after the 2000s (Campbell and Shorrocks 2023). These changes in political behaviour tell an interesting story about how economic changes and changing values combine to shape the way people vote.

Scholars have also begun to investigate gender gaps among low- and middle-income countries. We will consider some of the findings from this growing research agenda in this case study.

Blaydes and Linzer (2008) analyse women's support for fundamentalist Islam. The puzzle they're interested in is why Muslim women, and not only Muslim men, often support fundamentalist movements that romanticize the past and call for a return to traditionalist values and the re-establishment of men's power over women. The authors show that economic incentives play an important role. In systems where women lack economic opportunities in the labour market, women prioritize marriage as a source of financial stability. Adopting fundamentalist beliefs increases the likelihood of achieving financial stability through marriage, as these views make women more attractive as prospective partners. The findings of Blaydes and Linzer's study suggest that the political opinions of women in Muslim-majority countries are influenced by their situation in the labour market and by the relationships between women and men within families—which are the same factors that have influenced the changing gender gap in the Global North.

Moving to a different part of the world, Gottlieb, Grossman, and Robinson (2018) study 27 sub-Saharan African countries and ask if African men and women differ in their preferences over public policy. This study found that in most countries, by a small margin, women tended to prioritize poverty, water, and health to a greater extent than men. Men, on the other hand, tended to prioritize issues such as the economy, infrastructure, and agriculture. Overall, the gender gaps found in this study were statistically significant, but quite small: women were on average 2–3 percentage points more likely to prioritize water and health and 7 percentage points more likely to prioritize poverty, whereas men were on average 2 percentage points more likely to prioritize the economy, infrastructure, and agriculture. However, the authors also found that these gender gaps vary between and within countries, and the largest differences could be found in places where women enjoy little financial independence and social empowerment. Like the other findings we've discussed in this case study, Gottlieb, Grossman, and Robinson's results suggest that the political differences between women and men are not innate, but depend on the relationship between women and men in the labour market and how women and men form families.

12.3.3 Psychological explanations

Psychological theories emphasize traits, attitudes, and behaviours at the individual level rather than the joint behaviour of social groups, such as working-class and middle-class voters, women and men, and immigrants and natives (which are the sorts of distinctions that sociological theories tend to highlight).

One ongoing scholarly debate in comparative politics concerns the effects of underlying psychological traits, such as conscientiousness and openness, on people's political behaviour. Another contemporary debate concerns the effects of emotions such as anger, resentment, and fear on political attitudes, party choices, and political behaviour. Young (2019) reports the result of an experiment in Zimbabwe, in which opposition supporters were asked to participate in an exercise that induced mild fear. The results suggest that people who experience fear are less likely to voice their dissent in an authoritarian regime. (We studied the history of opposition movements in Zimbabwe in Case Study 9.1 in Chapter 9.)

Although the different types of explanation we've discussed so far rely on different theories of why people think and vote as they do, they're not mutually exclusive—it's quite possible for all of the factors we've discussed in this section to have an effect on people's opinions and vote choices. Moreover, it's often difficult in practice to distinguish between different explanations. For example, does education influence people's vote choices because of how it shapes their outlooks, opportunities, and attitudes in the long run, which is something sociological theories can explain? Or does it cause people to vote as they do because people with jobs that require different types of education have different political interests, which is something that rationalist theories can account for? Or does education perhaps change the way people process information and regulate their emotions, which is something psychological theories can help us understand? In many contexts, it is difficult to separate these different effects.

12.3.4 Institutions and comparative political behaviour

Political institutions help to explain why public opinion and electoral behaviour vary so much between countries.

The theories of prospective voting that we discussed in the section on rationalist approaches to electoral behaviour propose that political parties adopt electoral platforms outlining the policies they would like to implement. Voters then choose among the platforms on offer, and the party or parties that win the election enact the policies they promised. Comparative research has shown that political parties are more likely to keep their promises in countries with single-party governments than in countries with coalition governments (Thomson et al. 2017). Moreover, where parties must form coalitions to govern, voters take this into account when casting their votes. For example, Kedar (2005) has shown that voters sometimes choose more extreme parties over moderate alternatives, since they anticipate that their policies will be diluted through political bargaining after the election.

Institutions matter for retrospective voting too. Scholars have long observed that the relationship between economic downturns and voting against the government is significantly stronger in some countries than others. One theory that explains this pattern is that it's easier for voters to punish governments that perform badly when there is greater 'clarity of responsibility' in the political system (Powell and Whitten 1993). This means that economic-voting effects are stronger where political power is less fragmented—in countries with single-party majority governments, for instance—and weaker in countries were political power is shared more widely because of coalition governments, minority governments, or other political arrangements that divide political power between several institutions, parties, and individuals (see Chapter 8).

Sociological theories of electoral behaviour and public opinion instead direct our attention to how social circumstances vary from country to country—circumstances such as average incomes, the composition of the labour force, the education system, the role of voluntary associations and interest groups such as trade unions, female labour-force participation, and family norms. For example, as we've already noted, there is an important literature in political science and sociology on differences in class voting among countries (Evans 1999). In some countries, the relationship between social class and voting remains much stronger than in others. Most importantly, class voting is strong where trade unions are strong.

Finally, since psychological explanations for electoral behaviour and public opinion are mainly concerned with the psychological traits and dispositions of individuals, they may seem ill-equipped to explain differences among countries, but just as political institutions influence the calculations of rational voters in rationalist models and the social structure in sociological models, institutions help to explain why psychological factors have different effects among countries. For example, scholars who study the role of emotions in politics have observed that voters are more likely to feel animosity towards their political opponents in some countries than others.

12.4 VOTER TURNOUT

LEARNING OUTCOMES

After reading Section 12.4, you'll be able to:
- Describe differences in electoral turnout between countries
- Apply different theories of electoral turnout
- Describe the relationship between turnout and other forms of political participation.

In the previous section, we learned about some of the main explanations for why people vote as they do in different countries around the world. Another important question that scholars of political behaviour have long studied is why people vote at all—or, as is often the case, why they don't. This question is about electoral participation, or turnout—that is, how many of those who have the right to vote actually vote.

In democracies, turning out to vote is the most important form of political participation. But people can participate in politics in many other ways. We will learn about two other important forms of political participation in Chapter 13—on the one hand, joining an interest organization or voluntary association; on the other hand, participating in protests.

One of the reasons that scholars of comparative politics are interested in turnout is that it varies a lot among countries. You can see this in Figure 12.2, which describes the level of turnout in the most recent elections to the national legislature in all countries in the world that hold such elections.

We see immediately that some of the countries in the world with the highest rates of electoral turnout are authoritarian regimes such as Cuba in North America, Belarus in Europe, Ethiopia in Africa, Uzbekistan in Central Asia, North Korea in East Asia, and Laos in South-East Asia. As we discussed in Chapter 5, authoritarian leaders often use elections to mobilize support for the regime and demonstrate to the world that they have a strong hold on power.

There are also many democracies that have high levels of turnout. As Figure 12.2 shows, among democracies with a turnout rate of more than 80 per cent in the most recent election before 2024, we find Chile and Uruguay in the Americas; Belgium, Denmark, and Sweden in Europe; Botswana in Africa; and Australia in Oceania.

In many other democracies, however, turnout is significantly lower than that. Among the established democracies in the world that had a turnout rate of less than 60 per cent in the most

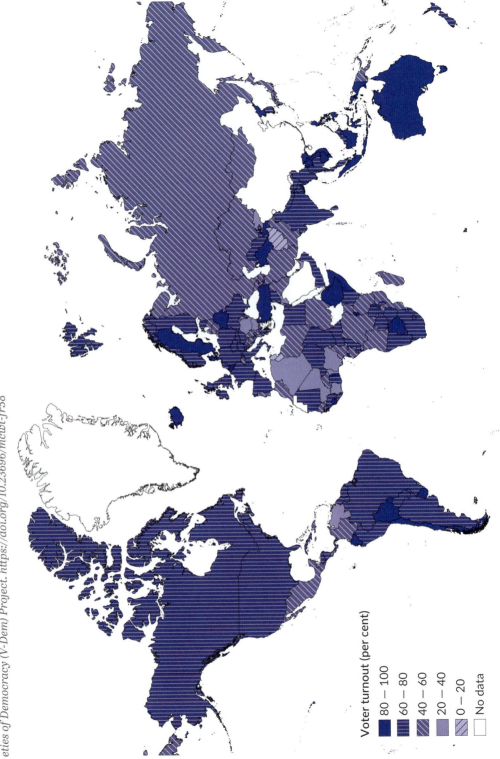

Figure 12.2 The level of turnout in legislative elections varies greatly among the world's countries (the data are from 2023 or from the most recent legislative election before that year). *Source: Author's own work, based on data from Coppedge et al. (2024), "V-Dem Country–Year Dataset v14" Varieties of Democracy (V-Dem) Project. https://doi.org/10.23696/mcvt-fr58*

recent legislative election before 2024 were Colombia and Mexico in the Americas, Switzerland in Europe, and Japan in East Asia.

Scholars have identified many different factors that are associated with high voter turnout. At the national level, aggregate turnout is associated with political institutions such as compulsory-voting rules (of the high-turnout countries we listed, Australia, Belgium, and Luxembourg have all made voting compulsory, which is reflected in their exceptionally high turnout rates), district magnitude (larger districts mean higher turnout), and electoral laws (proportional elections are associated with higher turnout) (see, for example, Blais 2006). On an election-by-election basis, turnout is associated with factors such as the closeness and decisiveness of elections, for when there's more at stake, people are more motivated to vote (Franklin 2004). At the individual level, finally, turnout is higher among the well educated and people with high incomes (Verba, Schlozman, and Brady 1995).

You will learn more about two examples of elections with high and low levels of turnout in Case Study 12.2, and you'll be able to think more about the reasons for high and low turnout if you turn to Research Prompt 12.1.

CASE STUDY 12.2
High and low turnout in Norway and Algeria

In the local elections in Norway in 2019, turnout increased by approximately 5 percentage points, from 60 per cent in 2015 to 65 per cent four years later. According to Bergh, Christensen, and Holmås (2021) and Saglie et al. (2021), two of the main reasons for this increase were the government's efforts to improve turnout through so-called get-out-the-vote initiatives and the fact that the election revolved around issues voters cared greatly about.

The Norwegian government organized two large get-out-the-vote campaigns in the period leading up to the elections. The Directorate of Elections sent out text messages to all eligible voters in Norway and letters to all eligible voters with immigrant backgrounds, who in Norway have a history of low participation. Based on evidence from get-out-the-vote experiments performed in 2015, Bergh, Christensen, and Holmås (2021, 110) conclude that the two government campaigns increased turnout in 2019 by approximately 2 percentage points.

At the same time, there was an intense national debate about environmental policy and climate change, which became the most salient issues in the 2019 campaign (Saglie et al. 2021, 40). They were especially salient among younger voters and, not coincidentally, turnout increased more among the young than in other groups. As Bergh, Christensen, and Holmås (2021, 110) note, 'the election revolved around issues that the voters cared about, and these issues seem to have had an engaging and mobilizing effect'. As we discussed in the main text, people are much more likely to turn out if they feel there's a lot at stake in the elections.

For an example of a recent election in which turnout was low since many voters were *not* engaged and mobilized, consider the constitutional referendum in Algeria in 2020. Turnout in Algerian elections has varied between 35 and 60 per cent in recent years (Sardar 2018, 78), but in the constitutional referendum, it was a mere 23 per cent.

In the year before the referendum, there were anti-government protests all over Algeria, which has an unpopular electoral-authoritarian regime (see Figure 12.3). In response to this protest movement—the 'Revolution of Smiles'—Algeria's government proposed a new constitution, which

Figure 12.3 In 2019, the year before the constitutional referendum, there were many anti-government protests in Algeria. *Source: Saad-Bakhouche / Shutterstock*

it said would restrict the power of political elites, strengthen the parliament and the judiciary, and guarantee civil liberties. But many Algerians felt that these changes were largely cosmetic and didn't go far enough in addressing important issues such as the role of the military in politics or the widespread political corruption in the country (Altman and Sánchez 2021, 43). They therefore chose to boycott the referendum.

Even if voters in Algeria were deeply concerned about how the country's political system works, many appear to have lacked motivation to vote in the referendum since it failed to address the issues that people cared about the most.

 RESEARCH PROMPT 12.1
Turnout in South America

Figure 12.4 zooms in on one corner of the world map we looked at in Figure 12.2: South America. As you can tell from the figure, turnout varied a lot in this region: from less than 60 per cent in Colombia to more than 90 per cent in Uruguay. What might explain these big differences across South America?

Select two South American countries, consult the Inter-Parliamentary Union's database on legislatures around the world (you can use the search function to retrieve information about the

Figure 12.4 Turnout varied greatly in legislative elections in South America in the late 2010s and early 2020s. *Source:* Author's own work, based on data from Coppedge et al. (2024), "V-Dem Country–Year Dataset v14" Varieties of Democracy (V-Dem) Project. https://doi.org/10.23696/mcwt-fr58

legislatures of the countries you're interested in) and a reputable news source that covers elections in Latin America, and use what you've learned in this section to identify explanations for the cross-country differences you see. Try to find out if turnout has decreased or increased over time in the countries you've selected. The explanations you propose are more plausible if they can also explain these trends within countries.

As with all questions about the effects of political institutions (see Chapter 2), it is often difficult to determine whether the relationship between voter turnout and institutions such as compulsory-voting laws are causal—in the sense that if the compulsory-voting laws were repealed, turnout would decrease. But when it comes to the effects of the electoral system, we can be fairly confident. Several scholarly articles in recent years have complemented earlier cross-country studies of turnout with detailed studies of electoral-system reforms in individual countries, using state-of-the-art methods to estimate the effects of changes in electoral rules in countries such as France (Eggers 2015) and Norway (Cox, Fiva, and Smith 2016). Proportional elections are consistently associated with higher voter turnout.

There are many reasons for scholars of comparative politics to take an interest in why voter turnout varies so much among countries and over time. Let's take two examples.

- As we discussed in Chapter 11, most political parties face a trade-off between appealing to 'core voters', which are their most loyal supporters, and 'swing voters', which are voters who hesitate between different parties. If they appeal to core voters, they risk alienating the swing voters. But, importantly, if they appeal to swing voters, they risk alienating their core voters. When it comes to their core voters, the risk parties run is that they will abstain from voting. In other words, turnout is both a cause and a consequence of the political strategies that parties pursue.
- As you will learn in Section 12.5, another important theme of scholarship in comparative politics is political responsiveness—the extent to which changes in public opinion are reflected in changes in public policy. When studying this important question, it is important to keep in mind that political decision makers aren't necessarily responsive to the people as a whole; they are responsive to *those who actually vote*. To understand how democratic responsiveness works, we therefore need to understand when and why people turn out to vote in elections.

Because low turnout among certain groups of voters often exacerbates other economic, social, and political inequalities, scholars have long been interested in explaining differences in turnout between high- and low-income voters, men and women, the old and the young, and different ethnic and religious groups. For example, after women got the right to vote in many countries in the late nineteenth and early twentieth centuries, it typically took a long time for women to catch up with men in electoral participation.

There are many other forms of participation besides voting, including writing letters to politicians, participating in marches and demonstrations, joining interest organizations and cause groups, as well as civil disobedience and more dangerous and violent forms of direct action. We'll come back to some of those forms of participation in Chapter 13, where you'll learn about the role of interest groups in different political systems and about the politics of protests around the world. One key thing to keep in mind is that some types of participation are complements to voting—that is, where turnout is high, those types of participation are also common—while others serve as substitutes for voting, arising in response to the perceived failures of electoral democracy.

12.5 THE STRUCTURE OF PUBLIC OPINION

LEARNING OUTCOMES

After reading Section 12.5, you'll be able to:
- Analyse the main dimensions of political opinion in different countries
- Distinguish between different meanings of political polarization
- Identify different approaches to studying political responsiveness.

So far, we have mainly discussed the factors that explain whether individuals vote, why voters vote as they do, and how people form their political opinions. In this section, we will discuss the structure of public opinion in the electorate as a whole. First, we will analyse the main dimensions of political opinion—that is, the primary ways in which people's opinions differ from each other. Then we'll turn to polarization—that is, the extent to which the electorate is divided into two or more distinct political groups.

12.5.1 Dimensions of conflict

One key question in contemporary scholarship on political behaviour concerns the main *dimensions* of political opinions.

People have opinions about all kinds of things, of course, but many beliefs and attitudes tend to go together. For example, those who are opposed to high taxes are usually not eager to see the government redistribute income from those with high incomes to those with low incomes, but they tend to favour letting private companies conduct business without being constrained by laws and regulations. We usually think of people who hold these opinions as being right wing on economic issues, while those who want to increase taxes, redistribute income from high-income to low-income groups, and regulate companies are considered left wing. This means that there is a left–right *dimension* in politics, which describes people's views on redistribution and the role of the state in the economy. As we discussed in Chapter 11, there is an economic left–right dimension in most party systems around the world. The reason is that there are high-income people and low-income people in all countries, and the conflict between them often shapes political competition. When we do empirical research, we use various left–right 'scales' to study the positions of parties and voters along the left–right dimension.

But there are other dimensions in politics, and throughout history, the terms 'left' and 'right' have been used to describe a wide range of issues, not just economic ones. Many scholars believe that politics in contemporary democracies is structured around the economic left–right dimension on the one hand and, on the other, a 'sociocultural' dimension that reflects different views on political issues such as immigration, gender equality, crime and punishment, and the environment. This dimension is referred to by different names in the literature. Hooghe, Marks, and Wilson (2002) call it the 'GAL–TAN' dimension, where 'GAL' stands for 'green, alternative, and libertarian', and 'TAN' stands for 'traditional, authoritarian, and nationalistic'.

The dominance of the economic left–right dimension in many countries during the twentieth century may have been an exception, not the rule. In the nineteenth and early twentieth centuries, the most intense political conflicts in many countries concerned social and cultural issues such as the role of the government in the education system, and in many countries around the world, issues related to religion, ethnicity, and language have long been just as important as, and often more important than, economic conflicts over distribution and redistribution (see, for example, Lijphart 1979). In other words, the multidimensional nature of politics in contemporary democracies is a normal state of affairs, both historically and in comparative perspective.

12.5.2 Polarization

Another key debate in contemporary scholarship on comparative political behaviour concerns **polarization**, which is a term political scientists use to describe differences in political opinions in the population and among political parties. It is important to understand the magnitude of polarization, as it is related to the stability of democracy (see Chapter 5) and because it can explain the problem of 'democratic paralysis'—an inability to adopt new policies (see Chapter 15).

The term 'polarization' has at least two different meanings, which are often confused. One refers to an increase in the ideological distance between parties. Another, subtly different meaning is that the representatives of different parties cluster in distinct groups instead of being spread more evenly across the political spectrum. When this is the case, politics becomes a binary conflict between two separate teams. Importantly, it is possible to have polarization in the first sense without polarization in the second sense, and vice versa.

Some explanations of polarization emphasize the incentives that politicians and political parties have to seek out more extreme positions and differentiate themselves from their opponents. Other explanations focus on which issues are most politically salient, as compromise is more difficult on some issues than others. Still other explanations emphasize changes in political communication, such as the rise of cable television and the internet—as we will discuss in Chapter 14.

12.5.3 Responsiveness

Once we have a sense of how political opinions are distributed in the population, it becomes possible to ask questions about the relationship between the opinions of the electorate and the public policies that political leaders pursue. We say that the political system is *responsive* if greater public support for a policy is associated with a higher likelihood that it's actually adopted (so, if more people want to raise taxes, it becomes more likely that taxes will in fact be raised).

One important strand of scholarship in this area concerns the effects of political institutions on responsiveness. For example, according to Powell (2000), countries with proportional electoral systems are on average more responsive than those with majoritarian electoral systems. More recently, Powell (2019) has noted that this relationship has become weaker, and he now argues that the effect of the electoral system depends on other factors.

Other scholars have studied a phenomenon known as 'dynamic' representation. In this view, the main question isn't whether public policies correspond to public opinion at any given time, but whether *changes* in public opinion are reflected in *changes* in public policy (Stimson, Mackuen, and Erikson 1995). One version of this idea is the 'thermostatic' model (Soroka and Wlezien 2010), according to which the public tends to vote against incumbents who veer too far left or too far right—in other words, the electorate acts as a thermostat that regulates the 'temperature' in the political system so it doesn't become too hot or too cold.

A third theme of the literature on responsiveness concerns political inequality. Inspired by an influential study from the United States (Gilens 2012), scholars around the world have recently sought to develop new evidence on whether some groups of voters are more influential than others. Many studies, including Gilens (2012), have found that high-income voters have significantly more political influence than others. Other studies have questioned this finding. For example, Elkjar and Iversen (2020) argue, based on cross-country data, that in the long run, it's not high-income voters but rather middle-income voters who get what they want in representative democratic systems.

12.6 CONCLUSION

In this chapter, you have learned about different approaches to the study of electoral behaviour and public opinion. Given that this is a book about comparative politics, we have emphasized how electoral behaviour and public opinion vary among and within countries. We began by discussing the methods scholars use to study political behaviour and the main theoretical approaches to explaining differences in electoral behaviour and public opinion over time. We then examined differences in voter turnout around the world. In the chapter's final section, you learned about some of the most important debates concerning the *structure* of public opinion in contemporary democracies—debates about the dimensionality of public opinion, polarization and its consequences, and the relationship between public opinion and public policies, which is known as 'responsiveness'.

In the next chapter, we will continue discussing how ordinary citizens participate in politics in different countries. Instead of emphasizing electoral behaviour and the relationship between voters and politicians, we will study the role of voluntary associations that try to influence public policies without competing for public office. We will also examine the causes and consequences of political protests, which have become an increasingly common form of political participation in the twenty-first century.

SUMMARY

- Scholars rely on two main methods when studying electoral behaviour and public opinion: comparisons between regions and localities within countries; and surveys of randomly selected citizens.
- There are many different approaches to electoral behaviour and public opinion, ranging from rationalist models, which assume that voters choose the party they think will bring them the most benefits, to sociological models, which assume that voters are shaped by their upbringing, their jobs, and their education.
- Comparative studies of electoral behaviour and public opinion reveal that political institutions shape political behaviour, opinions, and attitudes across national, regional, and local contexts.
- The level of voter turnout varies greatly among both democratic and authoritarian states.
- Among democracies, turnout is on average higher in countries with compulsory voting and proportional elections, but it also depends on other factors such as the average level of education and the closeness and decisiveness of elections.
- The structure of political opinion—especially the number of salient dimensions of opinion and the degree of polarization within those dimensions—is an important factor in politics in both democratic and authoritarian regimes.
- In many contemporary democracies, public opinion is best understood as two-dimensional, with political attitudes varying along an economic left–right dimension and a sociocultural liberal–conservative dimension.
- With the help of empirical evidence on public opinion, it becomes possible to study the level of democratic responsiveness in different political systems—that is, the extent to which changes in public opinion are associated with changes in policy—both for the electorate as a whole and for different groups within the electorate.

STUDY QUESTIONS

1. As we discussed in Section 12.4, political parties and candidates face two types of risk when they decide which policies to run on. One risk is that they will fail to appeal to pivotal 'swing' voters, who may therefore choose to vote for another party. Another risk is that they will alienate their 'core' voters, who may therefore choose to abstain from voting, since they feel betrayed by their old party. Now that you've learned more about the main explanations for why people vote as they do, in which circumstances do you think parties feel this trade-off most keenly?
2. Throughout the chapter, we have discussed rationalist, sociological, psychological, and institutional explanations for electoral behaviour. Which approach seems most helpful to you when it comes to explaining cross-country differences in political behaviour?

FURTHER READING

Russell J. Dalton and Hans-Dieter Klingemann (eds.), *The Oxford Handbook of Political Behiavor* (2007).
Provides a comprehensive overview of the field of political behaviour.

Rafaela M. Dancygier, *Dilemmas of Inclusion* (2017).
Analyses the electoral behaviour of Muslim immigrants in Western countries and the challenges for political parties that wish to appeal to those voters.

Peter A. Hall, Georgina Evans, and Sung In Kim, *Political Change and Electoral Coalitions in Western Democracies* (2023).
Presents an up-to-date analysis of the electoral behaviour of different occupational groups in Europe.

CHAPTER 13

INTEREST GROUPS AND PROTESTS

CHAPTER GUIDE

13.1 Introduction
13.2 Interest Groups and Social Movements
13.3 Interest Groups around the World
13.4 State–Society Relations
13.5 Protests
13.6 Conclusion
Summary
Study Questions
Further Reading

13.1 INTRODUCTION

The most important form of political participation in modern representative democracies is elections. That's why we spent so much time on electoral systems and electoral behaviour in Chapters 7 and 12. Each individual voter's measure of political influence may be small, but the combined influence of large groups of voters can be decisive. At least that's how elections are supposed to work. It's also the idea behind most democratic constitutions. Consider South Africa's democratic constitution from 1996, to take just one example. Article 1 states that politics in South Africa is based on the value of 'Universal adult suffrage, a national common voters roll, regular elections and a multi-party system of democratic government, to ensure accountability, responsiveness and openness'. Accountability, responsiveness, and openness are the goals; effective, well-run, multi-party elections are the principal means of reaching those goals.

But people only vote on election day. Between the elections, individuals, groups, and organizations that strive for political influence must use other methods. South Africa's constitution guarantees the right of individuals and groups to use those channels, too. Most importantly, Article 18 provides that everyone 'has the right to freedom of association', and Article 17 provides that everyone 'has the right, peacefully and unarmed, to assemble, to demonstrate, to picket and to present petitions'. In other words, South Africa's constitution protects the right to form interest organizations and other political associations and the right to engage in political protests.

This chapter studies the role of interest groups and the politics of protest across political systems. Section 13.2 discusses the differences between sectional interest organizations and cause groups, which are the two main forms of interest groups studied by scholars of comparative politics, and how they seek to influence political processes. Section 13.3 examines some of the main explanations for the varying strength of interest organizations among countries. Section 13.4 analyses the relationship between interest groups, political parties, and state institutions—or 'state–society relations'—across political systems. Finally, Section 13.5 discusses what political protests are, why people protest, and what scholars of comparative politics have learned about the causes and consequences of protests in different political regimes.

13.2 INTEREST GROUPS AND SOCIAL MOVEMENTS

LEARNING OUTCOMES

After reading Section 13.2, you'll be able to:

- Distinguish between sectional interest organizations and cause groups
- Analyse the role of interest groups in democratic systems
- Describe the relationship between interest groups and social movements.

As we noted in Chapter 11, the main difference between **interest groups** and political parties is that interest groups seek to influence public policy indirectly, not directly. We defined political parties as organizations that put up candidates for public office. By definition, then, political parties try to control lawmaking and policymaking directly, by getting their candidates elected to the legislature and by forming or participating in governments. That's not what interest groups do. They want political influence, but their methods are different.

There are two main types of interest group. The first type represents citizens—or companies or other associations—that have certain social, economic, and political interests in common. For example, workers are represented by trade unions, employers are represented by business associations, and farmers are represented by agricultural organizations. There are different terms for this first type of group, including 'pressure group' (emphasizing their ability to put pressure on politicians) and 'interest organization' (emphasizing their role of representing the specific interests of their members). We'll use the more specific term **sectional interest organizations**, since the most important characteristic of this sort of organization is that they represent a particular segment of society.

The other type of group works to promote more general ideals, values, and principles. For example, the organization Amnesty International, founded in 1961, advocates for human rights; the organization Oxfam, originally founded in Oxford in 1941, is dedicated to disaster relief and the fight against poverty; and the World Wide Fund for Nature, also founded in 1961, works for the protection of the natural environment (see Figure 13.1). These types of groups are sometimes called public-interest organizations or idea-based organizations, but we'll use the term **cause groups**, which emphasizes that they work for a general cause, not for the particular interests of their own members. Table 13.1 summarizes the main differences between sectional interest organizations and cause groups, and anticipates the discussion of insider and outsider strategies later in this section.

It isn't always possible to make a sharp distinction between sectional interest organizations and cause groups. For example, one way to think of the late-nineteenth- and early-twentieth-century movements for women's suffrage that we discussed in Chapter 4 is that they were made up

Figure 13.1 In the 2000s and 2010s, the World Wide Fund for Nature cooperated with the French artist Paulo Grangeon on the art installation '1600 Pandas', touring the world to raise awareness of the threats to the survival of the giant panda. *Source: DocChewbacca / Flickr (CC BY-SA 2.0)*

Table 13.1 The main types of interest organization

Type of group	Main characteristic	Examples	Typical strategies
Sectional interest organizations	Represent the interests of their members	Trade unions, business associations, and farmers' organizations	Insider strategies such as lobbying, cooperation with political parties, and collective bargaining
Cause groups	Represent general ideas and ideals	Environmental groups, human rights organizations, and humanitarian associations	Outsider strategies such as petitions, protests, and awareness-raising campaigns

of interest organizations that fought for the social, economic, and political rights of their women members. But one might also think of them as made up of cause groups that fought for the principle of political equality between women and men (and at least some suffrage organizations admitted men as members).

That said, the distinction between sectional interest organizations and cause groups is important since these two types of group typically face different challenges, use different methods for achieving their aims, and interact in different ways with politicians and public officials.

We'll discuss the organizational challenges faced by different groups in Section 13.3, which examines the main explanations for why the strength of interest groups varies among countries and across policy areas. In this section, we'll concentrate on the methods that interest groups use to influence political decision makers. The main distinction here is between **insider** and **outsider** strategies.

Many groups rely on a combination of insider and outsider strategies, but the difference between the two remains important. As Dür and Mateo (2016) put it, some interest groups seek to 'establish direct contacts with decision makers', relying on their access to executive institutions, whereas other groups 'rely more strongly on tactics that are aimed at mobilizing the public or changing public attitudes'. Insider strategies include making financial contributions to political candidates and campaigns; lobbying individual politicians, groups of politicians, or public officials; strengthening the ties between interest groups and individual political parties; and engaging in consultations and negotiations with politicians and other organizations in political systems where such contacts are a part of the regular decision making process (see Section 13.4). Outsider strategies include conducting media campaigns, building grassroots organizations, using legal advocacy, and engaging in political protests (see Section 13.5). There is no one-to-one relationship between different types of interest group and different methods of influence, but on average, sectional interest organizations are more likely to pursue insider strategies and cause groups are more likely to pursue outsider strategies. For example, Dür and Mateo (2016) find that business organizations are much more likely to rely on insider methods than what they call 'citizen groups', a category that includes environmental organizations and other cause groups. Trade unions and professional associations occupy a middle ground between these two extremes—they sometimes resemble business organizations and sometimes citizen groups.

Both insider and outsider strategies can be effective, but resource-strong sectional organizations such as business groups often have better and more frequent access to policymakers. This difference between sectional interest organizations and cause groups can have important consequences for political representation. To see how, turn to Case Study 13.1, which examines lobbying by different types of interest group in the Swiss parliament.

> **CASE STUDY 13.1**
> Interest groups in Switzerland
>
> When interest groups influence policymakers, it can affect the relationship between politicians and their voters. But how? One possibility is that interest groups persuade policymakers to adopt policies their voters disapprove of, which would be harmful for political responsiveness. Alternatively, interest groups might promote policies that the voters approve of, which would strengthen political responsiveness. A third possibility is that different types of interest group have different effects on the political system.
>
> Evidence from Switzerland supports this third view. In their article 'Voting Against Your Constituency?', Giger and Klüver (2016) investigate the political consequences of the activities of two types of interest group: sectional interest organizations, which represent special interests such as specific industries, and cause groups, which represent more general ideals or values, such as
>
>

human rights or the protection of the environment. Their main hypothesis is that since cause groups advocate for broader ideals, their lobbying should make politicians *more* likely to adopt policies their voters want. Conversely, since sectional groups advocate for narrow interests, their lobbying should make politicians *less* responsive to their voters.

To test these theoretical expectations, Giger and Klüver conduct an empirical analysis of Swiss public policymaking across various areas, from immigration laws to maternity leave. As expected, they find that lobbying has different effects on democratic responsiveness depending on the type of interest group that's involved: if sectional interest organizations are influential, politicians tend to vote against the wishes of their voters; if cause groups are influential, politicians become more likely to vote for policies their voters want. These results hold for both individual representatives and political parties.

Although their results indicate that the lobbying efforts of cause groups are on average more effective than those of sectional groups, Giger and Klüver conclude by noting that sectional interest organizations have more resources and therefore find it easier to mobilize the groups they represent. 'Sectional groups outnumber cause groups, so significantly more MPs [members of parliament] are lobbied by sectional groups than by cause groups. They dominate the parliamentary sphere and are therefore able to bias legislative outcomes in their favour' (2016, 202).

Why are interest groups able to influence political decision makers, when the main channel of political participation and influence in modern democracies is supposed to be elections? They do this by offering the decision makers something they want (such as direct financial contributions), by threatening them with something they don't want (such as withholding the votes of their members at the next election), or by shaping public opinion (changing the terms of the political debate). One important factor that may not be immediately obvious is that interest groups have a lot of knowledge in their respective fields. This is true both for sectional organizations (think of the European Chemical Industry Council, which lobbies European institutions for companies in the chemical sector and knows the ins and outs of that industry), and for cause groups (think of environmental organizations such as the World Wide Fund for Nature, which employs scientists and biologists with detailed knowledge of threats to the natural environment). As we discussed in Chapter 3, the modern state is a complex organization that regulates many domains of economic and social life, and it is usually impossible for government ministers, members of the legislature, or even public officials to match the specialized knowledge that interests groups have in their field.

We end this section by noting that an important tradition of scholarship treats interest groups as manifestations of broader **social movements**, such as the labour movement, the women's movement, the peace movement, the environmental movement, and the lesbian, gay, bisexual, and transgender movement. 'Social movement' is a term that sociologists and political scientists use to describe networks of 'informal interactions, between a plurality of individuals, groups or associations, engaged in a political or cultural conflict, on the basis of a shared collective identity' (Diani 1992, 13). Research on social movements has shown that modern societies go through waves of political mobilization in which large groups of citizens start to think of themselves as having similar political concerns and interests and gradually develop a collective identity (such as 'feminist' or 'environmentalist'). Such movements often result in the formation of new interest groups, including both sectional organizations, such as the trade unions that grew out of the labour movement, and cause groups, such as the environmental associations that grew out of the environmental movement. As we discussed in Chapter 11, social movements can also result in the formation of new political parties, such as modern green parties.

13.3 INTEREST GROUPS AROUND THE WORLD

LEARNING OUTCOMES

After reading Section 13.3, you'll be able to:
- Analyse the challenges interest groups face
- Explain why interest groups are better organized in some countries than in others.

Now that we know what interest groups do, what types of interest group there are, what methods they use, and how they're related to broader social movements, we're ready to discuss the strength and role of interest groups in comparative perspective. Interest organizations and cause groups are better organized in some countries than in others, use different methods depending on the political systems in which they operate, and vary greatly in their political success. Scholars of comparative politics, always eager to understand similarities and differences among political systems, have long sought to understand how the role of interest groups varies across countries. The discussion in this section is mainly concerned with democratic regimes.

One type of interest organization that has attracted a lot of attention from scholars is **trade unions**. Trade unions emerged in the nineteenth century to represent the interests of workers in relation to employers and to the state. Today, trade unions exist in almost all countries in the world, but they are much stronger in some regions than others. We'll use trade unions as our main example when we discuss the strength, behaviour, and influence of interest groups, but we will also mention other examples along the way.

One reason that trade unions are better understood than other interest groups is that scholars have access to high-quality cross-country comparative data on union density—the percentage of all employees who are members of trade unions—which are compiled by the International Labour Organization in Geneva, one of the specialized agencies of the United Nations. Figure 13.2 describes the level of union density in the more than 150 countries for which data are available from the 2000s and 2010s (the oldest data in this graph are from 2007; the newest data are from 2020).

As these figures show, trade union density varies between more than 90 per cent of all employees in Iceland and close to 0 per cent in Venezuela. Among high-income democracies in Europe, North America, and the Asia-Pacific region, trade unions are strongest in the Nordic countries, in which most people who have a job are members of a trade union, and in Belgium, Italy, and Canada. Among democracies elsewhere, trade unions are strongest in the southern parts of South America (Argentina and Uruguay) and Africa (Botswana and South Africa). Perhaps you remember from our discussion of South Africa at the beginning of this chapter that the country's constitution from 1996 protects everyone's right to 'picket'. Picketing—protesting outside a particular location—is something trade unions do, typically to keep people from entering the premises of a company that is involved in a labour conflict. The fact that South Africa's constitution specifically protects picketing is a result of the fact that trade unions had a lot of political influence in the country when the constitution was drafted after the end of the racist apartheid system.

Figure 13.2 Trade union density—the proportion of all employees who are members of trade unions—varies between more than 90 per cent in Iceland and close to 0 per cent in Venezuela.

Source: Author's own work, based on data from International Labour Organization (2020), courtesy of International Labour Organization (2020)

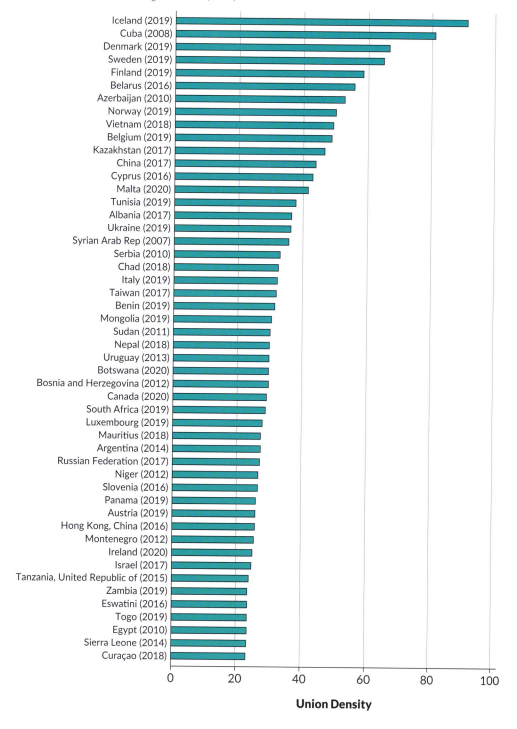

Figure 13.2 (Continued)

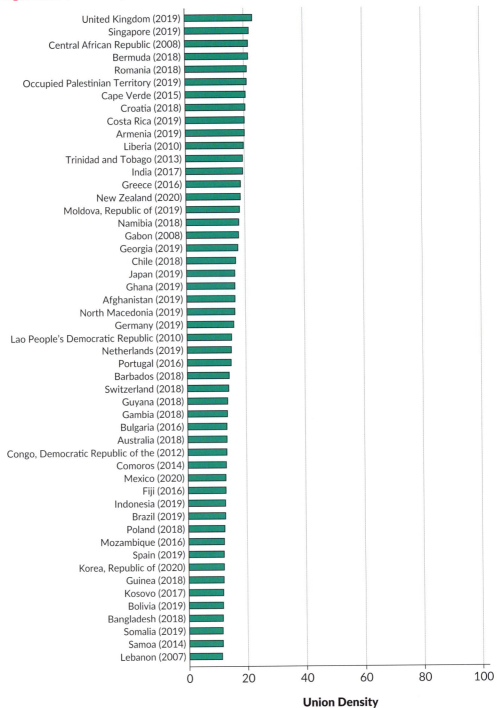

Union Density

Figure 13.2 (Continued)

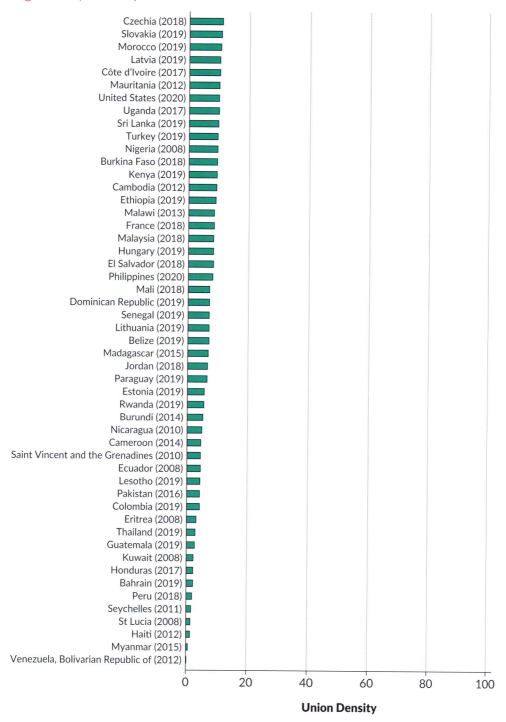

Trade unions can teach us five broad lessons about interest groups.

1. In democratic systems, interest groups are part of a **civil society** that is distinct from the state and the government; in authoritarian systems, by contrast, the difference between the state and civil society is often indistinct, or even non-existent. Trade unions organize a large proportion of all employees in communist or formerly communist authoritarian states such as Cuba, Belarus, and Vietnam. However, as we'll discuss in more detail in Section 13.4, interest groups tend to have a very different role in authoritarian systems than in democracies.

2. It's often difficult to mobilize and organize people, even if they have many interests in common. There are fewer than 20 countries in the world in which more than a third of all those who have jobs are trade union members, and that number is declining—in many parts of the world, especially among high-income democracies, trade unions used to be a lot stronger than they are now. In the United Kingdom, to take just one example, union density was approximately 50 per cent in the early 1980s; today, as Figure 13.2 shows, it is only 23 per cent.

    One theory that explains why it is hard to persuade people to join organizations and associations that promote their interests is the theory of **collective action**, which was developed by the economist Mancur Olson in his book *The Logic of Collective Action* (1965). The main idea behind the theory of collective action is that it's often individually rational for people *not* to join and support interest groups and other voluntary associations, even if they agree with their goals, for if the organization is successful in its endeavours, non-members often benefit just as much as the members do—they are able to 'free ride'. For example, if a trade union lobbies the government to put in place more stringent protections for workers with hazardous jobs, all employees in the affected industries will benefit from those efforts, whether they're union members or not.

    Many comparative studies of interest groups are concerned with how interest organizations and cause groups in different countries and in different periods have sought to overcome this problem. In Section 13.2, we noted that sectional interest organizations that represent business interests are often more effective than citizen-based cause groups. One of the explanations for this pattern is that cause groups tend to have more diffuse and general goals, which makes it more difficult for them to offer their supporters the sorts of tangible, material benefits that narrow sectional interest organizations can provide.

3. How interest groups act to promote their members' interests depends on how **encompassing** they are—that is, whether they have broad or narrow groups of supporters. In countries where trade unions are very strong overall, trade union members come from all sectors of the economy and represent many different occupations. In countries where trade unions are weak overall, their members tend to be concentrated in specific groups, such as among public-sector employees. For example, in Sweden, where trade union density in the early 2020s was just under 70 per cent, the difference between the private and the public sector was relatively small (63 versus 79 per cent); in the United States, where trade union density was around 10 per cent, the difference was much larger (6 versus 33 per cent) (see Kjellberg 2020; Bureau of Labor Statistics 2023). Encompassing organizations often take a broader view of social, economic, and political issues than more narrowly based organizations do.

4. The political influence of interest groups depends on the resources they have and the methods that are available to them. The strength of trade unions depends on their membership

numbers and the fees the members pay to the organization. Resources are important to all organizations, but their effects appear to be strongest for sectional interest organizations that engage directly with politicians (Dür and Mateo 2016). The most important method of influence for trade unions is strikes—work stoppages that are meant to put pressure on the employers and sometimes also the government. This is a method that is unique to trade unions. Other types of organization use different methods.

5. Finally, whereas interest groups and political parties are different types of organization, interest groups in general and trade unions in particular often work closely with allies among the political parties. South Africa is again an example, for the leading trade union confederation in that country, COSATU (the Congress of South African Trade Unions), is allied with the country's ruling party, the ANC (African National Congress). South Africa is far from unique—across the world, unions are often associated with left-of-centre political parties, and business organizations often have close links with parties on the right. Other types of organization are associated with other sorts of parties. For example, as we discussed in Chapter 11, green parties typically grew out of the environmental movement and many of them remain closely associated with environmental organizations.

We have used the example of trade unions to draw lessons that apply to interest groups more broadly. All the five lessons we've discussed here are relevant for a wide variety of interest groups across countries and over time.

13.4 STATE–SOCIETY RELATIONS

LEARNING OUTCOMES

After reading Section 13.4, you'll be able to:
- Explain the role of voluntary associations in democratic and authoritarian regimes
- Distinguish between the pluralist, corporatist, and statist models of state–society relations.

In Sections 13.2 and 13.3, we discussed what interest groups are and do, and we analysed some of the main explanations for why interest groups vary among countries. In this section, we'll discuss the place of interest groups within the political system. There are important differences among countries when it comes to how interest groups engage with state institutions and political leaders—and vice versa. Scholars of comparative politics regard the interaction between interest groups and the political system as one aspect of the broader topic of state–society relations, a term that describes how politicians and government officials engage with associations in civil society.

We have already come across one way in which interest groups may interact with the state when we discussed the role of trade unions in authoritarian regimes in Section 13.3. We noted that in many authoritarian regimes, there is no clear distinction between the state and civil society, and, to the extent that voluntary associations are permitted, rulers make them subservient to the state and require them to perform services for the government and follow its lead. One extreme but striking historical example is the role played by organizations for midwives in Nazi Germany in the 1930s and 1940s (Ansell and Lindvall 2021, Chapter 9). The national-socialist government in Germany introduced legislation that strengthened the midwifery profession and offered new social-insurance benefits for midwives—but it also expected midwives to assist in the registration of 'hereditary diseases' and, later, in the mass killing of children with genetic variations such as Down Syndrome. As Lisner (2006, 259) puts it, 'Loyalty to the Nazi state and commitment to the implementation of the state's racist population policy were prerequisites of the professionalization and upgrading of the midwifery profession during the Nazi era', and midwives became the 'arm of the state reaching into every apartment'.

In democracies, interest groups are not subservient to political leaders. Indeed, as we discussed in Chapter 4, many theorists treat the freedom of association as a core element of the very *definition* of democracy. But there are nevertheless many different views among countries and across political parties of what role interest groups ought to have in a democratic political system. According to one view, interest groups ought to be kept at arm's length from political decision makers, to ensure that politicians are guided by the views of the voters, not the views of narrow, well-organized groups. According to another, very different view—which is especially prevalent in continental Europe and which has long influenced policymaking within the European Union—interest groups play an important role in politics as 'social partners' that ought to be encouraged to participate in policymaking processes by consulting and negotiating with each other and with political decision makers and officials.

Scholars have long distinguished between three models of the relationship between interest groups, state institutions, and political decision makers in modern democracies.

The first model is known as **pluralism**. In a pluralist system, there is a wide range of interest groups, which are all allowed to express their political opinions and make their voices heard, and political institutions don't favour some organizations over others. The pluralist model has traditionally been associated with English-speaking democracies such as the United States and the United Kingdom, but as usual with ideal-typical descriptions of political arrangements, there are exceptions. For example, there was a period in the 1970s when the United Kingdom tried to put in place corporatist political institutions that were modelled on institutional arrangements in northern Europe, where interest organizations such as trade unions and employer associations play a more active role in political decision making (see Grant 2000).

Corporatism is the second model of interest mediation we will consider here. It means that interest groups are concentrated in a relatively small number of peak-level organizations, and then the government, the legislature, and public authorities engage in negotiations and bargaining with selected organizations that they regard as especially important representatives of key groups in society. This sort of system first emerged in the context of industrial relations—that is, in the world of trade unions and employer organizations—but in countries with corporatist traditions, it has later been extended to other sorts of associations. There are strong corporatist traditions in northern Europe and in Latin America. Corporatism has existed both in authoritarian systems, such as fascist Italy in the 1920s and 1930s and Latin American dictatorships in the middle of the twentieth century, and in democratic systems, where interest groups have interacted closely with political leaders and the state without compromising their autonomy as civil society organizations.

The third model of the relationship between interest groups and the state is **statism**, which means that interest groups are discouraged from trying to influence politics or at least kept at arm's length from political decision makers and the halls of power. This is a model that is typically associated with the case of France, in which republican doctrines are influential that 'denounce intermediary bodies which come between the State and the citizen', as Williams and Harrison put it in their book on the French Fifth Republic (1971, 145). It's a different approach from the pluralist view, which expects that democracy works best if there is a wide diversity of groups that represent different interests and viewpoints. It's also different from the corporatist view, which sees politics as an ongoing process of negotiations among the principal interest groups in society.

These different traditions of state–society relations have had important consequences for how modern democracies work. They matter for political parties (Chapter 11), since parties are organizations that mediate between society and the state. They matter for public policymaking (Chapter 15), since the influence of organized interests is one of the key factors that explain why political decision makers adopt different policies across different political systems. But they also matter for public administration, for although the primary function of interest organizations and cause groups within political systems is to advocate for certain interests and values, trying to influence the legislature, the executive, and administrative agencies, governments sometimes rely on interest groups to provide essential services or to perform other public functions. For example, there are several countries in Europe in which unemployment insurance is administered by trade unions and voluntary associations, not by a government agency. Across the world, charity organizations, religious orders, and other voluntary associations also provide health care and other basic services to millions of people. In other words, analysing the role of interest groups and civil society organizations in contemporary political systems is essential not only for our understanding of political decision making but also for our understanding of the scope of the state (Chapter 3) and the implementation of public policies (Chapter 10).

13.5 PROTESTS

LEARNING OUTCOMES

After reading Section 13.5, you'll be able to:
- Distinguish between different approaches to explaining why people protest
- Describe the increasing frequency of political protests in today's world
- Analyse how governments respond to political protests.

One form of political participation that is becoming increasingly important is *protests*.

13.5.1 Theories of protests

According to the political scientist Michael Lipsky's classic definition (1968, 1145), protests are 'a mode of political action oriented toward objection to one or more policies or conditions, characterized by showmanship or display of an unconventional nature'. There are two things to note about this definition. First, a protest is an *unconventional* action, in the sense that it occurs outside the domain of regular, institutionalized politics (see also Della Porta and Fillieule 2003). Second, a protest is a *reaction* (or 'objection') to a policy or a state of affairs: people protest since they wish to voice their opposition to political leaders, the policies those leaders pursue, or, more generally, the economic, social, and political situation at the local, national, or international level.

There are many forms of protest, including marches, anti-government demonstrations, boycotts, political strikes (work stoppages that are directed not against an employer but against the political authorities), civil disobedience, and other forms of direct action. These different methods are sometimes referred to as the 'repertoire' of political protest. Some of the methods are more unconventional than others—for example, some are typically legal, whereas others, such as civil disobedience, are by definition illegal. The repertoire of political protest is evolving, varies from country to country, and is shaped by historical events and experiences. Protests are an old form of political participation. Indeed, in pre-democratic periods in which the people weren't expected to participate in politics at all, protests were one of the few forms of participation that were available to most people.

In Chapter 2, we distinguished between four main types of theoretical approach in comparative politics: rationalist theories, sociological theories, psychological theories, and institutionalist theories. The idea of a 'repertoire' of political protest is closely associated with sociological theories of politics. But rationalist, psychological, and institutionalist theories have been used to study protests too.

- From a rationalist perspective, organizing and participating in protests is something that organizations and individuals do for instrumental reasons: they want to achieve some political goal; protests are the best, or perhaps the only, method that's available to them, and they judge that the potential benefits—the likelihood that they will reach their goal—exceed the costs.
- From a psychological perspective, people participate in protests because they want to express their opinions and their emotions or because they strongly support the message of the protesters and relate to that group. In this view, people don't engage in protests because they have a certain political goal in mind and choose the method that's available to them; instead, people engage in protests because of the act of protesting itself.
- From an institutionalist perspective, when people choose to organize and participate in protests, they do so largely because of the institutional environment they're in. We'll come back to this approach in our discussion of the concept of political opportunity structures later in this section.

Turn to Research Prompt 13.1 to explore some of the reasons that people engage in political protests.

RESEARCH PROMPT 13.1
Covid-19 protests

Scholars of comparative politics seek to understand what drives people to protest, how governments respond, and how likely protesters are to achieve their political goals. In this research prompt, you will explore these important questions.

During the Covid-19 pandemic that began in the spring of 2020, there were protests in many countries against the public health policies that governments adopted to prevent the spread of the virus (see Figure 13.3). Your task is to choose one particular country where such protests occurred and answer the question below. Among the countries you may want to consider are the United States, where state governments faced significant protests related to mask mandates, school closures, and vaccine requirements; Germany, where the government faced protests from groups advocating for personal freedoms; Brazil, where both supporters and critics of the government's handling of the pandemic engaged in protests; and India, which also experienced protests related to the government's response to the pandemic.

Figure 13.3 During the Covid-19 pandemic, anti-government protests were common.
Source: Michael Swan / Flickr

Consult a reliable news source and learn more about the nature of the protests and the demands the protesters put forward. Do you think people's decision to organize and participate in protests during the pandemic are best explained by rationalist, sociological, psychological, or institutionalist theories of politics?

13.5.2 Protests around the world

Protests are a more important form of political expression and participation than ever before. Throughout the 2010s and 2020s, countries have been affected by major protest movements, from the Yellow Vests protests in France in 2018–2019 to the Black Lives Matter protests in the United States in 2020; from the protests in Chile in 2019 that we'll discuss in Case Study 13.2 to the protests in Iran after the death of a young woman in police custody in 2022, and the protests against Covid restrictions in China in 2022 that led to the government stepping back from its harsh public health policies. Citizens are increasingly taking to the streets to voice their political demands. According to Ortiz et al. (2022), the number of major protest events increased in all world regions between the late 2000s and the late 2010s, with total numbers almost doubling. Another recent study concluded that protests had increased in all regions at a rate of over 11 per cent per year on average (Brannen, Haig, and Schmidt 2020).

Figure 13.4, which is based on data from the ACLED project (Armed Conflict Location and Event Data Project; Raleigh, Kishi, and Linke 2023), shows how the average number of protests per year varied among countries in the first two decades of the twenty-first century (the two types of event that are included in the dataset used for the map are 'protests' and 'riots', which includes violent demonstrations and mob violence). We need to keep in mind that these are raw numbers that don't take the size of the population into account. It's only natural that countries with large populations have a greater number of protests.

That said, we find some interesting patterns in this map. First of all, there are more protests in democracies than there are in authoritarian states, even if we take population into account. We can see examples of the differences between more democratic and more authoritarian states by comparing, for instance, India and China, both of which have approximately 1.4 billion inhabitants. But the pattern also holds true on average. If we were to rework the data to show the number of events per head of population—instead of simply the total number of events in each country—we would find that in an average-sized democracy, there are approximately 1,000 more protests per year than in an average-sized authoritarian state. Of course, there is a risk that we are undercounting the number of protests in authoritarian regimes—as we'll see in Chapter 14, authoritarian governments often use their influence over the media to make sure citizens don't learn about protests within the country, which may also cause foreign observers to undercount protests in authoritarian systems. The main explanation, however, is likely to be that whereas engaging in peaceful protests is seen as a right in all democratic regimes, in most authoritarian regimes it's not.

We also learn from the map, however, that there are important differences among both democratic and authoritarian states. For example, the average number of protests per year was three times as high in Chile (1,800) as in Ecuador (640), although they're both democracies and their populations are almost identical. We can also find examples of authoritarian states with thousands of protests per year (such as Iran) and almost no protests at all (such as North Korea).

Political institutions help to explain many of these differences among countries. On the one hand, the grievances that motivate people to engage in protests are often associated with the structure and functioning of political institutions. If formal channels of political influence are open to citizens, there is less reason for them to take to the streets, so protests are more likely to occur if people don't trust political institutions to work and lack faith in their political leaders. On the other hand, the strength of social movements depends on what's known as the **political opportunity structure** in a society. This is a term that scholars of political protests use to describe the political circumstances that shape the ability of protest movements and activists to organize and promote their causes (McAdam 1999). The term has been used to describe the openness of formal political institutions, the likelihood of repression by the police or the military, the presence of potential elite allies among the leading political parties and interest organizations, and the availability of different methods of political influence. Political institutions thus matter greatly both for the reasons that people protest in the first place and for their opportunities to succeed if they do.

Another important theme of comparative-politics scholarship on political protests concerns the response of the political authorities. On the one hand, political leaders and political authorities can respond to protests by accepting some of the demands of the protesters, or by 'conceding'. On the other hand, political authorities can use repression to break up the protests and punish the protest leaders. Interestingly, political authorities often do both, especially in authoritarian

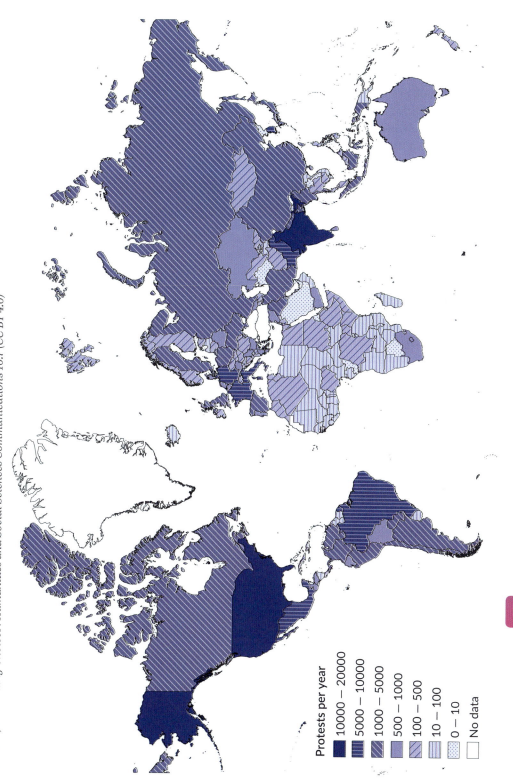

Figure 13.4 The number of protests per year varied greatly around the world in the early twenty-first century. *Source: Author's own work, based on data from Raleigh, Clionadh, Roudabeh Kishi, and Andrew Linke. 2023. 'Political Instability Patterns are Obscured by Conflict Dataset Scope Conditions, Sources, and Coding Choices'. Humanities and Social Sciences Communications 10:7 (CC BY 4.0)*

regimes, relying on a combination of 'carrots' and 'sticks' to protect the government and try to persuade people to leave the streets. One might think that state repression lowers the likelihood of protests, but it has also been shown to have the opposite effect. For example, Hager and Krakowski (2022) have shown that in communist Poland, state repression caused widespread anger that led to more protests, not fewer.

A third, related theme is the study of the circumstances in which political protests are successful, in the sense that the protesters achieve their political goals. To read more about one recent protest movement that persuaded the government to call a referendum on a new constitution, see Case Study 13.2.

CASE STUDY 13.2
Protests and constitutional reform in Chile

In 2022, Chile held a referendum on a new constitution. The referendum was the result of widespread protests that began in October 2019, sparking a movement known in Spanish as the *estallido social*, or 'social outburst'. The immediate cause of the protests was an increase in subway fees, but the protest movement quickly evolved to address wider issues of social and economic inequality, with protesters expressing frustration over the perceived divide between the political elites and society, and the rising costs of services such as education and health care (Garcés 2019; Gonzalez and Foulon 2020; Somma et al. 2021).

The protests were led by adolescents, building on earlier student movements in 2006 and 2011. There was no clear leadership or organizational structure. Instead, scholars have identified the use of social media as a key tool in mobilizing citizens and facilitating communication and coordination (on social media and protests, see also Chapter 14).

In response to the protests, Chile's president, Sebastián Piñera, declared a state of emergency and implemented a curfew and ban on public gatherings. There were reports of violent, repressive methods used by the police. Indeed, traumatic eye damage was so common in Chile in 2019 that international observers suspected the police of deliberately targeting the eyes of young protesters, to incapacitate, to maim, and to discourage others (see 'A Bullet to the Eye Is the Price of Protesting in Chile', *New York Times*, 19 November 2019).

As we discussed in the main text, however, governments that are faced with protests often combine aggressive policing with political concessions and negotiations. That's what Chile's government did, too, announcing a social policy agenda that included an increase in pensions for low-income households, a raise in the minimum wage, higher taxes for the wealthy, and a halt to electricity price increases. But the protests continued.

The government eventually agreed to hold a referendum on writing a new constitution, which took place in October 2020. The vote was overwhelmingly in favour of drafting a new constitution. A constitutional assembly was formed, made up of 155 members representing a diverse range of political and social groups.

In the short run, the protest movement was successful. In the long run, the story is a little more ambiguous. The election of a left-wing president, Gabriel Boric, in 2022, was in part a consequence of the protest movement. But when a second referendum was held in 2022 on the proposal put forward by the constitutional assembly, the vote was overwhelmingly negative, since most voters regarded the assembly's proposal as too radical.

13.6 CONCLUSION

In this chapter, we have examined two important ways for citizens, groups of citizens, and private organizations such as business firms to express their political opinions and seek political influence between elections: forming political associations and organizing and participating in protests.

We began by studying the role of interest groups in different political systems. After distinguishing between sectional interest organizations and cause groups, and between insider and outsider methods, we used the example of trade unions to discuss some of the main explanations for why interest groups are stronger in some countries than others and use different methods across political systems. We then reviewed some of the main models of 'state–society relations' in comparative politics—that is, different ways in which interest groups engage with political decision makers. Finally, we learned about the increasing importance of political protests as a form of political participation around the world, reviewed some of the main theories of protests, and discussed a few of the questions contemporary scholars are asking about the politics of protest in different countries.

In the next chapter, we'll investigate the role of the media across political systems and discuss how people learn about politics from print, broadcast, and digital media. In other words, we'll move from the topic of political *participation* to the topic of political *communication*. But as with most of the topics we're studying in this book, the topics of political participation and political communication are closely connected to each other. As we saw in Case Study 13.2, modern protest movements often begin on social media networks. That's a topic we'll come back to in Chapter 14.

SUMMARY

- There are two main types of interest group—sectional interest organizations and cause groups that work towards more general and abstract ideals.
- Interest groups use two main types of method: insider methods and outsider methods.
- The strength of interest groups varies greatly among countries.
- The theory of collective action offers one explanation for this variation: it is generally difficult to build organizations that work towards common goals, and due to various social, economic, and political factors, this problem is easier to overcome for some groups than others.
- In democracies, voluntary associations are a part of civil society, which is a social sphere that is distinct from the state.
- In authoritarian regimes, rulers typically try to control voluntary associations and make them subservient to the state and its institutions.
- Among democracies, some countries have a tradition of keeping interest groups at arm's length from political decision makers, but in other countries, interest groups are encouraged to participate and may even be invited to take part in negotiations about new public policies.
- Protests are an increasingly important form of political participation.
- Scholars of comparative politics are especially interested in what makes people protest, how governments respond when they do, and how likely protesters are to achieve their political goals.

STUDY QUESTIONS

1. In Section 13.5, we discussed the relationship between political institutions and protests. On the one hand, protests are often a response to the perceived failures of political institutions. On the other hand, institutions are part of the political opportunity structure and therefore make protests more or less likely by influencing the perceived costs and benefits of protesting. Consider all the things you've learned about different forms of political institutions in this book—from our discussion of regimes in Chapters 4 and 5 via our discussion of electoral systems, legislatures, and executives in Chapters 7 and 8 to our discussion of the judiciary in Chapter 9. What sorts of institutions do you think make protests more or less likely?

2. Consider the examples of protests we have discussed in this chapter. How would you categorize the interest groups that engage in protests, using the categories we discussed at the beginning of the chapter?

FURTHER READING

Heike Klüver, *Lobbying in the European Union: Interest Groups, Lobbying Coalitions, and Policy Change* (2013).
Examines lobbying within the European Union.

Andreas Dür and Gemma Mateo, *Insiders versus Outsiders: Interest Group Politics in Multilevel Europe* (2016).
Studies the role of interest groups at different levels of government in Europe.

Hanspeter Kriesi et al., *Contention in Times of Crisis: Recession and Political Protest in Thirty European Countries* (2020).
Studies recent political protests in Europe.

Erica Chenoweth, *Civil Resistance* (2021).
Analyses the political effects of non-violent protests.

CHAPTER 14

THE MEDIA

CHAPTER GUIDE

14.1 Introduction
14.2 The Freedom of the Press
14.3 Politics and the Media
14.4 Media Effects
14.5 Digital and Social Media

14.6 Conclusion
Summary
Study Questions
Further Reading

14.1 INTRODUCTION

How do you keep yourself informed about politics? If you're like most people, you rely on print or digital media such as newspapers and magazines, broadcast media such as radio and television, or digital-only social media such as Facebook and TikTok. Because so many of us depend on the media for political information, the relationship between the media and the political system is a topic of central importance across the social sciences, from communication studies via sociology and economics to political science. In this chapter, we'll study the relationship between politics and the media from a comparative perspective and examine the regulation, ownership, and impact of print, broadcast, and digital media in different political systems.

In Section 14.2, we'll analyse the relationship between politics and the media in different types of regime, continuing the discussion of democracy and authoritarianism that we began in Chapters 4 and 5. Most authoritarian governments try to control the media, which they use to disseminate propaganda, while denying access to print, broadcast, and sometimes even digital media to their opponents. In democracies, by contrast, the freedom of the press is widely regarded as a basic political right. As we'll see in Section 14.3, the relationships between media organizations, political decision makers, and the state also vary greatly among democratic states. After considering these broad differences between political regimes and among democratic systems, we'll turn to the effects of the mass media on political campaigning, voting, policymaking, and other important political processes in democratic regimes (Section 14.4). In Section 14.5, finally, we'll examine the political consequences of the expansion of internet access and the pervasiveness of social media in the twenty-first century. We'll put these contemporary events in context by comparing the spread of the internet with historical transformations in political communication, such as the increasing circulation of newspapers in the nineteenth century and the coming of television in the twentieth.

Comparative research on political communication and the mass media has enriched our understanding of modern politics. The evidence we'll consider in this chapter suggests that if we want to understand contemporary politics, it's not enough to understand how political parties and interest groups are organized, how voters vote, or how political decision makers in legislatures, governments, high courts, and administrative agencies make their decisions. We must also understand how media corporations, editors, journalists, public relations professionals, and social media activists influence the flow of ideas and information in society, shaping how citizens think about political issues.

14.2 THE FREEDOM OF THE PRESS

LEARNING OUTCOMES

After reading Section 14.2, you'll be able to:

- Describe the variation in the freedom of the press across the world
- Analyse the relationship between democracy and the freedom of the press
- Explain how authoritarian regimes use propaganda.

As we discussed in Chapter 4, the right of journalists and media organizations to publish and disseminate information freely is central to most definitions of democracy. We still use the old term **the freedom of the press** to denote this bundle of rights. The term **media freedom** is also widely used, since 'the press', strictly speaking, only refers to print media such as newspapers and magazines, not broadcast and digital media.

The idea of freedom of the press goes back to the era of the Enlightenment in Europe in the eighteenth century (for a discussion of the concept and its history, see, for example, Graber 2017, 238). Many European scholars and political leaders in that period of intellectual and political change believed that economic, social, and political progress depended on the free flow of ideas in society.

This didn't necessarily make these intellectuals and political leaders democrats. For example, in his essay 'What Is Enlightenment?' (1784) the philosopher Immanuel Kant, whom we encountered in Chapter 1, encouraged citizens to 'Argue as much as you want and about what you want, but obey!' But the Enlightenment's ideas about freedom of expression and of the press were important in their own right and influenced many eighteenth-century constitutions. In 1766, for example, the Swedish parliament adopted the Freedom of the Press Act, which, in its revised 1949 form, remains part of the Swedish constitution to this day. In 1789, in the early days of the Great Revolution, the French National Assembly adopted a Declaration of the Rights of Man, which stated that 'The free communication of ideas and opinions is one of the most precious of the rights of man' and that every citizen could 'speak, write, and print with freedom' (Article 11). Two years later, in 1791, the United States ratified the First Amendment to the constitution, which provided, among other things, that 'Congress shall make no law ... abridging the freedom of speech, or of the press'.

Let us consider some cross-country evidence on the freedom of the press today. Figure 14.1 is based on the World Press Freedom Index, which is compiled every year by the international non-profit organization *Reporters sans frontières* (Reporters without Borders). The map describes the

Figure 14.1 The freedom of the press varied greatly across the world in 2023. *Source: Author's own work, based on data from Reporters without Borders (RSF) 2024 World Press Freedom Index*

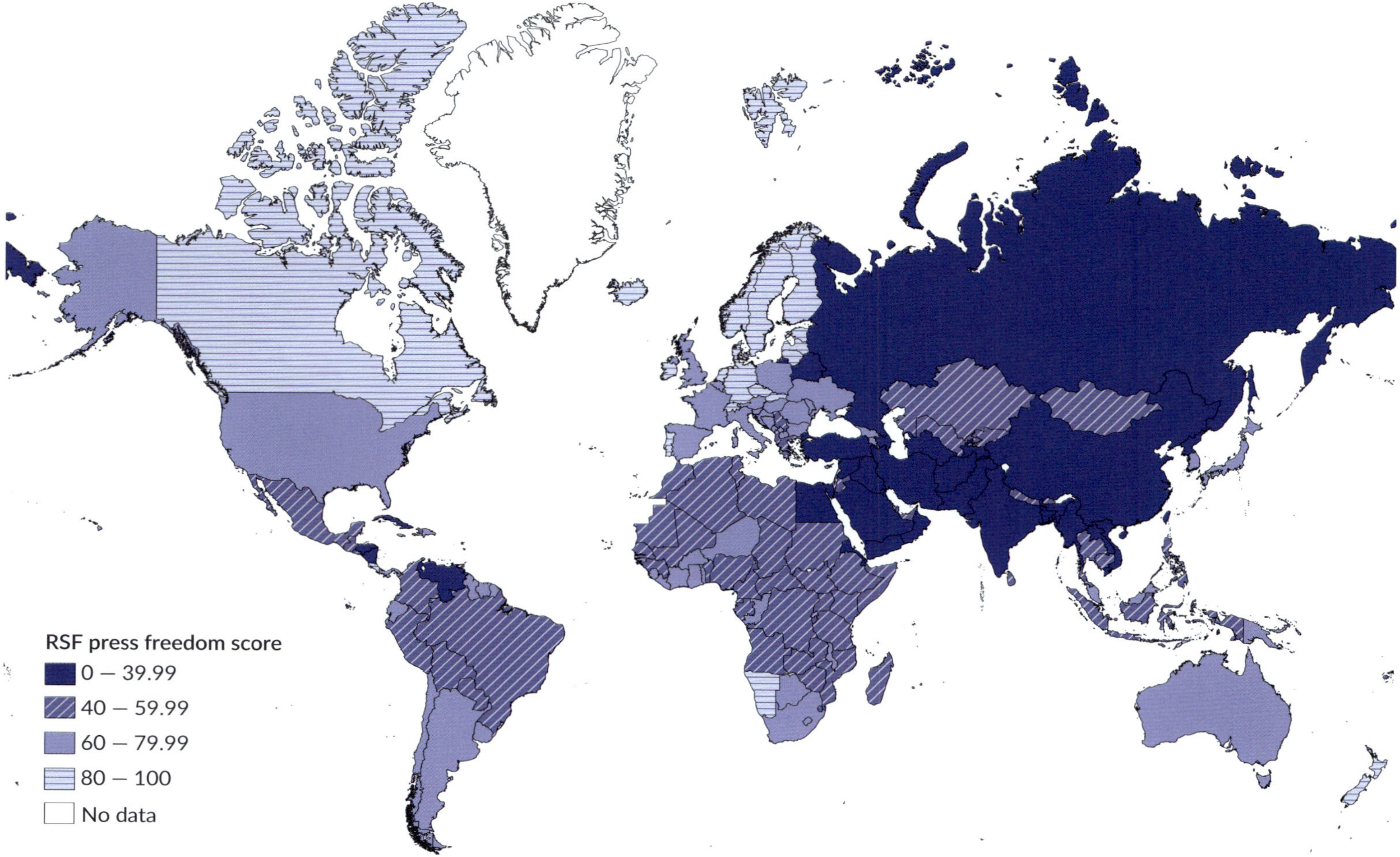

RSF press freedom score
- 0 – 39.99
- 40 – 59.99
- 60 – 79.99
- 80 – 100
- No data

environment for journalism in early 2023. The freedom of the press is defined, here, as 'the ability of journalists as individuals and collectives to select, produce, and disseminate news in the public interest independent of political, economic, legal, and social interference and in the absence of threats to their physical and mental safety'. This is a complex definition that goes beyond legal protections for journalists by taking into account the actual conditions that reporters and news organizations face. Consequently, the evidence in the figure relies on numerous indicators of constitutional rules, the concentration of media ownership, and various threats faced by editors and journalists.

A cursory look at the map in Figure 14.1 is enough to determine that there is a close relationship between press freedom and democracy (keeping in mind the maps of democratic and authoritarian regimes that we studied in Chapter 4). The reason is simple: a democracy cannot function without a free press, for elections lose their meaning if the voters cannot make an informed choice when they vote, and governments aren't accountable if they can keep failures and abuses of power secret. Democratic government needs to be transparent, so citizens can learn what's going on. But transparency is not enough. There also needs to be a group of people who work actively to keep citizens informed about current affairs, since most of us are too busy with other things to follow politics closely. For hundreds of years, that group has been made up of reporters and other journalists.

As we learned in Chapter 5, a transition from democracy to authoritarianism often begins with a struggle over the mass media. This happens quickly in a *coup d'état*. For example, when the military began its attempt to overthrow the government of Niger in July 2023, forces loyal to the incumbent president, Mohamed Bazoum, were immediately deployed to protect the state broadcasting organization, Office de Radiodiffusion et Télévision du Niger, or ORTN. In the evening of 26 July, however, the leaders of the coup appeared on one ORTN television channel, Télé Sahel, to announce that they had taken control over the government (see Figure 14.2).

Figure 14.2 On 26 July 2023, the leaders of the *coup d'état* in Niger announced on state television that they had removed President Mohamed Bazoum from power. *Source: BBC News, 'Niger Coup: President Mohamad Bazoum in good health, says France', Tchima Illa Issoufou & Lucy Fleming, 28 July 2023*

When a transition from democracy to authoritarianism occurs more gradually, through an incumbent takeover, the government typically enhances its control over state media and increases its pressure on independent media organizations step-by-step, not all at once. If you go back to Case Study 5.2, which dealt with the fate of democracy in Hungary, you will find that several of the events that we discussed there concerned the government's efforts to increase its influence over the mass media. Note, for instance, the creation of a new National Media Authority in 2011, the biased media coverage of the parliamentary election of 2014, and the closure of Hungary's largest independent newspaper in 2017.

Today, scholars of authoritarian politics are paying particularly close attention to the relationship between politics and the media, since most twenty-first-century authoritarian governments rely less on violent repression and persecution than authoritarian regimes did in the past. Instead, they hold on to power by using the media to disseminate propaganda that portrays the authoritarian regime in a good light and discredits opposition groups. According to Guriev and Treisman's 'informational theory of autocracy' (2023), twenty-first-century authoritarian rulers often survive in office by convincing the general public that they are competent leaders and administrators, not by promoting a particular ideology, as twentieth-century authoritarian regimes typically did. They persuade the public to accept the authority of the regime by producing state propaganda, censoring independent media organizations, and co-opting economic, social, and political elites. Political influence over the media is thus an important mechanism through which contemporary authoritarian rulers accomplish their principal political goals. As research by Gohdes (2023) has demonstrated, contemporary authoritarian regimes also use digital media effectively for purposes of surveillance and repression.

One illustrative example of how authoritarian media achieve their political objectives can be found in the work of Otlan et al. (2023), who conducted a detailed study of how Russian media have reported on political protests outside of Russia. Although one might have expected authoritarian media to refrain from covering foreign protests, since doing so might inspire domestic opponents of the regime to organize protests of their own, Otlan et al. demonstrate that the opposite is true: Russian media have in fact covered foreign protests extensively. But they also show that the Russian media have reported very selectively on protests in democracies, in order to convey the idea that an active citizenry can be disruptive and disorderly. They also note that reporting on foreign protests has tended to decline when there have been protests inside Russia, presumably because such coverage might have encouraged people to engage in domestic protest activities. As this example from Russia shows, a contemporary authoritarian government can use its control over the media carefully and deliberately to increase support for the regime.

Before we conclude our discussion of the freedom of the press, it's important to note that the legal framework around the principle of the freedom of the press varies among democracies. As we discussed in the beginning of this section, the First Amendment to the United States constitution provides that 'Congress shall make no law . . . abridging the freedom of speech, or of the press', and the United States Supreme Court interprets the phrase 'make no law' to mean that almost all restrictions on the freedom of the press are unconstitutional. In European states, the freedom of the press is usually less absolute. These legal differences between the United States and western Europe are significant, since they influence political debates about the role of the media in a democratic society. Indeed, as we'll learn in Section 14.3, there are many other important differences between the world's democratic states when it comes to the relationship between the media and the political system.

14.3 POLITICS AND THE MEDIA

LEARNING OUTCOMES
After reading Section 14.3, you'll be able to:
- Describe the main differences between media systems in democracies
- Analyse the relationship between the media system and other important institutions.

The first major comparative study of the relationship between media and politics was Siebert, Peterson, and Schramm's *Four Theories of the Press* (1956). From their vantage point in the middle of the Cold War, Siebert, Peterson, and Schramm distinguished between two non-democratic models of the relationship between the media and the political system: an old 'authoritarian' model, which they argued went back to the autocratic regimes in Europe in the eighteenth and nineteenth centuries, and a newer 'Soviet communist' model that had emerged in the twentieth century. But they also distinguished between two different *democratic* models of the relationship between the media and the political system, which they referred to as the 'libertarian' and 'social responsibility' models. The libertarian model was based on the idea that the government ought to interfere as little as possible in the media. The social responsibility model, on the other hand, was based on the idea that the media industry can have pernicious social and political effects and therefore needs to be regulated.

Later generations of scholars have grouped countries differently, but the general idea that the relationship between the media and the political system varies a lot among democracies continues to hold. One influential study from the early 2000s, Hallin and Mancini (2004), argued that democratic countries can be sorted into three groups with different 'media systems', which they referred to as the liberal model, the democratic-corporatist model, and the polarized-pluralist model. These concepts were applied mainly to democratic states in North America, western Europe, and the Asia-Pacific region, but later, the authors sought to extend the framework beyond that group of countries (Hallin and Mancini 2011). Hallin and Mancini categorized the media systems of individual countries on the basis of evidence on four concepts: the inclusiveness of the media market (whether the news media reach many different groups in society), professionalism (how professional journalists are and how well they're trusted by citizens), political parallelism (how autonomous the media are from political groups and parties), and the state's role (whether there is a public broadcasting corporation and how the state funds or regulates private media organizations).

- The liberal model, much like the 'libertarian' model discussed in *Four Theories of the Press*, is characterized by a high degree of press freedom and minimal government intervention in the media. Among the high-income democracies in Europe and North America, Hallin and Mancini argued that Britain, Canada, Ireland, and the United States resembled the liberal model.
- The democratic-corporatist model is characterized by more coordination between the government, the mass media, and other sectors, and the media are expected to mediate conflicts between different groups in society. This model bears a close resemblance to the media systems in central and northern European countries such as Austria, Belgium, Denmark, Finland, Germany, Netherlands, Norway, Sweden, and Switzerland.
- The polarized-pluralist model, finally, is characterized by a high level of political polarization and a weak tradition of press freedom. In this third model, the media are often used as a tool for particular political factions or groups (in Italy, for instance, the public television channels

were long divided between the major political parties). In Europe, Hallin and Mancini argued that the polarized-pluralist model resembles the media systems in southern European states such as France, Greece, Italy, Portugal, and Spain.

If you think back to what we've discussed in previous chapters, you'll note that in their work on the media, Hallin and Mancini (2004) used concepts that we recognize from other areas of comparative politics. For example, the way in which they grouped European and North American countries is reminiscent of how scholars of comparative politics have grouped the advanced democracies when it comes to the role of interest groups in political decision making (see Chapter 13) and the organization of the welfare state (see Chapters 3 and 15). Such typologies are useful, since they encourage us to think about the most important differences among countries. But they can also give the impression that political arrangements are more stable and coherent than they actually are. We must always keep in mind that all real-world media systems, like real-world interest-group systems and welfare states, combine traits that are associated with different stylized models.

In one of the most recent attempts to group countries according to the relationship between the media and politics, Humprecht et al. (2022) try to establish how the rise of digital and social media in the twenty-first century has influenced the media systems in the democratic states in Europe and North America. Their main findings are presented in Figure 14.3, which describes

Figure 14.3 The media systems in European and North American states varied greatly in the early 2000s. *Source: Author's own work, based on data from Edda Humprecht, Laia Castro Herrero, Sina Blassnig, Michael Brüggemann, Sven Engesser, 'Media Systems in the Digital Age: An Empirical Comparison of 30 Countries',* Journal of Communication, *Volume 72, Issue 2, April 2022, pp. 145–164, (c) Oxford University Press 2022*

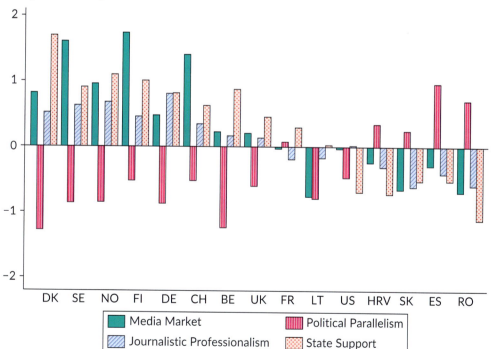

the level of professionalism among journalists, the inclusiveness of the media market, the nature of state support for the media, and the degree of political parallelism in 30 countries in the 2010s and 2020s. As the figure shows, the democratic states in northern and continental Europe have media systems that resemble Hallin and Mancini's democratic-corporatist model, because of their professional, state-supported media, their inclusivity, and their low levels of political polarization. There is also a group of countries that corresponds to Hallin and Mancini's polarized-pluralist model, with politicized media that are weakly supported by the state. This group includes many eastern European countries that were not studied by Hallin and Mancini. Finally, there is a group of countries that Humprecht et al. refer to as 'hybrid' since their models are neither democratic-corporatist nor polarized-pluralist. The United Kingdom is included in this group.

The main thing to keep in mind, as we move from these broad institutional differences among countries to more specific questions about how the mass media shape political processes, is the simple observation that democratic countries organize the relationship between the media and the political system in very different ways. One might have expected the proliferation of increasingly global cable television, digital media, and social media to make countries more alike, but many important differences remain. Some countries continue to be dominated by national newspapers, television networks, and radio stations; other countries have more decentralized media. In some countries, media organizations are associated with particular political parties; in other countries, political parties keep their distance. Finally, in some countries, public media corporations, such as the British Broadcasting Corporation (BBC) in the United Kingdom, continue to play an important role in radio, television, and digital media; in other countries, public broadcasters are small or non-existent, and private corporations dominate the media industry.

In Case Study 14.1, we will study the role of the media in the context of a hybrid political regime: we will learn about the political consequences of the concentration of media ownership in the hands of a few powerful businessmen in Ukraine in the decades after the fall of communism in the early 1990s. As the case study shows, we can think of the Ukrainian media system—with its many media corporations controlled by powerful 'oligarchs'—as an extreme example of the polarized-pluralist model that Hallin and Mancini described.

CASE STUDY 14.1
Who owns the news? Lessons from Ukraine

After the end of communism, Ukraine, like its neighbours in eastern Europe, dismantled its old state monopoly on media, and a new, more decentralized and privatized media landscape emerged. But Ukraine's experiences in the 1990s, 2000s, and 2010s demonstrate that formal press freedom isn't enough for media organizations to be independent and act as a check on political institutions and leaders.

As Ryabinska (2011) points out, private media companies need advertisement revenue for a strong media sector to emerge. Ukraine's economy has been weak, and 15 national broadcasting stations have competed for the available revenue, so this condition for a vibrant media sector has not been met. Much of the revenue has instead come from political advertisements.

> Ryabinska also highlights how the remaining state-owned outlets in Ukraine have hampered the development of new media: they have been able to offer cheaper prices to consumers and advertisers, as well as making more lucrative job offers.
>
> But what's perhaps most notable about the Ukrainian media landscape after the end of communism is the predominance of ownership by powerful 'oligarchs'. These powerful businessmen have their main economic operations outside of the media sector, especially in the banking and steel industries, and have used their media empires to promote their business interests. The most illustrative example is the aggressive campaign that the media corporation Inter TV waged against Ukraine's prime minister, Yulia Tymoshenko, in 2009, because of a conflict around gas supplies between one of the TV corporation's owners and the prime minister and her team (Ryabinska 2011, 10).
>
> In other words, because of the vast economic power of a few businessmen—a result of the rapid privatization of nationalized industries in the 1990s, after the end of the Cold War—private media companies in Ukraine have often served the political interests of their owners.

14.4 MEDIA EFFECTS

LEARNING OUTCOMES

After reading Section 14.4, you'll be able to:

- Distinguish between agenda setting and framing
- Analyse media effects in different political systems
- Explain how political parties and decision makers are influenced by the media.

When journalists and media organizations report on politics, they can influence how voters think about political issues. Scholars of political communication distinguish between two main types of media effect: agenda-setting effects and framing effects. By reporting on certain issues and not others, the media can influence the political agenda—that is, which issues voters pay attention to and regard as important. But the media can also influence how voters *interpret* the issues that are on the political agenda. They do so by framing issues in a manner that leads readers, listeners, and viewers to associate them with particular expectations, ideas, and values.

Let's consider an example. If the media devote a lot of their coverage to environmental issues (as opposed to, say, defence procurement or education spending), environmental policy is likely to rise to the top of the voters' agenda (but defence and education are less likely to do so). The voters will pay more attention to the issue the media report on, which may ultimately influence which party they vote for. But the media can also emphasize different aspects of environmental policy when they cover that issue—in other words, they can 'frame' the issue in different ways. For example, if the government has proposed a tax on fossil fuels, the media can emphasize the effects of the new tax on carbon dioxide emissions, but they can also emphasize its effects on fuel costs for rural and suburban voters who depend on cars for transportation. These two different frames—which we might call the carbon dioxide frame and the rural–urban frame—are likely to influence how people view the government's proposal (Figure 14.4).

Figure 14.4 The media might frame fuel taxes as a response to climate change—or as a burden on rural citizens. *Source: A: Toa55 / Shutterstock; B: sportpoint / Alamy Stock Photo*

(A) Lower emissions…   (B) …or higher living costs?

For scholars and students of comparative politics, what's most interesting about the media's agenda setting and framing of political issues is that they vary systematically between countries with different political institutions and media systems (De Vreese 2017). For example, a comparative study of election campaigns in the United States and Sweden in the early 2000s, inspired by the comparative research on media systems that we discussed in Section 14.3, demonstrated that newspapers in the two countries covered election campaigns very differently, giving voters a different sense of what politics is about (Strömbäck and Dimitrova 2006). In particular, American newspapers were more likely to engage in 'horserace' journalism—emphasizing the election campaign per se—whereas Swedish media were more likely to cover substantive political issues.

The media don't just influence how ordinary citizens perceive political issues, parties, and candidates; they also influence many of the political institutions and organizations we have covered in this book. Consider parliaments, which we discussed in Chapter 8. In a recent paper, Yildirim et al. (2023) show that members of parliament who appear often in the media also make more speeches in the legislature. More senior members of the governing party tend to benefit the most from the increased attention they get by being featured in the media. Or consider political parties, which we discussed in Chapter 11. Scholars such as Strömbäck and Van Aelst (2013) have demonstrated that modern political parties have adapted both their organizational structures and their communication strategies to the demands of the intense media environment they're in. Some scholars of political parties have even argued that the growing importance of the mass media in modern societies has led to major changes in party organizations since the middle of the twentieth century by making party leaders more independent of their parties' members and activists (Katz and Mair 1995). In the twenty-first century, changes in the media landscape have contributed to the rise of 'personalist' parties that are dominated by single individuals. It is worth keeping in mind that two of the foremost populist politicians of the early twenty-first century—Silvio Berlusconi, who used to be prime minister of Italy, and Donald Trump, president of the United States from 2017 to 2021 and from 2025—both made their careers in the television industry (in both cases after first pursuing a career in the real-estate industry).

In Chapter 15, we'll discuss the factors that influence public policymaking in democratic political systems. The mass media can have powerful effects on policymaking too. Indeed, as noted by Grossman (2022), the rise of digital and social media seems to have forced politicians to become more reactive to the media agenda, responding to conflicts that play out on the internet, where as previous generations of politicians were often able to influence the media and use that influence to further their own political goals.

One important goal of contemporary comparative-politics scholarship on the media is to estimate the political effects of the establishment of new newspapers, radio stations, television stations, or internet sites. The reason is methodological. The effects of news consumption on political behaviour are difficult to assess empirically, since people decide for themselves what news to consume, which means that correlations between news consumption and political behaviour typically cannot be interpreted causally. People who consume left-wing media tend to have left-wing views, and people who consume right-wing media tend to have right-wing views, but the most plausible explanation for these correlations is that people consume newspapers and television programmes they agree with—not that the media change people's attitudes. What we have here is another example of the general problem of causality that we discussed in Chapter 2.

However, scholars have come up with some ingenious solutions to this problem, and many studies of the political effects of the media go beyond mere correlations between media consumption and political attitudes and behaviours, emphasizing how people's attitudes and behaviours change when a new communication technology or a new form of broadcasting becomes available in a particular geographical area. The results of such studies give us stronger reasons to believe that the media have causal effects on attitudes and behaviour. For example, DellaVigna and Kaplan (2007) analysed the spread of the right-wing television channel Fox News in the United States and found a positive effect on the Republican vote share in presidential elections in the late 1990s and 2000s when Fox News reached different parts of the country. We'll discuss these sorts of studies in Case Study 14.2.

CASE STUDY 14.2
CNN or Fox News?

As we've just discussed in the main text, it is inherently difficult to study the relationship between the media that people consume and their political preferences. Especially in countries with highly politicized media and polarized political systems, people's media habits and their political attitudes and electoral behaviour are highly correlated, which might be taken to suggest that consuming particular newspapers, television news, radio broadcasts, or digital media has a powerful effect on political behaviour. But then you realize that people's media habits are themselves shaped by their political attitudes and loyalties, which raises the possibility that the media have no effects at all—our media habits may simply be a reflection of our underlying political orientations.

Over the last few years, social scientists have sought to estimate the effects of the media on political attitudes with the help of methods that go beyond mere correlations and come closer to identifying the causal effects of exposure to particular media. In the United States, scholars have been especially interested in studying the effects of exposure to the television network that is most closely associated with the party on the right, Fox News, and the television network that is most popular among more left-of-centre viewers, CNN.

In one influential study, DellaVigna and Kaplan (2007) took advantage of the fact that as the Fox News channel was introduced, it wasn't available immediately in all media markets in the United States—it spread gradually, and became available in different US cities at different times.

By studying what happened to people's political attitudes and party choices when Fox News became available in new markets, the authors could estimate the effect of the network with great precision. The main result of their study is that the vote share of the Republican candidate in the presidential elections increased by somewhere between 0.4 and 0.7 percentage points in towns were Fox News was available, compared with towns in which it wasn't.

The DellaVigna and Kaplan study relied on what's called a 'quasi-experimental' method—by studying what happened as Fox News became available in new media markets, the authors in effect learned about the effect of Fox News as if an experiment had been run, whereby some voters in the United States were exposed to Fox News but others weren't. In a later study, Broockman and Kalla (2022) used an actual experiment—a 'field experiment'—to study the effect of switching from one television network to another. They identified a group of American voters who watched Fox News a lot and paid some of them to instead watch the liberal-leaning television network CNN for a month. They found that watching CNN had a discernible, if not very large, effect on political attitudes. In other words, like the effect identified by DellaVigna and Kaplan, the effect was 'statistically significant', in the sense that it was unlikely that there was no effect at all, but it was not very strong, since people's political opinions didn't move very much.

The quasi-experimental study by DellaVigna and Kaplan (2007) and the field experiment by Broockman and Kalla (2022) are examples of how scholars are able to assess the ability of the media to sway public opinion and change people's political behaviour. Their findings suggest that the effects are real, but not as large as one might be led to believe by observing how closely related media habits and political preferences are.

In another study of the United States, Gentzkow (2006) demonstrated that the roll-out of cable television had a negative effect on voter turnout, probably because cable television replaced other media that had a richer content of political information. But here we again see that effects can vary a lot between different media systems and political systems, for in a very different setting—rural Norway—Sørensen (2019) showed that the roll-out of public television broadcasting had a *positive* effect on turnout.

14.5 DIGITAL AND SOCIAL MEDIA

LEARNING OUTCOMES

After reading Section 14.5, you'll be able to:
- Compare access to the internet across the world
- Assess the political effects of new communication technologies
- Analyse the role of social media in twenty-first-century politics.

Today, many people get their news from news websites and from social media such as Facebook, X, Instagram, and Tiktok. Scholars of political communication have therefore been eager to learn more about how digital and social media have influenced election campaigns, public discourse, and public policy.

Compared with print media such as newspapers and magazines and broadcast media such as radio and television, digital-only media and social media have only been around for a short time. As recently as in the early 2000s, very few people in the world had access to the internet. By the early 2020s, by contrast, most people did. We can see this in Figure 14.5, which describes the level of internet connectivity in different countries in 2020, using data from the World Bank. As the figure shows, major differences remain between the world regions—with internet access in sub-Saharan Africa being especially patchy—but in most countries, more than half of the population used the internet regularly.

Online-only and social media differ from print media and broadcast media in at least three important respects.

- Producing and communicating content that can be distributed via digital networks is much cheaper than producing and distributing newspapers, magazines, and radio and television programmes. Since anyone can start a blog, a media channel on YouTube, or a podcast, not just large corporations, the media have become more heterogeneous, decentralized, and fragmented.
- Print and broadcast media are highly institutionalized, with long-established legislation, codes of conduct, and ethics rules governing the work of journalists and editors. Online-only and social media are not governed by such dense rules.
- Social media are interactive. The broadcast media that emerged in the twentieth century—radio and television—are one-way technologies: one sender, usually a radio or television corporation, sends out a signal that reaches many radio and television receivers, which cannot themselves send out signals. Social media are by definition not one-way.

Because of these three differences between digital-only and social media and traditional print and broadcast media, the spread of the internet has changed the nature of political communication in the twenty-first century.

That said, it's important to remember, as we evaluate the effects of the spread of the internet, that this isn't the first time that a new technology has revolutionized political communication. Television changed politics when it emerged in the middle of the twentieth century. Radio arguably changed politics even more dramatically when advances in wireless technology after the First World War made mass broadcasting possible for the very first time. Democratic political leaders such as President Franklin D. Roosevelt in the United States used the radio effectively to communicate with their voters, while dictators such as Adolf Hitler in Germany used radio broadcasting to spread regime propaganda.

Long before the coming of radio, in the nineteenth century, modern newspapers also changed political communication fundamentally. In the late nineteenth and early twentieth centuries, powerful 'newspaper barons'—such as Lord Northcliffe (Alfred Harmsworth) and Lord Beaverbrook (Max Aitken) in the United Kingdom—developed reputations for being able to make or break political careers: politicians knew that they crossed these powerful men at their peril. One technological innovation that revolutionized the newspaper industry in the nineteenth century was the electric telegraph, which has been called the 'Victorian internet' (Standage 1998), since it created the first worldwide electronic communication network. The telegraph seems like a slow and antiquated technology to us now, but it changed political communication forever. For example, with the arrival of the telegraph, it became possible to relay news between North America and

Figure 14.5 By 2021, most people in the world used the internet regularly, but great disparities remained among countries. *Source: Author's own work, based on data from Teorell et al. (2024)*

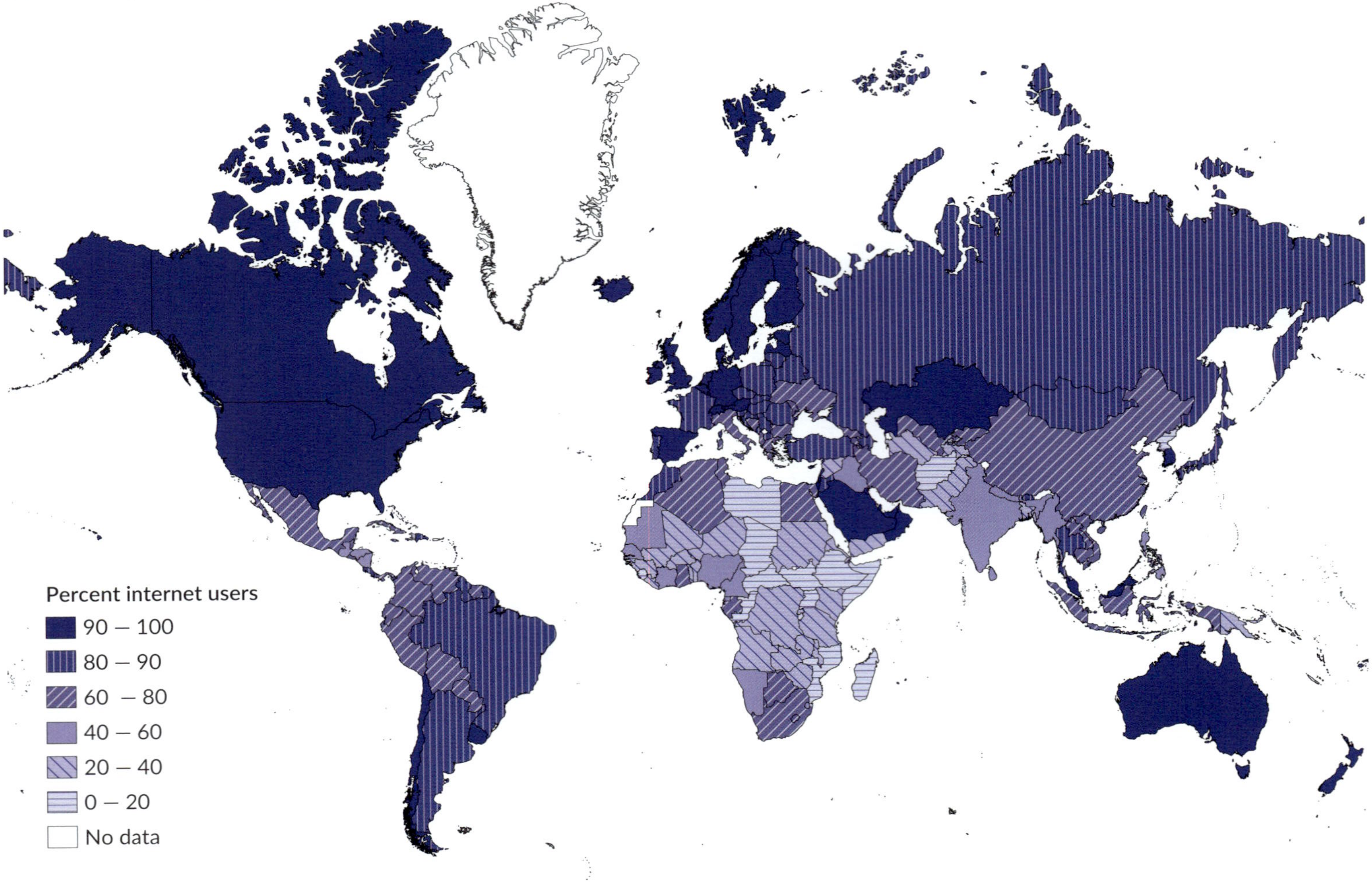

Europe in a matter of hours, even minutes; before the telegraph, it usually took months for news from America to reach Europe and vice versa.

Going even further back, the printing press, which was invented in the middle of the fifteenth century, arguably had more profound effects on political communication than any other technology before or since. The term 'global village'—which we use today to describe the highly connected world that social media have made—was introduced decades ago in a book about the world the *printing press* made (McLuhan 1962). We understand the effects of new technologies such as the internet better if we think of them as a phase in an ongoing revolution of media systems and political communication that began centuries ago.

Political scientists have asked many different sorts of questions about the political effects of social media.

Social media can facilitate the exchange of ideas and information, which can, in turn, lead to increased political participation. We know this from studies of modern protest movements, which, as we mentioned in Chapter 13, often begin online, with the leaders of the movements using social media to mobilize activists and to plan and publicize protest events. Empirical studies of contemporary protest movements have shown that social media networks have sometimes brought together disparate groups into broad political coalitions, such as the combinations of liberals, ethnic minorities, religious communities, and others who opposed authoritarian regimes in North Africa and the Middle East during the Arab Spring. For example, Tufekci and Wilson (2012) find in a study of protests in Europe that social media users were more likely to attend protests than citizens who depended on telephone or email. The attack on the Capitol Building in Washington, DC in January 2021 that we discussed in Chapter 2 was also coordinated via social media networks.

But digital-only and social media can also be used to spread misinformation and propaganda. Social media channels are particularly vulnerable to misinformation, which can have powerful political effects. There are strong reasons to believe that the election of Donald Trump as president of the United States in 2016 was influenced by the distribution of misinformation via social media channels: most of the false news stories that circulated on these channels during the 2016 election tended to favour Trump and discredit his opponent, Hillary Clinton. Specifically, Allcott and Gentzkow (2017) found that 115 pro-Trump false stories were shared on Facebook 30 million times, whereas 41 pro-Clinton false stories were shared only 7.6 million times—and one in four Americans visited websites distributing misinformation. In the 2024 election, there was a fairly uniform swing towards Trump across geographical areas and demographic groups, which suggests that the election wasn't decided by the spread of information or propaganda through specific social networks.

The fragmented media landscape that has emerged as a result of the proliferation of digital-only and social media has contributed to the increase in political polarization that we discussed in Chapter 12. One of the reasons is that digital-only and social media tend to facilitate the creation of online communities in which people don't discuss or engage with those who have different opinions from theirs, but instead only with those they already agree with. For example, with the help of experimental methods, Levy (2021) shows that exposure to 'counter-attitudinal' news that speaks against people's political opinions tends to reduce political polarization, but the algorithms that select news stories for users of social media sites such as Facebook limits their exposure to such counter-attitudinal information.

Another effect of the proliferation of digital and social media is that most people today live in what communication scholars call 'high-choice media environments', which forces us all to be more discerning as we consume news and which has transformed political communication (Van Aelst et al. 2017). We consider political communication in high-choice media environments in Research Prompt 14.1.

>
> **RESEARCH PROMPT 14.1**
> Spoiled for choice
>
> One of the most important consequences of the spread of digital and social media is that citizens today have access to many more sources of news and political information than they did two or three decades ago. Choose a country whose language you can read and consult the website of one of its major political parties—perhaps one of the parties you studied in Research Prompt 11.2 in Chapter 11. Browse the website for recently issued press releases, news items, and campaign materials, and list all the traditional media channels and social media channels the party has relied on to get its message out and engage with voters. Can you spot a pattern in how the party uses different channels to communicate different messages to different groups of voters? Then think about the party's messaging from the point of view of voters. What challenges do voters face in a high-choice media environment as they try to keep themselves informed about politics?

14.6 CONCLUSION

In this chapter, we have studied the role of the media in politics. We began with the differences between authoritarian and democratic regimes. Then we examined the relationship between the media and the political system in the established democracies in Europe and North America. As we learned in Section 14.3, the countries in these regions have long had different 'media systems', and they continue to do so today, despite the global reach of modern broadcast and digital media. We then studied the effects of the media on different sorts of processes in democratic politics. Finally, we learned about the main differences between digital-only media and social media on the one hand and more traditional print and broadcast media on the other, and we discussed some of the problems that scholars of comparative political communication are most eager to understand better, including the role of social media in political protests and the relationship between digital media and political polarization.

The media perform an indispensable function in a democratic political system. As voters, we depend on newspapers, magazines, radio and television programmes, and digital and social media for information about the political parties and their platforms, and we're only able to hold the government accountable if we can keep ourselves informed about the government's policies and how successful they've been. This also means that the media can wield great influence in a democracy—but they do so in very different ways in different countries, since the organization of the media industry and the relationship between the media and the political system vary so much among democracies. In Section 14.4, we studied several examples of how the media influence important political processes, from election campaigns to party politics and legislative procedures. But we could have considered other examples, from other chapters in this book. For instance, the high courts we studied in Chapter 9 are acutely aware of how the media report on their trials and judgments.

In Chapter 15, we'll study public policymaking. You will find that the media can influence public policy too.

SUMMARY

- The freedom of the press varies greatly among countries, and it is closely related with democracy, since voters depend on the media to make an informed choice when they vote and hold the government to account.
- Contemporary authoritarian governments often use their power over the media to spread propaganda and silence dissenting voices.
- The relationship between media organizations and the political system also varies greatly among democratic states.
- Some democracies have polarized pluralist media sectors while others have public broadcasting companies with a more independent role in relation to political parties and interest groups.
- The media can influence public opinion through agenda-setting and framing effects.
- To learn about the effects of the media on political attitudes and behaviour, scholars often study the consequences of the adoption and roll-out of new media technologies. Many studies have used such methods to establish how the media influence political attitudes and political participation.
- Digital-only and social media are different from traditional mass media, especially because of the low costs of producing and distributing content and the interactive nature of digital technologies.
- But changes in media technologies have revolutionized political communication before, notably in the nineteenth century, when modern newspapers emerged, and in the beginning and middle of the twentieth century, with the coming of radio and television.

STUDY QUESTIONS

1. In Section 14.5, we compared the political effects of digital-only and social media with earlier revolutions in political communication, such as the rise of the modern newspaper in the nineteenth century and the coming of broadcast media in the twentieth. Think back to our discussion of the freedom of the press in Section 14.2, our discussion of different media systems in Section 14.3, and our discussion of media effects in election campaigns in Section 14.4. In which area do you think the transition from traditional print and broadcast media to digital media will have the greatest effects?
2. The media can influence how we think about political issues by covering some issues and not others, and by framing the issues they do cover in particular ways. But who influences the choices journalists and editors make about what to report on and how? Do you think they act autonomously, or can political parties and interest organizations exert influence over the media?

FURTHER READING

Daniel C. Hallin and Paolo Mancini, *Comparing Media Systems* (2004).
   An influential study of the relationship between politics and the media in western European and North American democracies.

Aeron Davis, *Political Communication: An Introduction for Crisis Times* (2023).
   A recent introduction to the field of political communication.

Claes de Vreese, Frank Esser, and David Nicolas Hopmann, *Comparing Political Journalism* (2017).
   A comparative overview of how the conduct of political journalism varies among countries.

CHAPTER 15

PUBLIC POLICYMAKING

CHAPTER GUIDE

15.1 Introduction
15.2 Comparative Public Policy
15.3 Studying Policymaking and Public Policies
15.4 Getting Things Done
15.5 Authoritarian Regimes and Global Challenges

15.6 Conclusion
Summary
Study Questions
Further Reading

15.1 INTRODUCTION

In this chapter, you'll learn more about public policies and how they come about, which is a process known as policymaking. Public policies are the end result of the struggle for power and influence among parties and interest groups, and they have profound effects on how we live our lives. It affects us personally when we're required to follow the law or are asked to pay our taxes. It also affects us personally when we receive public benefits, goods, and services—or when they're denied to us. Scholars of comparative politics are eager to understand why public policies and public policymaking vary so much among countries and how they influence people's lives.

Public policies are decisions, actions, and programmes implemented by legislatures, executives, and government agencies to achieve specific objectives. For example, economic policies regulate economic life and influence economic activity, education policies regulate and provide funding for schools and universities, and environmental policies regulate activities that impact the environment.

If you're not from an English-speaking country, the distinction between 'policy' and 'politics' may not be intuitive to you, as many languages don't have separate words for the concepts of policy (as in 'economic policy') and politics (as in 'party politics'). Instead, they use a single word for both, such as the French *politique*, the German *Politik*, or the Russian политика. There are interesting historical reasons for these linguistic differences (Heidenheimer 1986). For now, though, you just need to know that languages are different. If you speak a language that distinguishes between 'policy' and 'politics', such as English or modern Chinese, it's good to know there are languages that don't. If you speak a language that doesn't, it's good to know there are languages that do.

In Section 15.2, we'll examine a few main explanations for why policies vary over time, among countries, and between policy areas. In Section 15.3, we'll learn how scholars of public policy study the policymaking process and the development of public policies in specific areas such as economic policy. In Section 15.4, we'll discuss why legislatures and executives sometimes fail to adopt new policies even if they agree on the need for change. Finally, in Section 15.5, we will study policymaking in authoritarian regimes and go through some of the main policy challenges in the twenty-first-century world. What these challenges have in common is that they have an international or even global character, which blurs the distinction between comparative politics and another field of political science, international relations.

15.2 COMPARATIVE PUBLIC POLICY

LEARNING OUTCOMES

After reading Section 15.2, you'll be able to:
- Describe how public policies vary among countries
- Distinguish between different explanations for this variation
- Analyse the relationship between political institutions and policymaking.

Let's begin by considering an example of how public policies vary among countries, over time, and between policy areas. Figure 15.1 describes the percentage of states around the world in which old-age pensions, sickness benefits, maternity benefits, child and family benefits, and unemployment benefits were either mandated by legislation or provided by the government between 1900 and 2020. The data, which are recorded at five-year intervals, display the evolution of **social policies** around the world. They were compiled by the International Labour Organization for 186 of its 187 member states (all of the member states of the United Nations except seven).

It's a simple graph, but we can infer several important things from it.

1. First of all, social policies have changed a lot *over time*. Before the Second World War, only a few states provided benefits for the elderly, the sick, mothers, and families. Today, most countries do. The slopes of the lines in the graph tell us about the rate of change in different periods. We see that a lot of new social programmes were introduced in the first decades after the Second World War, which are sometimes called the 'golden age of the welfare state'.

2. Social policies vary *between countries*. By 2020, approximately two thirds of all countries in the world provided some form of family benefits or required employers to do so. That means a third don't. Approximately half of all countries provide unemployment benefits. That means the other half don't. These sorts of differences across countries intrigue scholars of comparative politics in general and scholars of comparative public policy in particular.

3. Finally, social policies have varied a lot *between different areas*. Old-age pensions are almost universal today, as are sickness benefits and maternity benefits. But family benefits and unemployment benefits are not. There seems to be something about these programmes that makes states less likely to adopt them. We will come back to the differences between different types of policy in Section 15.3.

Figure 15.1 In the twentieth century, most countries in the world began to provide old-age pensions and other social insurances. *Source: Author's own work, based on data from ILO. 2022.* World Social Protection Report 2020–2022. *Geneva: International Labour Organization. Figure 2.1. Copyright © International Labour Organization (CC BY 4.0)*

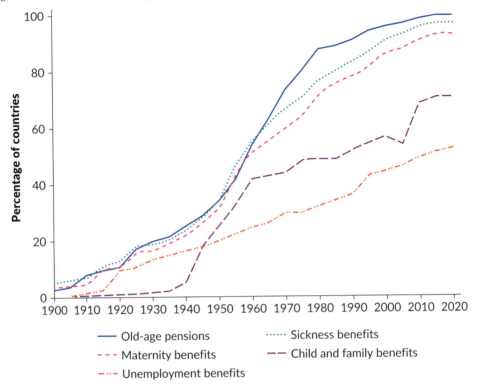

There are many things we *don't* learn about social insurances from Figure 15.1. Most importantly, the data in the figure only tell us if some form of benefit exists at all in a country. It doesn't tell us how many people are covered. For example, does everyone get a pension when they grow old or only a few? Nor does it tell us how generous the benefits are that people receive. For example, do child benefits make a real difference to the incomes of families with young children, or are they merely symbolic? To examine the ILO's data on social programmes in more depth, turn to Research Prompt 15.1.

> **RESEARCH PROMPT 15.1**
> **Social policies around the world**
>
> Figure 15.1 is based on data from the International Labour Organization's *World Social Protection Report*. In addition to the basic data on legislation that are summarized in Figure 15.1, the *World Social Protection Report* contains a lot of useful information about the coverage of social programmes and how much money governments spend on them. Consult the latest edition of the *World Social Protection Report* and find this evidence on coverage and spending. What differences do you see between the main regions of the world? And what differences do you see between democratic and authoritarian countries?

But what Figure 15.1 does tell us is already quite a lot. We'll therefore refer back to this figure when we discuss the explanations that scholars of comparative public policy typically consider when they try to make sense of why policies differ over time, between countries, and between policy areas. Those factors can be summarized by five words that all begin with the letter 'i': 'interests', 'ideas', 'internationalization', 'individuals', and 'institutions' (Peters 2020).

The claim that *interests* influence public policies is based on the straightforward notion that political decision makers pay a lot of attention to the interests of powerful groups in society when they make policy. In this view, to explain differences in public policy, we simply need to determine which groups have political influence and what the interests of those groups are. Some interest groups are relatively small in number but nevertheless very influential. For example, if the automobile industry is important to a country's economy, political decision makers are likely to pay a lot of attention to the interests of car manufacturers. Other interest groups are broader and more diffuse. For example, voters with university degrees have some interests in common, but they are a highly diverse group and are typically not well organized.

What would an interest-based explanation for the patterns in Figure 15.1 look like? When it comes to differences over time, an interest-based explanation might emphasize that the working class, which usually benefits the most from social insurances and benefits, often won the right to vote at the beginning of the twentieth century and was especially influential in politics in the first decades after the Second World War (see Figure 15.2). This explanation for the growth of social programmes even has a name: it's called the power-resources theory of the welfare state (Korpi 1983; Huber and Stephens 2001). When it comes to differences between policies, an interest-based explanation might emphasize that employers and business organizations have strong reasons to oppose generous unemployment benefits, since they wish to keep wages

Figure 15.2 Nurses at a polling station for the UK's 1945 general election. The enfranchisement of the working class is one interest-based explanation for the trends in social policies after the Second World War. *Source: piemags/archive/military / Alamy Stock Photo*

low (they cannot offer wages that are lower than the benefits people would receive if they were unemployed).

But it isn't always clear what is in the interest of different groups in society (or, indeed, which groups there are in the first place). That's one of the reasons why *ideas* matter in politics. Ideas can influence how individuals, groups, parties, organizations, and decision makers think about things. They can influence our values—that is, what we care about and what goals we try to achieve. They can also influence our beliefs about how the world works, and they can influence our norms—the things we take for granted and regard as natural or obvious. An ideas-based explanation for the patterns in Figure 15.1 might emphasize changes in how people perceive social problems such as poverty and inequality, the emergence of new ideas about how policies ought to be designed to tackle those problems, or generational shifts in values and norms.

In many policy areas, political decision makers take into account not only what happens in their own country but also what happens in other states. That's why *internationalization* matters. One pattern in Figure 15.1 that suggests internationalization influenced the growth of the welfare state is the *S*-shape of the curves for old-age pensions, sickness benefits, and maternity benefits. We often see these sorts of *S*-shaped curves when we study how innovations spread in society (Rogers 1962). The explanation is that at first, only a few early adopters put the policy in place. Then more and more countries follow, until most countries have adopted it and the rate of adoption begins to slow down again.

Sometimes, particularly influential *individuals* can bring about changes in public policy through their charisma, influence, or ability to communicate ideas. An explanation of the development of the welfare state that involves individuals might emphasize the role played by Otto von Bismarck, whose government introduced the world's first social insurances in the German Empire in the 1880s; William and Janet Beveridge, the social-policy experts whose report on the welfare state during the Second World War influenced the development of social policies in that period; or Jawaharlal Nehru, the first prime minister of India, who sought to build a welfare state on the Indian subcontinent after independence from Britain in 1949 attempting to find a middle way between the capitalist and communist systems.

There are often deeper explanations for why individuals such as Bismarck, the Beveridges, and Nehru did what they did, so scholars of comparative politics tend to be sceptical of the idea that powerful individuals shape public policy of their own accord. But there are strong reasons to think that individuals can at least make a difference on the margins, in combination with some of the other factors we're discussing in this section—that is, by mobilizing interests, spreading ideas, absorbing international influences, and, importantly, navigating political institutions.

This brings us to the last of the 'five Is': *institutions*. As we have discussed throughout this book, political institutions vary greatly among countries, and as a consequence of this variation, governments adopt different policies in different countries. Institutions influence public policies for several reasons. Perhaps most importantly, they decide whose voices are heard and whose interests are taken into account in the decision making process. In other words, to understand how factors such as interests and ideas influence public policymaking, we first need to understand how institutions privilege some interests over others and channel the flow of ideas in the political system.

Going back to Figure 15.1, there are strong reasons to believe that political institutions have influenced the evolution of the welfare state in different countries. For example, there is broad agreement that the level of public spending tends to be higher in countries with proportional representation than in countries with majoritarian institutions (Bawn and Rosenbluth 2006; Persson and Tabellini 2003). In proportional representation systems, there are usually many parties, and with each party having its own favourite programmes it would like to spend money on, political bargains often lead to higher expenditures overall.

One of the main challenges when we explain why policies vary over time, between countries, and between programmes is that it's often difficult to disentangle the effects of interests, ideas, internationalization, individuals, and institutions. For example, if we observe an association between an institution, such as proportional elections, and an outcome, such as public spending, can we be sure that the electoral institutions caused the level of spending (so if the electoral system changed, spending would go up), or might there be deeper explanations, such as interests or ideas, that influenced both the electoral system and the level of spending? What we have here is yet another example of the general problem of causality that we discussed in Chapter 2.

15.3 STUDYING POLICYMAKING AND PUBLIC POLICIES

LEARNING OUTCOMES

After reading Section 15.3, you'll be able to:

- Distinguish between different theories of the policy process
- Analyse the relationship between politics and the economy
- Describe how clientelist systems work.

One of the central ideas of scholarship on comparative public policy is that if we wish to understand how policymaking works, we need to go beyond the general explanations we considered in Section 15.2 and analyse the policies themselves, the evolution of policies over time, the nature of the policymaking process, and the context in which the policies are carried out.

15.3.1 Differences among policies

To understand how policies are made and what effects they have across societies, it's important to consider the nature of the policies themselves. Policies are very different from each other, and the differences matter greatly to the politicians who adopt them and the public officials who implement them.

Let's consider two ways in which policies might differ. First of all, as we noted in Section 15.2, there seems to be something about family benefits and unemployment benefits that makes states less likely to adopt those policies than old-age pensions and sickness benefits, which are almost universal in today's world. The explanation is most likely that family benefits and unemployment benefits directly influence power relationships in two of the most important social institutions in people's lives—the family and the workplace—to a much greater extent than old-age pensions and sickness benefits.

Second, some policies can be applied immediately in a wide range of cases without requiring major investments in new administrative organizations. Giving every mother with a young child a fixed monthly maternity benefit is one example. Other policies require careful case-by-case judgements by public officials. Providing care for people with mental health problems is an example of this type of policy. When policymakers consider policy proposals, they typically take into account whether the new policy will be straightforward for public officials to implement faithfully and consistently, or whether it will require a costly bureaucracy.

15.3.2 Path dependence

One of the main reasons that scholars of public policy pay close attention to the characteristics of individual policies is that many policies are **path-dependent**. Path dependence is an important phenomenon in politics and in social life more generally, but it's especially important in public policymaking. It refers to the notion that past decisions by policymakers, public officials, and other political agents—that is, the 'path' they chose when they were confronted with the problems of their time—have powerful effects on the options that are available policymakers and public officials today.

One example of path dependence is infrastructure investments such as railways and roads. Once these investments are made, the presence of railways and roads in specific locations create economic, social, and political effects that shape future political decisions. As a result, decision makers face a completely different landscape than they would have if those investments had never occurred. For example, in most of the United States, public transportation is much less developed than in Europe, because once people had adapted to a car-dependent lifestyle it became very hard to change course toward a model in which public transport played a greater role.

We see a similar dynamic when big social policy programmes are created. In Case Study 15.2, we will study pension reforms in the 1980s, 1990s, and 2000s. One important difference between the European countries we will discuss in that case study is that some countries have many different pension regimes for different groups in the labour market, whereas other countries have more uniform pension systems where different labour market groups have similar rights, conditions, and expectations. Reforming a country's overall pension system becomes much more difficult when there are many different pension regimes for different groups. The fact that conditions were so different across countries resulted from a series of historical contingencies and unforeseen events related to the circumstances in which pension programmes were originally introduced (for example, whether they were created piece by piece for different groups or established through a comprehensive pension reform covering a large proportion of the population). These events were historical accidents, but they shaped policymaking for decades to come. This illustrates how path dependence influences political conditions in different countries.

15.3.3 The policy process

Another important idea in the literature on public policymaking is that to understand how policies come about, we need to consider the nature of the policy process—that is, which steps politicians, public officials, and other agents take before a policy is adopted and implemented.

There are many different models of the policy process (see, for example, Weible and Sabatier 2017), and not enough room here to go through them all, but we will briefly discuss some of the main alternatives.

At one end of the spectrum, we find rational models, which assume that policymaking is a systematic and orderly process, where political decision makers, assisted by public officials, begin by identifying social problems that need to be solved, then specify their main objectives, define all the alternative solutions to the problems they've identified, evaluate the alternatives, select the one they prefer, and present a proposal. After an authoritative decision has been made by the executive or the legislature, or both, the policy is implemented by government agencies, and the outcomes of the policy are monitored and assessed before the whole process starts over again.

At the other end of the spectrum, we find models that portray policymaking as a much more complex and disorderly process, where different types of agent are involved—including experts (see Chapter 10), interest organizations (see Chapter 13), and the media (see Chapter 14). These agents are constantly advocating for ideas and trying to make themselves heard, with policy solutions often emerging before the problems they're supposed to solve—rather than the other way around, as would be expected in a more rational framework. One version of this type of model is the 'multiple streams' framework, which was proposed by Kingdon (2003). Kingdon's idea is that policymaking involves the interaction between three 'streams' of ideas and other inputs: the 'problem stream' (problems that get attention from politicians and the public), the 'policy stream' (ideas that are developed by experts), and the 'political stream' (political factors such as interest-group lobbying and public opinion). His main prediction is that policy change happens when the three streams are 'coupled'—that is, when problems, policy ideas, and political factors align.

15.3.4 Political economy

In the part of comparative politics that is known as comparative political economy, scholars study the relationship between the state and the market, or, more generally, between politics and the economy. For scholars of comparative political economy, the starting point when analysing public policymaking across countries is each country's economic system—the needs of the sectors of the economy that matter most, how different interest groups are organized in business associations, trade unions, and other organizations, and how the country fits into the international economy through trade, financial flows, and chains of production. For a concrete example of how scholars of comparative political economy think about how policymaking works, see Case Study 15.1.

CASE STUDY 15.1
Regulating Uber in different countries

Scholars of comparative political economy are interested in how the structure of the economy and the activities of interest organizations influence economic policymaking, and they're suspicious of approaches to public policymaking that omit these factors.

The company Uber provides a 'ride-sharing service' through which individual car drivers sell rides to individuals. When Uber was established, it was a new type of service that had become possible because of the development of digital technologies that matched drivers with passengers, and because of the ubiquity of smartphones, which meant that many people could access Uber's services when they were looking for transportation. Historically, ride services have been provided by taxi companies, which didn't use advanced digital technologies but relied on a central switchboard that people could call when they needed to get somewhere. When Uber entered the market, taxi companies came under threat from this new type of service.

In her article 'Regulating Uber', Thelen (2018) analyses what happened when Uber sought to establish itself in different countries. She studies the United States, which is widely regarded among comparative political economists as a 'liberal' market economy, and Germany and Sweden, which are usually categorized as 'coordinated' market economies that regulate private enterprises to a greater extent than liberal economies, seeking to embed them in a system of legislation and requiring them to bargain with trade unions, business associations, and other groups.

Thelen's main conclusion is that understanding why the response to Uber varied so much between the three countries requires examining the broader social and economic structure in each society. It would not be enough to study what the main political parties said and did in the legislature, or what regulations governments proposed.

In the United States, Uber used the country's fragmented political system to its advantage. 'Positioning itself as a champion of free markets and consumer choice', Thelen writes, 'the company rallied its users against unpopular taxi lobbies in one jurisdiction after another, pressuring politicians while tying up labor advocates in protracted court battles'.

In Germany's social market economy, by contrast, taxi companies were able to respond more effectively to the threats posed by Uber: 'Together with allies in public transportation, they positioned themselves as defenders of consumers whose interest in high quality, reliable services was best served by well-regulated markets, and isolated Uber as a threat to public order and the rule of law'.

In Sweden, finally, a sort of compromise was reached, whereby Uber could establish some of its services while respecting the ground rules of the Swedish political economy. 'In Sweden, . . . taxes emerged as the central regulatory flashpoint, and served as a common focal point for a broad coalition that included taxi companies, labour unions, and state actors in defense of the norms of fairness on which the Swedish social system rests'.

15.3.5 Clientelistic and programmatic representation

The final contextual factor we will consider concerns the differences between policymaking in systems with 'programmatic' parties and in systems with 'clientelistic' parties (see Chapter 11).

In a clientelistic system, which is a common form of political representation in countries with lower average incomes, there is a reciprocal relationship between a political leader or party and the leader's or the party's supporters—the supporters get certain benefits in return for the political support they offer. Hence the term 'clientelism': the voters in effect become the 'clients' of the political leader or party. As Allen Hicken (2011, 294) puts it, 'What is unique about clientelist exchange is that the chief criterion for receiving the targeted benefit is political support, typically voting'. Politicians and parties appeal to specific groups of voters in all systems—as we discussed in Chapter 11, the very word 'party' refers to the idea that the electorate is divided into groups. What sets a clientelistic system apart is the *transactional* nature of the relationship between politicians and parties and their supporters.

The main alternative to clientelism is *programmatic* representation. When politics is programmatic, politicians and parties try to put together broad-based programmes and electoral platforms that they think will appeal to a majority or at least a large proportion of the voters, and they don't make benefits and services conditional on political support, trading benefits for votes. In clientelistic systems, they do, and there is an expectation on both sides that this transactional relationship between the politicians and the voters will endure.

It is sometimes hard to distinguish between clientelistic and programmatic politics in practice, but it remains an important distinction. One reason is that the role of political parties differs entirely between a clientelistic system and a programmatic system.

As we discussed in Chapter 11, political parties are both associated with the state, since they organize groups of politicians within the legislature and other state institutions, *and* a part of society, since they appeal to the electorate and often have membership-based mass organizations. That's what lets political parties mediate between the state and society and represent the views of different groups of voters.

But what does it mean for parties to 'mediate' between state and society? Both clientelistic and programmatic parties do it, but they do it in different ways. In systems where politics is programmatic, parties formulate broad programmes and then the voters get to choose between those programmes before the election (prospective voting) and hold the government accountable after the election (retrospective voting). As Susan Stokes (2005) has argued in an influential study, clientelism, or 'machine politics', turns the idea of accountability on its head, for clientelism means that parties and politicians hold the people accountable for how they vote, not the other way around. All that voters expect and get in a clientelistic system are the clientelistic benefits, goods, and services the parties and politicians deliver to them.

Scholars of comparative politics have taken a keen interest in how clientelistic and programmatic systems work, conducting detailed empirical studies of public opinion, electoral behaviour, the role of parties, and how policies are made. In systems with clientelistic parties, scholars have sought to understand the role played by the local-level 'brokers' who facilitate the clientelistic exchange of goods and services for votes (Stokes et al. 2013). In systems with programmatic parties, by contrast, scholars have concentrated on the interaction between the electorate as a whole and the legislature and the government. For example, many scholarly studies have investigated the dynamic relationship between the political opinions of the voters and the public policies that legislatures and executives adopt (see, for example, Powell 2000; Soroka and Wlezien 2010).

In one influential study of a shanty town on the outskirts of Buenos Aires, the capital of Argentina, Javier Auyero (2000) describes in great detail how clientelism works in practice. He begins by establishing that the residents of the shanty town of Villa Paraíso have such low incomes that they cannot meet their basic needs in life. He then notes that the only organization that is capable of providing food, medicine, and other necessities is the local organization of the dominant political party in Argentina, the Justicialist, or Peronist, Party (named after the populist leader of Argentina in the 1950s, Juan Perón). That is where the residents of the shanty town turn when they're in need. Auyero identifies five 'brokers' for the Peronists: Matilde, Juan, Cholo, Andrea, and Norma. Those five people are surrounded by a circle of followers who carry out much of the work for the residents of the shanty town. Meanwhile, voters come to depend on the brokers and their helpers for information about politics, and become loyal voters for the party they represent.

In Case Study 15.2, we discuss pension reforms in the high-income democracies in Europe, and see how politics revolves around broad compromises and deals between programmatic political parties and large interest organizations at the national level. In a clientelistic system, people perceive politics differently. Instead of national-level politics, people care about deals struck at the local level, as votes and political loyalties are traded for life's necessities.

15.4 GETTING THINGS DONE

LEARNING OUTCOMES

After reading Section 15.4, you'll be able to:

- Distinguish between different explanations for the ability of legislatures and executives to change policies
- Analyse the relationship between political institutions and policy change.

One question that has long interested scholars of comparative politics is why legislatures and executives sometimes fail to adopt new policies even if they agree on the need for change. Scholars of politics have many names for this type of situation. One is 'gridlock' (a traffic metaphor; see Figure 15.3). Another is 'logjam' (a lumber-industry metaphor). A third is 'stalemate' (a chess metaphor). A fourth is 'paralysis' (a medical metaphor). The idea is the same, though: all these metaphors are meant to capture the idea that a political system can get stuck and immobile (Lindvall 2017, Chapters 1–2). In Section 15.2, we discussed what politicians *do* in different countries, periods, and policy domains. In this section, we'll discuss whether politicians can *get things done* in the first place.

This is an important topic for at least two reasons. First of all, if there's an urgent need for action, failing to get things done can cause economic and social harm. For instance, if there is a financial crisis, resolute action by the government can increase people's confidence in the financial and economic system, whereas doing nothing can lead to a deep and drawn-out economic depression. Second, failing to get things done can have damaging political consequences and may even

Figure 15.3 The term 'gridlock' is often used to describe the situation in which legislatures and executives agree on a need for change, yet fail to bring new policies into effect. *Source: Thomas Wyness / Shutterstock*

undermine the support for democratic institutions. For example, as we learned in Chapter 5, democratic institutions are vulnerable in deep economic crises.

There are many explanations for why legislatures and executives sometimes fail to get things done. Perhaps they simply lack ideas and don't know what to do (Section 15.2). Or perhaps they know what they would like to do, but can't get it done since the state is too weak (Chapter 3) or the bureaucracy is ineffective or corrupt, or both (Chapter 10). Or perhaps the government itself is corrupt and unresponsive and doesn't care about getting things done in the first place.

But in this section, we will concentrate on a longstanding argument about the role of institutions that is closely related to several other themes we have discussed throughout this book. Going back more than a century, many scholars of comparative politics have argued that effective government requires a *concentration of power*. If we want a government that can get things done, the argument goes, we ought to put in place a majoritarian electoral system that identifies a clear winner in each election (Chapter 7), and then we ought to let the government govern without having to negotiate with sub-national governments (Chapter 6) or with other parties in the legislature (Chapter 8), or worry that the courts will declare its policies unconstitutional or unlawful (Chapter 9). In short, we ought to leave the governing party *alone*, so it can get on with the business of running the government.

The idea is simple. Political parties that share power—within the executive, within the legislature, or across levels of government—often disagree with each other, and these disagreements sometimes keep governments from responding to important economic, social, and political problems. If reforms that benefit large groups can be blocked by a single party because of that party's particular interests and objectives, the government as a whole may become ineffective or even paralysed.

In Europe, the idea that governments become ineffective if power is shared among several parties and institutions was especially prominent in the inter-war years in the 1920s and 1930s, since many scholars blamed the rise of fascism in Italy and the rise of national socialism in Germany on the weakness of Italian and German coalition governments in the 1920s and 1930s (Finer 1924; Hermens 1941).

The main argument *against* the view that effective government requires a concentration of power is that there are many examples of countries in which power is shared among several parties and institutions that have nevertheless proven to be both politically stable and capable of changing their policies when necessary. In his book *Patterns of Democracy*—which we discussed in Chapter 2—Arend Lijphart (2012) describes the British constitution as an extreme example of power concentration. The United Kingdom has only had coalition governments a few times since it democratized a hundred years ago: in almost every election, one party has won a clear majority of the seats in the House of Commons, enabling that party to form a single-party government. Meanwhile, the ruling party's power is less constrained by other institutions than in most other democracies. Switzerland, on the other hand, is an extreme example of power sharing, since Switzerland's government, the Federal Council, is a semi-permanent coalition of four parties. Those four parties have divided the seven cabinet seats among themselves since the late 1950s (and by then, Switzerland had already been governed by a semi-permanent coalition of parties since the end of the nineteenth century). Yet it's far from clear that Switzerland is a less stable democracy than Britain is. Nor is it clear that Switzerland—where citizens have a much higher level of average income than the United Kingdom—has failed to adopt important policy reforms that have benefited its economic and social development (in 2022, according to the OECD, GDP per capita in Switzerland and the United Kingdom was US$70,085 and 44,745, respectively).

The argument that effective government requires a concentration of power may underestimate the ability of political parties in countries where power is widely shared to come together and overcome political gridlock through negotiations, compromises, and political deals. On the other hand, negotiations, compromises, and deals require mutual trust and confidence in the political system, so it is possible that only countries with a long history of political compromise can combine power sharing with effective government. Other countries may face a starker choice between effective government on the one hand and inclusive, representative government on the other.

One of the policy areas we discussed in Section 15.2 was old-age pensions, which are government benefits paid to eligible persons who have reached a certain age. Case Study 15.2 shows that when it comes to reforming pension systems in Europe, countries in which power is shared among many parties and institutions have in fact adopted and implemented more far-reaching pension reforms than countries in which power is concentrated.

CASE STUDY 15.2
Reforming pensions in Europe

Ever since the 1980s, the reform of old-age pension programmes has been one of the most salient political issues in European democracies. In this period, experts and politicians came to believe that existing pension programmes had become unsustainable—primarily, but not exclusively, because people live longer today than they did a few decades ago (see, for example, OECD 2005).

To improve the financial stability of the pension system, it is typically necessary for governments to impose short-term costs (by cutting benefits or raising contributions or taxes), and those costs fall more heavily on some people than others, which leads to political conflict. So all pension reforms involve conflicts between different generations, between different occupational groups, and between men and women.

One might think that these sorts of reforms are easier for parliaments and governments to carry out if power is concentrated in a single party, but that is not what scholars have found when they have studied pension reforms in Europe.

In one of the first major comparative studies of this trend, Giuliano Bonoli observed that significant reforms have been possible both in systems with many veto players and in systems with few veto players (on 'veto players', see Case Study 2.1), noting that even 'governments enjoying low levels of power concentration' had been 'able to achieve some change' since they had found ways of negotiating compromises between different groups (2000, 172). A few years later, Schludi (2005, 241) concluded, similarly, that many pension reforms have depended either on a deal between the government and the parliamentary opposition or on a deal between the government and the trade unions; he noted that 'even weak governments . . . can use their agenda-setting powers to obtain union consent to cuts in pension spending if they offer them attractive compensation payments'.

Five more years later, an influential study of France, Germany, and Switzerland by Silja Häusermann (2010) went further, arguing that a high number of formal veto players, such as political parties, and a high number of informal veto players, such as interest organizations, can be a political *asset* for reform-oriented governments. Häusermann argued that political fragmentation allows for 'coalitional engineering' and broad compromises that facilitate reform.

One of the broadest overviews of European pension reforms to date—the Oxford *Handbook of European Pension Politics* (Immergut, Anderson, and Schulze 2007)—also found flaws in the theory that big reforms require a concentration of power. This is especially noteworthy since one of the editors wrote an early contribution to the scholarly literature on how fragmented power inhibits reform (Immergut 1992). The authors were puzzled 'that some countries with few veto players and no veto points . . . pulled back from controversial pension reforms when they encountered voter resistance [whereas] countries with many veto players and effective veto points . . . adopted significant legislation' (Immergut and Anderson 2007, 24).

15.5 AUTHORITARIAN REGIMES AND GLOBAL CHALLENGES

LEARNING OUTCOMES

After reading Section 15.5, you'll be able to:
- Identify factors specific to policymaking in authoritarian regimes
- Describe policymaking in areas with an important international dimension.

We will end this chapter with a discussion of policymaking in authoritarian regimes and by considering the challenges of policymaking in areas in which countries are highly interdependent, in the sense that what individual countries do depends greatly on what other countries do.

15.5.1 Policymaking in authoritarian regimes

We have already mentioned policymaking in authoritarian regimes a few times in this chapter, and many of the factors we have discussed are relevant in both democracies and authoritarian regimes. For example, the 'five Is' that we discussed in Section 15.2—interests, ideas, internationalization, individuals, and institutions—are relevant in authoritarian regimes, too, as are mechanisms such as path dependence and clientelism (Section 15.3). But there are also many differences between authoritarian and democratic regimes, and we will review two of them here.

First of all, political power is on average more concentrated in authoritarian regimes than in democratic regimes, so political leaders in authoritarian regimes are less likely to find themselves in a 'gridlock' or 'logjam' or 'stalemate' (see Section 15.4)—that is, a situation in which it's difficult to get things done because of disagreements among politically powerful groups. The definition of an authoritarian regime is that power doesn't flow from the people as a whole, but from a smaller group. There may be disagreements within that smaller group that prevent policymakers from taking action—as we discussed in Chapter 5, political power in an authoritarian regime is often shared among the elite groups that have access to power—but on average, authoritarian rulers are less constrained than democratic rulers.

This is not necessarily an advantage, though. As we also discussed in Chapter 5, one important feature of personalistic authoritarian regimes—the fastest-growing type of regime in the world today—is that policymaking can become haphazard and erratic when policymakers and officials follow the whims of a single individual who wields great power in the state, as opposed to a formal organization or group such as a political party.

This brings us to a second important characteristic of policymaking in authoritarian regimes. Because they aren't accountable to the people, authoritarian rulers are more likely than democratically elected leaders to adopt wasteful policies that give the leader prestige and attention but don't benefit the population as a whole. For example, Gjerløw and Knutsen (2019) have analysed the construction of skyscrapers—buildings that are taller than 150 metres—in different countries around the world, and show that controlling for plausible alternative explanations such as economic prosperity and the size of the population, there are many more skyscrapers built in authoritarian states than in democracies.

15.5.2 Global challenges

In some policy areas more than others, policymakers in individual countries must always take into account what policymakers in other countries are doing.

The first challenge we'll consider is climate change. When fossil fuels such as coal and oil are extracted from the Earth and burned for energy, the carbon in those fuels reacts with oxygen and forms carbon dioxide that is released into the atmosphere. Before the middle of the eighteenth century, the concentration of carbon dioxide in the atmosphere had remained stable at a level just below 300 parts per million (ppm) for thousands of years. In 2022, the concentration of carbon dioxide in the atmosphere was more than 420 ppm. The Intergovernmental Panel on Climate Change, or IPCC, has shown in a series of reports that unless rapid action is taken to reduce the world's reliance on fossil fuels, the average temperature on Earth will keep increasing, which is likely to have catastrophic consequences for agriculture and for other systems and processes that support human life on Earth (see, for example, IPCC 2023).

What sets climate change apart from many of the other political issues that we have discussed in this book is that the problem is truly global. It doesn't matter where on the planet fossil fuels are burned—the carbon dioxide that's released into the atmosphere will spread, and the consequences will affect everyone on the planet. As a report headed by the British economist Nicholas Stern argued in 2007, climate change is 'the greatest and widest-ranging market failure ever seen'. In other words, market mechanisms aren't enough to solve the problem, since the benefits of burning fossil fuels for energy are concentrated among those who use and produce the energy, but the costs affect everyone. This is a type of problem that is commonly called a 'collective-action problem', and as we discussed in Chapter 1, those are the very sorts of problems we have politics to solve.

As a result of this situation, efforts have been made during the past three decades to take urgent action to reduce humanity's reliance on fossil fuels and to stop the rise in the concentration of carbon dioxide in the atmosphere. The global nature of the problem means that those efforts have also been global: governments around the world are trying to coordinate the policy responses to meet the unprecedented challenge to humanity. Discussions about how to do this involve profound conflicts among countries, for the largest emitters of carbon dioxide are high-income countries (see Figure 15.4). Countries with lower incomes are arguing that high-income countries—whose economies have benefited from industrialization driven by the burning of fossil fuels in the past—should do more to address the problem of climate change without keeping low-income countries from developing their own economies and improving the quality of life for their citizens.

The second challenge is international migration. In many high-income countries, immigration is one of the most important topics for voters. For example, among citizens in the member states

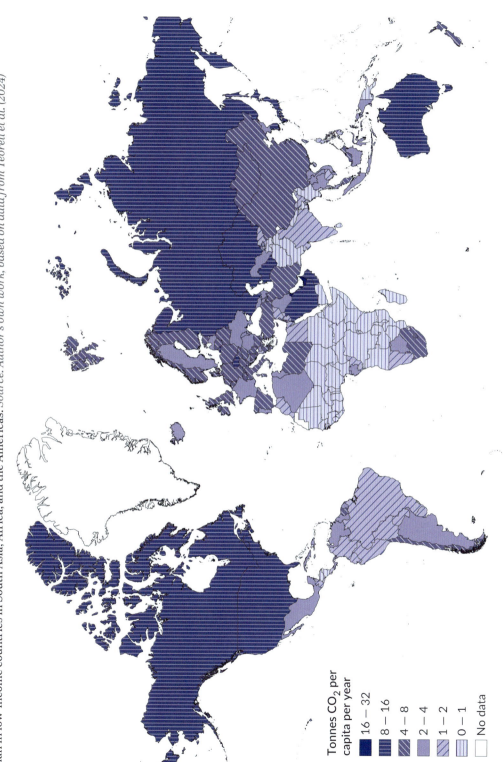

Figure 15.4 Carbon dioxide emissions per capita are much higher in high-income countries in North America, Europe, and the Asia-Pacific regions than in low-income countries in South Asia, Africa, and the Americas. *Source: Author's own work, based on data from Teorell et al. (2024)*

Figure 15.5 While national policies on labour migration have become less open over time, national policies with regard to refugees have, on average, become *more* open. *Source: Data from Peters, Margaret, Frida Boräng, Sara Kalm, J. Lindvall, and Adrian Shin. 2024. 'Historical Immigration Policies: Trends and Lessons'.* International Studies Quarterly *68:3, sqae084*

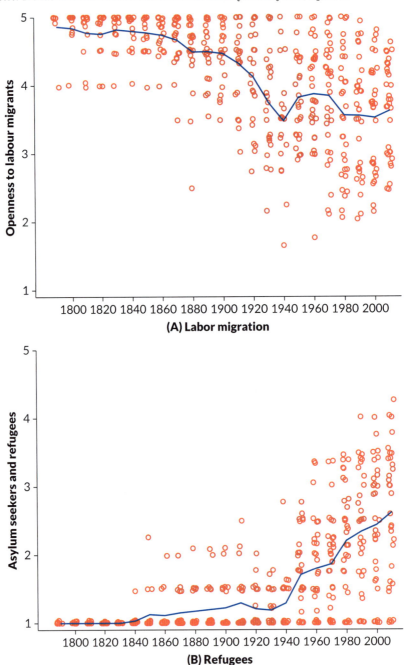

of the European Union, immigration has long ranked as one of the most important issues facing Europe, and in recent elections in the United States, immigration has been one of the issues that have divided voters the most.

What is special about conflicts over migration? One way to think about this is that the issue of immigration divides groups that typically agree with each other on public policy. Many of the main interest groups in high-income democracies are organized around issues of distribution and redistribution—that is, how to distribute income and wealth among different groups in a society. But the question when it comes to migration isn't how to distribute income and wealth among different members of society; it's who gets to be a member of society in the first place. For this reason, immigration is different from many other policy issues.

It is also an area, like climate change, where domestic politics and international politics meet, and indeed, it is difficult to see the distinction between them. Although individual states adopt their own immigration policies, international immigration is, by definition, something that happens in the international system—it isn't limited to particular countries. International treaties and other institutions also play an important role in the domain of immigration policy. As Figure 15.5 shows, states have become more and more restrictive when it comes to admitting labour migrants in recent years, but in the second half of the twentieth century, they became considerably more willing to make exceptions for refugees and asylum seekers. One of the main reasons is that states have ratified international conventions that obligate them to admit refugees and asylum seekers—the 1951 Geneva Convention and its 1967 Supplementary Protocol.

The two problems we have discussed in this section are closely related to each other. For example, in the future, climate change is likely to lead to increased migration from parts of the world that are becoming uninhabitable to parts of the world with more temperate climates. It is evident that the distinction between domestic and international affairs becomes increasingly porous when we think of these important contemporary problems, which means that the field of comparative politics begins to blend with another subfield of political science, international relations.

15.6 CONCLUSION

In Section 15.2, we explored the variations in public policies among countries and over time. Scholars grapple with understanding this diversity. Section 15.3 elucidated the dichotomy between broad-based *programmatic* policies and *clientelistic* policies. In Section 15.4, we learned about the problem of 'democratic paralysis'—why policymakers sometimes fail to get things done. Finally, in Section 15.5, we examined twenty-first-century policy challenges, many of which transcend national borders, blurring the lines between comparative politics and international relations.

This chapter has brought together many of the themes of the book. We began our discussion of central problems in politics in Chapter 3 with the growth of the state, which was the result of the adoption of new types of public policies. Since then, we've studied topics such as political regimes, legislatures and executives, bureaucracies, political parties, voluntary associations, mass political behaviour, and the media, all of which contribute to shaping public policymaking. Few things in comparative politics can be understood in isolation.

SUMMARY

- Scholars of comparative politics investigate why public policies vary over time, among countries, and between policy areas.
- Among the explanatory factors that scholars of comparative politics consider when they explain differences in public policy are interests, ideas, internationalization, individuals, and institutions.
- In many political systems, politicians tend to offer narrow, local, 'clientelistic' policies instead of broad-based 'programmatic' policies.
- The differences between clientelistic and programmatic policies have profound implications for political representation.
- Another central question in comparative public policy is when political decision makers are able to adopt new policies in the first place—and when they're not, a situation commonly referred to as 'gridlock', 'stalemate', or 'paralysis'.
- According to one prominent but not universally accepted theory, gridlock is typically an outcome of power sharing among several political parties and institutions.
- The most controversial and consequential political issues in today's world are international—they are not confined to, and cannot be adequately addressed within, one particular country.
- These issues call into question the separation between the field of comparative politics and the related political-science field of international relations.

STUDY QUESTIONS

1. In this last chapter, we have studied public policies and how they come about. But we have actually learned a lot about public policies throughout the book. Let's consider a few examples. Conflicts between legislatures and executives (Chapter 8) are typically the result of a clash between the executive's and the legislative majority's policy agenda. Federal constitutions (Chapter 6) state which policy areas the national government has power over and which policy areas are left to regional governments. And when appeal courts and constitutional courts declare laws and decrees unconstitutional (Chapter 9), it is often because they believe the government's policies violate fundamental rights.

    Some people believe that the best way to evaluate political institutions is by examining the policies they bring about. Do you agree with that view, or do you think there are other criteria that are more important when we ask questions about how well political institutions work?

2. At the beginning of this chapter, we learned about 'five Is' that can be used to explain why policies vary over time, between countries, and between policies: interests, ideas, internationalization, individuals, and institutions. The chapter also dealt with the global challenge of climate change. Pick two countries in Figure 15.4. Try to use the 'five Is' to understand why they differ and how.

FURTHER READING

Robert Goodin, Michael Moran, and Martin Rein (eds.), *The Oxford Handbook of Public Policy* (2008).
Provides an overview of the main approaches to the study of public policy in political science.

CONCLUSION

We have reached the end of the book. It has taken us on a journey around the world and through centuries of human history. We have learned that there are profound differences between the world's political systems. Those differences have emerged for a variety of historical reasons, such as warfare, colonialism, social conflicts, the spread of ideas and social movements, and the invention of new ways for humans to govern themselves. We have also learned that the differences between political regimes and systems have important consequences for how economic, social, and political conflicts play out, and for the relative power of rich and poor, men and women, old and young, and different ethnic and religious groups. Finally, we have learned that political institutions and systems are always changing. Sometimes change is immediate, dramatic, and apparent to everyone. More often it is gradual, creeping, and difficult to grasp.

Our task as scholars and students of comparative politics is to look for the roots of political conflicts, learn how political systems work, and think of ways in which political institutions might be reformed to improve the way we live together. Our job, then, is comparable to that of an architect. Architects try to figure out how the built environment influences how humans live together in buildings and cities. Scholars of comparative politics try to figure out how political systems influence how humans live together in societies. In Chapter 1, we noted that Aristotle was the first philosopher who engaged in what we would now think of as empirical research on the similarities and differences between political systems. But he wasn't the first scholar of politics. In Book 1, Part VIII of *Politics*, Aristotle identifies a man called Hippodamus of Miletus as 'the first person not a statesman who made inquiries about the best form of government'. Aristotle wasn't particularly impressed with Hippodamus's theory of government and doesn't seem to have thought very highly of him as a person (he writes that many people found Hippodamus 'affected' since he would 'wear flowing hair and expensive ornaments'). But he does give him credit for being first (he wasn't familiar with the work of the Chinese philosopher Confucius, who was born approximately 50 years before Hippodamus). Today, however, Hippodamus is best remembered for his day job: 2,500 years ago, he was one of the foremost architects in Greece. So Hippodamus, one of the very first scholars of politics, was also an architect.

We study comparative politics because we want to know how to build a world where we can live together. You're ready now to join in this endeavour.

GLOSSARY

Agenda-setting effects The media influence public perceptions of political issues by choosing which topics to emphasize.

Alternative voting An electoral system in which the votes of the least successful candidates are reallocated to the second choices of their voters until one candidate has a majority.

Appellate courts Higher courts responsible for hearing cases that have already been tried in lower courts.

Authoritarianism Political power is concentrated in a small group, such as the wealthy, the military, or a political party.

Ballot structure The format and appearance of the document that voters hand in when they vote.

Behaviour, political What people do when they participate in politics.

Bicameral Refers to a legislature with two chambers.

Budget, state A document that projects the state's income and allocates its expenditures, typically on a yearly basis.

Caucusing Members of a legislative body or political party meet to discuss and coordinate their activities.

Causality The relationship between cause and effect: how one thing leads to another.

Cause groups Organizations representing general ideals, values, and principles.

Central banks Institutions managing monetary policy and ensuring that the payments system is secure.

Civil society Voluntary associations and autonomous institutions that are neither part of the market nor part of the state.

Clientelism A system in which political parties compete by offering material benefits to particular groups in exchange for their votes.

Coalition governments Governments that are made up of two or more parties.

Collective-action problem When a group fails to achieve a shared goal because individuals act in their own interest.

Committees Groups of legislators that are tasked with studying particular political issues before they are debated by the whole legislature.

Commonwealth, the An international organization composed mainly of former British colonies.

Comparative politics A field of study within political science that is concerned with similarities and differences between political systems.

Compulsory voting A system in which voters face penalties if they do not participate in elections.

Concepts General ideas used to name and categorize things, organizing our thinking.

Confidence vote A procedure through which the government in a parliamentary system declares that it will resign if it loses a specific vote in the legislature.

Constitution A set of principles and rules that define the organization of a political system.

Constitutional courts Courts with special authority to interpret and uphold the constitution.

Corporatism Interest groups are concentrated in peak-level organizations, which interact closely with the state and political decision makers.

Correlation Two or more things often appear together.

Corruption The misuse of public office for private gain.

Counterfactual definition of causality A caused B if B wouldn't have occurred if A hadn't occurred first.

Coup d'état A small group of conspirators, often made up of military officers, takes power in the state.

Court An institution that administers justice.

Cross-sectional comparison A form of comparison that involves observing two or more units at one particular point in time.

Dataset A repository of information in which each row is an observation and each column is a variable.

Decentralization Political decisions are made by local or regional authorities instead of the central government.

Definition A statement that clarifies the precise meaning of a word.

Deliberative democracy A theory emphasizing that democracy is a form of communication that fosters mutual learning and understanding.

Democracy A political system where the people can replace their leaders through elections.

Democratic breakdown The process of becoming more authoritarian or shifting from democracy to authoritarianism.

Democratic peace The theory that democracies are unlikely to go to war with each other.

Democratic theory A branch of political theory that explores different forms of democracy and the arguments for and against them.

Democratization The process of becoming more democratic or shifting from authoritarianism to democracy.

District magnitude The number of candidates who are elected from each district.

Dominant-party regime A regime in which one political party effectively controls the government.

Duverger's Law The idea that majoritarian elections tend to reduce the number of parties while proportional elections tend to increase it.

Ecological-inference fallacy Erroneously drawing conclusions about individuals from observations of groups.

Electoral districts The geographical areas in which elections are conducted.

Electoral formula The method used to convert votes into seats, determining which candidates are elected and how seats are distributed in the legislature.

Electoral system The rules that govern how elections are conducted and how the votes are counted.

Empirical evidence Facts, figures, and other observations that are used to support a conclusion.

Encompassing interest organizations Interest organizations that represent broad groups, such as trade unions encompassing workers across industries.

Executive The branch of government responsible for executing laws and implementing public policies, often called 'government' in parliamentary systems.

Executive–legislative relations The strategic interaction between the executive and legislative branches of government.

Expert survey A method of data collection that relies on the advice of experts.

Federalism A political system where power is divided between central and regional governments.

First-past-the-post An electoral system in which the candidate with the most votes in a district wins, even if they don't secure a majority.

Foreign intervention When foreign powers force a country under their control to change its political system.

Framing effects The way in which mass media shape public opinion by influencing the public's interpretation of political issues.

Game theory A mathematical theory concerned with strategic interactions among rational agents.

Gross domestic product (GDP) per capita The total value of goods and services produced in a country divided by the size of the population.

Government agencies Administrative bodies staffed by non-elected officials who carry out the government's policies.

Grand corruption Large-scale corruption such as high-value bribes or the misappropriation of public funds.

Head of government The leader of the executive.

Head of state The ceremonial or symbolic leader of a country, representing the state in foreign relations.

High court A court at the apex of the hierarchy of courts in a country.

Hybrid regime Regimes where rulers hold elections but manipulate state institutions and the media to stay in power.

Ideal types Stylized models of complex real-world phenomena, used as conceptual tools in research.

Incumbent takeover The government, having risen to power legally, transforms the political regime from within.

Insider strategies When interest groups engage directly with policymakers to influence policy.

Institutionalism A school of thought that emphasizes the role of institutions in politics, society, and economic life.

Interest group An organized group that seeks to influence public policy but doesn't put up candidates for public office.

Internal democracy Party leaders are appointed by and accountable to the party members.

Judicial independence The principle that judges should make decisions based on their interpretation of the law, free from external influence.

Judicial review The power of courts to declare laws and government regulations unconstitutional or illegal.

Legislative election An election to a legislative body such as a parliament.

Legislature An assembly that makes laws and decides on the state's budget, known as a 'parliament' in parliamentary systems.

Linkage The connection between the state and society, often through political parties or other organizations.

Longitudinal Refers to a research method comparing data points over time.

Majoritarian electoral system An electoral system with single-member districts in which the candidate with the most votes wins.

Majority government A government formed by a party or coalition controlling more than 50 per cent of the seats in the legislature.

Media freedom The right of journalists and media organizations to report and publish without government interference.

Meta-analysis A statistical study combining findings from many studies.

Method A way of reaching a conclusion.

Military regime A government controlled by the military, often after a coup.

Minority government A government formed by a party or coalition controlling less than 50 per cent of the seats in the legislature.

Mixed electoral system An electoral system combining elements of majoritarian and proportional representation.

Modernization theory The theory that economic growth and social modernization contribute to the rise of democracy.

Monarchy A political system in which a monarch holds the highest office in the state, typically after inheriting it.

Multi-party system A system where more than two parties compete for power.

Observations Individual data points or records on which evidence is collected.

Office-motivated Refers to political parties that prioritize forming or being part of the government over other political goals.

One-party system A system with only one legal political party.

Operationalization Turning an abstract concept into something we can measure empirically.

Outsider strategies When interest groups seek influence by raising awareness of the issues they care about among the public.

Panel A dataset with repeated observations of the same cases over time.

Parliamentarism A system in which the government cannot survive if it's opposed by the legislature.

Party An organization that puts up candidates for public office.

Party discipline The methods political parties use to maintain unity.

Party financing The sources of income of political parties.

Party lists Lists of candidates drawn up by political parties in proportional electoral systems.

Party system The interactions among the parties within a political system.

Path dependence The idea that past political decisions have powerful effects on future policy choices.

Personalism A regime in which political power is concentrated in a single individual.

Petty corruption Small-scale corrupt activities, such as bribery, that are associated with everyday events.

Pluralism A political system where multiple interest groups can influence decision making.

Plurality voting A system where the candidate with the most votes wins, regardless of whether they have a majority.

Polarization The increasing distance and division between opposing political views.

Policy-motivated Refers to political parties that prioritize getting their policies implemented over other political goals.

Political institutions Rules that structure a country's political system, as well as the organizations that apply and maintain those rules.

Political opportunity structure Political circumstances that influence the ability of social movements and activists to achieve their political goals.

Political participation The various ways in which ordinary citizens take part in the political process and try to influence public policy.

Political science A scholarly discipline concerned with politics and government.

Political system An encompassing term that describes how the political regime, political institutions, and people's political behaviour interact within a community.

Presidentialism A system in which the head of government isn't responsible to the legislature but is directly or indirectly elected by the people.

Principal–agent problem The relationship between a principal who delegates authority and an agent who acts on the principal's behalf.

Programmatic Refers to parties that compete by presenting clear policy programmes that address broad issues.

Proportional electoral system A system in which the number of seats each party receives in the legislature is directly related to its share of the total vote across the country.

Psychological theories Theories of politics that emphasize how thoughts, beliefs, emotions, and other psychological factors influence political behaviour.

Public administration The implementation of public policies and the management of the operations of the state.

Quantitative evidence Information that can be stored in a database and analysed with the help of computer programs.

Rationalist theories Theories of politics that assume political agents are forward-looking, goal-oriented, and do what they can to reach their goals.

Regime The basic political arrangements that decide who has power in a state.

Representative democracy A system in which the people elect representatives who make political decisions on their behalf.

Research question A precise question that guides scholarly inquiry.

Resources (of parties) The financial, staffing, and organizational assets of political parties.

Reversal of democracy The process of becoming more authoritarian or shifting from democracy to authoritarianism.

Revolution A regime change from below that results in major changes in how a state is governed.

Run-off election A follow-up election that is held between the top two candidates when no candidate achieves a majority.

Sectional interest organizations Interest groups that represent specific categories of people, such as workers, employers, or farmers.

Semi-presidentialism A system with two heads of government—usually called president and prime minister—who share power.

Single-party government A government made up of one party.

Social movements The collective behaviour of groups mobilized around shared political concerns and identities.

Social policy A policy designed to provide social protection and improve the welfare of the citizens.

Social science A scholarly discipline focused on societies, such as economics, political science, or sociology.

Social trust A shared belief that most people can be trusted.

State An organization that controls a particular territory, upholds its laws, and carries out public policies.

State–society relations The interactions of politicians and government officials with civil society organizations.

Statism A political system in which interest groups are kept at arm's length from political decision makers.

Suffrage The right to vote.

Survey A data-collection method involving interviews with many individuals.

Systemic corruption Corruption so widespread that it affects nearly all parts of society.

Technocracy A system in which experts, not politicians, make important political decisions.

Technocratic government A government made up of experts and civil servants, not politicians.

Theocracy A political system where religious leaders hold political power.

Theory A combination of ideas that explain why things happen the way they do.

Time series Data that include observations over time within a single case.

Trade unions Organizations that represent workers and other wage earners, defending their economic, social, and political interests.

Turnout The percentage of eligible voters who participate in elections.

Two-party system A political system where only two parties can realistically compete for power.

Unicameral Refers to a legislature with a single chamber.

Unitary state A system in which political power is concentrated at the national level (unlike in a federal state).

Vote of no confidence A parliamentary procedure through which the legislature can force the government to resign.

Vote-motivated Refers to political parties that prioritize getting many votes over other political goals.

Welfare state A state that puts in place public services and income transfer programmes to ensure the welfare of its citizens.

REFERENCES

Abdulai, Abdul-Gafaru. 2023. 'Political Settlement Dynamics and the Emergence and Decline of Bureaucratic Pockets of Effectiveness in Ghana'. In *Pockets of Effectiveness and the Politics of State-Building and Development in Africa*, edited by Sam Hickey. Oxford: Oxford University Press, 61–90.

Aberbach, Joel D., Robert D. Putnam, and Bert A. Rockman. 1981. *Bureaucrats and Politicians in Western Democracies*. Cambridge, MA: Harvard University Press.

Abts, Koen, Poznyak Dmitriy, and Swyngedouw Marc. 2012. 'The Federal Elections in Belgium, June 2010'. *Electoral Studies* 31 (2): 448–452.

Acemoglu, Daron, Suresh Naidu, Pascual Restrepo, and James A. Robinson. 2019. 'Democracy Does Cause Growth'. *Journal of Political Economy* 127 (1): 47–100.

Acemoglu, Daron and James A. Robinson. 2019. *The Narrow Corridor*. New York: Penguin.

Ágh, Attila. 2016. 'The Decline of Democracy in East-Central Europe'. *Problems of Post-Communism* 63 (5–6): 277–287.

Ahmed, Amel. 2012. *Democracy and the Politics of Electoral System Choice*. Cambridge: Cambridge University Press.

Aimer, Peter and Raymond Miller. 2002. 'Partisanship and Principle: Voters and the New Zealand Electoral Referendum of 1993'. *European Journal of Political Research* 41 (6): 795–809.

Allcott, Hunt and Matthew Gentzkow. 2017. 'Social Media and Fake News in the 2016 Election'. *Journal of Economic Perspectives* 31 (2): 211–236.

Altman, David and Clemente T. Sánchez. 2021. 'Citizens at the Polls'. *Taiwan Journal of Democracy* 17 (2): 27–48.

Alvarez, Michael, José Antonio Cheibub, Fernando Limongi, and Adam Przeworski. 1996. 'Classifying Political Regimes'. *Studies in Comparative International Development* 31 (2): 3–36.

Anckar, Carsten and Cecilia Fredriksson. 2019. 'Classifying Political Regimes 1800–2016'. *European Political Science* 18 (1): 84–96.

Anderson, Benedict. 1983. *Imagined Communities*. London: Verso.

Andersson, Per and Thomas Brambor. 2019. 'Financing the State: Government Tax Revenue from 1800 to 2012. Version 2.0'. Lund: Lund University.

Andeweg, Rudy B., Robert Elgie, Ludger Helms, Juliet Kaarbo, and Ferdinand Müller-Rommel, editors. 2020. *The Oxford Handbook of Political Executives*. Oxford: Oxford University Press.

Ansell, Ben and Johannes Lindvall. 2021. *Inward Conquest*. New York: Cambridge University Press.

Aristotle. 1885 [c. 350 BC]. *Politics*. Oxford: Clarendon Press.

Auyero, Javier. 2000. 'The Logic of Clientelism in Argentina'. *Latin American Research Review* 35 (3): 55–81.

Bäck, Hanna, Marc Debus, and Jorge M. Fernandes, editors. 2021. *The Politics of Legislative Debates*. Oxford: Oxford University Press.

Bawn, Kathleen and Frances Rosenbluth. 2006. 'Short versus Long Coalitions: Electoral Accountability and the Size of the Public Sector'. *American Journal of Political Science* 50 (2): 251–265.

Beasley, William G. 1990. *The Rise of Modern Japan*. New York: St. Martin's Press.

Beitz, Charles R. 1989. *Political Equality*. Princeton, NJ: Princeton University Press.

Beramendi, Pablo. 2007. 'Federalism'. In *The Oxford Handbook of Comparative Politics*, edited by Carles Boix and Susan C. Stokes. Oxford: Oxford University Press, 752–781.

Bergh, Johannes, Dag Arne Christensen, and Tor Helge Holmås. 2021. 'Mobiliseringsvalget 2019'. In *Lokalvalget 2019*, edited by Jo Saglie, Signe Bock Segaard, and Dag Arne Christensen. Oslo: Cappelen Damm Akademisk, 87–115.

Bergman, Torbjörn, Hanna Bäck, and Johan Hellström. 2021. 'Coalition Governance Patterns across Western Europe'. In *Coalition Governance in Western Europe*, edited by Torbjörn Bergman, Hanna Bäck, and Johan Hellström. Oxford: Oxford University Press, 680–726.

Bermeo, Nancy. 2002. 'A New Look at Federalism: The Import of Institutions'. *Journal of Democracy* 13 (2): 96–110.

Bermeo, Nancy. 2003. *Ordinary People in Extraordinary Times*. Princeton, NJ: Princeton University Press.

Bersch, Katherine, Sérgio Praça, Matthew M. Taylor, and Dinsha Mistree. 2017. 'Bureaucratic

Capacity and Political Autonomy within National States: Mapping the Archipelago of Excellence in Brazil'. In *States in the Developing World*, edited by Miguel A. Centeno, Atul Kohli, and Deborah J. Yashar. Cambridge: Cambridge University Press, 157–183.

Bertsou, Eri and Daniele Caramani, editors. 2020. *The Technocratic Challenge to Democracy.* London: Routledge.

Besley, Timothy and Torsten Persson. 2011. *Pillars of Prosperity.* Princeton, NJ: Princeton University Press.

Blais, André. 2006. 'What Affects Voter Turnout?' *Annual Review of Political Science* 9: 111–125.

Blaydes, Lisa and Drew A. Linzer. 2008. 'The Political Economy of Women's Support for Fundamentalist Islam'. *World Politics* 60 (4): 576–609.

Boix, Carles. 1999. 'Setting the Rules of the Game: The Choice of Electoral Systems in Advanced Democracies'. *American Political Science Review* 93 (3): 609–624.

Boix, Carles, Michael Miller, and Sebastian Rosato. 2013. 'A Complete Dataset of Political Regimes, 1800–2007'. *Comparative Political Studies* 46 (12): 1523–1554.

Bolin, Niklas, Nicholas Aylott, Benjamin von dem Berge, and Thomas Poguntke. 2017. 'Patterns of Intra-party Democracy across the World'. In *Organizing Political Parties*, edited by Thomas Webb, Pauland Poguntke, and Susan E. Scarrow. Oxford: Oxford University Press, 158–184.

Bonoli, Giuliano. 2000. *The Politics of Pension Reform.* Cambridge: Cambridge University Press.

Bormann, Nils-Christian and Matt Golder. 2013. 'Democratic Electoral Systems around the World, 1946–2011'. *Electoral Studies* 32 (2): 360–369.

Bovens, Mark and Anchrit Wille. 2017. *Diploma Democracy.* Oxford: Oxford University Press.

Box-Steffensmeier, Janet M., Henry E. Brady, and David Collier, editors. 2008. *The Oxford Handbook of Political Methodology.* Oxford: Oxford University Press.

Bozóki, András and Dániel Hegedűs. 2018. 'An Externally Constrained Hybrid Regime: Hungary in the European Union'. *Democratization* 25 (7): 1173–1189.

Brambor, Thomas and Johannes Lindvall. 2018. 'The Ideology of Heads of Government, 1870–2012'. *European Political Science* 17: 211–222.

Brambor, Thomas, Johannes Lindvall, Ann-Ida Gyllenspetz, and Annika Stjernquist. 2024. 'The Ideology of Heads of Government, 1870–2012'. Version 2.0. Gothenburg: Department of Political Science, University of Gothenburg.

Brannen, Samuel J., Christian S. Haig, and Katherine Schmidt. 2020. 'The Age of Mass Protests'. Washington, DC: CSIS Risk and Foresight Group.

Brierley, Sarah. 2020. 'Unprincipled Principals: Co-opted Bureaucrats and Corruption in Ghana'. *American Journal of Political Science* 64 (2): 209–222.

Broockman, David and Joshua Kalla. 2022. 'Consuming Cross-Cutting Media Causes Learning and Moderates Attitudes: A Field Experiment with Fox News Viewers'. Unpublished manuscript, University of California Berkeley.

Burgess, Michael. 2000. *Federalism and the European Union.* London: Routledge.

Caldeira, Gregory A., R. Daniel Kelemen, and Keith E. Whittington. 2008. *The Oxford Handbook of Law and Politics.* Oxford: Oxford University Press.

Campbell, Rosie and Rosalind Shorrocks. 2023. 'The Evolution of the Gender Gap?' London: National Centre for Social Research.

Caramani, Daniele. 2017. 'Will vs. Reason: The Populist and Technocratic Forms of Political Representation and Their Critique to Party Government'. *American Political Science Review* 111 (1): 54–67.

Caramani, Daniele, editor. 2023. *Comparative Politics.* Oxford: Oxford University Press, 6th edition.

Cavaille, Charlotte and John Marshall. 2019. 'Education and Anti-immigration Attitudes: Evidence from Compulsory Schooling Reforms across Western Europe'. *American Political Science Review* 113 (1): 254–263.

Centeno, Miguel Angel, Atul Kohli, and Deborah J. Yashar, editors. 2017. *States in the Developing World.* Cambridge: Cambridge University Press.

Chenoweth, Erica. 2021. *Civil Resistance.* Oxford: Oxford University Press.

Chhibber, Pradeep K. and Rahul Verma. 2018. *Ideology and Identity: The Changing Party Systems of India.* Oxford: Oxford University Press.

Cleveland, William S. 1979. 'Robust Locally Weighted Regression and Smoothing Scatterplots'. *Journal of the American Statistical Association* 74 (368): 829–836.

Colagrossi, Marco, Domenico Rossignoli, and Mario A. Maggioni. 2020. 'Does Democracy Cause Growth? A Meta-analysis (of 2000 Regressions)'. *European Journal of Political Economy* 61: 101824.

Collier, Ruth Berins. 1999. *Paths toward Democracy.* Cambridge: Cambridge University Press.

Colomer, Josep M., editor. 2004. *The Handbook of Electoral System Choice.* Basingstoke: Palgrave.

Coppedge, Michael, John Gerring, Carl Henrik Knutsen, Staffan I. Lindberg, Jan Teorell, David Altman, Fabio Angiolillo, Michael Bernhard, Cecilia Borella, Agnes Cornell, M. Steven Fish, Linnea Fox, Lisa Gastaldi, Haakon Gjerløw, Adam Glynn, Ana Good God, Sandra Grahn, Allen Hicken, Katrin Kinzelbach, Joshua Krusell, Kyle L. Marquardt, Kelly McMann, Valeriya Mechkova, Juraj Medzihorsky, Natalia Natsika, Anja Neundorf, Pamela Paxton, Daniel Pemstein, Josefine Pernes, Oskar Rydén, Johannes von Römer, Brigitte Seim, Rachel Sigman, Svend-Erik Skaaning, Jeffrey Staton, Aksel Sundström, Eitan Tzelgov, Yi-ting Wang, Tore Wig, Steven Wilson, and Daniel Ziblatt. 2024. 'V-Dem Country–Year Dataset v14'. Gothenburg: Varieties of Democracy (V-Dem) Project.

Cornell, Agnes and Marcia Grimes. 2015. 'Institutions as Incentives for Civic Action: Bureaucratic Structures, Civil Society, and Disruptive Protests'. *Journal of Politics* 77 (3): 664–678.

Cornell, Agnes, Jørgen Møller, and Svend-Erik Skaaning. 2020. *Democratic Stability in an Age of Crisis*. Oxford: Oxford University Press.

Costa Lobo, Marina and Isabella Razzuoli. 2017. 'Party Finance and Perceived Party Responsiveness'. In *Organizing Political Parties*, edited by Thomas Webb, Pauland Poguntke, and Susan E. Scarrow. Oxford: Oxford University Press, 187–207.

Cox, Gary W. 1990. 'Centripetal and Centrifugal Incentives in Electoral Systems'. *American Journal of Political Science* 34 (4): 903–935.

Cox, Gary W. 1997. *Making Votes Count*. Cambridge: Cambridge University Press.

Cox, Gary W., Jon H. Fiva, and Daniel M. Smith. 2016. 'The Contraction Effect: How Proportional Representation Affects Mobilization and Turnout'. *Journal of Politics* 78 (4): 1249–1263.

Dahl, Robert A. 1971. *Polyarchy*. New Haven, CT: Yale University Press.

Dahl, Robert A. 1998. *On Democracy*. New Haven, CT: Yale University Press.

Dahlström, Carl and Victor Lapuente. 2022. 'Comparative Bureaucratic Politics'. *Annual Review of Political Science* 25 (1): 43–63.

Dalton, Russell J., David M. Farrell, and Ian McAllister. 2011. *Political Parties and Democratic Linkage*. Oxford: Oxford University Press.

Dalton, Russell J. and Hans-Dieter Klingemann, editors. 2007. *The Oxford Handbook of Political Behavior*. Oxford: Oxford University Press.

Dancygier, Rafaela M. 2017. *Dilemmas of Inclusion*. Princeton, NJ: Princeton University Press.

Darrieux, Rodolfo. 2019. 'Political Institutions and the Legislative Success of Brazilian Presidents'. *Brazilian Political Science Review* 13 (1): 1–23.

Davenport, Christian and David A. Armstrong. 2004. 'Democracy and the Violation of Human Rights'. *American Journal of Political Science* 48 (3): 538–554.

David, Roman and Ian Holliday. 2018. *Liberalism and Democracy in Myanmar*. Oxford: Oxford University Press.

Davis, Aeron. 2023. *Political Communication: An Introduction for Crisis Times*. Cambridge: Polity, 2nd edition.

De la Torre, Carlos. 2017. 'Populism in Latin America'. In *The Oxford Handbook of Populism*, edited by Cristóbal Rovira Kaltwasser, Paul Taggart, Paulina Ochoa Espejo, and Pierre Ostigu. Oxford: Oxford University Press, 195–213.

De Vreese, Claes. 2017. 'Comparative Political Communication Research'. In *The Oxford Handbook of Political Communication*. Oxford: Oxford University Press, 287–300.

De Vreese, Claes, Frank Esser, and David Nicolas Hopmann, editors. 2017. *Comparing Political Journalism*. London: Routledge.

De Vries, Catherine and Sara Hobolt. 2020. *Political Entrepreneurs: The Rise of Challenger Parties in Europe*. Princeton, NJ: Princeton University Press.

Della Porta, Donatella and Olivier Fillieule. 2003. 'Policing Social Protest'. In *The Blackwell Companion to Social Movements*, edited by David A. Snow, Sarah A. Soule, and Hanspeter Kriesi. Oxford: Blackwell, 217–241.

DellaVigna, Stefano and Ethan Kaplan. 2007. 'The Fox News Effect: Media Bias and Voting'. *Quarterly Journal of Economics* 122 (3): 1187–1234.

Diamond, Larry. 2002. 'Elections without Democracy: Thinking about Hybrid Regimes'. *Journal of Democracy* 13 (2): 21–35.

Diani, Mario. 1992. 'The Concept of Social Movement'. *Sociological Review* 40 (1): 1–25.

Dickson, Bruce J. 2016. 'The Survival Strategy of the Chinese Communist Party'. *Washington Quarterly* 39 (4): 27–44.

Djuve, Vilde Lunnan, Carl Henrik Knutsen, and Tore Wig. 2020. 'Patterns of Regime Breakdown since the French Revolution'. *Comparative Political Studies* 53 (6): 923–958.

Döring, Holger, Alexandra Quaas, Maike Hesse, and Philip Manow. 2023. Parliaments and Governments Database (ParlGov): Information on Parties, Elections and Cabinets in Established

Democracies. Development Version. https://parlgov.org.

Downs, Anthony. 1957. *An Economic Theory of Democracy*. New York: Harper & Row.

Dür, Andreas and Gemma Mateo. 2016. *Insiders versus Outsiders: Interest Group Politics in Multilevel Europe*. Oxford: Oxford University Press.

Duverger, Maurice. 1951. *Les partis politiques*. Paris: Colin.

Duverger, Maurice. 1963. *Political Parties*. New York: Wiley.

Dzinesa, Gwinyayi. 2012. 'Zimbabwe's Constitutional Reform Process: Challenges and Prospects'. Cape Town: Institute for Justice and Reconciliation (IJR).

Eckersley, Robyn. 2004. *The Green State*. Cambridge, MA: MIT Press.

Eggers, Andrew C. 2015. 'Proportionality and Turnout: Evidence from French Municipalities'. *Comparative Political Studies* 48 (2): 135–167.

Egreteau, Renaud. 2016. *Caretaking Democratization: The Military and Political Change in Myanmar*. Oxford: Oxford University Press.

Elkins, Zachary and Tom Ginsburg. 2021. 'What Can We Learn from Written Constitutions?' *Annual Review of Political Science* 24 (1): 321–343.

Elkins, Zachary and Tom Ginsburg. 2022. 'Characteristics of National Constitutions, Version 4.0'. Comparative Constitutions Project. Last modified: 24 October 2022. Available at comparativeconstitutionsproject.org.

Elkjær, Mads Andreas and Torben Iversen. 2020. 'The Political Representation of Economic Interests'. *World Politics* 72 (2): 254–290.

Escobar-Lemmon, Maria C., Valerie J. Hoekstra, Alice J. Kang, and Miki Caul. Kittilson. 2021. *Reimagining the Judiciary: Women's Representation on High Courts Worldwide*. Oxford: Oxford University Press.

Evans, Geoffrey, editor. 1999. *The End of Class Politics?* Oxford: Oxford University Press.

Evans, Peter and James E. Rauch. 1999. 'Bureaucracy and Growth'. *American Sociological Review* 64 (5): 748–765.

Fariss, Christopher J., Therese Anders, Jonathan N. Markowitz, and Miriam Barnum. 2022. 'New Estimates of Over 500 Years of Historic GDP and Population Data'. *Journal of Conflict Resolution* 66 (3): 553–591.

Fearon, James and David Laitin. 2003. 'Ethnicity, Insurgency, and Civil War'. *American Political Science Review* 97 (1): 75–90.

Figueroa, Valentín. 2021. 'Political Corruption Cycles: High-Frequency Evidence from Argentina's Notebooks Scandal'. *Comparative Political Studies* 54 (3–4): 482–517.

Finer, Herman. 1924. *The Case against Proportional Representation*. London: Fabian Society.

Finer, Samuel E. 1997. *The History of Government*. Oxford: Oxford University Press.

Franklin, Mark. 2004. *Voter Turnout and the Dynamics of Electoral Competition in Established Democracies since 1945*. Cambridge: Cambridge University Press.

Freeden, Michael, Lyman Tower Sargent, and Marc Stears, editors. 2013. *The Oxford Handbook of Political Ideologies*. Oxford: Oxford University Press.

Gandhi, Jennifer and Ellen Lust-Okar. 2009. 'Elections under Authoritarianism'. *Annual Review of Political Science* 12 (1): 403–422.

Gandhi, Jennifer, Ben Noble, and Milan Svolik. 2020. 'Legislatures and Legislative Politics without Democracy'. *Comparative Political Studies* 53 (9): 1359–1379.

Ganguly, Sumit. 2020. 'Is Empowered Hindu Nationalism Transforming India?' *Current History* 119 (816): 123–127.

Garcés, Mario. 2019. 'October 2019: Social Uprising in Neoliberal Chile'. *Journal of Latin American Cultural Studies* 28 (3): 483–491.

Gazibo, Mamoudou. 2005. 'Foreign Aid and Democratization: Benin and Niger Compared'. *African Studies Review* 48 (3): 67–87.

Geddes, Barbara. 1999. 'What Do We Know about Democratization after Twenty Years?' *Annual Review of Political Science* 2 (1): 115–144.

Geddes, Barbara, Joseph Wright, and Erica Frantz. 2014. 'Autocratic Breakdown and Regime Transitions'. *Perspectives on Politics* 12 (2): 313–331.

Geddes, Barbara, Joseph Wright, and Erica Frantz. 2018. *How Dictatorships Work*. Cambridge: Cambridge University Press.

Geddis, Andrew. 2006. 'A Dual Track Democracy? The Symbolic Role of the Māori Seats in New Zealand's Electoral System'. *Election Law Journal* 5 (4): 347–371.

Gellner, Ernest. 1983. *Nations and Nationalism*. Ithaca, NY: Cornell University Press.

Gentzkow, Matthew. 2006. 'Television and Voter Turnout'. *Quarterly Journal of Economics* 121 (3): 931–972.

Gerring, John and Strom C. Thacker. 2010. *Centripetal Democratic Governance*. Cambridge: Cambridge University Press.

Gerring, John, Strom C. Thacker, and Carola Moreno. 2009. 'Are Parliamentary Systems

Better?' *Comparative Political Studies* 42 (3): 327–359.
Giger, Nathalie and Heike Klüver. 2016. 'Voting Against Your Constituents? How Lobbying Affects Representation'. *American Journal of Political Science* 60 (1): 190–205.
Gilens, Martin. 2012. *Affluence and Influence: Economic Inequality and Political Power in America*. Princeton, NJ: Princeton University Press.
Gingerich, Daniel W. 2013. 'Governance Indicators and the Level of Analysis Problem'. *British Journal of Political Science* 43 (3): 505–540.
Gingerich, Daniel W., Virginia Oliveros, Ana Corbacho, and Mauricio Ruiz-Vega. 2016. 'When to Protect? Using the Crosswise Model to Integrate Protected and Direct Responses in Surveys of Sensitive Behavior'. *Political Analysis* 24 (2): 132–156.
Gingrich, Jane and Silja Häusermann. 2015. 'The Decline of the Working-Class Vote, the Reconfiguration of the Welfare Support Coalition and Consequences for the Welfare State'. *Journal of European Social Policy* 25 (1): 50–75.
Gjerløw, Haakon and Carl Henrik Knutsen. 2019. 'Leaders, Private Interests, and Socially Wasteful Projects: Skyscrapers in Democracies and Autocracies'. *Political Research Quarterly* 72 (2): 504–520.
Gohdes, Anita R. 2023. *Repression in the Digital Age*. Oxford: Oxford University Press.
Golden, Miriam A. and Lucio Picci. 2005. 'Proposal for a New Measure of Corruption, Illustrated with Italian Data'. *Economics and Politics* 17 (1): 37–75.
Golder, Sona N., Laura B. Stephenson, Karine van der Straeten, André Blais, Damien Bol, Philipp Harfst, and Jean-François Laslier. 2017. 'Votes for Women: Electoral Systems and Support for Female Candidates'. *Politics and Gender* 13 (1): 107–131.
Gonzalez, Ricardo and Carmen Le Foulon. 2020. 'The 2019–2020 Chilean Protests'. *International Journal of Sociology* 50 (3): 227–235.
Goodin, Robert, Michael Moran, and Martin Rein, editors. 2008. *The Oxford Handbook of Public Policy*. Oxford: Oxford University Press.
Górecki, Maciej A. and Michal Pierzgalski. 2023. 'Electoral Systems, Partisan Politics, and Income Redistribution'. *Comparative Political Studies* 56 (14): 2165–2200.
Gottlieb, Jessica, Guy Grossman, and Amanda Lea Robinson. 2018. 'Do Men and Women Have Different Policy Preferences in Africa? Determinants and Implications of Gender Gaps in Policy Prioritization'. *British Journal of Political Science* 48 (3): 611–636.
Graber, Doris A. 2017. 'Freedom of the Press'. In *The Oxford Handbook of Political Communication*, edited by Kate Kenski and Kathleen Hall Jamieson. Oxford University Press, 237–248.
Grant, Wyn. 2000. *Pressure Groups and British Politics*. Basingstoke: Macmillan.
Grimm, Jannis, Kevin Koehler, Ellen Lust, Ilyas Saliba, and Isabell Schierenbeck. 2020. *Safer Field Research in the Social Sciences*. London: SAGE Publications.
Gromes, Thorsten. 2010. 'Federalism as a Means of Peace-Building: The Case of Postwar Bosnia and Herzegovina'. *Nationalism and Ethnic Politics* 16 (3–4): 354–374.
Grossman, Emiliano. 2022. 'Media and Policy Making in the Digital Age'. *Annual Review of Political Science* 25 (1): 443–461.
Guriev, Sergei and Daniel Treisman. 2023. *Spin Dictators*. Princeton, NJ: Princeton University Press.
Hadenius, Axel and Jan Teorell. 2007. 'Pathways from Authoritarianism'. *Journal of Democracy* 18 (1): 143–157.
Hager, Anselm and Krzysztof Krakowski. 2022. 'Does State Repression Spark Protests?' *American Political Science Review* 116 (2): 564–579.
Haglund, David G., Jennie L. Schulze, and Ognen Vangelov. 2022. 'Hungary's Slide toward Autocracy'. *Political Science Quarterly* 137 (4): 675–713.
Hall, Peter A., Georgina Evans, and Sung In Kim. 2023. *Political Change and Electoral Coalitions in Western Democracies*. Cambridge: Cambridge University Press.
Hall, Peter A. and Rosemary C. R. Taylor. 1996. 'Political Science and the Three New Institutionalisms'. *Political Studies* 44 (5): 936–957.
Hallin, Daniel C. and Paolo Mancini. 2004. *Comparing Media Systems*. Cambridge: Cambridge University Press.
Hallin, Daniel C. and Paolo Mancini, editors. 2011. *Comparing Media Systems beyond the Western World*. Cambridge: Cambridge University Press.
Hamilton, Alexander, James Madison, and John Jay. 2003 [1787–1788]. *The Federalist*. Cambridge: Cambridge University Press.
Hanson, Jonathan K. and Rachel Sigman. 2021. 'Leviathan's Latent Dimensions'. *Journal of Politics* 83 (4): 1495–1510.
Harbers, Imke. 2015. 'Taxation and the Unequal Reach of the State'. *Governance* 28 (3): 373–391.

Harbers, Imke and Abbey Steele. 2020. 'Subnational Variation across States'. *Latin American Politics and Society* 62 (3): 1–18.

Häusermann, Silja. 2010. *The Politics of Welfare State Reform in Continental Europe*. Cambridge: Cambridge University Press.

Heidenheimer, Arnold J. 1986. 'Politics, Policy and Policey as Concepts in English and Continental Languages'. *Review of Politics* 48 (1): 3–30.

Heilmann, Sebastian. 2016. *China's Political System*. Lanham: Rowman & Littlefield.

Hermens, Ferdinand A. 1941. *Democracy or Anarchy?* Notre Dame: University of Notre Dame.

Hicken, Allen. 2011. 'Clientelism'. *Annual Review of Political Science* 14 (1): 289–310.

Hickey, Sam, editor. 2023. *Pockets of Effectiveness and the Politics of State-Building and Development in Africa*. Oxford: Oxford University Press.

Hirschl, Ran. 2007. *Towards Juristocracy*. Cambridge, MA: Harvard University Press.

Hobbes, Thomas. 2009 [1651]. *The Leviathan*. Oxford: Oxford University Press.

Hooghe, Liesbet, Gary Marks, Arjan H. Schakel, Sandra Chapman-Osterkatz, Sara Niedzwiecki, and Sarah Shair-Rosenfeld. 2016. *Measuring Regional Authority*. Volume I. *A Postfunctionalist Theory of Governance*. Oxford: Oxford University Press.

Hooghe, Liesbet, Gary Marks, and Carole J. Wilson. 2002. 'Does Left/Right Structure Party Positions on European Integration?' *Comparative Political Studies* 35 (8): 965–989.

Hooghe, Marc. 2012. 'The Political Crisis in Belgium (2007–2011)'. *Representation* 48 (1): 131–138.

Huber, Evelyne and John D. Stephens. 2001. *Development and Crisis of the Welfare State*. Chicago, IL: University of Chicago Press.

Humprecht, Edda, Laia Castro Herrero, Sina Blassnig, Michael Brüggemann, and Sven Engesser. 2022. 'Media Systems in the Digital Age'. *Journal of Communication* 72 (2): 145–164.

Huntington, Samuel P. 1991. *The Third Wave*. Norman, OK: University of Oklahoma Press.

ILO. 2022. *World Social Protection Report 2020–2022*. Geneva: International Labour Organization.

Immergut, Ellen M. 1992. *Health Politics*. Cambridge: Cambridge University Press.

Immergut, Ellen M. and Karen M. Anderson. 2007. 'Editors' Introduction: The Dynamics of Pension Politics'. In *The Handbook of West European Pension Politics*, edited by Ellen M. Immergut, Karen M. Anderson, and Isabelle Schulze. Oxford: Oxford University Press, 1–45.

Immergut, Ellen M., Karen M. Anderson, and Isabelle Schulze, editors. 2007. *The Handbook of West European Pension Politics*. Oxford: Oxford University Press.

Inglehart, Ronald and Pippa Norris. 2000. 'The Developmental Theory of the Gender Gap'. *International Political Science Review* 21 (4): 441–463.

Inglehart, Ronald and Christian Welzel. 2010. 'Changing Mass Priorities: The Link between Modernization and Democracy'. *Perspectives on Politics* 8 (2): 551–567.

Inter-Parliamentary Union. 2021. 'Parline Database'. Available from https://data.ipu.org/women-ranking.

IPCC. 2023. *Climate Change 2023*. Geneva: Intergovernmental Panel on Climate Change.

Ivarsflaten, Elisabeth and Rune Stubager. 2012. 'Voting for the Populist Radical Right in Western Europe: The Role of Education'. In *Class Politics and the Radical Right*, edited by Jens Rydgren. London: Routledge, 122–137.

Iversen, Torben and David Soskice. 2006. 'Electoral Institutions and the Politics of Coalitions'. *American Political Science Review* 100 (2): 165–181.

Jackson, Keith and Alan McRobie. 2019. *New Zealand Adopts Proportional Representation*. New York: Routledge.

Jaffrelot, Christophe and Gilles Verniers. 2020. 'The BJP's 2019 Election Campaign: Not Business as Usual'. *Contemporary South Asia* 28 (2): 155–177.

Kalyvas, Stathis N. 1996. *The Rise of Christian Democracy in Europe*. Ithaca, NY: Cornell University Press.

Kam, Christopher J. 2009. *Party Discipline and Parliamentary Politics*. Cambridge: Cambridge University Press.

Kant, Immanuel. 1991a [1784]. 'Idea for a Universal History with Cosmopolitan Purpose'. In *Political Writings*. Cambridge: Cambridge University Press, 41–53.

Kant, Immanuel. 1991b [1795]. 'Perpetual Peace'. In *Political Writings*. Cambridge: Cambridge University Press, 93–130.

Kant, Immanuel. 1991c [1784]. 'What Is Enlightenment?' In *Political Writings*. Cambridge: Cambridge University Press, 54–60.

Katz, Richard S. and Peter Mair. 1995. 'Changing Models of Party Organization and Party Democracy'. *Party Politics* 1 (1): 5–28.

Kedar, Orit. 2005. 'When Moderate Voters Prefer Extreme Parties'. *American Political Science Review* 99 (2): 185–199.

Kendall-Taylor, Andrea, Erica Frantz, and Joseph Wright. 2016. 'The New Dictators'. *Foreign Affairs*, 26 September.

Kingdon, John W. 2003. *Agendas, Alternatives, and Public Policies*. London: Longman.

Klüver, Heike. 2013. *Lobbying in the European Union*. Oxford: Oxford University Press.

Kölln, Ann-Kristin. 2015. 'The Value of Political Parties to Representative Democracy'. *European Political Science Review* 7 (4): 593–613.

Kommers, Donald P. 1994. 'The Constitutional Law of Abortion in Germany'. *Journal of Contemporary Health Law and Policy* 10 (1): 1–32.

Kornai, János. 2015. 'Hungary's U-Turn'. *Society and Economy* 37 (3): 279–329.

Korpi, Walter. 1983. *The Democratic Class Struggle*. London: Routledge & Kegan Paul.

Kottasová, Ivana. 2021. 'Convicted for "Advertising" Abortion, German Doctors are Fighting to Share the Facts'. CNN, 7 June.

Krause, George A. 1999. *A Two-Way Street: The Institutional Dynamics of the Modern Administrative State*. Pittsburgh, PA: University of Pittsburgh Press.

Kriesi, Hanspeter, Jasmine Lorenzini, Bruno Wuest, and Silja Häusermann, editors. 2020. *Contention in Times of Crisis: Recession and Political Protest in Thirty European Countries*. Cambridge: Cambridge University Press.

Kurer, Thomas. 2020. 'The Declining Middle'. *Comparative Political Studies* 53 (10–11): 1798–1835.

Laakso, Markku and Rein Taagepera. 1979. 'Effective Number of Parties'. *Comparative Political Studies* 12 (1): 3–27.

Larsen, Signe Rehling. 2021. *The Constitutional Theory of the Federation and the European Union*. Oxford: Oxford University Press.

Lee, Jong-Wha and Hanol Lee. 2016. 'Human Capital in the Long Run'. *Journal of Development Economics* 122 (C): 147–169.

Levitsky, Steven and Lucan A. Way. 2010. *Competitive Authoritarianism*. Cambridge: Cambridge University Press.

Levitsky, Steven and Daniel Ziblatt. 2018. *How Democracies Die*. New York: Crown.

Levy, Ro'ee. 2021. 'Social Media, News Consumption, and Polarization'. *American Economic Review* 111 (3): 831–70.

Lewis, David G. 2020. *Russia's New Authoritarianism*. Edinburgh: Edinburgh University Press.

Lijphart, Arend. 1968. *The Politics of Accommodation*. Berkeley, CA: University of California Press.

Lijphart, Arend. 1979. 'Religious vs. Linguistic vs. Class Voting: The Crucial Experiment of Comparing Belgium, Canada, South Africa and Switzerland'. *American Political Science Review* 73 (2): 442–458.

Lijphart, Arend. 2012. *Patterns of Democracy*. New Haven, CT: Yale University Press, 2nd edition.

Lindvall, Johannes. 2017. *Reform Capacity*. Oxford: Oxford University Press.

Linz, Juan J. 1990. 'The Perils of Presidentialism'. *Journal of Democracy* 1 (1): 51–69.

Lipset, Seymour Martin. 1959. 'Some Social Requisites of Democracy'. *American Political Science Review* 53 (1): 69–105.

Lipset, Seymour Martin and Stein Rokkan. 1967. *Party Systems and Voter Alignments*. New York: Free Press.

Lipsky, Michael. 1968. 'Protest as a Political Resource'. *American Political Science Review* 62 (4): 1144–1158.

Lisner, Wiebke. 2006. *Hüterinnen der Nation*. Frankfurt: Campus Verlag.

Loughlin, John, John Kincaid, and Wilfried Swenden, editors. 2013. *Routledge Handbook of Regionalism and Federalism*. London: Routledge.

Lust, Ellen, editor. 2022. *Everyday Choices*. Cambridge: Cambridge University Press.

McAdam, Doug. 1999. *Political Process and the Development of Black Insurgency 1930–1970*. Chicago, IL: University of Chicago Press, 2nd edition.

McAdam, Doug, Sidney Tarrow, and Charles Tilly. 2001. *Dynamics of Contention*. Cambridge: Cambridge University Press.

Macaulay, Fiona. 2017. 'Dilma Rousseff (2011–2016): A Crisis of Governance and Consensus in Brazil'. In *Women Presidents and Prime Ministers in Post-transition Democracies*, edited by Verónica Montecinos. London: Springer, 123–140.

McLuhan, Marshall. 1962. *The Gutenberg Galaxy*. Toronto: University of Toronto Press.

Magaloni, Beatriz. 2008. 'Credible Power-Sharing and the Longevity of Authoritarian Rule'. *Comparative Political Studies* 41 (4–5): 715–741.

Majone, Giandomenico. 1998. 'Europe's "Democratic Deficit"'. *European Law Journal* 4 (1): 5–28.

Manjari, Katju. 2019. 'The History of Hindu Nationalism in India'. In *The Oxford History of Hinduism*, edited by Torkel Brekke. Oxford: Oxford University Press, 203–215.

Mann, Michael. 1984. 'The Autonomous Power of the State'. *Archives européennes de sociologie* 25 (2): 185–213.

Mann, Michael. 2005. *The Dark Side of Democracy*. Cambridge: Cambridge University Press.

Marinov, Nikolay and Hein Goemans. 2014. 'Coups and Democracy'. *British Journal of Political Science* 44 (4): 799–825.

Marshall, Monty G. and Keith Jaggers. 2016. 'Polity IV Project: Political Regime Characteristics and Transitions, 1800–2015'. College Park, MD: University of Maryland.

Martin, Shane, Thomas Saalfeld, and Kaare W. Strøm, editors. 2014. *The Oxford Handbook of Legislative Studies*. Oxford: Oxford University Press.

Mazzuca, Sebastián. 2021. *Latecomer State Formation*. New Haven, CT: Yale University Press.

Meguid, Bonnie M. 2005. 'Competition between Unequals: The Role of Mainstream Party Strategy in Niche Party Success'. *American Political Science Review* 99 (3): 347–359.

Migdal, Joel. 1988. *Strong Societies and Weak States*. Princeton, NJ: Princeton University Press.

Moore, Barrington. 1966. *Social Origins of Dictatorship and Democracy*. Boston, MA: Beacon Press.

Morgan, Kimberly J. and Ann Shola Orloff, editors. 2017. *The Many Hands of the State*. New York: Cambridge University Press.

Müller, Wolfgang and Kaare Strøm, editors. 1999. *Policy, Office, or Votes?* Cambridge: Cambridge University Press.

Munck, Gerardo L. and Richard Snyder. 2007. *Passion, Craft, and Method in Comparative Politics*. Baltimore, MD: Johns Hopkins University Press.

Mylonas, Harris and Maya Tudor. 2023. *Varieties of Nationalism*. Cambridge: Cambridge University Press.

Neto, Octavio Amorim and Gary W. Cox. 1997. 'Electoral Institutions, Cleavage Structures, and the Number of Parties'. *American Journal of Political Science* 41 (1): 149–174.

Nistotskaya, Marina, Stefan Dahlberg, Carl Dahlström, Aksel Sundström, Sofia Axelsson, Cem Mert Dalli, and Natalia Alvarado Pachon. 2021. 'The Quality of Government Expert Survey 2020 Dataset: Wave III'. Gothenburg: Quality of Government Institute, University of Gothenburg. http://www.qog.pol.gu.se DOI: 10.18157/qoges2020.

North, Douglass C. 1990. *Institutions, Institutional Change, and Economic Performance*. Cambridge: Cambridge University Press.

Nunes, Leonardo Loureiro. 2021. 'Brazil: Impeachment and the Conflicting Relationship between the Dilma Rousseff Government and the National Congress'. In *Imperialism and Transitions to Socialism*, edited by Rémy Herrera. Bingley, UK: Emerald, 223–236.

Nyrup, Jacob and Stuart Bramwell. 2020. 'Who Governs?' *American Political Science Review* 114 (4): 1366–1374.

O'Donnell, Guillermo. 2001. 'Democracy, Law, and Comparative Politics'. *Studies in Comparative International Development* 36 (1): 7–26.

OECD. 2005. *Ageing and Pension System Reform*. Paris: Organization for Economic Cooperation and Development.

Olken, Benjamin A. 2009. 'Corruption Perceptions vs. Corruption Reality'. *Journal of Public Economics* 93 (7–8): 950–964.

Olson, Mancur. 1965. *The Logic of Collective Action*. Cambridge, MA: Harvard University Press.

Ortiz, Isabel, Sara Burke, Mohamed Berrada, and Hernán Saenz Cortés. 2022. *World Protests*. Cham: Palgrave Macmillan.

Otlan, Yana, Yulia Kuzmina, Aleksandra Rumiantseva, and Katerina Tertytchnaya. 2023. 'Authoritarian Media and Foreign Protests'. *Post-Soviet Affairs* 39 (6): 391–405.

Palshikar, Suhas. 2015. 'The BJP and Hindu Nationalism'. *South Asia* 38 (4): 719–735.

Panebianco, Angelo. 1988. *Political Parties*. Cambridge: Cambridge University Press.

Pemstein, Daniel, Kyle L. Marquardt, Eitan Tzelgov, Yi-ting Wang, Juraj Medzihorsky, Joshua Krusell, Farhad Miri, and Johannes von Römer. 2024. 'The V-Dem Measurement Model'. V-Dem Working Paper No. 21, 9th edition, Varieties of Democracy Institute, University of Gothenburg.

Persson, Torsten and Guido Tabellini. 2003. *The Economic Effects of Constitutions*. Cambridge, MA: MIT Press.

Peters, B. Guy. 2020. 'Approaches in Comparative Politics'. In *Comparative Politics*, edited by Daniele Caramani. Oxford: Oxford University Press, 5th edition, 35–49.

Peters, Margaret, Frida Boräng, Sara Kalm, J. Lindvall, and Adrian Shin. 2024. 'Historical Immigration Policies: Trends and Lessons'. *International Studies Quarterly* 68: 3, sqae084.

Pitkin, Hanna F. 1967. *The Concept of Representation*. Berkeley, CA: University of California Press.

Platt, Brian. 2004. *Burning and Building. Schooling and State Formation in Japan, 1750–1890*. Cambridge, MA: Harvard University Asia Center and Harvard University Press.

Powell, G. Bingham. 2000. *Elections as Instruments of Democracy*. New Haven, CT: Yale University Press.

Powell, G. Bingham. 2019. *Ideological Representation: Achieved and Astray*. Cambridge: Cambridge University Press.

Powell, G. Bingham and Guy D. Whitten. 1993. 'A Cross-National Analysis of Economic Voting: Taking Account of the Political Context'. *American Journal of Political Science* 37: 391–414.

Przeworski, Adam. 2004. 'Institutions Matter?' *Government and Opposition* 39 (4): 527–540.

Przeworski, Adam. 2010. *Democracy and the Limits of Self-Government*. Cambridge: Cambridge University Press.

Przeworski, Adam, Susan C. Stokes, and Bernard Manin. 1999. *Democracy, Accountability, and Representation*. Cambridge: Cambridge University Press.

Raleigh, Clionadh, Roudabeh Kishi, and Andrew Linke. 2023. 'Political Instability Patterns Are Obscured by Conflict Dataset Scope Conditions, Sources, and Coding Choices'. *Humanities and Social Sciences Communications* 10: 74.

Rapoport, Anatol. 1960. *Fights, Games, and Debates*. Ann Arbor, MI: University of Michigan Press.

Reilly, Ben. 2002. 'Electoral Systems for Divided Societies'. *Journal of Democracy* 13 (2): 156–170.

Reporters sans frontières. 2023. 'World Press Freedom Index'. Available at https://rsf.org/en/index, downloaded on 14 December 2023.

Riambau, Guillem, Steven Stillman, and Geua Boe-Gibson. 2021. 'What Determines Preferences for an Electoral System?' *Public Choice* 186 (1): 179–208.

Riker, William H. 1975. 'Federalism'. In *Handbook of Political Science*, Volume 5, edited by Fred Greenstein and Nelson Polsby. Reading, MA: Addison-Wesley, 93–172.

Ríos-Figueroa, Julio and Jeffrey K. Staton. 2014. 'An Evaluation of Cross-National Measures of Judicial Independence'. *Journal of Law, Economics, and Organization* 30 (1): 104–137.

Roberts, Andrew, Jason Seawright, and Jennifer Cyr. 2013. 'Do Electoral Laws Affect Women's Representation?' *Comparative Political Studies* 46 (12): 1555–1581.

Rogers, Everett M. 1962. *Diffusion of Innovations*. New York: The Free Press of Glencoe.

Rosenblum, Nancy. 2008. *On the Side of the Angels*. Princeton, NJ: Princeton University Press.

Rosenbluth, Frances and Ian Shapiro. 2018. *Responsible Parties*. New Haven, CT: Yale University Press.

Ross, Michael L. 2013. *The Oil Curse*. Princeton, NJ: Princeton University Press.

Rothstein, Bo. 1996. 'Political Institutions: An Overview'. In *A New Handbook for Political Science*, edited by Robert E. Goodin and Hans-Dieter Klingemann. Oxford: Oxford University Press, 104–125.

Rothstein, Bo and Jan Teorell. 2008. 'What Is Quality of Government?' *Governance* 21 (2): 165–190.

Rousseau, Jean-Jacques. 1762. *Du contrat social*. Amsterdam: Marc-Michel Rey.

Ryabinska, Natalya. 2011. 'The Media Market and Media Ownership in Post-Communist Ukraine'. *Problems of Post-Communism* 58 (6): 3–20.

Sachikonye, Lloyd M. 2013. 'Continuity or Reform in Zimbabwean Politics?' *Journal of African Elections* 12 (1): 178–185.

Saglie, Jo, Johannes Bergh, Jens Petter Gitlesen, and Hilmar Rommetvedt. 2021. 'Hva skjedde ved valget?' In *Lokalvalget 2019*, edited by Jo Saglie, Signe Bock Segaard, and Dag Arne Christensen. Oslo: Cappelen Damm Akademisk, 27–61.

Salmond, Rob. 2006. 'Proportional Representation and Female Parliamentarians'. *Legislative Studies Quarterly* 31 (2): 175–204.

Sardar, Minakshi. 2018. 'Parliamentary Elections in Algeria, 2017'. *Contemporary Review of the Middle East* 5 (1): 74–86.

Sartori, Giovanni. 1976. *Parties and Party Systems*. Cambridge: Cambridge University Press.

Schedler, Andreas. 2002. 'Elections without Democracy: The Menu of Manipulation'. *Journal of Democracy* 13 (2): 36–50.

Schleiter, Petra. 2020. 'Government Formation and Termination'. In *The Oxford Handbook of Political Executives*, edited by Rudy B. Andeweg, Robert Elgie, Ludger Helms, Juliet Kaarbo, and Ferdinand Müller-Rommel. Oxford: Oxford University Press, 294–313.

Schludi, Martin. 2005. *The Reform of Bismarckian Pension Systems*. Amsterdam: Amsterdam University Press.

Siebert, Fred S., Theodore Peterson, and Wilbur Schramm. 1956. *Four Theories of the Press*. Champaign, IL: University of Illinois Press.

Siegfried, André. 1913. *Tableau politique de la France de l'ouest sous la troisième république*. Paris: A. Colin.

Skocpol, Theda. 1979. *States and Social Revolutions*. Cambridge: Cambridge University Press.

Skocpol, Theda. 1992. *Protecting Soldiers and Mothers. The Political Origins of Social Policy in the United States*. Cambridge, MA: Belknap Press.

Skorge, Øyvind. 2023. 'Mobilizing the Underrepresented: Electoral Systems and Gender

Inequality in Political Participation'. *American Journal of Political Science* 67 (3): 538–552.

Snyder, Jack L. 2000. *From Voting to Violence*. New York: W. W. Norton & Company.

Soifer, Hillel. 2015. *State Building in Latin America*. Cambridge: Cambridge University Press.

Somma, Nicolás M., Matías Bargsted, Rodolfo Disi Pavlic, and Rodrigo M. Medel. 2021. 'No Water in the Oasis: The Chilean Spring of 2019–2020'. *Social Movement Studies* 20: 495–502.

Sørensen, Rune J. 2019. 'The Impact of State Television on Voter Turnout'. *British Journal of Political Science* 49 (1): 257–278.

Soroka, Stuart N. and Christopher Wlezien. 2010. *Degrees of Democracy*. Cambridge: Cambridge University Press.

Standage, Tom. 1998. *The Victorian Internet*. New York: Walker & Company.

Stimson, James A., Michael B. Mackuen, and Robert S. Erikson. 1995. 'Dynamic Representation'. *American Political Science Review* 89 (3): 543–565.

Stokes, Susan C. 2005. 'Perverse Accountability: A Formal Model of Machine Politics with Evidence from Argentina'. *American Political Science Review* 99: 315–25.

Stokes, Susan C., Thad Dunning, Marcelo Nazareno, and Valeria Brusco. 2013. *Brokers, Voters, and Clientelism*. Cambridge: Cambridge University Press.

Strøm, Kaare. 1990. *Minority Government and Majority Rule*. Cambridge: Cambridge University Press.

Strøm, Kaare, Wolfgang C. Müller, and Torbjörn Bergman. 2003. *Delegation and Accountability in Parliamentary Democracies*. Oxford: Oxford University Press.

Strömbäck, Jesper and Daniela V. Dimitrova. 2006. 'Political and Media Systems Matter: A Comparison of Election News Coverage in Sweden and the United States'. *Harvard International Journal of Press/Politics* 11 (4): 131–147.

Strömbäck, Jesper and Peter van Aelst. 2013. 'Why Political Parties Adapt to the Media'. *International Communication Gazette* 75 (4): 341–358.

Stubager, Rune. 2008. 'Education Effects on Authoritarian–Libertarian values'. *British Journal of Sociology* 59 (2): 327–350.

Svolik, Milan W. 2012. *The Politics of Authoritarian Rule*. Cambridge: Cambridge University Press.

Svolik, Milan W. 2015. 'Which Democracies Will Last? Coups, Incumbent Takeovers, and the Dynamic of Democratic Consolidation'. *British Journal of Political Science* 45 (4): 715–738.

Tate, C. Neal and Torbjörn Vallinder, editors. 1995. *The Global Expansion of Judicial Power*. New York: New York University Press.

Teele, Dawn Langan. 2018. *Forging the Franchise*. Princeton, NJ: Princeton University Press.

Teorell, Jan. 2010. *Determinants of Democratization*. Cambridge: Cambridge University Press.

Teorell, Jan, Aksel Sundström, Sören Holmberg, Bo Rothstein, Natalia Alvarado Pachon, Cem Mert Dalli, Rafael Lopez Valverde, and Paula Nilsson. 2024. 'The Quality of Government Standard Dataset', version January 2024. Gothenburg: Quality of Government Institute, University of Gothenburg. Available at https://www.gu.se/en/quality-government. doi: 10.18157/qogstdjan24.

Thelen, Kathleen. 2018. 'Regulating Uber: The Politics of the Platform Economy in Europe and the United States'. *Perspectives on Politics* 16 (4): 938–953.

Thomson, Robert, Terry Royed, Elin Naurin, Joaquín Artés, Rory Costello, Laurenz Ennser-Jedenastik, Mark Ferguson, Petia Kostadinova, Catherine Moury, François Pétry, and Katrin Praprotnik. 2017. 'The Fulfillment of Parties' Election Pledges'. *American Journal of Political Science* 61 (3): 527–542.

Tieku, Thomas. 2013. 'African Union: From Practical Federalism to Fantasy Union'. In *Routledge Handbook of Regionalism and Federalism*, edited by John Loughlin, John Kincaid, and Wilfried Swenden. London: Routledge, 573–583.

Tieku, Thomas. 2018. *Governing Africa*. London: Rowman & Littlefield.

Tilly, Charles. 1992. *Coercion, Capital, and European States*. Oxford: Blackwell.

Tingsten, Herbert. 1937. *Political Behavior*. London: P. S. King.

Transparency International. 2017. 'Global Corruption Barometer'. Available from https://www.transparency.org/research/gcb.

Tsebelis, George. 2002. *Veto Players*. Princeton, NJ: Princeton University Press.

Tsebelis, George and Jeannette Money. 1997. *Bicameralism*. Cambridge: Cambridge University Press.

Tudor, Maya. 2013. *The Promise of Power*. New York: Cambridge University Press.

Tufekci, Zeynep and Christopher Wilson. 2012. 'Social Media and the Decision to Participate in Political Protest'. *Journal of Communication* 62 (2): 363–379.

Van Aelst, Peter and Tom Louwerse. 2014. 'Parliament without Government: The Belgian Parliament and the Government Formation Processes of 2007–2011'. *West European Politics* 37 (3): 475–496.

Van Aelst, Peter, Jesper Strömbäck, Toril Aalberg, Frank Esser, Claes de Vreese, Jörg Matthes, David Hopmann, Susana Salgado, Nicolas Hubé, Agnieszka Stepińska, Stylianos Papathanassopoulos, Rosa Berganza, Guido Legnante, Carsten Reinemann, Tamir Sheafer, and James Stanyer. 2017. 'Political Communication in a High-Choice Media Environment: A Challenge for Democracy?' *Annals of the International Communication Association* 41 (1): 3–27.

Vanberg, Georg. 2015. 'Constitutional Courts in Comparative Perspective'. *Annual Review of Political Science* 18 (1): 167–185.

Verba, Sidney, Kay Schlozman, and Henry Brady. 1995. *Voice and Equality*. Cambridge, MA: Harvard University Press.

Veyne, Paul. 1983. 'Did the Greeks Invent Democracy?' *Diogenes* 31 (124): 1–32.

Vogler, Jan. 2023. 'Bureaucracies in Historical Political Economy'. In *The Oxford Handbook of Historical Political Economy*, edited by Cristóbal Rovira Kaltwasser, Paul Taggart, Paulina Ochoa Espejo, and Pierre Ostigu. 373–400.

Wahman, Michael, Jan Teorell, and Axel Hadenius. 2013. 'Authoritarian Regime Types Revisited: Updated Data in Comparative Perspective'. *Contemporary Politics* 19 (1): 19–34.

Wand, Jonathan N., Kenneth W. Shotts, Jasjeet S. Sekhon, Walter R. Mebane, Michael C. Herron, and Henry E. Brady. 2001. 'The Butterfly Did It: The Aberrant Vote for Buchanan in Palm Beach County, Florida'. *American Political Science Review* 95 (4): 793–810.

Webb, Paul, Thomas Poguntke, and Susan E. Scarrow, editors. 2017. *Organizing Political Parties*. Oxford: Oxford University Press.

Weber, Max. 1946. *From Max Weber*. New York: Oxford University Press.

Weber, Max. 1978 [1921]. *Economy and Society*. Los Angeles, CA: University of California Press.

Weible, Christopher M. and Paul A. Sabatier, editors. 2017. *Theories of the Policy Process*. London: Taylor & Francis, 4th edition.

Williams, Philip M. and Martin Harrison. 1971. *Politics and Society in de Gaulle's Republic*. London: Longman.

Wills-Otero, Laura. 2009. 'Electoral Systems in Latin America'. *Latin American Politics and Society* 51 (3): 33–58.

Yildirim, Tevfik Murat, Gunnar Thesen, Will Jennings, and Erik de Vries. 2023. 'The Determinants of the Media Coverage of Politicians'. *European Journal of Political Research* 62 (4): 1369–1388.

Young, Lauren E. 2019. 'The Psychology of State Repression'. *American Political Science Review* 113 (1): 140–155.

Zeldin, Theodore. 1958. *The Political System of Napoleon III*. London: Macmillan.

Ziblatt, Daniel. 2008. *Structuring the State*. Princeton, NJ: Princeton University Press.

INDEX

Tables and figures are indicated by an italic *t* and *f* following the page number.

A

abortion 167–8
African Union (AU) 96
agenda-setting effects
 media 253, 254
Algeria
 voter turnout 217–18
alternative voting systems 107, 114
appellate courts 162
Arab Spring 79, 82, 259
Argentina 26
 clientelism 271
 federalism in 100
Aristotle 1, 281
assumptions 19
authoritarianism 51, 84
 authoritarian monarchies 72–3
 categorization of authoritarian regimes 70–73, 75
 challenges for authoritarian rulers 81–2
 charismatic authority 73
 communist authoritarian regimes 73
 distribution of democratic and authoritarian regimes 2, 3*f*, 4
 dominant-party regimes 71
 electoral systems 83, 105–6
 executives 144–5
 freedom of the press, and 248, 249
 hybrid regimes 70, 73–7
 longevity of authoritarian regimes 83
 military regimes 71
 multiparty regimes 75
 personalist regimes 72
 political institutions, role of 82, 83, 84
 political parties 188–9
 'problem of authoritarian control' 81, 82
 'problem of authoritarian power sharing' 81
 propaganda and control over the media 249
 public policymaking 275–6
 rational-legal authority 73
 stability of authoritarian regimes 83–4
 traditional authority 73
 see also democratic reversals
autocracy 51
Auyero, J. 271

B

ballot structure 106, 110–13
Belgium
 government-formation processes 147–8
'bellicist theory of the state' 36
Benin
 democratization 64
Beramendi, P. 99
Berlin Wall, fall of 61, 61*f*
bicameralism 99–100, 139
Boix, C. 23, 24*t*, 56, 59
Bosnia and Herzegovina
 federal structure 101–2
Botswana
 ballot structure 110, 111*f*
Boulanger, G. 201–2
Brazil
 bicameralism 139, 140*f*
 constitution 129, 137
 executive–legislative relations 131, 132*f*, 149–50
 political regions 88*f*
 public administration 182–3
 budgets 136
 bureaucracy 172, 176
 'pockets of bureaucratic effectiveness' 183
 Weberian bureaucracy 177
 see also public administration
'butterfly ballot' 110, 111*f*

C

case studies 12
causality 16, 27–9
 correlation, and 27
 counterfactual definition of causality 27–8
 experiments 28
 scepticism 29
cause groups 226–9, 234
 see also interest groups
central banks 183–4
central government tax revenues
 as a percentage of GDP 35, 35*f*
chain of delegation 132
charismatic authority 73
Chile 74
 protests and constitutional reform 240
China
 Communist Party 188
 political system 71, 72
civil society
 interest groups 234
clientelistic parties 192, 193*f*
clientelistic systems
 public policymaking, and 270–71
climate change 276, 277*f*
closed-list electoral system 112
coalition governments 143, 143*f*, 144, 145*f*
codified constitutions 154
 see also constitutions
Cold War 78
collective-action problem 182, 234, 276
colonialism 36, 55
committee systems 140
communist authoritarian regimes 73

comparative politics 1, 2
  importance of 1
'competitive authoritarian'
  regimes 69–70, 74–7
compulsory voting 125–6
concentration of power, and
  public policymaking 273
concepts 8, 16
  defining 16
  ideal types 16
  operationalization 16
confidence vote 148
conflict 9–11
  democracy and capacity
    for resolving political
    conflicts 65–6, 67–8
  'fights', 'games', and 'debates' 11
  political institutions' influence
    on conflicts 9, 10, 11
consensus democracies 18
constitutional courts 162
constitutional monarchies 72
constitutions 154
  age distribution of the world's
    constitutions 154, 155t,
    156f, 157
  codified constitutions 154
  contents of 157, 157t, 158f,
    158–9
  effect of constitutions on
    political outcomes 159
contestation
  democracy, and 52
control group 28
core voters 220
corporatism
  state–society relations 236
correlation 4
  causality, and 27
corruption 26, 179–80, 182
  collective-action problem 182
  grand corruption 182
  level of corruption among
    countries 180, 181f
  'misuse of public office for
    private gain' 180
  petty corruption 182
  systemic corruption 182
  weak correlation between
    democracy and
    corruption 180
counter-attitudinal
  information 259

counterfactual definition of
  causality 27–8
coups d'état 78, 79
courts 161–3
  appellate courts 162
  constitutional courts 162
  court buildings 162f
  representation of women in
    high courts 162, 163f
  Supreme Courts 162
Covid-19 pandemic
  protests 238–9
  relationship between officials,
    and politicians 178–9
cross-sectional comparison 8
cross-sectional datasets 23

D

datasets 23, 24t
  cross-sectional datasets 23
  panel datasets 23
  time-series datasets 23
decentralization 89
decolonization 47, 61
deliberative theories of
  democracy 52–3
democracy 2
  capacity for resolving political
    conflicts 65–6, 67–8
  contestation 52
  defining democracy 51, 52,
    53, 54
  defining who constitutes 'the
    people' 53
  deliberative theories of
    democracy 52–3
  democratic peace 65
  dichotomous indicator of
    democracy 56, 59
  direct democracy 51–2
  distribution of democratic and
    authoritarian regimes 2, 3f,
    4, 55, 56
  economic development, and 65
  effects of democracy 65–6
  executives–parties
    dimension 18
  federal–unitary dimension 18
  freedom of the press 248
  gradual measure of
    democracy 56, 57f, 58, 61, 62
  indirect democracy 51–2

measuring democracy 52, 55,
    56, 58, 58t
  parliamentarism 52
  participation 52
  political equality, and 67, 68
  presidentialism 52
  relationship between
    judicial independence and
    democracy 164
  representative democracy 52
  'rule by the people' 51
  weak correlation between
    democracy and
    corruption 180
democratic-corporatist model of
  media 250
democratic reversals 78–9, 80
  causes of 80–1
  coups d'état 78, 79
  economic crises 81
  incumbent takeovers 78, 79
  international environment 81
democratic theory 51
democratization 59, 78–80
  drivers of 62–3
  ethnic and sectarian violence
    during 67
  international environment,
    and 64
  modernization theory 63
  revolutions 79
  waves of democratization 59,
    60f, 60–1, 62f, 62
Denmark 178
descriptive meaning of
  theory 17
descriptive representation 120
D'Hondt, V. 114
dictatorship 51
digital and social media 256–7
  access to the internet 257,
    258f
  comparison with traditional
    print and broadcast
    media 257
  misinformation and
    propaganda 259
  political effects of 259–60
  political participation 259
  political polarization 259
direct democracy 51–2
district magnitude
  106, 108

dominant-party regimes
　authoritarianism 71
Downs, A. 187
Duverger's Law 17, 124, 206

E

East African Community 96
ecological-inference fallacy 209
economic crises
　democratic reversals, and 81
economic development
　democracy, and 65
　state capacity, and 42, 44
education 36
　enrolment rates 36, 37f, 38f
Egypt 4, 6
　governorates 5f
　unitary state 6
'electoral authoritarian'
　regimes 69–70, 74–7
electoral districts 106, 108, 110
electoral formula 106, 113–14
electoral participation 6, 7, 125, 125t, 126, 215–20
　average voter turnout among democracies 6, 7f
　factors associated with different levels of turnout 217, 219–20
　variation among countries 215, 216f, 217
electoral systems 105, 106
　authoritarianism 83, 105–6
　ballot structure 106, 110–13
　characteristics of 106
　closed-list system 112
　compulsory voting 125–6
　development of different electoral systems 117–18
　D'Hondt method 114
　distribution of electoral systems around the world 115, 116f
　district magnitude 106, 108
　electoral districts 106, 108, 110
　electoral formula 106, 113–14
　electoral-system reform 119–20
　electoral thresholds 114
　first-past-the-post system 106–7, 114
　majoritarian systems 106, 107, 115, 126, 127

majority voting 114
mixed electoral systems 107, 115
multi-member districts 108
open-list system 112
party lists 107
plurality voting 107, 114
political representation 120–26
preferential voting systems 107, 114
proportional representation 107, 115, 118, 126, 127
representation of women 120, 121f, 121, 123, 124f
resolving social, economic, and political problems 126–7
run-off elections 107, 114
Sainte-Laguë method 114
single-member districts 108
see also electoral participation
electoral thresholds 114
empirical evidence 7, 8
Enlightenment 246
Ethiopia 4, 6, 98
　federal state 6
　regions 5f
ethnic and sectarian violence during democratization 67
European Union 94, 95f, 95–6
executive–legislative relations 148–50
executives 129
　authoritarian states 144–5
　coalition governments 143, 143f, 144, 145f
　constitutions 129
　democracies 143–4
　functions 142
　head of government 142
　majority governments 145
　ministers 142, 143f
　minority governments 145
　single-party governments 143, 143f, 144, 145f
　technocratic governments 144
executives–parties dimension democracy 17
experiments 28
expert surveys 58
explanatory meaning of theory 17

F

failed states 45
fascism 47, 73
federal–unitary dimension democracy 17
federalism 4, 6, 87
　African Union 96
　allocation of responsibilities in practice 89
　authority of regional governments 92, 93t
　bicameralism 99–100
　competition between regions 100
　continent-wide regional institution building 96
　defining 87
　distinct powers of central and regional governments 87, 89
　distribution of federal and unitary states in the world 90, 91f, 92
　East African Community 96
　European Union 94, 95f, 95–6
　judicial review 99
　list of federal states in the world 92t
　mitigating conflict within countries 100
　origins and causes of federalism 96–8, 103
　policymaking 99, 100
　'process of bargaining' 99
　shared power between central and regional governments 87
　variation in the structure of federal states 89
female political representation 120, 121f, 121, 123, 124f
female representation in high courts 162, 163f
female suffrage 53, 54f, 60, 63
first-past-the-post system 106–7, 114
foreign interventions
　regime changes 79
formalistic representation 120
forms of government 130
　changing systems 135
　distribution around the world 132, 134f
　effect on political processes 135

key differences between main
    forms of government 132*f*
  see also parliamentarism;
    presidentialism; semi-
    presidentialism
Forum of Federations 90, 92
framing effects
  media 253, 254
France 75
  change from parliamentarism
    to semi-presidentialism 135
  constitution 46, 188, 246
  democratization 63
  statism 236–7
Frantz, E. 70
'free riders' 234
freedom of the press 246
  authoritarianism, and 248, 249
  cross-country analysis 247*f*, 248
  democracy, and 248
  legal framework 249

G

game theory 19
Gazibo, M. 64
GDP per capita 4
Geddes, B. 70
gender gap
  electoral behaviour 212–13
Germany 54, 78, 167–8, 269–70
  ballot structure 112, 113*f*
  constitution 188
  Green Party 199–200
  path to federalism 97, 97*f*, 98
'gerrymandering' 11
Ghana 183
government agencies 171
  see also public administration
grand corruption 182
green parties 198–200
'green state' 40
gross domestic product (GDP) per
    capita 4

H

Hallin, D. 250–51
harmonized cross-country
    surveys 210
head of government 130–31, 142
high-choice media
    environments and political
    communication 259–60

high state capacity 42
Hippodamus 281
Hitler, A. 54, 73, 78
Hobbes, T. 9, 10
Humprecht, E. 251–2
Hungary
  government influence over
    mass media 249
  political regime 75, 76–7
hybrid regimes 69–70, 73–7

I

ideal types 16
ILO 263, 264*f*
impeachment 131
incumbent takeovers 78, 79
India
  Bharatiya Janata Party
    (BJP) 190–91
  democratic / authoritarian 4
  powers and responsibilities
    of central and regional
    governments 90
indirect democracy 51–2
insider strategies
  interest groups 228
institutionalism 20
  electoral behaviour 214–15
  protests 238
intellectual curiosity 1–2
interest groups
  cause groups 226–9, 234
  challenges 234–5
  civil society, part of 234
  collective-action problem 234
  encompassing
    organizations 234
  'free riders' 234
  insider strategies 228
  outsider strategies 228
  political influence of 234–5
  role of 226, 237
  sectional interest
    organizations 226–9, 234
  social movements, and 229–30
  'social partners', as 236
  specialized knowledge 229
  state–society relations 235–7
  ties with political parties 235
  trade unions 230–35
international environment
  democratic reversals, and 81
  democratization, and 64

International Labour
    Organization (ILO) 263, 264*f*
internet, access to 257, 258*f*
  see also digital and social media
Iran
  theocracy 71
Israel 47
Italy 26, 131
item-count technique 26

J

Japan
  state building 39–40
judicial independence 163–5
  level of judicial independence
    around the world 165*f*
  relationship between
    judicial independence and
    democracy 164
judicial review 99, 166–8
  controversial political
    issues 167–8
  strategic interaction between
    judges and politicians 166
'juristocracy' 184

K

Kant, I. 9, 10, 10*f*, 65, 246
Khrushchev, N. 82

L

legislatures 129, 136
  bicameralism 139
  budgets 136
  committee systems 140
  constitutions 129–30
  executive–legislative
    relations 148–50
  forum of debates 137, 141
  functions 136–7
  law making 136
  legislative chambers 137, 138*f*,
    138–9
  legislative elections 130
  oversight over the
    executive 136–7
  party discipline 140–41
  rules and procedures 140
  unicameralism 139
legitimacy of states 34
Levitsky, S. 75

liberal model of media 250
Lijphart, A. 18
linkage 189
longitudinal comparison 8
low state capacity 44

M

Madison, J. 187–8
majoritarian democracies 17
majoritarian systems 106, 107, 115, 126, 127
majority governments 145
majority voting 114
Mancini, P. 250–51
mass politics 208
media 245, 260
   agenda-setting effects 253, 254
   authoritarian regimes, propaganda, and control over the media 249
   counter-attitudinal information 259
   democratic-corporatist model 250
   framing effects 253, 254
   freedom of the press 246–9
   liberal model 250
   new forms of media and effects on people's attitudes and behaviour 255–6
   polarized-pluralist model 250–51
   policymaking, effects on 254–5
   political communication 257, 259–60
   political parties and decision makers influenced by the media 254
   relationship between media and politics 250–52
   see also digital and social media
Meiji Restoration 39–40
meta-analysis 65
methods 8, 22
   'most similar systems design' 25
   qualitative evidence 24–5
   quantitative evidence 22–4
   sources of information 25–6
Mexico 167
   conflicts between gangs and the state 44–5

migration 276, 278, 279*f*
military dictatorships 73–4
military regimes 71
Miller, M. 23, 24*t*, 56, 59
ministers 142, 143*f*
minority governments 145
misuse of public office for private gain *see* corruption
mixed electoral systems 107, 115
modernization theory 63
monarchies 72–3, 136
   authoritarian monarchies 72–3
   constitutional monarchies 72
'most similar systems design' 25
multi-member districts 108
multi-party authoritarian regimes 75
multi-party system 203
'multiple streams' framework 269
Myanmar
   rise and fall of democracy 66–7

N

nation states 46–8
national election studies 210
nationalism 46–8
nations
   contemporary challenges to the idea of the nation state 48
   'imagined' communities 47
   origins of nation states 46–7
'natural-resource curse' 4, 63
Nazi Germany
   midwives 235–6
Netherlands
   open-list system 112, 112*f*
New Zealand 60
   electoral-system reform 121, 122*f*, 122–4
newspapers and political communication 257
Niger
   coup d'état 248
Nigeria
   powers and responsibilities of central and regional governments 90
Norway
   voter turnout 217

O

observations 22
one-party system 203
open-list electoral system 112
operationalization 16
Otlan, Y. 249
outsider strategies
   interest groups 228

P

Palestine 47
panel datasets 23
Papua New Guinea
   electoral-system reform 118–19
parliamentarism 52, 130, 136
   chain of delegation 132
   formation and dissolution of governments 146–8
   head of government 130–31
   origins of 132
   vote of no confidence 130
parties *see* political parties
party discipline 140–41
party lists 107
party systems 203–6
   effective number of parties 203
   multi-party system 203
   one-party system 203
   origins of 205–6
   two-party system 203
path dependence 268
pension reforms 274
personalist regimes 72
petty corruption 182
picketing 230
Pinochet, A. 74, 74*f*
Pitkin, H. 120
pluralism
   state–society relations 236
plurality voting 107, 114
Poland 168
polarization 221–2
polarized-pluralist model of media 250–51
police 36
political communication
   high-choice media environments 259–60
   new technology revolutionizing political communication 257, 259

newspapers 257
printing press 259
radio 257
telegraph 257, 259
television 257
see also media
political economy 269–70
political equality
   democracy, and 67, 68
political inequality
   political influence of voters 222
political institutions 7
   authoritarianism, role in 82, 83, 84
   defining 10–11
   effects of 8
   influence on conflicts 9, 10, 11
   origins of 8
   protests, and 242
political opportunity structure 240
political participation 215, 223
   digital and social media 259
   see also electoral participation; interest groups; protests
political parties 186, 206
   authoritarian regimes 188–9
   clientelistic parties 192, 193f
   constitutions recognizing parties' contribution to democracy 188
   defining 187
   families of parties 196–7
   green parties 198–200
   interest groups' ties with political parties 235
   left–right dimension 196–7, 198f
   mainstream parties 192
   niche parties 192
   organizational structure 195–6
   origins of 194–5
   party discipline 140–41
   party lists 107
   party system 203–6
   'policy, office, and votes' 192
   populism 201–2
   programmatic parties 192, 193f
   regional parties 198
   religious parties 198
   role of 187–9
   strategies 191–2
political polarization 259
political regimes 7, 50
   see also authoritarianism; democracy
political representation 120–26
   descriptive representation 120
   electoral participation, and 125, 125t, 126
   formalistic representation 120
   representation of women 120, 121f, 121, 123, 124f
   substantive representation 120
   symbolic representation 120
political responsiveness 220, 222
political science 2
political systems 2
populism 201–2
power sharing and public policymaking 273–4
preferential voting systems 107, 114
presidentialism 52, 80, 131
   chain of delegation 131
   impeachment 131
   origins of 133, 135
   presidential elections 130
principal–agent problem
   public administration 172
   voters and politicians 212
printing press and political communication 259
programmatic parties 192, 193f
programmatic representation 270–71
proportional representation 107, 115, 118, 126, 127
prospective-voting approach 211–12, 214
protests
   definition 237
   forms of 237–8
   institutionalist perspective 238
   numbers of protests around the world 239, 240, 241f, 242
   political institutions, and 240
   political opportunity structure 240
   rationalist perspective 238
   response of the political authorities 240
   social-psychological perspective 238
psychological theories 20
   electoral behaviour 213–14, 215
   protests 238
public administration 170, 171
   'accountability vs. autonomy' 177
   bureaucracy 172, 176
   corruption 179–80, 182
   delegation of political power to experts 183–4
   government agencies 171
   impartiality 180, 182
   'law vs. management' 177
   level of professionalism among countries 175f, 176
   origins of public administration 171
   outsourcing 171
   pockets of effectiveness 183
   principal–agent problem 172
   relationship between politicians and public officials 172–4, 176–8
   technocracy 184
   types of public administration 177
public opinion and electoral behaviour 208–9
   core voters 220
   dimensions of political opinion 221
   ecological-inference fallacy 209
   electoral participation 215–20
   explanations of electoral behaviour 211–15
   gender gap 212–13
   harmonized cross-country surveys 210
   institutional approach to electoral behaviour 214–15
   national election studies 210
   polarization 221–2
   political responsiveness 220, 222
   prospective-voting approach 211–12, 214
   psychological approach to electoral behaviour 213–14, 215
   rationalist approach to electoral behaviour 211–12
   retrospective-voting approach 211–12, 214
   sociological approach to electoral behaviour 212, 214–15

public opinion and electoral behaviour (Continued)
  studying public opinion and electoral behaviour 209–11
  surveys 210
  swing voters 220
public policymaking 262–3
  authoritarian regimes 275–6
  clientelistic systems 270–71
  climate change 276, 277f
  complex and disorderly process 269
  concentration of power 273
  failure to implement policies 273
  ideas influence public policies 266
  influential individuals 266
  institutional influences 266–7
  interests influence public policies 265–6
  international dimension of policies 276–8
  internationalization influences 266
  media, effects of 254–5
  migration 276, 278, 279f
  'multiple streams' framework 269
  nature of policies 267
  path dependence 268
  policymaking process 268–9
  political economy 269–70
  power sharing 274–5
  programmatic representation 270–71
  rational models 268
  variation of policies over time, countries, and policy areas 263, 264f, 264–7
Putin, V. 74

Q

qualitative ('small-N') evidence 24–5
quantitative ('large-N') evidence 11–12, 22–4

R

radio and political communication 257
randomized-response technique 26

Rapoport, A. 11
rational-legal authority 73
rationalist theories 19
  electoral behaviour 211–12
  protests 238
  public policymaking 268
regime changes 78–80
  coups d'état 78, 79
  democratic reversals 78–9, 80, 81
  democratization 78–80
  foreign interventions 80
  incumbent takeovers 78, 79
  revolutions 79–80
regional parties 198
religious parties 198
representative democracy 52
research prompts 12
research questions 2, 4, 6
retrospective-voting approach 211–12, 214
revolutions 79
Riker, W. 87
Rosato, S. 23, 24t, 56, 59
Rousseau, J.-J. 9, 10
Rousseff, D. 131, 132f, 149–50
run-off elections 107, 114
Russia 74
  democratic constitution 64
  invasion of Ukraine 180
  media reporting on political protests 249
Ryabinska, N. 252–3

S

Sainte-Laguë, A. 114
Sartori, G. 187
scepticism
  causality, and 29
scholarly discipline, comparative politics as a 7–9
  systematic and transparent research 15
sectional interest organizations 226–9, 234
  see also interest groups
semi-presidentialism 130, 131
  chain of delegation 132
single-member districts 108
single-party governments 143, 143f, 144, 145f
social media see digital and social media

social movements
  interest groups, and 229–30
  'social partners', interest groups as 236
social policies 36, 37, 263, 264f, 264–7, 268
social sciences 19
social trust 65
sociological theories 19–20
  electoral behaviour 212, 214–15
  protests 238
South Africa
  constitution 188, 225
  trade unions 235
Soviet Union 82
Spain
  federalism in 100
state capacity
  defining 41
  economic development, and 42, 44
  failed states 45, 46
  government-effectiveness indicator 42, 43f
  high state capacity 42
  low state capacity 44
  measures of 42, 44
  variation in state capacity within countries 44, 45
state–society relations 235–7
  corporatism 236
  pluralism 236
  statism 236–7
states 32
  'bellicist theory of the state' 36
  colonialism 36
  defining the state 33
  education 36
  'green state' 40
  historical origins of 32–3
  legitimacy 34
  'monopoly on violence' 33
  nation states 46–8
  police 36
  political conflicts 40
  relationship between war and state building 36
  scope of the state 35, 36, 37, 38, 40, 41
  social insurances 40
  state building 38–39, 41
  welfare state 40

statism
  state–society relations 236–7
substantive representation 120
Supreme Courts 162
surveys 210
  harmonized cross-country surveys 210
Svolik, M. 81, 83
Sweden 178, 179*f*, 269–70
  Freedom of the Press Act 246
  trade unions 234
swing voters 220
Switzerland
  interest groups 228–9
  party system 203–5
symbolic representation 120
systemic corruption 182

T

tax revenues as a percentage of GDP 35, 35*f*
technocracy 144, 184
telegraph and political communication 257, 259
television and political communication 257
theocracy 71
theories 8, 16–18, 19
  assumptions 19
  combining theoretical ideas 21–2
  descriptive meaning of theory 17
  explanatory meaning of theory 17
  institutionalism 20
  psychological theories 20
  rationalist theories 19
  sociological theories 19–20
time-series datasets 23
trade unions 230–35
  picketing 230

union density 230, 231*f*, 234
traditional authority 73
treatment group 28
Trotsky, L. 33
Trump, D. 201–2
  rioting at the Capitol Building in Washington, DC 21–2
Tsebelis, G. 18
Türkiye
  district magnitude 108, 110*f*
Tunisia 56, 82*f*
two-party system 203

U

Uber 269–70
Ukraine
  corruption 180
  media system 252–3
unicameralism 139
unitary states 87
United Arab Emirates
  political regions 88*f*
United Kingdom
  bicameralism 139
  constitution 154
  devolved powers 98
  direct democracy 51
  party system 203–4
  suffragettes 53, 54*f*
United States 21–2, 269–70
  CNN and Fox News' effect on political attitudes 255–6
  constitution 157, 246, 249
  electoral ballots 110, 111*f*
  National Marine Fisheries Service 173
  powers and responsibilities of central and regional governments 90
  single-member districts 108, 109*f*

Supreme Court dissenting opinions 162
trade unions 234
Uppsala Conflict Data Program 66

V

Varieties of Democracy (V-Dem) project 55, 56, 57*f*, 58, 61, 62
'veto players' 18, 19
vote of no confidence 130, 148
voter turnout *see* electoral participation
voting behaviour *see* public opinion and electoral behaviour

W

war
  relationship between war and state building 36
Way, L. 75
Weber, M. 16, 33–4, 73, 172, 176, 177
welfare state 37
'Westminster Model' 137
World Bank
  government-effectiveness indicator 42, 43*f*
World Press Freedom Index 246, 247*f*
World Wide Fund for Nature 227*f*
Wright, J. 70

Z

Zimbabwe
  constitutional reform 159–61
Zionism 47